M000208652

"An inspiring and practical 'how to' guide to leading by example and from the heart in a complex world."
Mike Attwood, *Florence Nightingale Foundation, UK, and former NHS CEO*

"*Transpersonal Leadership in Action* brings together a number of enlightening approaches to assist leaders on this journey towards becoming the better versions of themselves – much needed, much appreciated."
Prof. Dr Antoinette Weibel, *University of St Gallen, Switzerland*

"I am convinced that leaders must embrace transpersonal action to enable thriving in and out of work – we must urgently put our egos in place and be radical, ethical, authentic and emotionally intelligent in as many contexts as possible."
Dr Tony Wall, *Head of the International Centre for Thriving, UK*

"*Transpersonal Leadership in Action* may not change your desire to be a transpersonal leader; however, it can and will change your ability to become the leader the business world, actually our entire world, needs now."
Marty Wolff, *Founder Partner in Contractor Succession, USA*

"*Transpersonal Leadership in Action* is a must-read for those who lead and those who aspire to be leaders."
Caroline Dowd-Higgins, *VP Career Coaching and Employer Connections, Ivy Tech Community College, USA*

Transpersonal Leadership in Action

How can leaders promote diversity, equality and inclusion? What does it mean to let go of leadership? How do learning, feedback and coaching help us become better leaders?

Following the success of *Leading Beyond the Ego*, this book shows how to apply transpersonal leadership – practiced leaders who are radical, ethical, authentic and act beyond their own interests to create high-performing organisations – in a wide range of contexts. It considers the attributes of transpersonal leaders and how they transform organisations by building strong, collaborative relationships and a caring, sustainable and performance-enhancing environment.

Shining a light on the way forward for senior leaders and HR and talent professionals, the book covers:

- Characteristics of transpersonal leaders such as purpose, ethics and adult development
- Impact of transpersonal leaders on global organisations, during digital transformation and change and through crises
- Case studies of transpersonal leadership in different contexts including in India and East Asia, when leading remotely, in HR and politics

Transpersonal Leadership in Action is essential reading for senior leaders, HR professionals and those responsible for leader and organisational development.

Duncan Enright is a Director of LeaderShape Global.

John Knights is the Co-founder and Chair of LeaderShape Global.

Danielle Grant is a Director of LeaderShape Global.

Greg Young is the Co-founder and CEO of LeaderShape Global.

Transpersonal Leadership in Action

How to Lead Beyond the Ego

Edited by Duncan Enright, John Knights, Danielle Grant and Greg Young

Routledge
Taylor & Francis Group

LONDON AND NEW YORK

LeaderShape

Shaping Transpersonal Leaders

Image Credit: © Getty Images

First published 2022
by Routledge
2 Park Square, Milton Park, Abingdon, Oxon OX14 4RN

and by Routledge
605 Third Avenue, New York, NY 10158

Routledge is an imprint of the Taylor & Francis Group, an informa business

British Library Cataloguing-in-Publication Data
A catalogue record for this book is available from the British Library

Library of Congress Cataloging-in-Publication Data
Names: Enright, Duncan, editor.
Title: Transpersonal leadership in action: how to lead beyond the ego /
edited by Duncan Enright, John Knights, Danielle Grant and Greg Young.
Description: Abingdon, Oxon; New York, NY: Routledge, 2022. |
Includes bibliographical references and index. |
Identifiers: LCCN 2021035537 | ISBN 9780367713881 (hardback) |
ISBN 9780367713898 (paperback) | ISBN 9781003150626 (ebook)
Subjects: LCSH: Leadership. | Executive coaching.
Classification: LCC HD57.7 .T7325 2022 | DDC 658.4/092—dc23/eng/20211027
LC record available at https://lccn.loc.gov/2021035537

ISBN: 978-0-367-71388-1 (hbk)
ISBN: 978-0-367-71389-8 (pbk)
ISBN: 978-1-003-15062-6 (ebk)

DOI: 10.4324/9781003150626

Typeset in Bembo
by codeMantra

Contents

Figures

Tables

Acknowledgements

When embarking on a book like this, as well as drawing on the expertise of the LeaderShape Global family (including the contributors to this book, to whom many thanks), we rely on the support of our actual families too. We learn from you and we lean on you – thank you always.

We would also like to acknowledge the leaders we have met including our partners in the United Kingdom, Sweden, the United States, Kazakhstan, Japan, Tanzania, South Africa, Germany, Italy and Brazil. All over the world, there are great leaders learning from each other and helping new leaders develop.

In particular, Duncan would like to thank his friends at Evidence-based Networks Ltd in North America, Kazakhstan, New Zealand, Moldova, Kyrgyzstan, Ukraine and the United Kingdom. You have been extraordinary and inspiring.

Contributors

Pavan Bakshi – Chapter Author

Pavan is LeaderShape's Managing Partner in India and an accredited Master Facilitator and Faculty Member of LeaderShape Global. He is also CEO of our Indian Business Partner, Prime Meridian Consulting India Pvt Ltd. Pavan is a distinguished Veteran Colonel, who is a Certified Executive Coach and trainer from the Army War College, Military College of Telecom Engineering. He has also been a trainer in the prestigious Indian Military Academy, Dehradun. Pavan specialises in the field of performance, growth, leadership, crisis, transition and change management. His coaching experience ranges from coaching senior executives in leadership positions in multinational companies to large Indian corporate organisations.

Pavan's Coaching Certification is from the NeuroLeadership Group, having been awarded "Results Certificate on Coaching Skills", "Coach Toolkit" (a set of tools to assist clients to stretch their thinking shift paradigms, and improve EI and performance) and Executive Coaching (Integration of Business and Personal Development needs).

He has been a Consultant Facilitator in India and South Asia and facilitated curriculums on personal and inter-personal effectiveness, leadership, productivity, trust, project management and execution. He has experience in developing programmes on coaching conversation skills for leaders/managers, and performance leadership, building a leadership pipeline and creating coaching cultures in organisations. He has also "trained the trainer", enabling participants to become ICF accredited in Coaching Skills. More details at https://www.leadershapeglobal.com/pavan-bakshi-2.

Sue Coyne – Chapter Author

Sue is an associate at LeaderShape Global. She spent 20 years as a business leader, and has been a sought-after leadership and team coach since 2003. She

is a thought leader and speaker on leadership issues and complements her work with expertise in neuro-science. Sue is the author of *Stop Doing Start Leading: How to Shift from Doing the Work Yourself to Becoming a Great Leader* (Coyne, 2016). She is a contributor to *Leadership Team Coaching in Practice: Developing High-performing Teams* by Peter Hawkins (Hawkins, 2014) and *Enabling Genius* (Downey, 2016) by Myles Downey. See her full bio here: https://www.leader-shapeglobal.com/sue-coyne.

Alison Hill – Chapter Author

Alison is a public health doctor. She held board-level leadership positions in the NHS for 25 years, including 10 years as director of public health in Buckinghamshire and Milton Keynes. She was managing director of Solutions for Public Health, an NHS consultancy that set up the National Obesity Observatory and developed the national suite of local authority health profiles. From 2012 to 2014, she was Public Health England's Deputy Chief Knowledge Officer. Within this role, she had responsibility for strategic leadership and business management within Public Health England's knowledge directorate, was managerially responsible for 600 staff and oversaw the delivery of a wide range of health information and evidence products and services.

After she retired from her public health roles, she completed a Diploma in coaching and mentoring at Oxford Brookes University. She currently undertakes pro-bono mentoring of chief executives and directors of charities based in Oxfordshire through Oxfordshire Charity Mentors. Alison was a LeaderShape faculty member until 2018. She has had a long-standing interest in the role that cycling can play in improving population health. She is now a cycling activist, chairing Cyclox the cycle campaign group for Oxford. She also chairs the Bikeability Trust, which manages the grant for Bikeability training in primary schools in England.

Frederick Hölscher – Chapter Author

"I like to challenge thought paradigms and stimulate new thinking that will support leaders and organisations on their transformational journey in the new world of work."

Frederick holds a PhD and has developed and applied innovative and academically sound concepts to produce tangible results in the workplace.

He worked with global consulting firms, and various tertiary educational institutions for more than 30 years and built up a wealth of experience in various industries across the globe.

He currently holds a position as Adjunct at Hult Ashridge Executive Education and is Visiting Professor at other business schools. He has a particular interest in how leaders and organisations respond to the disruptions facing them in the new world of work. He is co-author of *Agile Leadership for Turbulent Times: Integrating Your Ego, Eco and Intuitive Intelligence* searching for a new leadership logic in the space of transpersonal leadership.

Robert Jarvis – Chapter Author

Robert is a Chartered Fellow of the Chartered Institute of Personnel and Development, with over 20 years of experience in Human Resources. Robert is a Masters (Human Resources Management) graduate from Middlesex University Business School. He has undertaken senior roles in several sectors, including Retail, the NHS, Consultancy, Energy and most latterly in a Global role in Financial Services and Real Asset Advisory. Robert has been a long supporter of LeaderShape Global and the concepts of Transpersonal Leadership and has developed programmes for coaching and developing leaders. Robert has undertaken the Transpersonal Leadership Coaching qualification with LeaderShape Global and seeks opportunities to use transpersonal leadership in his daily life. Robert's chapter explores the connectivity between transpersonal leadership and HR activities by using the CIPD Profession map.

Heather Katz – Chapter Author

Heather is a member of the LeaderShape Global Faculty. Her career epitomises teaching, learning, development and change. Her passion is to inspire leaders, managers and teams to unleash their hidden potential and move towards becoming transpersonal leaders leading beyond their ego. Since 2005, as one of the first few coaches in the University of Oxford Saïd Business School's (SBS) Executive Education, she worked as a coach and facilitator on Advanced Management and Leadership

Programmes and also coaches MBA and EMBA students. In 2008 and 2009, as part of a team within SBS, she delivered leadership and personal development programmes to senior civil service leaders in Abu Dhabi. Heather also worked for several years in Oxfordshire as Senior Programme Director for Common Purpose, a non-profit international leadership and educational development organisation. She brings to her practice a unique blend of 18 years executive coaching and leadership development in the United Kingdom; ten years education, training and practice in Washington DC and New York as a Licensed Clinical Social Worker (MSW) and Family Systems Therapist; and 19 years business experience in marketing support, sales, training, product management and education with IBM in South Africa. Heather's lifelong passion is to continue to learn and develop, whilst often stepping outside her comfort zone. More details at https://www.leadershapeglobal.com/heather-katz.

Maiqi Ma – Chapter Author

Maiqi, known as Maggie, has been a project manager and professional trainer for over 15 years. She has been involved in several joint venture negotiations with a value of tens of millions of RMB, and has also engaged with the integration of the largest nationwide online real estate trading platform and online forum. Her footprint covered many Chinese cities and extended to neighbouring countries in south-east Asia. She published four business books whilst residing in China.

Maiqi believes life is a journey, to experience differences and enjoy challenges. In 2008, Maiqi moved to the United Kingdom. After a period of adjustment to the unfamiliar culture, she realised her Chinese academic and business background could benefit many western businesses that are seeking to expand into China. She set up a training and consultancy business in 2010. In the past five years, she has travelled and worked in many cities in the United Kingdom and mainland Europe. Nearly a thousand professionals have enjoyed and acclaimed Maiqi's training.

She has recently published her first book in English, which is a seminal guide to doing business with China. "*Win with China Volume 1 – Acclimatisation for Mutual Success Doing Business with China.*" Bite-Sized Books Ltd, October 2016. She is also the author of a number of articles and blogs and is a founder and director of China business training consultancy MOLAES. Maiqi holds a BA in English teaching and an MSc in Management, both gained in China, and an MA in Education from the United Kingdom, plus various other qualifications such as fashion design and nutrition. More details at https://www.leadershapeglobal.com/maggie-ma

Jenny Plaister-Ten – Chapter Author

Jenny is a member of the LeaderShape Global faculty and is dedicated to the development of global leaders and their teams. Following a stellar international career in the IT industry during which she lived and worked in the USA, Asia/Pacific and Europe, she ran her own consulting practice working in over 30 countries. Jenny is now a thought leader on the impact of culture in the coaching relationship and upon global leaders. Her book, *The Cross-Cultural Kaleidoscope: A Systems Approach to Working Amongst Different Cultural Influences*, was published in 2016. She is also a contributing author to *Intercultural Management* (Barmeyer and Franklin, 2016). See her full bio here: http://www.leadershapeglobal.com/jenny-plaister

Otti Vogt – Chapter Author

Otti is an inspirational global transformation leader and passionate about "igniting the human spark" to build better and more sustainable organisations. With over 20 years of experience in implementing strategic change in multi-cultural, complex businesses, he is an expert in crafting agile learning organisations to deliver sustainable value and "happiness at work". Educated at a humanistic gymnasium in Germany, Otti commenced his career as an entrepreneur in a successful start-up in Italy, before studying management in Bologna, Reims, Berkeley and London. During University, Otti gained ample experience in not-for-profit management, leading a global student association and staging a highly impactful national "Leaders of the Future Forum". Following his studies and several attempts to kick start an innovative internet venture during the dot-com crash, Otti joined strategic consulting and eventually British Telecom's global Enterprise division in the United Kingdom. Since then, in many international executive roles – across transformation, M&A, professional services, operations and IT – Otti developed extensive leadership skills and earned an MBA from London Business School. In 2016, Otti joined ING Group's leadership council in Amsterdam to support the "most radical transformation in European banking". As COO and Chief Transformation Officer for ING's global business line, he was accountable for ING's digital transformation programme and operations for more than 28m customers across Europe, Asia and Australia until 2021. Otti is also an INSEAD-qualified executive coach, associate of the Globally Responsible Leadership Initiative (GRLI) and international speaker on business transformation and was named Top 20 Global Thought Leader on Agile by Thinkers36.

Duncan Enright – Lead Editor and Chapter Author

Duncan is a Director of LeaderShape Global. Duncan has also worked with the team twice as a client in the NHS and in publishing, which means he has an extra appreciation of the value LeaderShape can offer any board or senior management group.

Duncan has been a senior director with over 30 years of experience in the publishing industry, as well as a decade as a Vice Chair and Non-Executive Director of an NHS Trust and 14 years as a councillor in various local authorities. Duncan is an experienced director, influencer and communicator who has been both elected and appointed to senior roles in NHS, policy and local government. He is used to analysing complex situations and communicating aims to persuade, influence, drive change, optimise performance and improve team understanding.

Alongside his professional career, Duncan has been involved in politics, spending a decade advising government on a range of policy areas as a National Policy Commissioner. He has stood for Parliament on three occasions, once against the Deputy Prime Minister and once against the Prime Minister, and again in a by-election in 2016. He has stood for European Election twice, and served on the board of organisations engaged in European engagement and electoral reform. He is a Councillor on town, district and county councils, currently serving on the County Cabinet, and spent a year as Mayor of Witney. More details at https://www.leader-shapeglobal.com/duncan-enright.

John Knights – Editor and Chapter Author

John's business life changed when in 1998 he had the serendipitous opportunity to learn to coach other chief executives and started to understand the real issues around leadership. His passion and purpose is to support leaders on their journey to become excellent Transpersonal Leaders. John, Chairman of LeaderShape Global, is an experienced senior executive, coach and facilitator, and an expert in emotional intelligence, transpersonal leadership and neuro-leadership. He has been a senior executive in major international corporations, a serial entrepreneur and lecturer at Oxford University. He is an author of the acclaimed text book, *Leading Beyond the Ego: How to Become a Transpersonal Leader*, and many other publications including a white paper on Ethical Leadership published by Routledge, which has been downloaded over 10,000 times, and the peer-reviewed "Developing 21st century leaders, a complete new process" published in the *Journal of Work-Applied Management*. John focuses on growing LeaderShape globally. More details at http://www.leadershapeglobal.com/john-knights-1

Danielle Grant – Editor and Chapter Author

Danielle's career epitomises embracing change. She held director-level positions in UK, US and European blue chip and executive search businesses, including Disney. In 2004, she gained her Advanced Diploma in Executive Coaching and embarked on a journey that fulfils her passion for growing transpersonal leaders. Danielle, a Director of LeaderShape Global, is an accomplished coach and facilitator, and an expert in the development of neuroscientifically based leadership programmes, using leading-edge blended methodologies for which she achieved an MA with distinction; she focuses on developing LeaderShape's team capability and leading-edge programmes globally. She is an accredited University Lecturer and has led Masters' programmes in leadership and coaching. Danielle is a contributing author of *Leadership Assessment for Talent Development* and an editor, general contributor and author of *Leading Beyond the Ego*. More details at http://leadershapeglobal.com/danielle-grant

Greg Young – Editor and Chapter Author

In a Damascene moment in Greg's first role as MD, he realised that instead of measuring his day by what he did, a more effective assessment was what he caused to happen. Embracing non-directive leadership styles, building a sense of vision, values, and coaching those around him to achieve more than they felt they were capable of, achieved greater results. He is a founding Director and CEO of LeaderShape Global, and has been a thought leader in the field of leadership development for over ten years following careers in the Life Sciences and Telecommunications. He is a contributor to *The Invisible Elephant & the Pyramid Treasure: Tomorrow's Leadership – the Transpersonal Journey* (2011) and *Leadership Assessment for Talent Development* (2013), and an editor and general contributor to *Leading Beyond the Ego*. Greg has authored a white paper published by Routledge on Women in Leadership, a theme to which he is committed. See http://leadershapeglobal.com/greg-young

Introduction

Transpersonal leadership in action

Duncan Enright

> The pursuit of transpersonal leadership is a journey, not a destination.
> Greg Young, CEO, LeaderShape Global

Overview

Transpersonal leadership is a concept whose time has come. It means thinking beyond narrow self-interest to become a truly effective leader; meeting our commitments to ourselves and others at work and home; safeguarding the interests of colleagues, stakeholders and the planet; and fulfilling our promise as individuals.

The route map for the transpersonal journey is set out in the important book *Leading Beyond the Ego* (Knights, Grant and Young, 2018) and summarised in Chapter 2. This work sets out the concept of transpersonal leadership and offers a practical approach to becoming an authentic, ethical, caring and more effective leader. The term 'transpersonal leader' has been developed by the team at LeaderShape Global and is rooted in real-life experience as senior leaders in a range of industry sectors, from media to pharmaceuticals, communications to publishing, engineering to public service. The concept of 'transpersonal psychology' has been studied for decades, and explores our experiences and development of consciousness beyond the personal to encompass wider aspects of humankind, life and the world around us. Transpersonal leaders, therefore, operate beyond their ego, not denying it but developing consciousness beyond it, to become radical, ethical, authentic while emotionally intelligent leaders.

In this book, *Transpersonal Leadership in Action*, we explore the concept of transpersonal leadership in a number of contexts, bringing into focus the importance of radical, ethically authentic leaders in our world today. Our team of authors describe various aspects of the transition to becoming a transpersonal leader in the first section. There follows an exploration of how transpersonal leaders make a difference in a number of settings. The third section shows how transpersonal leaders put their values into action in different situations. The whole book illustrates clearly the importance of transpersonal leaders and sets out the path to follow for those aspiring to become one.

DOI: 10.4324/9781003150626-1

Introducing LeaderShape Global

This volume of work has been written by a team of authors connected to or working for LeaderShape Global. The LeaderShape family grew from work by John Knights, an engineer who spent a career in senior positions in multinational companies, as well as founding and leading his own. John's great insight is that although leaders are encouraged to change the world around them by force of personality, it is only by changing yourself that you can become a radical, ethically aware, authentic and effective leader. John co-founded LeaderShape Global 20 years ago to conduct research and share insights, helping leaders to explore their own development. A worldwide community of senior executives who are trained coaches, now offering leadership development and coaching, LeaderShape offers programmes to individuals, teams and organisations in public, private and third sectors using a suite of tools and techniques developed over two decades.

The vision is to create a movement to develop transpersonal leaders who embrace the disruptors of the 21st century by operating beyond the ego.

Introducing this book

Our shared aim as authors is to illustrate the ideas behind transpersonal leadership and paint a picture of what you can do to become a radical, ethical, authentic leader who is emotionally intelligent.

An introductory chapter on transpersonal leadership itself, summarising the ideas in *Leading Beyond the Ego*, is followed by chapters in three parts:

1   Becoming a transpersonal leader – sharing what we have learned about the journey. This will offer you the tools you need to think differently about leadership and find a new way to go further.
2   The impact of a transpersonal leader – how you can make a difference, exploring key themes and challenges of our time such as digital transformation and change, diversity and inclusion, stakeholder management and leading at a time of crisis, such as the COVID-19 pandemic.
3   Transpersonal leadership in action – examples through different lenses of how bringing values to full consciousness, using emotional intelligence and empathy and letting core purpose and an ethical touchstone can change your world, and the world of those around you.

How to use this book

Of course, this book can be read from start to finish! However, we have tried to make it one you can dip into and use as a resource. Each of the chapters in the third section, for example, can be read as standalone contributions to stimulate your thinking, or as the basis for a discussion for you and your team.

If you are starting on the journey to discover yourself as a leader, we recommend the first section as a way in to the thoughts and processes of transpersonal leadership. For further reading, we provide many references, and previous works from LeaderShape such as *Leading Beyond the Ego* (Knights, Grant and Young, 2018), *Leadership Assessment for Talent Development* (Wall and Knights, 2013) and *The Invisible Elephant and the Pyramid of Treasure* (Knights and Manwaring, 2012) are also useful. If you are responsible for developing others to achieve their full potential as leaders, chapters on adult development, how to develop next-generation leaders, modern learning principles and how to develop transpersonal leaders – an HR perspective – offer a rich source.

Alongside this book, a number of resources are available at our website www.leadershapeglobal.com. You may also find that our podcast series, *Leadership Comes Alive* at https://www.leadershapeglobal.com/podcast, has resonance and again can provide a starting point for discussion and debate – or give you pause for thought. Several chapters in this book are updated and edited contributions based on a series published by Routledge between 2016 and 2019: The Transpersonal Leadership White Papers ('LeaderShape – The Transpersonal Leadership White Paper series', 2019).

Case studies provide stories to illustrate points, and some chapters such as those on China and political leadership have messages for those who have no involvement in either arena. Our objective is to provide insights and stimulate further thought. If you would like to share these thoughts with us, please get in touch as, like you, we are on this journey of discovery and believe that continuing professional development is just that – always continuing.

References

Knights, J., Grant, D. and Young, G. (2018). *Leading Beyond the Ego: How to Become a Transpersonal Leader*. London: Routledge.

Knights, J. and Manwaring, T. (2012). *The Invisible Elephant and the Pyramid of Treasure*. London: Tomorrow's Company.

LeaderShape – The Transpersonal Leadership White Paper series (2019). London: Routledge. https://www.leadershapeglobal.com/white-papers. Accessed February 9, 2021.

Wall, T. and Knights, J. (2013). *Leadership Assessment for Talent Development*. London: Routledge.

1 Understanding transpersonal leadership

Greg Young and John Knights

> Everyone thinks of changing the world, but no one thinks of changing himself.
>
> Leo Tolstoy

Overview

It is becoming more generally accepted that there is a need to develop a new kind of leader to meet the needs of our 21st century volatile, uncertain, complex, ambiguous (VUCA) world. The bookcases are full of volumes that describe "what" great leaders should do, but "how" to develop such leaders is usually limited to a macro or systemic solution rather than focusing on granular behavioural change of the individual. Our book 'Leading Beyond the Ego – How to Become a Transpersonal Leader' published in 2018 (Routledge 2018) describes the qualities and characteristics of transpersonal leaders, then focuses on developing these leaders through a new codified process that introduces readers to the concepts of transpersonal leadership and the journey an individual might undertake to move closer to it.

This new book seeks to continue to build on that initial concept and provide useful contexts in the practical application of transpersonal leadership. After all, a recipe might look great on paper, but it is only when the dish is prepared, cooked and consumed that we fully understand the feast as intended.

Introduction

We know that the climate and culture of organisations is an echo of the behaviours of its leaders, especially the Leader, the CEO or President.

Imagine if you worked in a place that had a clear sense of purpose that you and your colleagues shared, and that sense of purpose was ethical, authentic and caring whilst also being sustainably successful; taking care not only of shareholders, but of all the stakeholders. Imagine too, if that sense of purpose and environment allowed the organisation to be so nimble that it was able to respond to radical shifts in the environment with equally radical solutions.

DOI: 10.4324/9781003150626-2

An environment where input, initiative and innovation are encouraged; people valued, listened to and cared about with strong relationships between colleagues with an expectation of competence to get on with things. Wouldn't that be a place you would want to work?

So often we hear of organisational environments where knowledge is power, where there is a lack of engagement, brought about by managers relying on carrot and stick methods to motivate staff and where managers often have, for any variety of reasons, their own interests at the forefront of their minds. In addition to job security, those reasons could include the desire for power, prestige, recognition or reward. We've probably all experienced a boss like that at some stage in our careers. It may well have been a reason for us moving on from an organisation; it's rarely a positive experience.

An organisation that is a great place to work, like the one described above, needs to be led by exceptional people. They have become exceptional not only because they are demonstrably great leaders but because they have developed a level of self-awareness of their own strengths and weaknesses. They have also brought into full consciousness who they are in terms of values, ethics and beliefs and they know what they want to do with who they are; their motivation, courage, resilience and aspiration. They know their purpose, and they don't let self-interest get in the way. They are leading beyond the ego.

The news channels and social media are becoming increasingly full of instances where organisations have suffered financial penalties or even collapse because they have been found to have operated in ways that are unethical or they have failed to adapt to a change in context or disruptive technology. These might sound quite different things, but at their centre is the organisational ego set by the top leaders. That self-interest is getting in the way, driven either by placing personal reward over ethics, perhaps by the size of their personal income and bonus, or the fear that being radical will place their own position, power or income under threat. This is so often echoed throughout the organisation, mirroring the behaviour of those at the top.

There's a term for a person who acts beyond their ego, it's called being *transpersonal*. Transpersonal Leaders have developed the emotional intelligence (EI) to lead in ways that mean people follow them, there is empathy, trust and inspiration; all the things that equip someone to be an effective leader. When you have followers, you can afford to be radical in the knowledge that people will stay with you with a shared sense of values and purpose, understanding that you are making decisions in the interests of the greater good. That way organisations stay around, building a sustainable future that continually performs well, builds trust with its customers, staff, suppliers, shareholders, communities and making a valuable contribution to the world we live in.

That's an organisation many would go out of their way to work in.

There are many leaders who aspire to be like the Transpersonal Leader, but for one reason or another find the road to that goal challenging. If this is your desired path, then the first step we would encourage you to take is our previous publication, 'Leading Beyond the Ego – How to Become a Transpersonal

Leader' (Routledge 2018). It sets out a structured journey in practical steps towards becoming a Transpersonal Leader, which we will describe briefly in this chapter to provide you with a taste of what is involved.

The journey

Having completed the first 20 years of the 21st century, we have a VUCA world in which we are still in the early stages of the post-industrial information age. (VUCA stands for "Volatile, Uncertain, Complex and Ambiguous". Originally used by the American military to describe extreme conditions in Afghanistan and Iraq, but more recently as the state of the world in general.)

Just like the industrial revolution before, it needed different kinds of leaders, so does the information age. Hierarchical leadership does not work effectively any more in this increasingly complex world in which society is also changing rapidly. Such a world requires collaboration, participation, delegation and distribution of leadership. We need leaders who are more self-aware, emotionally intelligent and who can use a variety of leadership styles for different situations. They need all these attributes to be able to build a performance-enhancing culture in their organisations. But in addition to that, in order to create a culture that is also ethical, caring and sustainable, they need to bring their values to a higher level of consciousness. They must think radically, be authentic, lead beyond their ego and work for all the stakeholders of the organisation – and that includes the planet. And no one can achieve that without continuous personal and professional development. We call them Transpersonal Leaders (Knights et al., 2018).

To attain these heights of leadership competence, a leader needs to reach an advanced level of adult development (Kegan, 1982; Garvey Berger, 2006). But if we allow this to happen by serendipity, it will at least take until late middle-age, and then only 5% or so of the population will attain it.

So, our goal is to develop as many Transpersonal Leaders as possible and as young as possible. Then, we might start to change the world. To achieve this, the approach we have used is to enable leaders to rewire their own brains proactively based on the knowledge we provide, the insights they create, regular practice (primarily in the workplace) and regular reflection (Schon, 1983; Rock and Schwartz, 2007; Rock, 2009; Patterson, 2017). What we have developed over the last 20 years is a programme that uses state-of-the-art blended learning together with a process of learning that is in the most effective order to encourage embedding of the learning and the forming of new habits (Knights et al., 2018 – Ch22).

The journey of development

As we can see from Figure 1.1, the entire "Transpersonal leadership development journey to excellence" is made up of a programme to the intermediate level, followed by one to the advanced level. To reach the intermediate

REAL Transpersonal leadership development journey to excellence

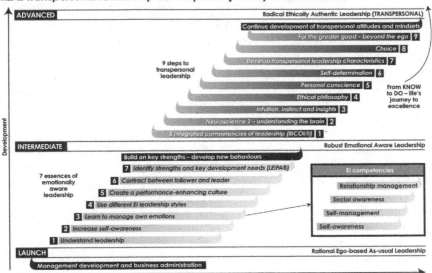

Figure 1.1 Transpersonal leadership development journey

level, leaders must understand what leadership is about in the 21st century, investigate how the brain actually works in the context of leadership, learn to increase self-awareness and understand how emotions impact our behaviour and leadership styles impact culture.

To progress through the advanced level of development, participants must learn to bring their values, beliefs and purpose to full consciousness and then act on them by using the new and improved behaviours they have already learned at the intermediate stage, and other behaviours they still need to learn, in order to manage their ego. During this part of the advanced journey, they become better decision-makers, addressing ethical issues and developing other transpersonal characteristics of being caring, radical, authentic and sustainable as well as emotionally intelligent and performance-enhancing. This provides a deep level of consciousness, allowing leaders to make their own choices, work for the greater good and lead beyond their ego.

At the very start of the journey, using our "REAL" mnemonic, participants function as a *"Rational, Ego-based, As-usual Leader" (REAL-1)*. What do we mean by this? Throughout our education (school, university, workplace and probably at home too), most of us are taught, told or persuaded to think logically and analytically; it is certainly what we are praised for and measured on. We are taught that our answers, responses and decisions should be thought out rationally and objectively. We are rarely (if ever) encouraged to think intuitively, emotionally or spiritually. By the time individuals are in a position of responsibility and take on a leadership role, most of us will have had any non-rational thinking "knocked" out of us. When we start our role as leaders, we usually have relevant job skills, know how to use them and also understand management processes and strategic planning (what we refer to as the "foundation" or "basic" level of leadership development). However, we often assume that other individuals think and act like us, although in reality, we all have different preferences. Every individual will have varying levels of innate intuitive thinking and emotional awareness, but most often, we will not be fully aware of our capabilities, and therefore will not be managing these attributes to maximise levels of self-management, relationships and performance. That takes care of "Rational".

In our early careers, both from a human maturity perspective and one of economics and sustainability, it is natural and usual to focus more on our personal needs. We want to get ahead with our careers, find the right partner, earn more money, get a nice car, buy a house, take care of our children and more. We want to establish ourselves and build our persona. It is primarily about "me". Fundamentally, we seek power, reward, prestige or recognition, or any combination of these. Usually, one or more of these needs will be the prime motivator for the leadership decisions we make. We are Ego-based. There is nothing wrong or immoral in any of this, and it is the nature of things, but as an employee and especially as we develop as a leader, we should instead be making decisions in the best interests of the organisation we work for and for the stakeholders of that organisation. Many of the corporate disasters during and since the financial crisis of 2008 were the result of the top leaders, unfortunately, never moving beyond being ego-driven.

Finally, let's explain what we mean by "As-Usual Leadership". For the vast majority of us, our default leadership style, the "As-usual" style, is to know everything and tell people what to do. That is what most people who have not learned otherwise think leadership is and is often counter-productive other than in specific circumstances. Many of those who have learned otherwise will nevertheless maintain this style as they feel it gives them power. Even those who, most of the time, make the effort not to lead like this will revert to it when stressed or hijacked by their emotions. Just think of any situation when you were "hijacked" in the last 24 hours. Wasn't your tendency just to want to do it your way without discussion? That is how our brain works genetically, in an attempt to reduce uncertainty (since that is experienced as an evolutionary existential threat) (Davachi et al., 2010).

Step by step – intermediate stage

The intermediate stage of the journey (Knights et al., 2018, Ch2–11) brings leaders to a level where they are *Robust, Emotionally Aware Leaders (REAL-2)*.

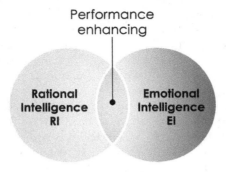

Figure 1.2 Creating performance enhancement

At this level, they possess a high level of EI and understand that sustainable performance can only be achieved by having the right kind of organisational culture. To do this, leaders must fully comprehend what leadership is about in today's world. This is achieved by appreciating how the brain actually works in the context of leadership, learning to increase self-awareness, understanding how emotions impact our behaviour (Goleman et al., 2002) and the way leadership styles determine the climate and culture of the organisation (Ogbonna and Harris, 2000). This is the foundation of the Transpersonal Leadership development journey, the ultimate objective of which is, of course, to provide improved, sustainable organisational performance. The essence of this part of the journey is to build on the rational intelligence of the leader to enhance performance through adding EI, as shown in Figure 1.2.

The first step (Figure 1.1) clarifies what leadership is, how it differs from management and how leadership needs to change to be successful in a VUCA world. We define what "we" mean by leadership and management and explain our default instincts about what "good" or "strong" leadership is (Covey, 1999; Landsberg, 2000). "As-usual" leadership was an acceptable and reasonably efficient style up to 25 years ago as it conformed to societal norms. However, it is no longer fit for purpose in this age of exponential social and technological changes.

We all have our instinctive views about inspirational leadership, but the reality is often surprising – such as "many leaders are introverts" (Farrington, 2019). A real understanding will give more people the confidence to be inspirational themselves. We identify some aspects of neuroscience that have a direct impact on how we lead. In particular, we focus on how much of our default behaviour is, on the one hand, based on how our brain developed to survive the stone age and, on the other, the environment needed to improve performance and productivity as well as create superior learning. We also explain how neuroscience helps us understand EI and why and how it is possible to improve our behaviours to better manage our emotions.

The second step helps leaders increase their self-awareness; a fundamental building block to enable our development as humans, especially as leaders. This self-awareness must be on several levels: our natural preferences, how we react to and deal with emotions, understanding our strengths and weaknesses, knowing how we use and react to our five senses, how we react in different situations and what our drivers are, how others react to us and why and how this is a life-long exercise.

The third step, managing emotions and EI, is one of the real core areas of learning and development that we all need and is a key building block to increasing performance. We discuss in detail the importance of EI as a part of leadership and how it can be developed. Having become aware of how our emotions impact our behaviour, we must now learn how to manage those emotions. We need to know which emotions and specific behaviours have the greatest impact, and so how to prioritise. This requires rewiring our brains and understanding exactly how we can do that. It is not just about managing our own emotions, but, as leaders, how we can impact more positively on the emotions of the people around us. We cover in detail how to improve our capability in the four competencies of EI: self-awareness, self-management, social awareness and relationship management – following the Goleman and Boyatzis model (Goleman et al., 2002).

The fourth step in the journey is about how to use different leadership styles. It is a critical step because it is about how to apply EI by using different styles in different circumstances and knowing when to adopt each style. Most of us have one preferred style, or at best two, which we tend to use all the time, but to be effective in all circumstances, we need to become competent in six styles (we use Goleman's six styles: visionary, coaching, affiliative, democratic, pace-setting and commanding as they correlate best with EI competencies and behaviours (Goleman et al., 2002)). This means honing four to five new styles which, in turn, means developing specific granular behaviours, which are not necessarily natural to us. All our research and experience, and that of others, have confirmed that of the six styles, the coaching style is the least used by leaders, even though it is the second most impactful (after the visionary style). The good news though is that it is the easiest to learn because there are many simple, proven techniques that can be used to develop and implement this style. A key role of leaders, which is often missing, is to help develop the people they are responsible for. The coaching style is the best style to use to help people learn in the workplace and develop to fulfil their potential.

In the fifth and sixth steps, we learn how to create a performance-enhancing culture and establish a mutually beneficial contract between leader and follower. These aspects are necessary to convert good leadership skills and styles into organisational effectiveness. Leaders learn how to develop the right kind of culture by first creating the right environment (climate) through their own consistent behaviour and values. Changing culture is longer term and requires the engagement of most of the people in the organisation. We use a model that has four parameters of culture (power, structure, achievement and support), and each parameter is specifically related to one or two of the six leadership styles (Harrison, 1972; Ogbonna and Harris, 2000). So, by identifying the "actual" and "ideal" cultures for an organisation using these parameters (we have a well-developed tool – LeaderShape Online Culture Shaper (LOCS) – to do just that), we can identify both the leadership styles the leaders need to use and granular behaviours the organisation needs to focus on in order to move towards the ideal. An important aspect of developing the right culture is the explicit contract between individual leaders and each person reporting to them, which has a psychological dimension as well as a practical one.

The seventh and final step in the intermediate stage of the journey is about identifying strengths and improving development areas. We use a specific tool (LEIPA®), developed by LeaderShape. LEIPA is the Leadership and Emotional Intelligence Performance Accelerator. Using best practice in a 360° format, LEIPA® identifies and compares the individual's habitual leadership styles to those which will have the greatest positive impact (http://www.leadershapeglobal.com/Leipa).

LEIPA enables leaders to identify their habitual granular behaviours and leadership styles that form the inherent strengths of their leadership competence and how to build on that. It also identifies those styles and capabilities that need developing or improving and explains how, usually, improving just two or three granular behaviours can have a major impact on a leader's competence and performance (Wall and Knights, 2013). This step also includes a detailed action plan.

Step by step – advanced stage

The advanced stage of the journey (Knights et al., 2018, Ch12–21) will take leaders towards becoming *Radical, Ethically Authentic Leaders (REAL-3)*, that is *Transpersonal Leaders*. This advanced journey is primarily about bringing our values, beliefs and purpose to full consciousness, and then acting on them by using the new and improved behaviours we have already learned during the intermediate stage, and other behaviours we still need to learn, in order to manage our ego.

For the purposes of this journey and to understand how we use the words, we think of *Awareness* as fundamentally about "observation" (knowing about self and others), whereas *Consciousness* is about "experiencing" (connecting with self and others) in the moment (OLD, 2017).

This advanced journey takes leaders on a voyage beyond EI, beyond our ego to the ultimate state of Transpersonal Leadership. It is about increasing our consciousness, and then learning and taking actions from that. In addition to bringing our values to full consciousness, we must gain a better understanding of our ego and how to manage it. Critically, we must also learn to improve our decision-making and judgement, so it takes into account the emotional, ethical and authentic aspects of any issue or challenge as well as the logic-analytical ones we are often more comfortable handling. Learning that this journey has direction but no end point or ultimate summit, and is life-long, is the final important lesson.

At the heart of the advanced part of the journey is the addition of spiritual intelligence to our rational and EI, as shown in Figure 1.3. This will enable us to define better what "performance" really means to a Transpersonal Leader. Unfortunately, the word "spiritual" in the Western world has negative connotations associated with the mystical and religious which for some people can throw up barriers. We like Cindy Wigglesworth's definition of spirituality, "the ability to behave with wisdom and compassion, while maintaining inner and outer peace, regardless of the situation" (Wigglesworth, 2012). In much of Asia, the word "spiritual" is more commonly used and rarely seen as uncomfortable. The Dalai Lama explains spirituality as being "concerned with those qualities of the human spirit — such as love, compassion, patience, tolerance, forgiveness, contentment, a sense of responsibility, a sense of harmony, which brings happiness to both self and others" (Craig, 2002). In the end, the spiritual is grounded in our values (Fry, 2003), and that cannot be ignored. It is thought that our spiritual intelligence manifests itself in the brain through synchronous neural oscillations which wave across the main parts of the brain (Grey et al. 1989; Zohar and Marshall, 2000).

The first step (referring to Figure 1.1) in this advanced journey is understanding the Eight Integrated Competencies of Leadership (8ICOL®) that take into account rational, emotional and spiritual intelligence and our innate personal preferences. We explain in detail the 8ICOL® model (see Figure 1.4) developed by LeaderShape to show how the different aspects of intelligence

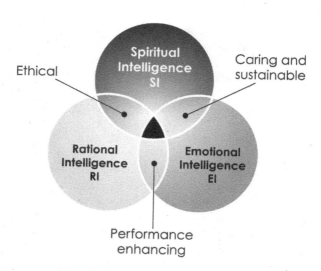

Figure 1.3 Transpersonal leadership integrates three intelligences

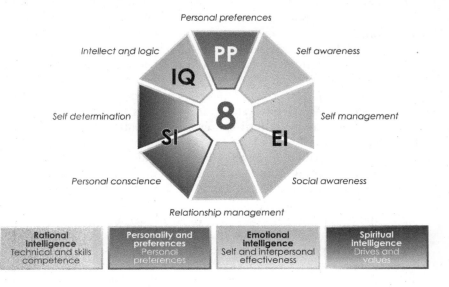

Figure 1.4 Eight Integrated Competencies of Leadership (8ICOL®)

and competence provide a holistic template for leadership development that includes explaining how behaviours are the foundation for values and ethical behaviour (Gardner, 1983; Lynn and Vanhanen, 2002; Goleman, 2004; Griffith, 2017). Uniquely, it introduces two new competencies of personal conscience and self-determination, which helps us to appreciate better the role and purpose in leadership of different kinds of values.

The second step brings the latest neuroscience research together with some relevant philosophy which focuses on consciousness and how the brain works to handle the spiritual, ethical and value-based aspects of leadership (Crick, 1995). Neurons connect in three different ways, but it is primarily the bonding through synchronous neural oscillations that we address in this step (Zohar and Marshall, 2000).

The third step, "Managing the Ego", explains that we need to know what drives us in order to manage our ego. Whereas emotions can hijack our behaviours, drivers can hijack our ego (Black and Hughes, 2017). Moving beyond the ego as an organisational leader requires us to focus on the stakeholders we are serving and the order of priority of those stakeholders in different contexts. It identifies who really are the stakeholders that will determine the sustainable success of the organisation. Where is the ethical balance between a leader taking care of their own needs versus those of the organisation?

Steps 4 and 5 introduce the importance of the 3Is (intuition, instinct and insight) and ethical philosophy in decision-making and improving our judgement. We are taught throughout our education and most of our lives to make decisions rationally and logically. Yet, in actual fact, we tend to use logic for explaining our decisions rather than making them. The three other subconscious, nonconscious and unconscious decision-making processes each come with their biases and prejudices that we need to be aware of and understand so that we can unpick and overcome them in order to make better judgements (Steare, 2006; Sadler-Smith, 2009).

Steps 6 and 7 propose a new framework to understand the role of values in leadership. We divide values into the areas of personal conscience and self-determination. Personal conscience is about "who I am" whereas self-determination is "what I am going to do with who I am" and is very leadership-focused (Ryan and Deci, 2000). We discuss the more common values that employees want in their leaders, but also the softer values such as "forgiveness" and "humility", and the difficult ones like "vulnerability" that need to be developed and implemented in order to become a Transpersonal Leader. Managing diversity and inclusion is another area that is critical for leaders to operate beyond their ego and in full consciousness, to establish creative, effective workplace cultures (Rosado, 2006; Plaister-Ten, 2017).

Developing Transpersonal Leadership characteristics or qualities (caring, radical, ethical, authentic, sustainable, emotionally intelligent, performance-enhancing), Step 8 in the advanced journey is underpinned by an inner journey, which includes mindfulness/meditation practice (Reitz and Chaskalson). Such practice supports the leader in being fully present and being aware of what is required in each moment from a leadership perspective. It also requires a growth mind-set and congruency of identity, values and beliefs. In addition, the leader needs to ensure that they are thriving as an individual so that they are able to create the conditions for their people to thrive. All of this promotes sustainable high performance and success.

Steps 9 and 10, "Choice" and "For the Greater Good" are interconnected. Choice is much more important than our abilities, and ultimately, to be a Transpersonal Leader, one has to make choices about what is right for all stakeholders, including the planet (Suddendorf, 2014; Santos and Rosati, 2015). To make those choices, it is important to understand one's own purpose and spiritual belief system, and how that manifests into ethical behaviour. In the end, how will I, YOU, WE leave the world a better place?

The continuing journey

Beyond the final step in the journey is continuous self-development. There are six levels of self-awareness, the highest level being *"No longer a struggle between Ego (what I want for myself) and the greater good"* – developed from the work by Wigglesworth (2006). Reaching this level of self-awareness plus continually working to improve and develop those behaviours that are barriers to leadership competence, as well as raising one's consciousness to live one's values, is a life-long journey of development. The process in itself requires many EI capabilities (e.g. initiative, achievement orientation, emotional self-awareness) and values (e.g. resilience, humility, motivation) to achieve. Continuous development can be aided by following transpersonal practices, which themselves are based on the complex-adaptive system of nature (Miller and Page, 2007; Zohar, 2016), by connecting with the various stages of human development (Kegan, 1982; Garvey Berger, 2006) and by using the evolution of intelligences as a guide (Knights et al., 2018 – Figure 21.2). With commitment and determination, leaders can reach the advanced level of the REAL journey to become radical, ethically, authentic leaders. In our experience, few leaders reach this level naturally. This is not because it is not possible for anyone with a slightly above-normal IQ, but because very few will chance upon the experiences, learning opportunities and support that are required to get there. Our goal is to remove the "chance" element and make it a proactive choice for anyone who has the will. Finally, let us review what the phrase *"Radical, Ethically, Authentic Leader"* means. To be *Radical* is critical because we need a new kind of leadership. We need to have the courage, fearlessness, conviction and ideas to move to unorthodox approaches, realise we might need alternatives to continuous growth and gauge societal success in measures other than gross domestic product (GDP). There may also be times when we need disruptive thinking for survival.

Acting *Ethically* means not only integrity, but also a social conscience and a willingness to follow the rules (or get them changed if that is what is needed). It means working for the greater good. And it is not only about "me" as an individual leader being ethical. We have a responsibility to create ethical cultures in organisations. Ethical leadership is defined in *How to Develop Ethical Leaders* (Knights, 2016) as the process of influencing people to act through principles and values and beliefs that embrace ethical behaviour. Ethical Behaviour is about acting in a way that is consistent with one's own principles and values which are characterized by honesty, fairness and equity in all interpersonal activities, be they personal or professional, and by respecting the dignity, diversity and rights of individuals and groups of people (see Chapter 5).

A Transpersonal Leader must also be *Authentic* because a leader must act as they truly are. They must be honest with themselves and others. Excellent leadership is not a game; it is not something we can pretend to do and get right. The human being is very good at seeing through the falseness of others, although often not in a conscious way. "Authentic" also implies that the leader is the same person (though may behave appropriately differently) in all circumstances – their values are operating at full consciousness and they don't leave them at the door to the office (Knights, 2011).

To become this kind of Leader, an individual needs to be emotionally intelligent in order to have sufficient inner self-confidence, awareness and empathy to be able to take this advanced journey. To become a Transpersonal

Leader, we must bring our values, beliefs and purpose to full consciousness and act on them.

Implications for practice and society

The Transpersonal Leadership development and training programmes described in this chapter have been developed over the last 20 years using a combination of best practice, sourced research, in situ evidence-based research and personal experiences. It has far-reaching implications for how we lead, how we impact the climate, culture and performance of our organisations, governments and societies in such an uncertain environment. This book aims to bring to life the way we have observed Transpersonal Leadership being applied to real, everyday situations in a variety of contexts.

References

Black, B. and Hughes, S. (2017), *Ego Free Leadership: Ending the Unconscious Habits that Hijack Your Business*, Greenleaf Book Group Press, Austin, TX.

Covey, S. (1999), *The 7 Habits of Highly Effective People*, Simon & Schuster, London.

Craig, M. (2002), *The Pocket Dalai Lama by the Dalai Lama (Abridged)*, Shambhala Publications, Boulder, CO.

Crick, F. (1995), *The Astonishing Hypothesis: The Scientific Search for the Soul*, Simon & Schuster, New York.

Davachi, L., Kiefer, T., Rock, D. and Rock, L. (2010), *Learning that Lasts through AGES*, available at: https://www.ahri.com.au/ data/assets/pdf_file/0016/16144/ Learning-that-lasts-through-AGES.pdf (accessed March 2017).

Farrington, J. (2019), "Is inspiration overrated? I Think Not", *HF Blog*, available at: https://www. jonathanfarrington.com/is-inspiration-overrated-i-think-not/.

Fry, L. (2003), "Toward a theory of spiritual leadership", *The Leadership Quarterly*, Vol. 14, pp. 693–727.

Gardner, H. (1983), *Frames of Mind: The Theory of Multiple Intelligences by Howard Gardner*, Fontana Press, London, 1781.

Garvey Berger, J. (2006), *Key Concepts for Understanding the Work of Robert Kegan*, Kenning Associates, Atlanta.

Goleman, D. (2004), *Emotional Intelligence & Working with Emotional Intelligence*, London: Bloomsbury.

Goleman, D., Boyatzis, R. and McKee, A. (2002), *Primal Leadership: Realizing the Power of Emotional Intelligence*, Harvard Business School Press, Brighton, MA, Published in the UK as "*The New Leaders*".

Grant, D. (2013), *Determining Key Design Principles to Help Embed Leadership Learning in a Blended Learning Programme*, Master's Degree Dissertation to University of Chester, UK, Unpublished Manuscript.

Grey, C., Konig, P., Engel, A. and Singer, W. (1989), "Oscillatory responses in cat visual cortex exhibit inter-columnar synchronization which reflects global stimulus properties", *Nature*, Vol. 338, pp. 334–337, doi: 10.1038/338334a0.

Griffith, R. (2017), *The Definition of Spiritual Intelligence*, SQI.CO, available at: http://sqi.co/definition- of-spiritual-intelligence/.

Harrison, R. (1972), "Understanding your organization's character", *Harvard Business Review*, Vol. 50, No. 3, pp. 119–128.

Kegan, R. (1982), *The Evolving Self*, Harvard University Press, Cambridge, MA.

Knights, J. (2011), *The Invisible Elephant & the Pyramid Treasure*, Tomorrows Company, London, available at: http://www.leadershape.biz/invisible-elephant.

Knights, J. (2016), *How to Develop Ethical Leaders*, White Paper by Routledge, NY and Oxford, available at: https://www.routledge.com/posts/9951.

Knights, J., Grant, D. and Young, G. (2018), *Leading Beyond the Ego: How to Become a Transpersonal Leader*, Routledge, NY and Oxford.

Landsberg, M. (2000), *The Tools of Leadership: Vision, Inspiration, Momentum*, Harper Collins, London.

Lynn, R. and Vanhanen, T. (2002), *IQ and the Wealth of Nations (Human Evolution, Behavior, and Intelligence)*, Praeger, Westport, CT, USA.

Miller, J. and Page, S. (2007), *Complex Adaptive Systems: An Introduction to Computational Models of Social Life (Princeton Studies in Complexity)*, Princeton University Press, Princeton, NJ.

Ogbonna, E. and Harris, L. (2000), "Leadership style, organisational culture and performance: Empirical evidence from UK companies", *The International Journal of Human Resource Management*, Vol. 11, No. 4, pp. 766–788.

OLD (2017), *Oxford Living Dictionary*, available at: https://en.oxforddictionaries.com (accessed 12 April 2017).

Patterson, E. (2017), "Waking up to the power of reflection to unlock transformation in people, teams and organisations in contemporary leadership challenges – Chapter 1", in Alvinius, A. (Ed.), available at: www.intechopen.com.

Plaister-Ten, J. (2017), *Leading across Cultures: Developing Leaders for Global Organisations*, Routledge, Oxford, New York, available at: http://bit.ly/2mbDuYm.

Rock, D. (2009), *Your Brain at Work*, Harper Collins Publishers, New York.

Rock, D. and Schwartz, J. (2007), *Neuroscience of Leadership*, Strategy & Business, New York.

Rosado, C. (2006), *What Do We Mean by "Managing Diversity"?*, Rosado Consulting for Change in Human Systems, Portland, available at: http://www.edchange.org/multicultural/papers/rosado_managing_diversity.pdf.

Ryan, R. and Deci, E. (2000), "Self-determination theory and facilitation of intrinsic motivation, social development and well-being", *American Psychologist*, Vol. 55, No. 1, pp. 68–78.

Sadler-Smith, E. (2009), *The Intuitive Mind: Profiting from the Power of Your Sixth Sense*, Chen Wiley and Sons, Chichester, UK.

Santos, L. and Rosati, A. (2015), "The evolutionary roots to human decision making", *Annual Review of Psychology*, Vol. 66, pp. 13.1–13.27.

Schon, D. (1983), *The Reflective Practitioner: How Professionals Think in Action*, Routledge, Oxford, New York.

Steare, R. (2006), *Ethicability: How to Decide What's Right and Find the Courage to Do it*, London: Roger Steare.

Suddendorf, T. (2014), *What Makes US Human? Huffington Post – The Blog*, available at: http://www.huffingtonpost.com/thomas-suddendorf/what-makes-us-human_b_4414357.html (accessed 08 February 2014).

Wall, T. and Knights, J. (2013), *Leadership Assessment for Talent Development*, Kogan Page, London.

Wigglesworth, C. (2006), "Why spiritual intelligence is essential to mature leadership", *Integral Leadership Review*, Vol. VI, No. 3, available at: http://integralleadershipreview.com/5502-feature-article-why-spiritual-intelligence-is-essential-to-mature-leadership/ (accessed May 2012).

Wigglesworth, C., 2012. Spiritual Intelligence: Living as Your Higher Self. [online] HuffPost, available at: https://www.huffpost.com/entry/spiritual-intelligence_b_1752145 (accessed 22 October 2021).

Zohar, D. (2016), *The Quantum Leader*, Prometheus Books, New York.

Zohar, D. and Marshall, I. (2000), *Spiritual Intelligence: The Ultimate Intelligence*, Bloomsbury, London.

Part 1

Becoming a transpersonal leader

Duncan Enright

> I am the master of my fate:
> I am the captain of my soul.
>
> William Ernest Henley, from the poem "Invictus"

Overview

How do you become a transpersonal leader? It might be fair to say that you never do. If you lean back in your swivel chair, gaze at the computer screen and declare "I have finally made it and am now without doubt a transpersonal leader," the odds are that you are not. The journey and not the destination is, as described in Chapter 2, what leads us to seek personal development and learning constantly, to seek to renew our approach to life, to find out more about ourselves and to apply our learning in ever-changing environments in a turbulent world.

I am in the second half of my life (unless I am very lucky, or medical science conquers ageing). I am still learning new things about myself, never mind the ways I learn about the fascinating, puzzling and inspiring people around me; not to mention gaining insights and marvelling as I try to make sense of the world and the universe beyond. As I write, a new mission has just landed on Mars to explore signs of ancient life. The discoveries it makes will change our view of our galaxy, bring new insights on the nature of being, alter the course of human history and, in its own small way, change me.

This section of the book explores a number of perspectives of that journey and the nature of transpersonal leadership. Each of these offers a fresh look at our development. You might think of this section as a journal, written by many hands, of the scenery as we travel, the mode of transport and how it operates, or our thoughts and feelings as we whizz through the countryside.

Hopefully by the end of this section, you will have a series of images to create your own map, personal to you and different for each of us, giving a clue to where you are going and why. If at every stage of the journey you have fresh insights and questions, that is all to the good. After all, the key to

DOI: 10.4324/9781003150626-3

transpersonal leadership is self-awareness, and through that we will understand how much more we have to learn if we are to grow as a leader.

Navigating the chapters in this section

Each chapter here describes the development of leaders. First is an account by John Knights and Danielle Grant of the role of 'purpose' – what is it that we are trying to achieve by becoming transpersonal leaders? What is the journey for? Not only will this give useful guidance on finding purpose, but it will help you to discover the motivation and energy to get travelling. John then explains ethical leadership and how we might look for and develop an ethical approach that matches our values and virtues. If in doubt, or facing challenges, there is great strength to be gained by relying on our values, and to do this we need self-knowledge and to have brought them to consciousness.

There follows work by Heather Katz and Alison Hill exploring adult development as it relates to transpersonal leadership development. Can we learn to operate with a self-transforming mind and how will that help our development? Sue Coyne shares thoughts about sustainable leadership, and how to achieve it. This includes advice on how we can change our thinking and habits to support our leadership practice. At LeaderShape, we have developed a 360-degree assessment tool we call LeaderShape Emotional Intelligence and Performance Accelerator (LEIPA). Its principles, how it is used to support leaders to change, and the results we have found over the decade and more of its use are shared in the next chapter. For many of us, the journey can be long and we are well into our careers with hard-to-shift habits by the time we can be aware of transpersonal leadership. If we are to change the world, we need to encourage next-generation leaders to become self-aware, and make the journey. Xenia Angevin describes how this can happen in a chapter on next-generation leadership development. As a result of our work, we have found time and again, across the world, women score more highly on average on most (nearly all!) transpersonal leadership qualities and skills. Greg Young explores this further in a chapter on women in leadership, which has lessons for all of us and shines a light on the work we need to do. Finally, Danielle Grant shares the latest learning methodologies and approaches which we know can all be put to use, by all of us, in our lifelong pursuit of change.

How to use this section

If you are reading about transpersonal leadership for the first time, this section follows neatly from Chapter 2 and will give you a three-dimensional picture in your mind about the principles. For those who have explored these ideas before, this is a guide to move from 'what' to 'how'.

No matter where you are on your journey, the aim here is to give you the ingredients you need to identify those aspects that most require attention, and ideas which will help you plan your development. If you are responsible for the development of others and looking for solutions, this section offers insights that can help you plan. If you are someone who is actively involved in leadership development, such as a trainer or a coach, the ideas here are yours to incorporate in your current toolkit and refresh your approach.

Every journey begins with the first step, and our aim in 'Becoming a Transpersonal Leader' is to introduce you to some of the dance moves that will get you going in the right direction.

2 Purpose and transpersonal leadership

Danielle Grant and John Knights

People want to do well and do good. They want to understand how they're making a difference in the world. Things change all the time, but your organization's purpose transcends any individual product or service.

Mark Weinberger, former CEO of Ernst & Young

Overview

Throughout the COVID-19 pandemic, there has been a growing trend to talk about 'purpose'.

The realisation that the human race is all connected on our small planet has been brought home to us vividly, as a small virus spread around the globe, affecting communities irrespective of size or geography. A striking feature has been that often-crowded cities in developed countries have been affected as much, if not more, than less developed nations. Why has this sparked our interest in and awareness of the importance of purpose? The purpose of the virus is very simple: infect more people and survive to replicate! In defence, perhaps, we have sought more meaning in our own lives, hence the focus on purpose.

This chapter explores the meaning of purpose and makes clear the difference between purpose, vision, mission and other strategic concepts. The impact of finding purpose is explained, and ways of divining individual and organisational purpose are explored.

Defining purpose

How can we define Purpose and differentiate it from the traditional 'corporate speak' of Vision and Mission? Purpose is at the pinnacle of who we are and our WHY both as individuals and organisations.

There is often confusion about the definition of Vision and Mission. In fact, we always used a series of 'easy to define' statements instead, which we called "A rose by any other name."

- A short externally focused memorable statement of what we do
- An externally focused statement of how we want the world to perceive us

DOI: 10.4324/9781003150626-4

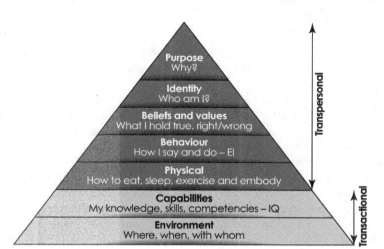

Figure 2.1 Hierarchy of developing purpose

- Internally *focused statement of the reason for the existence of the organisation*
- Internally focused statement of how we work
- What are the goals we want to achieve?

However, in essence: Vision is about WHAT, Mission is about HOW and Purpose is about WHY. So, the third statement referred to here is "A focused statement of the reason for the existence of the organisation" – and that is what purpose is all about (Figure 2.1).

Here are some examples of statements from leading companies. Can you identify others from the websites and corporate literature of companies you know well? What purpose do these statements serve?

Purpose (The Why):

Why do we do what we do (aside from commercial benefit).

"To accelerate the world's transition to sustainable energy." – Tesla

Vision (The Where):

Where is your brand going and what does that future brand look like?

"To become the world's most loved, most flown, and most profitable airline." – Southwest Air

Mission (The What):

What are you committed to in realising your vision?

"Build the best product, cause no unnecessary harm, use business to inspire and implement solutions to the environmental crisis." – Patagonia

Values (The How):

How will your brand go about its business in realising its vision for the future?

"Sell good merchandise at a reasonable profit, treat your customers like human beings, and they will always come back for more." – L.L. Bean

Individual purpose

The Japanese have a concept called Ikigai, which is a useful way to identify one's reason for being or, as Daniel Pink would say: 'start with Why? "The most deeply motivated people hitch their desires to a cause bigger than themselves" Daniel Pink (2018).

You can use Figure 2.2 to begin to explore what your own 'Why?' might be. It can be very helpful to explore this with a coach who can ask you questions you may not ask yourself. If you don't have a coach or buddy, ask yourself the question contained in each section, then see if you can distil your Ikigai from your responses.

This question of 'why?' is explored by the authors where it is related as a foundation of Self-Determination, which is termed the ultimate leadership competence: "Self-determination is the combination of having a purpose in life powered by the values that enable us to best use our personal conscience in order to make a positive contribution in whatever sphere we choose" (Knights, Grant & Young, 2018, Chapter 17).

To be a transpersonal leader requires us to have a purpose, something that at least starts to answer the question "what contribution can I make to improve the world, even if just a little bit?"

When you align your work with your purpose, you experience vitality, unleash your creativity, feel passionate and spend more time in flow. What

Figure 2.2 The concept of IKIGAI

is more, when you are on purpose, it is difficult for others to knock you off balance.

Organisational purpose

In his 2014 book, *Reinventing Organisations*, Frederic Laloux observes that "When the individual and organisational purpose enter into resonance and reinforce each other, extraordinary things can happen" (Laloux, 2014).

These days we speak far more about organisational purpose, and it is interesting to understand why it has become so important (Figure 2.3).

There is a marked increase in the prevalence today of companies focusing on purpose. Even venture capitalists (VCs) investing in start-ups are today more interested in purpose than vision. To some extent, it is because it is fashionable 'management speak' – like Agile and total quality management (TQM). It does not change the fundamentals.

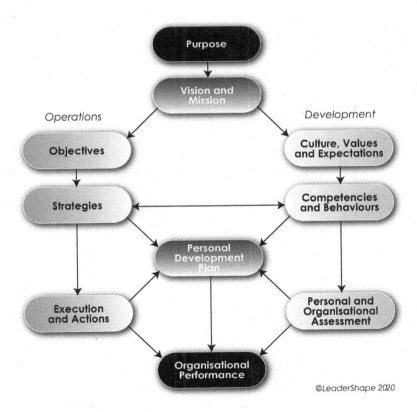

Figure 2.3 Purpose to performance

This 'fashionable' perspective is solidified through efforts like the commitment by 181 CEOs of major US companies in August 2019, to 'Profits with Purpose' (Business Roundtable, 2019). However, disappointingly, a peer-reviewed academic paper one year later identified that none of those CEOs had actually implemented anything meaningful (Colvin, 2020).

But the real importance of finding and aligning purpose is because purpose awakens our spiritual intelligence – the Why! In contrast, vision awakens our rational intelligence (What); and mission connects to our emotional intelligence (How). Purpose connects with us at a deeper level – it connects to our values and a deep human desire of wanting to do good (which, across all humans, is at very differing levels of consciousness).

Some of the changes to the old 'business as usual' can be found in a shift of perspective. To have a purpose means we go beyond a focus on shareholders to consider all the organisation's stakeholders, including the planet.

It is also good for business on many levels. Research from the Global Leadership Forecast (DDI World, 2018), EY (DiversityInc, 2018) and elsewhere shows that companies with high levels of purpose outperform the market by 42% per year (Figure 2.4). They also grow faster and have higher profitability. Companies like Unilever have seen quantifiable value of making purpose a core driver of growth and differentiation at brand level. Nearly half of the company's top 40 brands now focus on sustainability. These 'sustainable Living' brands, including Knorr, Dove and Lipton, are growing 50% faster than the company's other brands and delivering more than 60% of the company's growth.

Purposeful businesses are also better at innovation, as purpose promotes passion. And as we have seen so strikingly, innovation and agility have accelerated dramatically from the beginning of the COVID-19 pandemic. The common and aligned purpose of healing/saving lives harnessed the most innovative and rapid development in pharmaceuticals, business models, government and more. In Chapter 11, the importance of purpose as a point of 'pivot' when undergoing change, particularly digital transformation, is explored in more detail. Purpose keeps us focused on what is really important, while the 'how' and 'what' may change completely.

However, to make this approach endure in the day-to-day running of organisations, when we are not all aligned to the overarching purpose of defeating COVID-19, the link between purpose and profitability has to be explicit. It can only be ensured, if the senior team has been successful in diffusing that sense of purpose further down in the organisation, especially in middle management. The need is to provide strategic clarity throughout the organisation on how to achieve that purpose. That means great communication, trust and inspiring middle management to be champions.

The recent growth in emphasis on purpose is based on the fact that, in times of uncertainty, anxiety and fear, we want something we can hold onto to give us hope for and belief in the future. I think also that the experience of the pandemic is making us question whether the world, as we know it, is

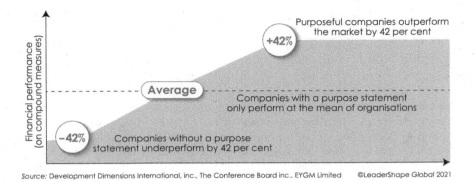

Source: Development Dimensions International, inc., The Conference Board inc., EYGM Limited   ©LeaderShape Global 2021

Figure 2.4 Impact of purpose on financial performance

what we want for the future. It feels like a time for reinvention and renewal once we are through the crisis and that requires us to have a purpose.

When we consider Purpose as 'what really matters', a Wisconsin University study (Center for Healthy Minds, 2020) showed that higher levels of purpose were better for maintaining good health, especially in relation to depression and anxiety – which is particularly important in times of crisis and uncertainty. Their centre for healthy minds found that a strong sense of purpose is associated with improved health outcomes and behaviours, including increased physical activity, decreased incidence of stroke, fewer cardiovascular events, reduced risk of death, lower health care utilisation and even better financial health.

Developing purpose

A recent Korn Ferry Institute survey showed that 79% of business leaders believe that purpose is central to an organisation's success and longevity, but only 34% agree that purpose guides their decision-making (Goleman, 2021). Yet, for this to embed, the leaders need to continually ensure that this purpose is expressed in every product, action and process. In short, organisational purpose has to align with that of the team and the organisation. Or to put it another way, it has to be simultaneously internal, external as well as being used to scan the horizon for new opportunities to express it. As a Deloitte Insights report in 2019 says "Purpose-driven businesses truly embed purpose in every action, aiming to leave an enduring impact on people's lives." The same report finds that employees and customers want to work in and engage with companies whose goals resonate with their own. They mention examples like Kellogg's aim to "nourish families so they can flourish and thrive" through nutritious breakfast cereals and Patagonia being "in business to save our home planet" (O'Brien, Main, Kounkel & Stephan, 2019).

Understanding that purpose is crucial, to organisations themselves as well as the individuals who work in them and their customers, results in a three-fold approach.

First, as individuals, we need to develop a purpose. So how do I do that? Let's start with an internal focus. This is a journey of increasing self-awareness (Knights, Grant & Young, 2018). This involves looking inward to get in touch with our personal conscience values (virtues), both those that are part of who we are as human beings and those that we may seek to develop. Just as crucial are those that allow us to express our purpose in the world. These are our Self-Determination values. By getting in touch with our own feelings, emotions and reactions, we can identify where in our lives we find meaning. The exercises in this chapter can be used to help you elicit your values, drivers, and from that emerges your purpose. That then allows us to appreciate how we can express this in our role, future direction and how it aligns with the purpose of the team and the organisation we belong to.

In Figure 2.5, we provide an example of one person's touchstone. As shown in Table 2.1, we split the Personal Conscience values into 'hard' and 'soft'. The Self-Determination values are how you bring your values to life in the real world; for example, it may take courage or resilience to offer forgiveness. This is not an exhaustive list and you could create your own touchstone by selecting your values (from this list or add your own). We suggest you choose two from the hard, two from the soft and two from the self-determination areas. You may want to include one or two that you wish to develop and others that are integral to your own sense of who you are. The Transpersonal Qualities (on the right of the image) are fixed as these are essential to being a transpersonal leader (Knights, Grant & Young, 2018, Chapter 20).

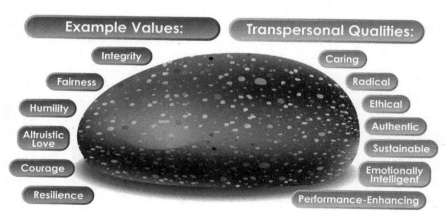

Figure 2.5 Ethical touchstone example

Table 2.1 Examples of values

Personal conscience values	Self-determination values
Hard	– Purpose
– Integrity	– Motivation
– Trustworthiness	– Power
– Truth & Honesty	– Energy
– Excellence	– Courage
Soft	– Resilience
– Humility	– Aspirations
– Vulnerability	– Drive (Intense Will)
– Patience	– Continuous Personal Development – CPD
– Fairness	
– Conscientiousness	
– Forgiveness	
– Altruistic Love	

We suspect that more people have a purpose than may immediately re-alise it. Like most things in the spiritual zone, the identification of purpose may be a 'sense' and something that is non-conscious. Of course, an important part of the transpersonal leadership journey is to increase our level of consciousness.

For those who know what they want to do in life, and particularly for those with a sense of vocation, finding your purpose is less difficult. The question to ask yourself is WHY do I want to do this? If I want to be a singer, is it because I want to be famous, because I want to make a lot of money, because I want to make people happy, or because I need a platform to promote human rights, for example? Or is it something I feel compelled to do, as a 'vocation'?

As well as the other exercises in this chapter, maybe start off with these four questions to yourself:

- What is the broader reason for my actions other than the actions themselves? (For example, do I help others because I feel it is part of who I am or because at some level I want thanks?)
- How is the direction I am taking consistent with my values? (For example, am I choosing a role just for the income, or is the business one that aligns with my values?)
- To what extent do I think strategically about my life and what is to be achieved for the greater good? (For example, if I am at a stage in life where my priority is earning an income for my family, can I identify extracurricular activities where I can serve the greater good?)
- What do I believe to be my goal in life and the purpose it represents? (For example, is my goal to accumulate spare wealth so as to support philanthropic work?)

Once we have greater clarity around our own purpose, we are enabled to begin to uncover purpose in those around us. By truly paying attention to those we work with, we can tune in to their values.

Why not get a whole team to create their touchstones and then identify the common values to create a team touchstone and from there, try asking pointed questions about the expressed values from an exercise like this, reflecting with your own observations of those around you (and actively listening to the answers). One simple question could be, "What matters most about what we do?" "Why is it important?" With answers to questions like this, you can make choices and engage them in those, for the benefit of the group. This approach to 'external' focus lets you better see how to align the individual and the team purpose, in support of that of the organisations.

Continuing on the theme of the 'external' focus, the next stage is to look towards the horizon. What is the widest view we can take of the organisation, its stakeholders, the broader community and, indeed, the world? What

---

Case study: PepsiCo

While we might not yet be aware of it, one household name, employing this approach to bridge the gap between values and action, is PepsiCo.

The company set an overarching goal of creating a healthier relationship between people and food. To embed this into their defined agenda, they created a 2025 plan entitled Performance with Purpose. This began with looking at the source of their raw materials, and all their ingredients. This led to an emphasis on sustainable farming, safe water access, nutrition, reducing sugar, providing clear labelling and responsible marketing. Sustainability has been a key objective in their business operations since 2006.

"Performance with Purpose is about the character of our company and managing PepsiCo with an eye toward not only short-term priorities, but also long-term goals, recognizing that our success—and the success of the communities we serve and the wider world—are inextricably bound together," explains PepsiCo's former Chairman and CEO, Indra K. Nooyi – the woman responsible for putting this initiative into action (PepsiCo, 2018).

This agenda has also inspired the launch of PepsiCorps, a global volunteer program created by the company's associates. "I've never seen anything stick as fast as this did across the company," said their chief personnel officer in an interview. "It's helped everyone remember that they serve a bigger mission and be able to think of the future in a positive way."

are the systemic connections? What can we notice about the ripple effect of what we do moving ever-outwards, to create a bigger purpose and a more impactful whole?

Alignment of individual and organisational purpose

Why is this coming of age now? In the past, most working people were considered as human machines who followed orders. This relates to the model of the organisation as a machine which emerged from the earlier industrial revolutions. And, it still happens in many places. But in the 21st century – in the information age, where people are more educated and informed; more and more people will want to work somewhere that treats them with respect and fairness. And also is doing something for the benefit of the planet in one way or another.

There is a lot of research showing that millennials and younger generations around the world put more importance on purpose and the working environment than older generations. It has to do with the growing sophistication of society too. In a recent survey, 63% of millennials—essentially workers under 35—said the primary purpose of businesses should be "improving society" instead of "generating profit." A study from the Society for Human Resource Management tells us that 94% of millennials want to use their skills to benefit a cause and 57% wish that there were more company-wide service days (Lou, 2017). No wonder the PepsiCo initiative was welcomed!

What happens when the organisation and individual purpose are not aligned? Since alignment creates greater engagement and effort, it stands to reason that a lack of alignment creates dissonance, so when individuals and teams are not aligned – that results in little or no discretionary effort and a related fall in productivity. If the organisational purpose does not align with that of the individual, then the individual is not going to be motivated, is not going to go that extra mile. A Deloitte study found 73% engagement in "purpose-driven" companies but only 23% engagement in those that are not (Vaccaro, 2014). Also, the 2018 Corporate Board/EY Global Leadership Forecast showed that companies without a purposed mission and vision underperformed the market by 40%.

Remember productivity in the end is about getting people to give that discretionary effort – which they won't do if they are not engaged and their own purpose is not aligned. So, for the self-interested leader having a purpose will have a direct impact on the bottom line. For the leader who is expressing their own purpose through their organisation, it is far more than the bottom-line results. It is what provides meaning and joy. But of course, the purpose has to be genuine, heartfelt and core to the organisation. And that is where many organisations fall down – it is just marketing spiel.

Exercise: the Purpose Wheel

This concept was inspired by Maslow's hierarchy of needs and what motivates human satisfaction. IDEO created a framework called the Purpose Wheel. The development of a sense of purpose starts by imagining various ways an organisation might have an impact on the world.

This can drive a productive conversation to elicit the purpose of the organisation and through which its leadership can align. Only then can they start to write out the statement that answers "the why."

The centre of the wheel proposes five ways a company or organisation might have an impact on the world. Each slice answers the "Why do we exist beyond profit?" question in a different way.

- We exist to Enable Potential… Creating impact by inspiring greater possibilities. (Tesla, Nike)
- We exist to Reduce Friction… Creating impact by simplifying and eliminating barriers. (Google, Spotify)
- We exist to Foster Prosperity… Creating impact by supporting the success of others. (Pampers, Warby Parker)
- We exist to Encourage Exploration… Creating impact by championing discovery. (Airbnb, Adobe)
- We exist to Kindle Happiness… Creating impact by inciting joy. (Dove, Zappos)

The outer wheel is there to push your imagination and force you to consider how your company might make an impact. With it, you continue to engineer your purpose statement: We exist to [insert phrase from inner wheel] through [insert phrase from outer wheel] to impact society for the better (Figure 2.6).

Questions and actions for personal development

1. Create your touchstone (if you do not yet have one) then consider:
    - How does your touchstone help support you in making decisions that align with living your purpose?
    - Which of the Transpersonal Qualities (CREASEP) would you say come most naturally for you?
    - Reflect on one way you have shown one of these qualities.
2. Consider a time when you have felt your work to be aligned with your values and purpose (or if never, when they have been dissonant) – how did this affect your engagement and quality of your work?
3. Using the organisational Purpose Wheel, set your desired organisational purpose – how does that inform your current work or your future career direction?
4. What do you think is the difference between a vocation and a purpose? Or are they interchangeable?

Purpose Wheel Framework
The Purpose Wheel is a tool that helps teams envision how a company might have impact in the world beyond profit. Start in the centre to imagine the company's desired impact. Work outwards to experiment with how the company might achieve this. The results are key ideas that can help shape the company's purpose statement.

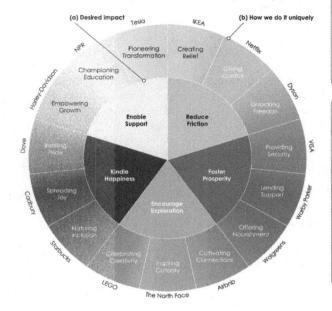

We exist to:
_____
(a) desired impact

by

_____
(b) how we do it uniquely

to impact society for the better

How this impacts the people we serve:
_____
_____
_____
Individual
_____
_____
Group
_____
_____
Society
_____

Adapted from The Purpose Wheel, designed by global design firm Ideo.   ©LeaderShape Global 2021.

Figure 2.6 The Purpose Wheel, designed by global design firm IDEO, is a tool that helps teams envision how a company might have an impact on the world beyond profit. Start in the centre to imagine the company's desired impact. Work outwards to experiment with how the company might achieve this. The results are key ideas that can help shape the company's purpose statement

References

Business Roundtable. 2019. Business Roundtable Redefines the Purpose of a Corporation to Promote 'An Economy That Serves All Americans'. *Businessroundtable.org.* https://www.businessroundtable.org/business-roundtable-redefines-the-purpose-of-a-corporation-to-promote-an-economy-that-serves-all-americans, accessed March 26, 2021.

Center for Healthy Minds. 2020. A Look into the Science of Well-Being and the Healthy Minds Framework from the Center for Healthy Minds at UW–Madison - Center for Healthy Minds. *Centerhealthyminds.org.* https://centerhealthyminds.org/about/why-well-being, accessed March 23, 2021.

Colvin, G. 2020. Revisiting the Business Roundtable's 'Stakeholder Capitalism,' One Year Later. *Fortune.com.* https://fortune.com/2020/08/19/business-roundtable-statement-principles-stakeholder-capitalism-corporate-governance/, March 26, 2021.

DDI World. 2018. Global Leadership Forecast 2018. *Ddiworld.com*. https://www.ddiworld.com/research/global-leadership-forecast-2018, accessed March 26, 2021

DiversityInc. 2018. EY Study: 6 Leadership Megatrends Changing the Workplace Worldwide. *diversityinc.com*. https://www.diversityinc.com/ey-study-6-leadership-megatrends-changing-workplace-worldwide/, accessed March 23, 2021.

Goleman, D. 2021. How to Make Employees Happier This Year. *kornferry.com*. https://www.kornferry.com/insights/articles/how-to-make-employees-happier-this-year, accessed March 26, 2021.

Knights, J., Grant, D., & Young, G. 2018. *Leading Beyond the Ego*. London: Routledge.

Laloux, F. 2014. *Reinventing Organizations*. Brussels: Nelson Parker.

Lou, E. 2017. Why Millennials Want More Than Just Work: The Importance of Your 'Double Bottom Line'. *forbes.com*. https://www.forbes.com/sites/theyec/2017/06/09/why-millennials-want-more-than-just-work-the-importance-of-your-double-bottom-line/, accessed March 26, 2021.

O'Brien, D., Main, A., Kounkel, S., & Stephan, A. 2019. Purpose is everything. *Deloitte Insights*. https://www2.deloitte.com/us/en/insights/topics/marketing-and-sales-operations/global-marketing-trends/2020/purpose-driven-companies.html, accessed March 23, 2021.

PepsiCo. 2018. PepsiCo Reports Significant Strides in Pursuit of Performance With Purpose 2025 Agenda. *PepsiCo, Inc. Official Website*. https://www.PepsiCo.com/news/press-release/PepsiCo-reports-significant-strides-in-pursuit-of-performance-with-purpose-2025-07112018, accessed March 26, 2021.

Pink, D., 2018. *Drive*. Edinburgh: Canongate Books.

Vaccaro, A. 2014. How a Sense of Purpose Boosts Engagement. *Inc.com*. https://www.inc.com/adam-vaccaro/purpose-employee-engagement.html, March 26, 2021.

3 Ethical leadership

How to develop ethical leaders

John Knights

Overview

The consequences of the lack of Ethical Leadership are in the news headlines virtually every day, whether it concerns the leaders of major countries, issues such as immigration, or organisations accused of tax evasion (or avoidance), negligence, misrepresentations, bribery, money laundering, financial manip-ulation and so on. Policy makers and legislators seem to be at a loss as to what to do, other than come up with new sticking plaster rules and regulations that lawyers and accountants then find ways around. The general public is angry, resulting in populist and idealistic politicians coming to the fore and extreme political parties gaining ground. Fake news and unsubstantiated allegations add to the forces driving polarisation.

It all seems quite a mess and quite frightening! But actually the fact that all these corporate misdeeds are coming to light demonstrates a positive under-lying development that is the result of the information and internet age we are living in. In the 20th century and earlier, organisations were much more easily able to hide their law-breaking and unethical behaviour. Slowly, very slowly, there is a realisation that fundamental changes need to take place. We need a new kind of leadership.

Ethical behaviour is a core element of Transpersonal Leadership and sits alongside "radical", "authentic", "caring" and "performance-enhancing" as its key purposes. Ethical leadership is one of those things that most of us know is important, but for which there are very few methodologies on how it can be achieved or examples of how it has been actually realised in organisations.

At the time of writing, "ethical leadership" gets over 47.9 million hits on internet search engines (compared to 3 million in 2016) with a main focus on what ethical leadership is and what leaders should do.

However, although I need to explain and define in this article what we mean by "ethical leadership", there are two other areas that require much more debate and development:

- Why do we need ethical leadership?
- How do we develop ethical leaders?

DOI: 10.4324/9781003150626-5

The second bullet is really critical. Unless we actually develop the leaders that can implement an embedded ethical way of operating within organisational cultures, the whole subject becomes a purely academic and unrealisable exercise.

I believe the reason there is little literature on how we actually develop ethical leaders is probably because we prefer – as a result of our standard education and training methodologies – to think logically and analytically about these subjects. Hence, the abundance of descriptions of what ethical leadership is and what needs to be done. Overwhelmingly, the solutions are process and structure based and focus on compliance. These processes tend not to deal with values and behaviour even though the only way that people will comply in spirit, rather than to the letter, is by using their values to ensure they behave ethically. The result, not only in today's world but since ancient times, is that it is morally acceptable to play the game by ticking the boxes while circumventing the rules. This is exemplified by the attitude of professional advisors around the world who hide behind compliance to the rules while undermining ethical behaviour.

Fixed rules and processes actually allow an abdication of personal leadership, accountability and responsibility if they are not underpinned by a strong ethical culture.

As someone who received his university degree in chemical engineering and spent most of his career in international business, I have come to realise that sometimes a logical and analytically trained brain like mine has its drawbacks and "thinking" needs to be balanced by "feeling" and "being". That is, actions need to be underpinned by behaviours and values.

Definitions

The English language, being what it is, contains many words that have different meanings depending on the context or who you ask. So it is with "ethics". The big confusion is between the words "ethics" and "morals". One reputable reference can define them exactly the opposite of one another. We need to define what these words mean in our discussion of Transpersonal Leadership in general, and for this chapter in particular, especially in terms of behaviour.

Ethical Behaviour: Acting in a way that is consistent with one's own principles and values which are characterised by honesty, fairness and equity in all interpersonal activities, be they personal or professional; and by respecting the dignity, diversity and rights of individuals and groups of people.

Moral Behaviour: Understanding there are Rules of Conduct of any group or society, which may differ from one to another, and behaving in accordance with these rules. These rules are based on conviction or convention, rather than proven evidence of efficacy, and may or may not be ethical as defined above.

In essence Ethical Behaviour is of a higher order than Moral Behaviour, and this is very important for any leader operating in a culture (be it a country or organisation) where what is accepted morally is not ethical in the view of that individual. Just think about how capital punishment or gay rights are treated in different societies and what your view is – and how you might need to act.

We also need to define the following in order to be able to communicate accurately:

Ethical Organisations can be defined as ones that have a culture that considers the implications of what they are doing and the effect it might have on all their stakeholders, which includes employees, customers, suppliers, the community, the shareholders, the planet and even the universe. An ethical organisation does the right thing (being honest, fair and equitable) through everyone in the organisation having a common touchstone defining what that is.

Leadership is usually a process which involves influencing others and/or oneself to take action and happens within the context of a group. Leadership involves goal attainment, and these goals are shared by leaders and their followers. The very act of defining leadership as a process suggests that leadership is not a characteristic or trait with which only a few certain people are endowed at birth. Leadership can be defined as a process which is a transactional event that happens between leaders and their followers and can happen anywhere in the hierarchy of the organisation (Rowe and Guerrero, 2013). Our experience suggests that leading oneself is an important first step in the journey in which an individual "just" needs to face and overcome fear to act (Barrett, 2010).

In summary, *Leadership* is the process of influencing others to achieve goals (*Van Buren*).

We can therefore define *Ethical Leadership* as:

The process of influencing people to act through principles and values and beliefs that embrace what we have defined as ethical behaviour.

Principles and practicalities of ethical leadership

The Western literature on ethical leadership generally refers to the five principles which can be traced back to Aristotle (ca. 384–322 BC). They are **Respect** and **Service** to others, **Justice** for others, **Honesty** towards others and **Building community** with others (DuBrin 2010; Northouse 2013). The words trip easily off the tongue, but they are extremely difficult to always put into practice.

As I am sure you have noticed, these principles are all about how the individual deals with "others". The key criterion to actually live these principles is to operate beyond the ego, to put others first. This not only potentially creates conflict between self and others but also between others and others. Our families are naturally our prime "others" but to be an ethical leader we also have to think about the greater good. Is there an order of priority of whom you take care of first or does it depend on the circumstances? This requires a really mature and high level of decision making and judgement which goes beyond rational thinking and requires effective use of the sub-conscious and unconscious neural processes of intuition, instinct and insight (Sadler-Smith 2007, 2009) as well as a sound personal ethical philosophy (Steare 2006) and as described in more detail in Chapter 16 of *Leading Beyond the Ego* (Knights et al., 2018).

In one important area, we live in a different world to Aristotle, Plato, Confucius and all the other revered ancient sages. They lived in a world of extreme hierarchy and ultimately they always honoured and respected their leader who felt the moral obligation and expectation to make all decisions. But to expect "<u>the</u> leader" to always come to the best solution alone is unrealistic, especially in our modern increasingly complex world.

Today, hierarchy is disappearing as leadership depends less on heredity, victory, power and secretly held knowledge. Just over the last 20 years, we have not only seen the arrival of the information age but also huge global societal change which is continuing to break down barriers. The consequence of all this is that people are becoming more equal as human beings – even though this change is still very slow in many cultures and the modern celebrity culture actually fights against this. Also counter to this trend is the growing wealth gap between the super-rich and the rest. Between 2004 and 2014, the number of US$ billionaires tripled to 1,645 according to *Forbes* Magazine with the number from the emerging world growing from 20% to 43% during the same period. Some of these billionaires are a result of the rapid growth of large companies, especially in Asia, but others are the result of cronyism (Freund 2016). Each will no doubt have their own story of ethical behaviour. In just the two months from 23 March to 22 May 2020 (at the height of the COVID-19 pandemic), 25 of the richest billionaires in the world gained $225 billion to bring their total net worth to nearly $1.5 trillion (Ponciano, 2020). Oxfam reported in January 2019 that the World's richest 26 people own as much as the poorest 50% (3.9 billion) (Elliott, 2019).

So, I would add a sixth principle, "**Human Equality**". This does not mean we have to be equal in our roles or in our living standards or in our salaries, but just being equal as human beings will inevitably reduce the extremes of excess and poverty which themselves are drivers for unethical behaviour. We should treat those at the bottom of society's hierarchy with the same dignity, respect, fairness and honesty as we do those at the top – think "janitor vs the Queen of England"! Both our ego and our emotions (especially "fear") need managing to be able to overcome this instinctive tendency.

Other chapters in this book (such as Chapters 13, 19, 20 and 21) address leadership, morals and hierarchy in various cultures and countries in more detail.

The impact of this change is that anyone can and should look to be a leader wherever they are in an organisation. Leadership is becoming more distributed, more informal, more shared. In this context, on the one hand, the role of senior Ethical Leaders is pivotal, and on the other, every single employee should be thinking of themselves as an ethical leader. This can only be achieved by creating an ethical culture.

The role of the ethical leader is not just about values and principles but also about behaviours. This personal experience explains why.

A few years ago on a business trip to India I met the CEO of a major insurance company. He was an extremely intelligent and urbane man who had studied at Harvard and was interested in developing the next generation of leaders in their organisation. He was keen to better engage the people in the organisation (there was a high turnover of staff), he wanted to genuinely improve customer service and he was keen to increase the involvement of the organisation in the communities where they operated. All good values and principles. After about 15 minutes, he phoned the HR Director (who he had spoken highly about) and told her she would be interested in what we were discussing and to come to the meeting right away! She arrived soon after but was obviously not able to concentrate, perhaps because she had been taken away from something that she considered very important.

Coincidently, during the same trip, I met the very mature CEO of a manufacturing organisation in the energy sector who had very similar issues. And after about 15 minutes or so, he phoned the HR Manager (the HRD was away visiting one of their factories) and asked him how he was. He explained that I was visiting and talking about leadership development in their organisation, and that he thought he might be interested to attend if he was available, although realised he should have informed him earlier. After a few seconds listening, the CEO said to the HR Manager that he understood, it was important that he attended the other meeting that had been arranged, and would brief him later.

They were both ethical leaders in their intent of service, justice and honesty, but one of them did not match up to the principles of "respect" and "human equality" through their behaviour.

This very simple yet important lesson demonstrates that a good intellect and good values alone are not sufficient to be a good ethical leader. Often what is lacking in real-life situations are the appropriate behaviours.

Why do we need ethical leadership?

It may seem obvious but a question that needs answering because of the evidence of the misdeeds of national leaders and large corporations alluded to earlier – and think of all those we don't know about yet!

This brief case study provides a good reason why!

Working with a major division of a global multinational, the CEO was very keen to develop and embed an ethical culture for the long-term success of the organisation, especially as they were becoming increasingly global with operations in different countries having a variety of moral codes. In a session with the senior leadership team, we asked the question "Why do you think being an ethical company is important for your organisation?" The response was the following list:

1   To create trust with our stakeholders to help overcome barriers
2   To create a safe environment
3   To attract and retain good people
4   To connect the personal to the corporate
5   To secure a long-term future as a business
6   To be able to sleep well at night
7   It's good for the corporate image – relevant and ethical
8   So everyone has the same ethical framework and knows where the line is
9   To create a positive environment which will positively impact on innovation
10   To reduce any "fear culture"
11   To get balanced decision making
12   To get consistency of culture in a changing environment
13   To make the right choices generating sustainability
14   To create transparency and all the benefits that brings

Then, we asked the question, "and how many of these are good for business?" The somewhat surprised answer was "they all are".

There is a strong default mentality in the corporate world that at the crux, business needs (success and competitiveness) override ethical concerns. The example above alone gives 14 reasons why we fundamentally disagree with this and believe that in the 21st century good ethics is increasingly important for a successful, sustainable business.

An additional reason for our view comes from a global study by IBM comparing the demands of different generations, which found that Millennials (between 23 and 36 years old in 2016) regard fairness and ethics in the workplace as even more important than recognition and opportunity (IBM 2015). This is a real shift, especially as nearly 50% of the working population in 2020 are composed of Millennials (Alton, 2017) who put more importance on company culture, sustainability, ethics and diversity. Many are both today's "followers" and young leaders, as well as the next generation of senior leaders. These findings have been replicated in various studies including one peer-reviewed paper that demonstrated Millennials (and especially female Millennials) have a greater orientation towards values than previous generations (Weber and Urick, 2016).

Compliance is not enough!

Many organisations today have compliance and ethics training as part of their strategy to meet national, industry or business sector codes. Often this is because leaders have a genuine desire for their organisations to operate ethically; other times, it may have been forced upon them because of past misdeeds. Unfortunately, compliance processes are usually just a tick-box exercise to meet regulatory requirements, or shareholder or market expectations.

We came across one organisation that had been taken to court because of a serious bribery issue in one of its subsidiaries. The company was ordered to install a process at considerable cost to ensure ethical compliance across the organisation. Unfortunately, it did not change the culture and too many people treated it as platform for making sure they did not get caught next time.

What is so important and often ignored is to embed ethical behaviours into the culture of the organisation, so it becomes the norm that members of that organisation will act ethically. This manifests itself in employees seeking advice if they have any sense of potential conflict, and that it is the accepted norm for anyone to challenge anything they believe may be unethical. Unfortunately, being unethical does not necessarily mean breaking the law, so the judgement has to appeal to the values of the individual and be supported by the culture of the organisation.

Whereas tick-boxing often gives license to finding a way around the rules, an ethical culture supports the notion that "this is the way we do things around here".

The first step in developing an ethical culture is for the leader(s) to establish the right climate, which is achieved by the standards they demonstrate and the values on which their behaviours are based. A leader needs to be both emotionally and spiritually intelligent in order to set the right climate. As an example, and regardless of your persuasion, consider the difference between the climates set by US Presidents Obama, Trump and Biden when they first came into office.

How do we develop ethical leaders?

The fundamental to developing ethical leaders is to increase values to a higher level of consciousness and to raise their awareness of how their behaviour impacts the performance of themselves and the people around them (Knights et al., 2018; Wall and Knights, 2013).

A core problem is that although most people fundamentally have good values and a real sense of what is right and wrong, organisations tend to ignore these traits when identifying future leaders. Instead, they favour traditional leadership characteristics of self-confidence, assertiveness, influence and achievement which without the good values to temper them regress to high-ego, aggression, manipulation and ruthlessness and an obsession for total control. It is therefore not surprising that 1 in 25 CEOs are considered psychopathic – four times higher than the general population (*Babiak 2010*) (*Dutton 2012*) – though personally, I would use the term "sociopathic" to describe these undesirable behaviours. Even those with good basic values have most often been taught to "leave values and ethics at the front door when you come to work".

Another challenge is that many potentially good ethical leaders (as well as unethical ones) are unable to motivate and engage staff to reach their potential in order to raise the sustainable productivity of the organisation. These leaders often generate stress and fear, releasing cortisol which in turn reduces creative thinking and openness to new ideas (Shiv 2012). However, we know clearly from neuroscience research that positive behaviours can be learned and negative behaviours unlearned in the same way we learn to drive a car and change from driving an automatic to a manual. And the methodologies and experience are available to enable real behavioural change (Knights et al., 2018; Wall and Knights, 2013).

During my life, I have come across many people who could have become excellent Transpersonal Leaders but were either not good at getting to the top (they didn't always put themselves first) and/or were not willing to make the ethical compromises. Organisations must change and start identifying leaders that will be the right kind of leader when they get there, not just effective at climbing to the top.

To look at some of the basics about how we identify and develop ethical leaders, we need to consider the hierarchy of intelligences (Zohar and Marshall, 2000) as shown in Figure 3.1.

The first level of intelligence is the intellectual – our rational and logical "thinking". The neural processes that enable this are through serial connections that are hard wired. To a large extent, our potential intellectual capacity is fixed from birth (although most people never reach anywhere near their capacity).

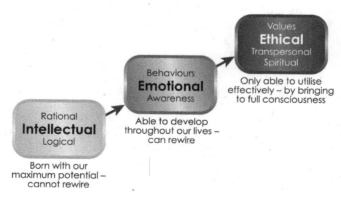

Figure 3.1 Hierarchy of intelligences

The second level is emotional intelligence which manages our emotions and impacts on our feelings and behaviours. The neural connections that enable this intelligence are associative. That means billions of neuro cells are loosely connected but desirable connections can be strengthened through practice and repetition (this is often referred to as the "plasticity" of the brain).

The highest level of intelligence is "spiritual" (which includes ethical) which manages, amongst other things, how we activate our values. Spiritual intelligence also has a unique way for our neurons to connect known as synchronous oscillations. First discovered by Singer & Grey in 1989 (Singer and Grey 1989), every neuron in the localised part of the brain involved emits oscillations in harmony and unison in the 40 Hz range. Raising one's level of consciousness, for example through mindfulness exercises, activates this mechanism.

The science of consciousness is still not fully understood and to some is the holy grail of neuroscience. Chapter 14 of *Leading Beyond the Ego* (Knights et al., 2018) gives a good synopsis of the latest developments. Let's now look at how these intelligences and the method of neural connections affect ethical leadership.

To be any excellent leader, one does need a certain level of intellect. But an IQ anything more than 15% above the norm makes no difference (Goleman, 2004) to the likelihood of success as a leader. So, whereas a reasonable intellect is a threshold necessity to becoming an excellent leader, it is not sufficient and certainly does not guarantee any competence in ethical leadership as such.

Have passed that threshold, the one thing anyone would accept is vital to be a good ethical leader is having good values which involves the highest level of intelligence. However, we really need to investigate which values are critical for "ethical" leadership. LeaderShape has developed a model that divides values into two separate categories: those that define Personal Conscience (who I am) and those that categorise Self-Determination (what I am going to do with who I am). The list developed over eight years, of the most common and relevant values for leadership, is shown in Tables 3.1 and 3.2 (Knights et al., 2018), with "Vulnerability" added to the list based on the latest data

Table 3.1 Virtues of personal conscience

Personal conscience	
Virtues	• ***Trustworthiness***
	• ***Truth & Honesty***
	• ***Excellence***
	• ***Integrity***
	• Humility
	• Vulnerability
	• Fairness
	• Conscientiousness
	• Patience
	• Forgiveness
	• Altruistic Love

Table 3.2 Virtues of self-determination

Self-determination	
Value driver	*Purpose*
Values	• Motivation • Aspiration • Drive (Will) • Power • Energy • Courage • Resilience • Continuous Personal Development (CPD)

as it is becoming more accepted that vulnerability in the right circumstances can be an important strength.

The most common desired values for leaders to possess, as cited by employees, are integrity, trust, honesty and excellence (Table 3.1 in bold). But to be an ethical leader, it is also necessary to specifically develop the "softer" personal conscience values of Fairness, Forgiveness and Altruistic Love, as well as Humility and Vulnerability; and the self-determination values of Courage and Resilience. This can only be achieved by the leader raising their level of consciousness so that a true understanding of each key value is used as a touchstone in every decision made. This takes time, practice and commitment, but can be achieved. The more it is done, the easier it becomes. A more complete explanation of this is provided in Chapter 20 of *Leading Beyond the Ego* (Knights et al., 2018).

The best practical way for a leader to bring a full armoury of values into their everyday working lives is to carry out a 360° values assessment (such as LeaderShape's 8ICOL – https://www.leadershapeglobal.com/8ICOL) and identify which of the values are core strengths and which might need focus and development. If each one of us looks at the values in Tables 3.1 and 3.2, and are really honest to ourselves, we can probably immediately choose a couple of values we personally have the most challenges in demonstrating.

As an example, let us consider Fairness. To answer the question "am I being fair?" can feel quite complex and daunting to answer but if we break it down into granular steps such as these four phrases for fairness:

• Treats everyone on an equal basis
• Appoints and promotes those best suited for the job
• Helps people to learn from genuine mistakes
• Supports those affected negatively by personal and family pressures

it suddenly becomes more manageable. Any value can be broken down into four to six granular behaviours and approached in the same way.

Building these values through their granular components into a touchstone for every decision made and action taken is a key step to developing into an ethical leader.

Unexpectedly, the key intelligence that is most important to successfully becoming an ethical leader is the second level in Figure 3.1, that of emotional intelligence. The combination of thinking (intellect) and being (spiritual) is useless as a leader unless they are translated into behaviours, and behaviours are the outcome of how we manage our emotions. The case described in the earlier section "Principles and practicalities of ethical leadership" is a perfect example of this.

The right behaviours can be learned but this is only achieved as a result of the individual leader becoming more aware of how their behaviours impact not only their own performance but also the performance of the people around them. Just think of the example of the Chief Executive of the insurance company. He not only caused the HRD to be ineffective during the meeting but also ruined whatever else she was trying to accomplish when interrupted. And this may have impacted her overall performance for some time after the event due to the negative emotions caused.

The way we recommend leaders identify which behaviours they need to improve is by carrying out an emotional intelligence and leadership 360° assessment (such as LeaderShape's LEIPA – https://www.leadershapeglobal.com/leipa) that identifies how they and their close network both observe and would desire their behaviour to be; and can thus isolate a few granular behaviours that will have the greatest impact on leadership performance.

Working either in a facilitated team or with a personal coach, or even better a combination, can lead to those with fundamentally good values becoming excellent ethical leaders.

If enough organisations embrace this approach to choose the right future leaders for development, we would be on our way to a better world for everyone.

Questions and actions for personal development

1. What is the difference between Ethical and Moral Behaviour and how might that have an impact on how you lead in your organisation and also in a global organisation (if yours is not one)?
2. How would you define Ethical Leadership in your own words? How does this compare with the definition in this chapter, and what are your reflections on the result?
3. What is the sixth principle of ethical leadership, why was it not included in the time of Aristotle (or other ancient sages), and how important do you think it is in the world of today and tomorrow?
4. Why do you think we need Ethical Leadership?
5. Why is compliance insufficient by itself to ensure ethical behaviour?
6. What do you think are key areas leaders need to develop to become ethical leaders?

References

Alton, L. (2017). *How Millennials Are Reshaping What's Important In Corporate Culture.* Forbes Online. https://www.forbes.com/sites/larryalton/2017/06/20/how-millennials-are-reshaping-whats-important-in-corporate-culture/#73acc68b2dfb Downloaded 18/11/20.

Babiak, P., Neumann, C. S. and Hare, R. D. (2010). *Corporate Psychopathy: Talking the Walk.* Behav Sci Law–Mar–Apr; 28(2):174–193. doi: 10.1002/bsl.925.

Barrett, R. (2010), *The New Leadership Paradigm* – www.valuescentre.com – self published.

DuBrin, A. (2010). *Leadership: Research Findings, Practice, and Skills* (6th ed.). Mason, OH: South-Western/Cengage

Dutton (2012). *The Wisdom of Psychopaths: What Saints, Spies, and Serial Killers Can Teach Us about Success,* FSG Books.

Elliott, L. (2019). World's 26 richest people own as much as poorest 50%, says Oxfam. *The Guardian Online.* https://www.theguardian.com/business/2019/jan/21/world-26-richest-people-own-as-much-as-poorest-50-per-cent-oxfam-report. Downloaded 28/11/20.

Freund, C. (2016). *Rich People Poor Countries: The Rise of Emerging-Market Tycoons and Their Mega Firms.* Peterson Institute for International Economics.

Goleman (2004), *Emotional Intelligence & Working with Emotional Intelligence.* Bloomsbury.

IBM (2015). *Myths, Exaggerations and Uncomfortable Truths: The Real Story behind Millennials in the Workplace.* IBM Institute for Business Value.

Knights, J., Grant, D. and Young, G. (2018). *Leading Beyond the Ego: How to Become a Transpersonal Leader.* Routledge.

Northouse, P. G. (2013). *Leadership: Theory and practice* (6th ed.). Sage.

Ponciano, J. (2020). *The Changing Fortunes of the World's Richest.* Forbes Online. https://www.forbes.com/sites/jonathanponciano/2020/05/22/billionaires-zuckerberg-bezos/. Downloaded 18/11/20.

Rowe W. G. and Guerrero L. (2013), *Cases in Leadership – 3rd Edition,* Sage.

Sadler-Smith, E. (2007). *Inside Intuition,* Oxford: Routledge.

Sadler-Smith, E. (2009). *The Intuitive Mind: Profiling from the Power of Your Sixth Sense,* Hoboken, NJ: John Wiley & Sons.

Shiv, B. (2012). *What Is the Path to Increased Innovation?* Insights by Stanford Business.

Singer and Grey (1989). *Oscillatory Responses in Cat Visual Cortex Exhibit Inter-Columnar Synchronization Which Reflects Global Stimulus Properties,* Nature 338:334–337 (23 March); doi:10.1038/338334a0.

Steare, R. (2006). *Ethicability: How to Decide What's Right and Find the Courage to Do It.* Roger Steare Consulting Limited.

Van Buren, J. A. (2015). *Ethical Leadership,* Noonmark Nonprofit Services. Downloaded 18/11/20 from https://www.uvm.edu/sites/default/files/ethical_leadership_factsheet.pdf.

Wall, T. and Knights, J. (2013). *Leadership Assessment for Talent Development,* Kogan Page.

Weber, J. and Urick, M. (2016). *Examining the Millennials' Ethical Profile: Assessing Demographic Variations in Their Personal Value Orientations.* Business and Society Review 122(4):469–506. https://www.researchgate.net/publication/313840681_Examining_the_Millennials'_Ethical_Profile_Assessing_Demographic_Variations_in_their_Personal_Value_Orientations.

Zohar, D. and Marshall, I. (2000) *Spiritual Intelligence – The Ultimate Intelligence.* London: Bloomsbury.

4 Adult development

Its role in the leadership journey

Alison Hill and Heather Katz

> If I am not for myself who will be for me? And when only for myself, what
> am I? And if not now, then when?
>
> Hillel the Elder, born 110 BC

Overview

As adults we should be on a continuous journey of development. The purpose
of this chapter is to explore how our development as a leader is closely connected to our development as an adult. Knowing where we are on our adult
development journey will help us understand both our own path towards
transpersonal leadership, leading beyond the ego and the development needs
of those we lead. This chapter provides an opportunity for further insights
into others and ourselves.

Introduction

If ever our world needed true leaders who can lead in increasingly uncertain,
complex and radically changing times, it is now.

Leaders need to manage and lead through enormous complexity, while
providing vision and assurance to their employees, stakeholders and shareholders. They need to understand themselves and their impact as well as understand their people, organisations and stakeholders, within both the local
and global context. The COVID-19 pandemic has highlighted the need for
leaders to be increasingly flexible, interconnected and reaching out beyond
safe space.

We are all products of our childhoods, environments, societies and many
different cultures and experiences, and even as adults, we may still wrestle
with issues of trust, self-confidence, empathy, conflict and much more. There
is still a widely held belief that once we are past adolescence we are fully
formed as adults. Rather there is the "possibility of life after adolescence" as
Kegan and Lahey (2009) so beautifully express in their book "Immunity to
Change".

DOI: 10.4324/9781003150626-6

A compelling body of evidence shows that development continues throughout adulthood. In the 1950s, Erik Erikson (1950) developed an accessible eight-stage psychosocial model illustrating life as a series of lessons and challenges, which help us develop from infancy to late-stage adulthood. Many others have built on this, including experts such as Kegan (1982), Cook-Greuter (2000), Laske (2006), Goodman (2002) and more recently Bachkirova (2011), whose model we draw on in this chapter.

This process of development has parallels with the "*Journey to Leadership Excellence*" described in Figure 4.1, which shows the main elements of leadership development required to become a Transpersonal Leader.

As can be seen from a different and more detailed view of the transpersonal journey model (Figure 4.2), most leaders start the journey with '*Rational Ego based As usual Leadership*', some will develop through '*Robust Emotionally Aware Leadership*' and fewer to '*Radical Ethical Authentic Leadership*'.

John Knights (Wall & Knights, 2013), Chairman of LeaderShape, developed this model. He believes that adult development can be accelerated as part of a behavioural and values-based leadership development programme.

To move towards 'Radical Ethical Authentic Leadership', we need to understand where we are on our own adult development path and continue to develop ourselves as leaders.

From our experience of leading ourselves, and supporting leaders to grow and change, we have some understanding about the qualities that make a

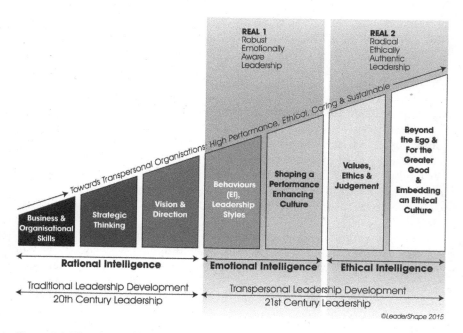

Figure 4.1 The LeaderShape journey to leadership excellence

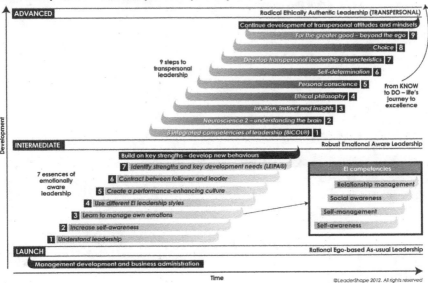

REAL Transpersonal leadership development journey to excellence

Figure 4.2 Transpersonal leadership development journey

great leader. We invite you to think about where you are in your own adult development and what impact this may have on your leadership. We hope to awaken your curiosity and encourage you to consciously take steps towards your own transpersonal leadership development. These steps require courage, insight, self-awareness, determination, humility, resilience and motivation to identify areas for development and to take action to change and develop.

Why recognising the impact of adult development is important

We are excited and challenged by the concept of adult development and its implications for our practice. Through our work, we are playing a small part as catalysts to enable leaders to enhance their personal insight into themselves, their people and organisations. We motivate and encourage them to take relevant actions to develop themselves further.

While it is impossible to summarise decades of research on adult development into a few paragraphs, we set out some of the concepts here that inform our argument.

Theories of adult development are based on the notion that 'as people develop they become more aware of and open to a mature understanding

The Relationship Between Leadership Development and Adult Development

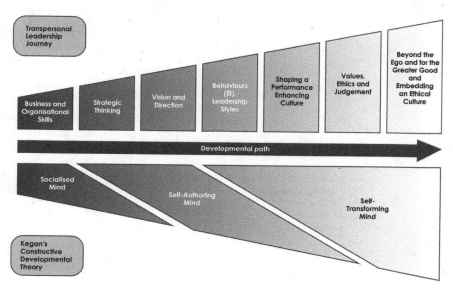

Figure 4.3 Adult development stages

of authority and responsibility, and display greater tolerance to ambiguity' (Ives & Cox, 2012).

Kegan's Constructive Developmental Theory (Kegan, 1982) describes adults as being in a continuous state of meaning making; that is, attempting to make sense of the world and their part in it. Kegan views adult development in terms of social maturity together with affective, cognitive and moral development. He describes three adult developmental stages that follow one after the other over a lifetime (see Figure 4.3). These are:

- **The socialised mind**: those (usually younger adults) who base their views of the world on role models and on the opinions of others. Many never go beyond this stage. Bachkirova (2011) in her book "Developmental Coaching" describes this stage as an 'unformed ego'.
- **The self-authoring mind:** those who step back from their social environment to form their own world view. This is usually thought of as the normal adult state, though many never reach this stage. Bachkirova describes this stage as a 'formed ego'.
- **The self-transforming mind:** those who have learned the limits of their own inner systems, can hold contradictions, work with ambiguity, find solutions from adversity and move from the linear to the holistic. Bachkirova describes this stage as a 'reformed ego'.

This simple three-stage model creates a narrow classification that hides a multiplicity of personal qualities. Kegan defined these stages through years of research, using a "Subject-Object" survey on thousands of participants, with consistent and replicable results.

He describes the journey through these stages as movement from Subject to Object. Subject is about self and being inward looking, whereas Object is about others and the external environment. Things experienced as Subject are unquestioned and felt as part of the self, whereas things experienced as Object can be examined objectively, questioned and possibly changed. When we move away from Subject towards Object, we are able to reflect on what we previously have taken for granted and thereby gain different perspectives.

We believe leaders can move more easily through the "REAL" developmental journey (Figure 4.2) towards becoming transpersonal leaders when they develop insight about where they and others are in their adult development. Figure 4.3 shows how the transpersonal leadership journey can be underpinned by Kegan's Constructive Developmental Theory, offering a leadership development path.

This three-stage approach has helped us think about the links between stages of adult development, and the approaches leaders and their coaches might take to make the leader's journey towards transpersonal leadership. In the next section, we suggest some approaches towards that development.

Emotional intelligence and adult development

Our experience with effective leaders is that they are often further along their adult development path than others. Here, we will explore the relationship between emotional intelligence (EI) and adult development.

Very often in re-organisations, leaders change structures and processes, thinking that personal and organisational development occurs through so-called "hard skills" training, such as project management or strategic planning. While these are important, our experience shows that overriding issues are primarily related to dysfunctional relationship management. This is highlighted in Chapters 7 and 13 by Sue Coyne and Jenny Plaister-Ten based on their white papers (Coyne, 2016; Plaister-Ten, 2017), where they each relate the importance and impact of emotionally intelligent relationship management to increased organisational success and sustainability.

The four domains of emotional intelligence

Goleman, Boyatzis and McKee, in their ground-breaking book on emotionally intelligent leadership (Goleman et al., 2002), highlight the concept of EI in leadership. Leaders need to practice high levels of awareness of self and others through self-awareness, self-management and relationship management (Figure 4.4). Goleman links these EI competencies to his six styles of leadership. John Knights has further developed this concept in his book, *Leading*

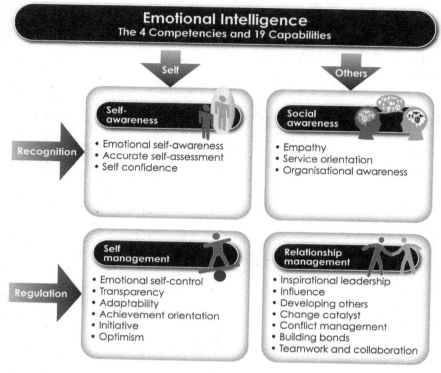

Figure 4.4 Emotional intelligence competencies and capabilities

Beyond the Ego (Knights et al., 2018). This is summarised in Table 4.1 where leadership styles are ordered by their degree of impact on an organisation. The most used and least effective are commanding and pacesetting leadership styles. The least used, yet second most effective, is the coaching style of leadership.

While the topic requires further research, Michael Shiner (2015), supervised by Kegan et al., suggests that there is a link between EI and adult development: a claim that we develop in this chapter.

Developing ourselves as leaders

What is out there to enable us to enhance our leadership capabilities and develop our people and organisations further?

Coaches, talent development managers and those with a background in human resources use many different approaches and techniques to help their clients develop. These include coaching, team facilitation, 360° feedback, psychometric testing, culture surveys, action learning sets and more.

In our experience, the most radical changes come about through an integrated, multifaceted, multimodal approach involving the whole

Table 4.1 Leadership styles and their impact

Six leadership styles and their key EI competencies	Impact on organisation
VISIONARY Leads people towards a shared vision	
Inspirational Leadership (Relationship Management)	**Most Strongly**
Self-Confidence (Self-Awareness)	**Positive**
Change Catalyst (Relationship Management)	+++
Transparency (Self-Management)	
COACHING Enables leaders to build capability in individuals	
Developing Others (Relationship Management)	**Strongly Positive**
Empathy (Social Awareness)	++
Emotional Self-Awareness (Self-Awareness)	
AFFILIATIVE Provides cohesiveness and harmony to a team, group or organisation	
Empathy (Self-Awareness)	**Positive**
Conflict management (Relationship Management)	+
Building bonds (Relationship Management)	
DEMOCRATIC Builds engagement, commitment and buy-in	
Self-Confidence (Self-Awareness)	**Positive**
Transparency (Self-Management)	+
Inspirational Leadership (Relationship Management)	
Change Catalyst (Relationship Management)	
PACESETTING Sets high standards by expecting followers to "do as I do"	
Achievement Orientation (Self-Management)	
Initiative (Self-Management)	**Often Negative**
Negative effect if missing:	–
Emotional Self-Awareness (Self-Awareness)	
Emotional Self-Control (Self-Management)	
Empathy (Social Awareness)	
Teamwork & Collaboration (Relationship Management)	
COMMANDING Demands immediate compliance to leader's agenda and decisions	
Achievement (Self-Management)	**Usually Highly**
Initiative (Self-Management)	**Negative**
Influence (Relationship Management)	– –
Negative effect if missing:	
Emotional Self-Awareness (Self-Awareness)	
Emotional Self-Control (Self-Management)	
Empathy (Social Awareness)	

Adapted and developed from Goleman et al. (2002).

executive team, board and senior and mid-range leaders. This approach creates an essential understanding and awareness of the culture and values of the organisation, which facilitates development of individuals, teams and the organisation. In this section, we describe approaches that have had real success.

We have seen transformational change come from programmes that combine a blend of online work-based learning courses, company culture surveys, face-to-face master classes on EI, leadership styles and other inputs. These can be supported through a blend of individual and team coaching, mentoring, action learning sets, peer group support and more.

The following case study describes such a transformative approach.

Case Study 1: An organisation–wide multimodal approach

The CEO of a large publicly funded organisation invited LeaderShape to undertake a one-year programme to develop, retain and prepare senior leaders for higher office.

The organisation provides specialist advice to the public, provided by a highly qualified cadre of professional staff. It had undergone a rapid period of growth over four years. There was significant turmoil at the top with three successive CEOs in post during the programme, with resulting confusion over vision and strategic direction. Because of the rapid growth, the established culture had been diluted. The organisation was made up of three 'tribes': the professionals, the case workers and the administrative staff. The professional staff regarded themselves as sapiential leaders, many using a commanding style of leadership.

Twelve people participated in the LeaderShape programme, organised into two multidisciplinary groups of six. LeaderShape ran a fully blended programme including team coaching and action learning. All participants had diagnostic interviews and all completed Myers Briggs, MBTI step 2 self-assessments. There were monthly masterclasses, and before each masterclass, participants had taken part in on-line learning modules, which aimed to increase their knowledge. The masterclasses embedded, extended and contextualised the learning, through challenge and stretch, using a variety of interventions, with a major focus on the coaching style of leadership. Everyone did a 360° assessment with feedback (see section on LEIPA® later in this chapter), with individual reports being collated into a team assessment. At the end of each masterclass, the facilitator asked for actions and takeaways.

Several people had that "Aha!" moment when they realised that their style of leadership did not bring out the best in the performance of their teams. All made a shift from a commanding to a less directive more coaching style. Several saw the improvement in performance that resulted from a simple shift in leadership style. Within each group, there was increased team work, more equality between members and greater comfort in challenge. The facilitator observed that most moved along the 'REAL' journey (see Figure 4.2).

The programme was fully evaluated looking at changes in behaviours and a return on investment assessment, by participants being asked to estimate the saving resulting from the improvements resulting from the programme. One participant alone estimated saving a staggering £900k in staff costs after just one year.

As well as team and organisation-wide interventions, when working with individuals, we often witness change through individual coaching, particularly when associated with psychometric testing and various types of 360° feedback.

Our experience shows that self-assessed psychometrics are valuable in raising self-awareness. However, unless psychometric testing is combined with 360° feedback and ongoing coaching, it doesn't usually lead towards significant sustained behavioural change.

We further think that for the development of the other EI competencies of self-management, social awareness and relationship management, 360° feedback increases insights into competencies that need development (see Table 4.1). The two purposes of 360° feedback are improving performance and supporting personal development (Fletcher, 2004). Feedback aims "to strengthen people's motivation to change" (McDowall, 2008) and allows a leader to learn how others see them, which gives them much greater insights.

There are many tools on the market, which give understanding and some personal insight. As coaches, our experience is with LEIPA® (LeaderShape, 2017) and is described in box below.

---

*LEIPA® (**L**eadership and **E**motional **I**ntelligence **P**erformance **A**ccelerator) is a development tool that engages raters (colleagues, peers, direct reports or managers who "rate" the leader's desired and observed behaviour in their role) in the leader's ongoing development process.*

It is a diagnostic development tool, the aim of which is to increase individual performance by enhancing self-awareness and appreciation of how we are experienced by others. It identifies granular inter-personal skills and behaviours that individuals and teams require to move towards excellence.

LEIPA® is different from many other 360° measurement tools because it compares observed behaviour of an individual's EI with the desired level of behaviour. Individuals who complete a LEIPA® receive a totally bespoke coaching debrief, where the individual decides on and chooses the behaviours they will change and the actions they will take. The candidate's chosen raters are then invited by the individual to support their process.

The strength of LEIPA® lies in its links with EI and leadership styles and works most successfully when it is part of an overall development programme.

We invite you to download a free app "LeaderShaper" (see links on the first page of this chapter), from which you can complete an abridged self-assessment version of LEIPA®.

Developing our people

In this section, we suggest how leaders can more effectively support their staff depending on their level of adult development. The primary ways that a leader directly supports staff in their development are through modelling appropriate behaviours (leading beyond the ego) and giving feedback directly or using 360° feedback tools. We explore how leaders can give feedback, in particular 360° feedback, using a coaching style of leadership (see Table 4.1). Other tools, such as psychometric self-assessments, can help with self-awareness, but feedback gives people insight into how they are perceived by others and is, therefore, uniquely important. Bachkirova (2011) also proposes that coaching involving feedback requires different approaches at different developmental stages.

Feedback for people with a socialised mind (or unformed ego)

Kegan and Lahey (2009) state that the "socialized mind ... strongly influences how information is *received* and *attended to*" (their italics). They suggest that the socialised mind is highly sensitive to the message and over-interprets it, creating other meanings well beyond that which the message was meant to convey. People with a socialised mind have an internalised view of how they are perceived because it is influenced by views of others.

Case Study 2: The socialised mind (see Figure 4.3)

OV is a middle manager in a non-governmental organisation. She requested 360° feedback, and since the organisation did not have a 360° process, she and her coach agreed to develop some questions that she felt were relevant to her role. Her coach collated anonymous feedback.

Even though she asked for the intervention, she could not cope with the impact of the feedback. She was still very much in 'subject' mode and was unable to take an 'object' learning view about herself. During the debrief, she was more concerned with who made specific comments and was troubled by the more negative observations.

Her response seems to parallel the message from peers and manager that she was not willing to engage with the rest of the organisation and unable to reflect on feedback. Despite encouragement, she chose not to explore the implications of these observations for her own development needs.

On reflection, the coach realised that she was at the level of the 'socialised' mind and was not ready for 360° feedback, as it appeared to reinforce some of her own subjective thinking. She was unable to take an objective view and was at the 'Rational Ego based As-usual Leadership level'. The coach needed to use a different approach relevant to her adult development level (described below).

360° feedback may not be useful for people with socialised minds (or unformed egos). Maxwell (2017) summarises other approaches that might be relevant, such as immediacy (Brockbank & McGill, 2006), feedforward (McDowall et al., 2014) and self-feedback (Whitmore, 2009), all of which may help the client explore self-perceptions and feelings, in a less threatening way than 360° feedback.

Bachkirova (2011) describes the complexity of coaching someone with an unformed ego, as the relationship could be seen as that of a 'good parent' providing a nurturing relationship. If feedback is not managed with skill and care, the staff member may become dependent, or may retreat into themselves, with the potential for harm.

The client in the case study above was in denial about her 360° feedback. Our experience shows that similar individuals are more likely to accept 360° feedback, when they first learn about EI, leadership styles and how EI Leadership impacts culture (see Case Study 1). This can then enable them to move towards a self-authoring mind.

Feedback for people with a self-authoring mind (or formed ego)

Kegan and Lahey (2009) consider that the self-authoring mind filters received messages, giving priority to the information it has sought. Other information that is not asked for does not get through the filter.

Often 360° feedback is better suited for people at this stage of their development (Bachkirova, 2011). People will be receptive to external views of themselves and will be more ready to accept and learn from the feedback.

Case Study 3: The self-authoring mind (Figure 4.3)

JK had recently moved into a director role. She had come from an operational role and needed to develop her leadership skills and become more strategic. She was worried that she was not bringing her authentic self to the job and asked for 360° feedback. The coach used the LEIPA® tool (see box above) to give her feedback.

She drew valuable messages from the LEIPA® feedback, which affirmed her leadership competencies and capabilities. This increased her confidence to take on the leader's mantle and develop her own authentic style. She created a SMART action plan, which she shared with her raters, to engage their support in her development. Her raters identified three EI capabilities that required development. These were empathy, building bonds and influence. She identified some key actions: listen more than speak; enable people to reach their own conclusions; and make more time to connect in person rather than by email.

The coach reflected that this was an appropriate intervention for this client as she was in the self-authoring mind stage of her adult development and was able to be objective. She welcomed feedback and was resilient and committed to taking action.

Case Study: A self-reflection from a LeaderShape faculty member

"About ten years ago, in the first few minutes of my bespoke LEIPA® feedback session, I needed to go no further than the first summary page to get the most benefit for myself. LEIPA®'s first page feedback summarises self and raters, rating the difference between Actual and Desired behaviours. I had totally underrated myself compared to my raters. The page was highlighted red with differences in perception. These are described as hidden strengths in LEIPA®. My immediate feeling was surprise and then determination to cease underrating and undermining myself and become more realistic about my actual strengths. The other aspects of the raters' feedback showed areas for development in certain emotional intelligence competencies. This enabled me to then decide and agree on which SMART actions to take. Working on these over time has enabled me to become a more effective leader and coach. LEIPA®, because of its specificity, proved to be a significant milestone in my adult development and my journey along the 'REAL' path".

Many formal rating tools, like LEIPA®, have a 'self' and 'other' rating (Heidemeier & Moser, 2009), which provides people with unique insights into how they perceive themselves compared to how others see them. This exposes hidden strengths and blind spots and gives the person an opportunity to explore these differences in perception.

People with a self-authoring mind (formed ego) are confident of their own views of themselves and they will get rich material from the feedback to support their ongoing development.

Feedback for people with a self-transforming mind (or reformed ego)

People with a self-transforming mind, who have 360° feedback, are usually undertaking it to develop themselves further in their leadership role. It is also possible that the feedback will be done as part of team as well as individual development.

360° feedback for executives with self-transforming minds needs to be tailored and made relevant, to address those aspects that feed their curiosity about themselves. They will want to make meaning of the feedback, and their curiosity is more likely to improve the quality of their perception (Bachkirova, 2011). The leader, using a coaching style of leadership (see Table 4.1), can play an important role here in helping someone with a self-transforming mind to identify where there are discrepancies in the feedback and to explore its meaning. They are ready and able to look at themselves from the many perspectives that a 360° tool might reveal and will also explore their emotions more objectively.

Concluding self-reflections

Through writing this chapter, we realised we wanted to give more thought to where we are in our own adult development and how we got here. As we reflect on our continued learning and development, we notice that we shift between self-authoring and self-transforming minds. In the 'REAL' model, this is equivalent to shifting between the **R**obust **E**motionally **A**ware **L**eadership and **R**adical, **E**thical, **A**uthentic **L**eadership.

We found this both challenging and humbling. We recognise how complex the adult development journey is and how easy it is to slide backwards to an earlier stage of development, particularly when stressed.

As the title of this chapter indicates, we hope we have encouraged and inspired you to think about where you are on your adult development path, and what impact this may have on your people, your organisation and your journey towards transpersonal leadership.

We hope we have captured your attention, encouraged you to read and think further around this subject and stimulated you to be bold enough to engage in a more developmental approach to your own learning and that of your teams and organisations.

Our greatest challenge is to *notice* what's happening, manage our state and choose to act as **R**adical, **E**thical, **A**uthentic **L**eaders.

Questions and actions for personal development

1. Where do you think you are on the transpersonal leadership journey now, and where would you like to be?
2. Reflecting on Kegan's adult development stages, where would you place yourself?
3. What assessments have you had and what value did you receive from them? What insights did you get on your emotional intelligence, your leadership style and on your own stage of development?
4. What (if any) hidden strengths do you consider yourself to have?
5. What actions do you need to take to support your people in their own development journey?
6. How are you going to do continue to develop yourself?

References

Bachkirova, T. (2011). *Developmental Coaching: Working with the Self*. Maidenhead, Open University Press.

Brockbank, A., & McGill, I. (2006). *Facilitating Reflective Learning through Mentoring and Coaching*. London, Kogan Page Ltd.

Cook-Greuter, S. R. (2000). 'Mature Ego Development: A Gateway to Ego Transcendence?' *Journal of Adult Development, 7*, 227–240.

Coyne, S. (2016). *Sustainable Leadership; Rewire Your Brain for Sustainable Success*. https://www.routledge.com/posts/10721.

Erikson, E.H. (1950). *Childhood and Society.* New York, W. W. Norton & Co.

Fletcher, C., 2004. *Appraisal and Feedback.* London: Chartered Institute of Personnel and Development.

Goleman, D., Boyatzis, R., & McKee, A. (2002). *Primal Leadership: Realizing the Power of Emotional Intelligence.* Cambridge, MA, Harvard Business School Press.

Goodman, R. G. (2002). 'Coaching senior executives for effective business leadership: The use of adult development theory as a basis for transformative change', in: C. Fitzgerald & J. Garvey Berger (ed.) *Executive Coaching. Practices and Perspectives.* Palo Alto California, Davies-Black, pp. 135–153.

Heidemeier, H., & Moser, K. (2009). 'Self–other agreement in job performance ratings: a meta-analytic test of a process model', *Journal of Applied Psychology*, 94, 353–370.

Ives, Y., & Cox, E. (2012). *Goal-focused Coaching. Theory and Practice.* London, Routledge.

Kegan, R. (1982). *The evolving self: Problem and Process in Human Development.* Cambridge, MA, Harvard University Press.

Kegan, R., & Lahey, L. L. (2009). *Immunity to Change: How to Overcome It and Unlock Potential in Yourself and Your Organization.* Harvard, Harvard Business School Publishing Corporation.

Knights, J., Grant, D., & Young, G. (Eds) (2018). *Leading Beyond the Ego.* Abingdon, Routledge.

Laske, O. E. (2006). *Measuring Hidden Dimensions. The Art and Science of Fully Engaging Adults. Volume 1.* Medford, MA, Interdevelopmental Institute Press.

LeaderShape (2017). *Leadership & Emotional Intelligence Performance Accelerator.* http://www.leadershapeglobal.com/Leipa.

Maxwell, A. (2017). 'The use of feedback for development in coaching: Using the coach's stance', in: T. Bachkirova, G. Spence, & D. Drake (ed.) *The SAGE Handbook of Coaching.* London: Sage, pp. 310–330.

McDowall, A. (2008). 'Using feedback in coaching', in: Passmore, J. (ed.) *Psychometrics in Coaching: Using Psychological and Psychometric Tools for Development.* London, Kogan Page Ltd, pp. 26–44.

McDowall, A., Freeman, K. & Marshall, S. (2014) 'Is Feedforward the way forward? A comparison of the effects of Feedforward coaching and Feedback', *International Coaching Psychology Review*, 9, 135–146.

Plaister-Ten, J. (2017). *Leading across Cultures: Developing Leaders for Global Organisations.* https://www.routledge.com/posts/11399.

Shiner, M. (2015). *7 Leadership Blind Spots: Adult Development, Emotional Intelligence, and Leadership Effectiveness among Biotech R&D Leaders.* Doctoral dissertation, Harvard Graduate School of Education. https://dash.harvard.edu/handle/1/16461059.

Wall, T. K., & Knights, J. (2013). *Leadership Assessment for Talent Development.* London, Kogan Page Ltd.

Whitmore, J. (2009). *Coaching for Performance: GROWing Human Potential and Purpose: The Principles and Practice of Coaching and Leadership*, 4th edition. London, Nicholas Brearley Publishing.

5 Sustainable leadership

Rewire your brain for sustainable success

Sue Coyne

Overview

In this chapter, we explore why we need a more sustainable approach to leadership and how we can shift from the old mechanistic view of leadership to a more sustainably effective one that is appropriate for the 21st century. It helps leaders become more relevant and less obsolete and lead in a way that sustains rather than drains themselves and others.

Introduction

At a conference on trust that I attended in London in October 2014, Sir Bob Geldof observed the following: "100 years later we are back where we were, a new world struggling with an old structure that is no longer fit for purpose. If businesses want to be successful, they need to be authentic, genuine and real". I was struck by this pattern of getting stuck in an old view of the world that is no longer appropriate and finding it difficult to shift as I had personally experienced this in my own life. Maybe you have too.

Sir Bob explained that after the 19th century it took two world wars to shift our perspective to one appropriate for the 20th century. We are now 21 years into the 21st century yet many of our institutions including our organisations and their leaders are stuck in a 20th-century mind-set. What is it going to take for us to shift to a perspective appropriate to the 21st century? What does this mean for the shift we need to make as leaders?

What is sustainable leadership?

When you search for sustainable leadership on Google, there is a lot of information about *environmental* sustainability. When we refer to sustainable leadership, we are looking at it from the *people* perspective. It is leadership that delivers sustainable high performance through creating the conditions in which everyone thrives, thereby ensuring that the organisation and all of its stakeholders experience sustainable success. As such, it is an integral part of Transpersonal Leadership.

DOI: 10.4324/9781003150626-7

Why do we need sustainable leadership?

Perhaps you are a leader in an organisation. Maybe you are a leader outside of work. But there is no maybe about whether you are the leader of your own life.

How many of us pay attention to how sustainable our approach to leading our life is? Very often, it takes a wakeup call to bring the message home. Having had cancer and burnout myself in 2000 followed shortly afterwards by divorce, I have personally experienced the impact these sorts of wakeup calls have on your life.

Following the sale of the business I was a director and shareholder of in 2002, I retrained as a coach so that I could support other leaders in finding a way to be successful without having the sort of wakeup call I had. So that's why sustainable leadership matters to me personally.

Let's examine why sustainable leadership matters from the bigger picture perspective.

The 20th-century view of the world sees organisations as machines and people as cogs inside them (Figure 5.1).

This mechanistic mind-set is based on the notion that profit is king and the purpose of businesses is to maximise profit for the owners or shareholders. This way of thinking dates from Adam Smith and other 18th- and 19th-century economists who ushered in the Industrial Revolution. It produces hierarchical organisations where superhero leaders use IQ, authority and a command-and-control style to get the cogs in the machine to do what they deem to be necessary for maximising profit.

Figure 5.1 People as cogs in a machine

This approach has enabled an unprecedented period of growth and innovation, but it is reaching the limit of its effectiveness due to:

- Globalisation
- The ever-increasing pace of change
- The impact of technology
- Widespread use of social media giving customers and other stakeholders more influence
- The changing needs of employees with Generations X (born between ca. 1960 and 1980) and Y or Millennials (born between 1980 and 1993) expecting engagement and fulfilment at work (IBM, 2015).

What are the costs of maintaining this mechanistic viewpoint beyond its useful life?

Erosion of trust in businesses and their leaders

As a result of numerous scandals and crises, including the financial crisis in the West created by the bankers in 2008 and Volkswagen falsifying emission tests in 2015, trust in business leaders was at a low ebb in 2015 (Knights, 2015). Since 2015, trust in both business and Government remained low, but interestingly in the 2020 Edelman Trust Barometer, 92% said they expect their employer's CEO to speak out on issues such as training for jobs of the future, the impact of automation on jobs, ethical use of tech, income inequality, diversity, climate change and immigration. Business leaders according to the 2020 results should take the lead on change rather than waiting for government to impose it. To build trust, businesses and their leaders need to be both ethical and competent. They need to involve their employees, invest in local communities, embrace an all-stakeholder model and partner with other institutions. There is a perception of increasing inequality with both Government and business serving the interests of only a few.

Sustainable leadership is about starting to reverse these low levels of trust and addressing increasing inequality.

Adverse effects on health and well-being

The transition from the 20th-century paradigm where people believed that you could not succeed without burning out has already started. It is, however, shocking to read the results of research studies that show that there is still a long way to go. In 2019, over half (56%) of respondents to Britain's Healthiest Workplace survey were suffering from at least one dimension of work-related stress (Financial Times, 2019). The survey signals that in the UK exhaustion as a result of being 'on' 24/7, longer commutes and working unpaid hours contributes to sleep problems which contribute to stress. Poor sleep costs the

UK £30bn a year with the loss of 200,000 working days (Hafner et al., 2016) and the US a massive $411 billion a year.

There is growing awareness of the impact of negative stress and of mental health issues. In a 2020 survey of the UK workforce by Perkbox of those who experienced work-related stress, 55% experienced anxiety as a result. The survey concluded that stress continues to be a significant contributor to poor mental health, low productivity and absenteeism in the UK workforce. Sustainable employers need to identify the causes of stress in their workplace and introduce strategies to ensure happier and healthier employees (Perkbox. com, 2020).

Stress is a massive opportunity cost for any business. If employees were not sick or underperforming due to stress and mental health issues, how much value could they be adding to the organisation?

I believe that leaders who create environments in which they and their people risk burn out will not only be unfit to lead, they will become obsolete and irrelevant.

Organisational brain drain

Then, there is an additional cost of stress that neuroscience has brought to light. The impact of on-going stress on the capacity of an individual's brain means that stress is reducing the collective brainpower of organisations. If you hire someone and put him or her under high pressure without the tools to handle the resultant stress, the likelihood is that he or she will lose brain capacity as a result (Goewey, 2014a).

Because of the impact of stress on collective brainpower, more organisations are working with experts on neuroplasticity to address this issue. Neuroplasticity and the ability to rewire your brain to access its optimal state will soon become the new competitive edge in organisations (Goewey, 2014b).

The fact remains that many organisations are not doing anything about workplace stress. In 2020, there is no excuse for this. The benefits at an individual as well as organisational level are exponential. It is up to sustainable leaders to start to address this issue.

Take a moment to reflect and ask yourself:

Why does sustainable leadership matter to me?

What is the shift required for sustainable leadership?

John Naisbitt has written extensively on futures studies, and one of his most famous observations is that "*The most exciting breakthroughs of the twenty-first century will not occur because of technology, but because of an expanding concept of what it means to be human*".

If we are to shift to a more sustainable view of leadership, a re-wiring of our collective brain is required. How do we do this? Our working memory has limited capacity. So, in order to cope with the huge amount of information the brain has to deal with, it identifies what is significant or occurs frequently and then "hardwires" it into our long-term memory, which has more capacity (McLeod, 2009).

So, what happens is your brain filters the information coming in to find things which confirm your already hardwired beliefs. These beliefs become your thoughts, which influence how you feel, what you do and the outcomes you get as a result. It becomes a self-fulfilling prophecy, which is not easy to break out of.

The reason it is difficult is that your brain likes certainty and does not like change. What this means is that in a world that is constantly and rapidly changing, your view of the world very quickly becomes outdated and holds you back or keeps you stuck.

The first step in re-wiring our collective brain is to identify the beliefs that have been hardwired into our psyche since the 19th century (and before) that are keeping us stuck in the outdated mechanistic view of the world. These are beliefs such as:

- Organisations are machines
- People are dispensable cogs in those machines
- People can't be trusted and must be told what to do and controlled
- Profit is king
- Success requires burnout

We then need to hard wire a set of new beliefs based on a more sustainable, human approach to leadership. These are beliefs such as:

- Organisations and the people in them are living systems and do not operate in isolation
- Organisations have multiple stakeholders all of whom need to benefit from its activities

Seventy percent of what happens in organisations comes from people imitating the leaders (Marlier and Parker, 2009). So, if we are to see a shift to this human, more sustainable approach to leadership, it starts with leaders themselves changing. Again, this comes down to re-wiring outdated beliefs at an individual level.

Most of the beliefs that form the basis of our way of thinking and behaving are hardwired into our subconscious mind by the time we are seven years old. As we are not taught about the need to update this wiring as we go through life (like updating the software on our laptop), most of us have a seven-year-old running our lives as adults (Rock and Page, 2009).

Learning to let go of the beliefs that hold you back is an important leadership skill. Examples of such limiting beliefs are:

- I need to be perfect to be a good leader
- I need to know everything to be a good leader

- I need to be right
- I need to work hard to prove I am good enough
- If I make a mistake or admit I don't know, others will think I can't do my job
- I have to fix everything

It can be really stressful for leaders to feel they have to know and control everything. When leaders behave in this way, people feel mistrusted and resentful. The negative impact it has on others makes it totally unsustainable in the longer term.

Leaders changing their beliefs will enable their behaviours to change with appropriate development support, and ultimately, we will see a collective paradigm shift.

What else needs to change in order to make this shift sustainable?

You will have heard the saying that what gets measured gets done. So, we need to shift from focusing too much on financial measures of success to consider a broader definition of success. This broader definition needs to recognise that organisations depend for their success on a complex global system made up of the natural environment, the social and political system and the global economy. This is referred to as the Triple Context (Tomorrow's Company, 2011) (Figure 5.2).

The definition of organisational success that takes this into account is the Triple Bottom Line. This was developed by John Elkington in 1994 (Elkington, 1997) and is a balanced scorecard which reports on the three Ps: profit, people and planet.

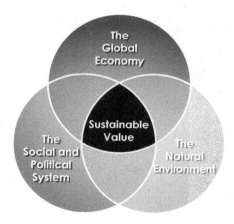

Figure 5.2 The Triple context

For organisations to be able to perform consistently well across the balanced score card of the Triple Bottom Line, they need leaders who can bring balance into their own lives (Figure 5.3).

Leaders are no different to most other people. There are three things they want in their life: happiness, health and success. This realisation led me to create "Triple H Leadership" (Coyne, 2016) to support leaders in adopting a wider definition of success that allows them to be happy, healthy and therefore sustainably high performing (Figure 5.4).

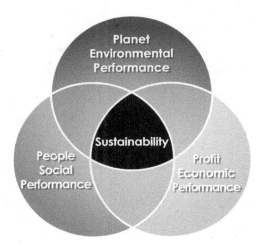

Figure 5.3 Triple Bottom Line

Figure 5.4 The three Hs of High Performance, Health and Happiness

Being a high-performing leader

There are three aspects to being a sustainable high performer: Purpose, Prioritising and Pausing.

Purpose

Identifying your **purpose** as a leader and the difference you want to make through your leadership gives you a strong "why". It enables you to be confident and authentic as a leader. This in turn means that people trust in you to do the right thing.

Prioritising

Once you are clear on your purpose, that acts as a filter for how you spend your time.

You need to identify your absolute priorities that will enable you to deliver on your purpose and make sure you focus on them each day. As you do this, the positive impact you are having increases. Your work/life balance will improve significantly too.

Prioritising is also about using the learning from neuroscience to work in a brain-friendly way:

• Schedule tasks requiring the most attention and energy when you have a fresh and alert mind.
• Doing multiple tasks leads to a big drop in accuracy or performance. Focus whenever possible on one thing at a time (Rock, 2009).
• Every time you allow yourself to be distracted by a call or e-mail, it takes more effort to focus and you have lower energy reserves to draw on. A study at London University found that constant e-mail and text-messaging reduces mental capacity by an average of 10 points on an IQ test. The effect is similar to missing a night's sleep (Rock, 2009).

Pausing

Because of the mechanistic view in many organisations, we are expected to perform at a high level 90% of the time. If we compare this to athletes, we see that they are only expected to perform at their best for 10% of the time. The rest of the time they are in training or recovery. If you are to avoid stress and burnout and be a sustainable leader, you need to build recovery breaks into your working day and make sure you get enough sleep (Loehr and Schwartz, 2003).

Being a healthy leader

Operating to a wider definition of sustainable success based on the three H's requires further re-wiring of your brain (more about how to do this later). The belief that we have had, and that many still have currently, is that it is okay to work long hours or to do whatever it takes to deliver on short-term financial objectives. We have seen the evidence already in this chapter, which shows that this leads to stress and ultimately burnout. So, what keeps us stuck in this mind-set?

Many of us have been brought up to believe that it's not okay to be selfish and put ourselves first. I have worked with clients who when asked to draw a picture of their own lives realised that they didn't even feature in them. This not only saddened them but also made them realise that they needed to change the limiting beliefs that created this situation.

The new belief that many of them have chosen to support themselves in becoming sustainable leaders is:

> I am the instrument through which I make my difference as a leader. It is therefore part of my job as a leader to look after that instrument before doing anything else. Only then will I be able to make a difference to the lives of others.

What benefits does being healthy bring?

Isn't it true that when you are fit and healthy, you handle stress better, you have more energy and you feel a greater sense of well-being?

According to research from the Centre for Creative Leadership, executives who are physically fit are considered to be more effective leaders than those who aren't. There is now evidence to link looking after your health with more sustainable high performance at work and enhanced leadership competence (Center for Creative Leadership, 2016).

When I refer to health for leaders, I regard it as having three key aspects:

- Brain health
- Stress management
- Healthy beliefs

Brain health – your competitive advantage

Science used to think that our brain was fixed once we became an adult and that it degraded with age. In the past decade, however, neuroscientists have discovered that our brain has neuroplasticity. This means that our brain has a lifelong capacity to change and rewire itself, meaning that we can continually learn throughout life (Pascual-Leone et al., 2011). So, brain health is about retaining the neuroplasticity of your brain.

As a leader, maintaining the neuroplasticity of your brain is part of your job.

How do you do this? Through continually learning things that you don't already know how to do; through regular exercise which gets more oxygen to the brain; through eating plenty of green vegetables and good oils; and through getting seven to nine hours sleep a night.

Stress – don't let it get you down

Another key aspect of the health and well-being of a leader is being able to handle stress.

Our brain is wired to sense danger and then put us into a state of fight/ flight/freeze to help us to survive the danger. Because we need all the energy to run or fight, our brain shuts down our pre-frontal cortex which is the executive centre where we have our short–term memory and do all of our best thinking and planning (Rock and Page, 2009). This completely disables us from operating effectively as leaders.

Also, stress hormones such as cortisol and adrenaline are released into our system. This is all right in short bursts, but as many leaders are operating in a stressful state for extended periods, the on-going presence of these hormones in the body can cause health problems.

In order to enhance our ability to cope with stress, we need to change our attitude.

Mindfulness can help with this; it slows us down, helps us remain calm and be more present in the moment (Siegel, 2016). For many, exercise is another effective way to reduce stress.

Your beliefs can keep you healthy

We have already said that our hardwired beliefs become outdated and hold us back. So, how do you update these hardwired, limiting beliefs? The first step is to bring these limiting beliefs to conscious awareness. As they have been in place for so long, they are buried deep in the subconscious and it takes patience and skill to bring them to the surface. Once you have identified your limiting beliefs, you can start to identify what would be a more empowering set of new beliefs given the outcomes you want to bring about.

Neuroscience has shown us that you can't just overwrite these existing beliefs, which are hardwired into neural pathways in your subconscious brain. The only way is to create new neural pathways for the new beliefs that you identify.

In order to hardwire a new belief, we need to focus on it enough over time that it becomes embedded in our subconscious. Learning to choose your thoughts and behaviour more consciously is important as a sustainable leader, given you have an impact on those around you.

Being a happy leader

Again much of what we need to do to be a happy leader involves looking at our beliefs and re-wiring them where necessary.

Is happiness something we find externally?

Many people have a tendency to believe that when we lose weight, earn more money or have the car/house/partner we are dreaming of we will be happy. Often, when you get whatever it is, the happiness is short lived. This is illustrated by the fact that personal incomes more than doubled between 1960 and the late 1990s, but the proportion of people who described themselves as happy remained stable at 30%. It seems that once you are above the poverty line, more money contributes less and less to your happiness (Stein and Book, 2011).

Many people think that if they work harder, they will be more successful and they'll be happier. Have you ever been so busy striving to achieve a goal that you got addicted to the destination and forgot to enjoy the journey? Happiness often gets indefinitely postponed, as the minute you achieve something you start trying to achieve the next thing.

Happiness is not about what is happening in the external world – only 10% of our long-term happiness is external. Ninety percent is how we process that external world (Achor, 2016).

So, if striving for external things and achieving our goals does not give us lasting happiness, what does?

Can happiness come from serving others?

Happiness research confirms that true happiness makes us naturally want to serve others. It motivates us to be generous and to use our success to support other people's success (Anik et al., 2009).

Is happiness something innate?

The Ancient Greeks defined happiness as the *joy* of moving towards our potential (Achor, 2010). This creates a very different picture of the connection between happiness and success. This inner joy enhances your performance at work, attracts positive relationships, generates a feeling of satisfaction with life and helps you to be healthier and live longer. Yes, there has actually been research that has proven that happier people live 14% longer than miserable people, increasing longevity by 7.5 to 10 years (Hamilton, 2016).

How can you create inner happiness?

There are two happiness chemicals in the brain – dopamine and oxytocin. Many studies suggest that as we age, we are constantly losing our stores of dopamine. The two best ways to increase your brain's dopamine production are smiling and exercise. Ways to increase levels of oxytocin include hugging people, stroking pets, having a massage, watching romantic films, dancing, meditating and making music, particularly in the company of others.

Does your brain have the chemistry of happiness?

A study by Richard Davidson, a professor of psychology and psychiatry at the University of Wisconsin, showed that when Buddhist Monks experienced bliss when deep in meditation, the left prefrontal lobe of their brain (above the left eyebrow) showed increased electrical activity. The findings in this study suggested that bliss or happiness is not just a vague feeling, but also a physical state of the brain (Time, 2005).

More importantly, this physical state can be induced deliberately. He refers to this as making a left shift. Many of the activities we have already discussed including exercise, meditation and mindfulness help to make a left shift.

How does happiness affect sustainable organisational success?

The evidence shows that companies with higher than average employee happiness have better financial performance and customer satisfaction (Achor, 2016). As a leader, it is your job to contribute to the happiness of your people. This starts with you developing a happiness mind-set. What makes a happy mind-set is the belief that creating happiness for yourself is not self-indulgent but a necessity, as it is a performance enhancer, for you and those around you. If you choose happiness in the moment, everything we can test for improves – intelligence, creativity and productivity (Warr and Clapperton, 2010).

Sustainable Leadership skills that enable your people to thrive over the long term

"Triple H" provides the foundations of sustainable leadership by enabling you to understand your "why", and how to deliver sustainable high performance in yourself.

You then become a role model and create a ripple effect that influences the behaviour of those around you, thus creating the climate and ultimately influencing the culture of the organisation. Your job is to ensure that this climate enables your people to thrive and deliver sustainable success.

The leadership capabilities that enable you to create this climate for sustainable success are:

- Building trust and rapport
- Understanding what is ethical, and the bigger picture, so that you can do the right thing for the team/organisation
- Developing your emotional intelligence
- Developing your awareness beyond emotional intelligence, so that you are present and centred in the moment, can sense what is needed in any situation and adjust your leadership style accordingly
- Empowering and developing people through coaching, feedback, utilising diversity and individual and team accountability

- Engaging all of your key stakeholders to create mutual sustainable success
- Developing your influencing, storytelling and collaboration skills
- Learning how to lead change in yourself and others through self-directed neuroplasticity

In short, you need to become a Transpersonal Leader.

Ultimately, this chapter is about your ability to change and lead change in order to bring about the shift to sustainable leadership. As a sustainable leader, you need to know how to rewire your brain so that you can be the change you want to see. You also need to enable others to do the same through creating an environment in which they feel safe and valued and as a result are willing to learn, grow, experiment and try out new ways of doing things/behaviours. Finally, you help to embed the change by focusing your people repeatedly on the behaviours you want to see.

Questions and actions for personal development

1. What is your definition of sustainable leadership?
2. What beliefs do you hold about leadership that stop you from becoming a more sustainable leader?
3. Why are you doing what you do? What is your purpose at work? Does knowing this help you become more optimistic, high-performing, or encourage those around you?
4. Describe an instance when you have been truly happy in your work. How did this affect people around you? How did it affect your own performance?
5. Write down three (or more) things you will do, as a result of reading this chapter, to move towards "Triple H" or sustainable leadership.

References

Achor, S. (2010). *The Happiness Advantage*. New York: Broadway Books.

Achor, S. (2016). *Transcript of "The Happy Secret to Better Work"*. Ted.com. Available at: https://www.ted.com/talks/shawn_achor_the_happy_secret_to_better_work/transcript?language=en.

Anik, L., Aknin, L., Norton, M. and Dunn, E. (2009). *Feeling Good About Giving: The Benefits (and Costs) of Self-Interested Charitable Behavior*. SSRN Electronic Journal.

Center for Creative Leadership (2016). *A Leader's Best Bet: Exercise - Center for Creative Leadership*. Available at: http://insights.ccl.org/multimedia/podcast/a-leaders-best-bet-exercise/.

Edelman (2020). *Edelman Trust Barometer*. https://www.edelman.com/trust/2020-trust-barometer (accessed 9 February 2021).

Elkington, J. (1997) *Cannibals with Forks: The Triple Bottom Line of 21st Century Business*. Capstone/John Wiley.

Financial Times (2019). Health at Work. Available at: https://www.vitality.co.uk/media-online/britains-healthiest-workplace/pdf/2019/health-at-work-2019_uk.pdf.

Goewey, D. (2014a). *Stress, the Brain and the Neuroscience of Success.* [Blog] The Huffington Post. Available at: http://www.huffingtonpost.com/don-joseph-goewey-/stress-success_b_5652874.html.

Goewey, D. (2014b). *The End of Stress: Four Steps to Rewire Your Brain.* New York, Atria Paperback, a Division of Simon & Schuster Inc.

Hafner, M., Stepanek, M., Taylor, J., Troxel, W. and Van Stolk, C. (2016). *Why Sleep Matters — the Economic Costs of Insufficient Sleep: A Cross-Country Comparative Analysis.* Rand Corporation. https://doi.org/10.7249/RR1791.

Hamilton, D. (2016). *Do Positive People Live Longer?* The Huffington Post.

IBM (2015). *Myths, Exaggerations and Uncomfortable Truths: The Real Story behind Millennials in the Workplace.* IBM Institute for Business Value.

Knights, J. (2015). *Now It Is the Auto Industry that Needs Transpersonal Leadership*, [online] London: Kogan Page. Available at: http://bit.ly/2dfLg08.

Loehr, J. and Schwartz, T. (2003). *The Power of Full Engagement.* New York: Free Press.

McLeod, S. (2009). *Short Term Memory.* Simply Psychology. Available at: http://www.simplypsychology.org/short-term-memory.html.

Marlier, D. and Parker, C. (2009). *Engaging Leadership.* Houndsmill, Basingstoke, Hampshire: Palgrave Macmillan, p. 59.

Pascual-Leone, A., Freitas, C., Oberman, L., Horvath, J. C., Halko, M., Eldaief, M., et al. (2011). Characterizing brain cortical plasticity and network dynamics across the age-span in health and disease with TMS-EEG and TMS-fMRI. *Brain Topography*, 24: 302–315.

Perkbox.com (2020). *The 2020 UK Workplace Stress Survey.* https://www.perkbox.com/uk/resources/library/2020-workplace-stress-survey.

Rock, D. (2009). *Your Brain at Work.* New York: Harper Collins Publishers.

Rock, D. and Page, L. (2009). *Coaching with the Brain in Mind.* Hoboken, NJ: Wiley.

Siegel, D. (2016) *Neuroplasticity and Mindfulness.* Available at: http://meditationscience.weebly.com/dr-dan-siegel-on-neuroplasticity-and-mindfulness.html.

Stein, S. and Book, H. (2011). *The EQ Edge.* Mississauga, Ont.: Jossey-Bass.

TIME.com. (2005). *Health: The Biology of Joy.* Available at: http://content.time.com/time/magazine/article/0,9171,1015863,00.html.

Tomorrow's Company. (2011). *Tomorrow's Stewardship: Why Stewardship Matters.* Tomorrow's Company, p. 2. Available at: http://tomorrowscompany.com.

Warr, P. and Clapperton, G. (2010). *The Joy of Work?* London: Routledge.

6 Use of feedback and coaching to improve leadership and emotional intelligence

Duncan Enright

Oh would some power the gift give us, To see ourselves as others see us.

Robert Burns

Overview

Feedback and reflection are important tools essential to growth as a leader. Research shows that a combination of multi-rater feedback and coaching improves leadership effectiveness by up to 60% (Thach, 2002). Here are described the benefits of 360° feedback accompanied by coaching.

As an example of this approach, details are given of a tool developed by LeaderShape Global to support transpersonal leaders in their development, and for coaches to use to help them. This tool is called the Leadership and Emotional Intelligence Performance Accelerator (LEIPA®). As well as describing how it works, examples are given of its use and comments from users to illustrate the value of this approach are shared.

The importance of feedback in leadership development

In every area of human endeavour, feedback and coaching provide a platform for improvement. When a leader works to develop their skills, this is very much the case, though care must be taken to match the feedback mechanisms and approach appropriate to the aims; for example, it is not effective to link performance management with leadership development (Conger & Toegel, 2002).

The counsel of a friend, the advice of a mentor or feedback from colleagues all provide valuable food for thought if you seek to improve your performance. The 360° feedback tool has become a trusted method of exploring ways to improve (Alimo-Metcalfe, 1998). The multi-rater system involving peers, direct reports, line managers and others allows a comprehensive picture of performance in specific areas. Not only does this give a rich source for reflection, it also has the potential to engage others in personal improvement and development.

DOI: 10.4324/9781003150626-8

Coaches who work with 360° feedback can help interpret the results, organise thoughts about next steps and encourage the coachee to explore options. Ideally, a leader should seek feedback constantly, informally and through more structured feedback routes like 360° assessments.

Benefits of 360° feedback and associated coaching

There are benefits to this approach for both leaders and for the organisation in which they operate. The impacts of feedback on the individual include:

- Independent input from trusted colleagues
- Ingredients for a personal development plan
- A new way to build trust within your working environment
- A springboard for positive change and to develop new habits
- Improved confidence through knowing more about your strengths and weaknesses

The benefits for an organisations are:

- Investing in the development of leaders, showing commitment and gaining greater involvement
- Information to drive improved performance
- Greater trust and sharing leading to a more healthy work culture
- New vocabulary to discuss personal and team development
- Improved leadership skills across the board, not just for the candidate, through understanding key behaviours and working on them across the organisation

To embed learning from 360° feedback on leadership, coaching is highly effective and has been proved to increase engagement and effectiveness, and lead to changes in leadership behaviour (MacKie, 2014).

Example: Leadership and emotional intelligence performance accelerator

Using the concepts of transpersonal leadership, the team at LeaderShape Global has developed a 360° assessment tool called LEIPA® – the Leadership and Emotional Intelligence Performance Accelerator. More details of the use of this tool are available elsewhere (Wall & Knights, 2013), but here, we will describe it in outline. First, it is important to note that the team at LeaderShape has worked hard to differentiate LEIPA® against other 360° assessment tools so it is considered first as a leadership performance accelerator; and secondary to that is its 360° style. It is essentially a coaching developmental tool rather than a straightforward diagnostic.

The approach is not to measure competence (how good someone is at a task), but frequency of observed behaviours. This allows greater suspension of judgement fuelled by positive or negative emotion towards the candidate and renders the instrument culturally neutral across and within different geographic and organisational cultures. Part of the reason for emphasising the observational focus is that if it were based on competency, then the questions and statements would require some validation against context. For an example of the complexities this can cause, see the work on development and validation of a 360°-feedback instrument for healthcare administrators by Garman, Tyler and Darnall (2004). Basing the instrument on behaviours, not competencies, overcomes this. LEIPA® compares different leadership styles against their importance in the executive's current role, providing a gap analysis (see Figure 6.2). The accelerator was developed from the proven Emotional Intelligence and Leadership Style Framework (Goleman, Boyatzis & McKee, 2013).

Scoring for desired behaviours is on a five-point scale (1 = low importance in this role, 5 = essential in this role) as is observed behaviours (1 = very rarely observed, 5 = always observed). There are 76 granular behaviours in the assessment, organised by emotional intelligence (EI) competency and capacity with an additional 16 behaviours relating to Communications, Trustworthiness and Conscientiousness. Raters are approached to invite them to contribute by the candidate and then contacted independently with an online survey. Results are compiled anonymously (other than where only one person is placed in a cohort – typically the boss). The results are presented in a report containing the following:

- A summary of the performance differences (desired less observed) by EI competency and capability for self and other raters, identifying those areas where the gap is larger according to others (blind spot) and self (hidden strength). The size of the gap is also noted and can lead to useful conversations; a gap of over 0.5 among other raters is worthy of note, and a gap of over 1 is a standout result (see Figure 6.1).
- Verbatim comments, anonymised as before, organised by behaviours to continue ('keep doing'), to develop ('do more of'), to commence ('start doing') and to address ('do less of').
- A report on leadership style priorities (see Knights, Grant & Young, 2018, Chapter 8) by rater cohort indicating styles in the order of importance, difference between desired and observed and EI capabilities pertaining to each.
- Ratings by EI capability and by rater cohort (i.e. self, boss(es), coworkers, direct reports, others, all excluding self).

Behaviours are described in short phrases, and some examples are given in Table 6.1.

LEIPA® provides a precise, defined plan for behavioural change, tailored to the individual's role within their organisation. The process ensures a

Performance Difference Desired less Observed

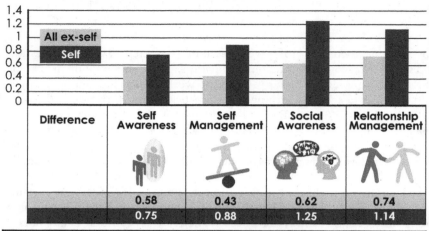

Difference	Self Awareness	Self Management	Social Awareness	Relationship Management
All ex-self	0.58	0.43	0.62	0.74
Self	0.75	0.88	1.25	1.14

	Self	Average ex-self
Self-awareness	**0.75**	**0.58**
Emotional self-awareness	1.00	0.98
Accurate self-assessment	0.75	0.81
Self-confidence	0.50	HS	– 006
Self-management	**0.88**	**0.43**
Achievement orientation	0.75	0.31
Optimism	1.00	HS	0.38
Emotional self-control	1.50	HS	0.33
Transparency	0.50	0.31
Adaptability	0.75	0.52
Initiative	0.75	0.71
Social awareness	**1.25**	**0.62**
Empathy	1.75	1.25
Organisational awareness	0.75	0.33
Service orientation	1.25	HS	0.27
Relationship management	**1.14**	**0.74**
Developing others	1.75	1.08
Inspirational leadership	0.75	0.33
Influence	2.00	0.73
Change catalyst	0.75	0.58
Conflict management	1.25	1.02
Building bonds	1.00	HS	0.29
Teamwork and collaboration	0.50	BS	1.10
Communications	**0.67**	**1.00**
Trustworthiness	**0.50**	**0.17**
Conscientiousness	**0.00**	**0.00**

BS = Potential Blind Spot, HS = Potential Hidden Strength

Figure 6.1 Desired less observed behaviours (sample) from a LEIPA® report

Table 6.1 Examples of granular behaviours and their associated EI competencies and capabilities

EI competency	EI capability	Granular behaviour
Self-Awareness	Accurate self-assessment	Aware of own strengths and weaknesses
Self-Management	Optimism	Is generally a positive person
Relationship Management	Conflict management	Encourages debate and open discussion
Social Awareness	Empathy	Listens attentively to what people say
Trustworthiness	n/a	Treats people with respect and dignity
Conscientiousness	n/a	Is considered to be reliable

Visionary		Coaching		Affiliative		Democratic		Pace-setting		Commanding	
Level of importance as scored by raters	**1**	Level of importance as scored by raters	**5**	Level of importance as scored by raters	**3**	Level of importance as scored by raters	**2**	Level of importance as scored by raters	**4**	Level of importance as scored by raters	**6**
PRIME:		**PRIME:**		**PRIME:**		**PRIME:**		**PRIME:**		**PRIME:**	
Self-confidence	-0.1	Emotional self-awareness	1.0	Empathy	1.3	Teamwork & collaboration	1.1	Achievement	0.3	Achievement	0.3
Inspirational leadership	0.3	Empathy	1.3	Conflict management	1.0	Conflict management	1.0	Initiative	0.7	Initiative	0.7
Change catalyst	0.6	Developing others	1.1	Building bonds	0.3	Influence	0.7			Influence	0.7
Transparency	0.3					Accurate self-assessment	0.8				
SECONDARY:		**SECONDARY:**		**SECONDARY:**		**SECONDARY:**		**SECONDARY:**		**SECONDARY:**	
Emotional self-awareness	1.0	Initiative	0.7	Emotional self-awareness	1.0	Empathy	1.3	Self-confidence	-0.1		
Optimism	0.4	Emotional self-control	0.3	Initiative	0.7	Adaptability	0.5				
TERTIARY:		**TERTIARY:**		**TERTIARY:**		**TERTIARY:**		Sub-total +ve	0.4	Sub-total	0.6
Initiative	0.7	Accurate self-assessment	0.8	Accurate self-assessment	0.8	Organisational awareness	0.3	**NEGATIVE EFFECT IF MISSING**		**NEGATIVE EFFECT IF MISSING**	
Empathy	1.3	Optimism	0.4	Transparency	0.3	Service orientation	0.3	Emotional self-awareness	1.0	Emotional self-awareness	1.0
Influence	0.7	Organisational awareness	0.3					Emotional self-control	0.3	Emotional self-control	0.3
								Empathy	1.3	Empathy	1.3
								Teamwork & collaboration	1.1		
								Sub-total	0.9	Sub-total	0.9
Overall score:	0.4	Overall score:	0.9	Overall score:	0.8	Overall score:	0.9	Overall score:	0.7	Overall score:	0.7

Figure 6.2 Leadership styles and ratings (sample) from a LEIPA® report

rounded view from both self-perception and colleagues, focusing on EI and leadership styles. Using best practice in a 360° format, LEIPA® identifies and compares the individual's habitual leadership styles to those which will have the greatest positive impact in their role. Specific behaviours to change, producing significant performance improvement are pinpointed, delivering a framework for action (see Figure 6.2).

Unlike most EI tools, LEIPA® relates competencies directly to leadership. By comparing this with raters' perceived importance of each leadership style, it is possible to identify the leadership style(s) the manager needs to develop. Focus can now be brought on the behaviours that the identified leadership style depends on. It measures competence in six leadership styles and compares that with the importance of each style in their own role and provides insights into the culture of the organisation. Objective focus is placed on observed against desired behaviours within the organisation, backed by verbatim comments. It is therefore an assessment not reliant on 'norms', and is therefore culturally neutral, so it can be used across any organisation or geography. The outcome is a specific action plan for immediate and future development.

The full report, which remains confidential to the candidate (unless they choose to share it), contains complete details of the data to enable thorough investigation of key points as detailed above. The candidate is guided to improve EI development areas that will have the greatest impact in their current role. This includes as mentioned before, and very importantly, identified areas where the candidate scores the gap between desired and observed behaviour to be lower than raters – known as 'blind spots'; and also highlights the areas where raters see the gap as smaller – 'hidden strengths'. Both blind spots and hidden strengths offer significant learning points.

The process includes the candidate engaging with raters to follow up on development areas. Training is available for LEIPA® facilitators (including undertaking a LEIPA® themselves); a cadre of facilitators therefore exists, all of whom are accredited executive coaches able to follow up the LEIPA® report debrief with on-going coaching where appropriate.

A description of how LEIPA® provided value for senior leaders in India is given in Chapter 15. Often as in this case, a 360° feedback process can be used simultaneously with an executive team, shining a light on areas for common development and offering some opportunities for reflection on diversity of thinking (a valuable attribute of any team, see Chapter 10).

LeaderShaper

Widely used in training as a self-assessment tool in EI and leadership styles, LeaderShaper is a free app available on Android and iOS devices. Resulting advice on behaviours and leadership styles provides a useful source of reflection and a platform for further work, particularly for new managers.

Further developments

LEIPA® is being made available in a range of languages, including Russian and Portuguese, to meet local demand for its use, though the content is universally the same.

LEIPA® also stores results in a data warehouse, providing the team with a bank of real-world information to fuel further research and development. There is also an ability to aggregate results across a team to facilitate thinking about team development needs and organisational design and development.

Comments on 360° feedback from users

Specific to LEIPA® but common to a range of appropriate feedback tools, users find the process highly effective in assisting them to improve their leadership skills and develop new habits.

"LEIPA made a strong contribution in improving my self-awareness, and provided an excellent tool to enable me to identify very specific areas I could work on to improve my leadership capability." Chris Tattersall, Managing Partner, SMART UK.

"The LEIPA was incredibly helpful in learning how others see me and very helpful in pin-pointing areas for change and development to improve my leadership style to maximise my effectiveness. LEIPA offers its greatest value when combined with on-going coaching and development." Kate Bennett, Director, Equality and Human Rights Commission, Wales, UK.

Questions and actions for personal development

1. In what ways does 360° feedback help you develop as a leader?
2. How might a 360° feedback process provide a coach with a basis for assisting a coachee in personal and leadership development?
3. Reflecting on a feedback process you have undertaken or been part of, what provided most value for you? For the candidate? For the organisation?
4. Consider whether now is a good time in your development to seek 360° feedback, and explore with your organisation how and when that might happen.

References

Alimo-Metcalfe, B. 1998. 360 Degree feedback and leadership development. *International Journal of Selection and Assessment*, 6(1): 35–44.

Conger, J., & Toegel, G. 2002. Action learning and multi-rater feedback as leadership development interventions: Popular but poorly deployed. *Journal of Change Management*, 3(4): 332–348.

Garman, A., Tyler, L., & Darnall, J. 2004. Development and validation of a 360-degree-feedback Instrument for Healthcare Administrators. *Journal of Healthcare Management*, 49(5): 307–321.

Goleman, D., Boyatzis, R., & McKee, A. 2013. *Primal Leadership*. Boston: Harvard Business Review Press.

Knights, J., Grant, D. and Young, G., 2018. *Leading Beyond the Ego*. Oxford: Routledge.

MacKie, D. 2014. The effectiveness of strength-based executive coaching in enhancing full range leadership development: A controlled study. *Consulting Psychology Journal: Practice and Research*, 66(2): 118–137.

Thach, E. 2002. The impact of executive coaching and 360 feedback on leadership effectiveness. *Leadership & Organization Development Journal*, 23(4): 205–214.

Wall, T., & Knights, J. 2013. *Leadership Assessment for Talent Development*. London: Kogan Page.

7 Women, naturally the best leaders for the 21st century?

Greg Young

> We have to free half the human race, the women, so that they can help free the other half.
>
> Emmeline Pankhurst

Overview

History is awash with examples of famous leaders that when asked one can bring to mind. Ask the question specifically whether one can name a notable woman leader and the task gets more challenging. The responses might include female monarchs: Cleopatra, Elizabeth 1st and 2nd, Victoria, or politicians: Golda Meir, Margaret Thatcher, Angela Merkel or Indira Gandhi. Take it a step further and ask the question relating to notable women business leaders and I am guessing that you will really struggle. Admittedly, for much of the time leading up to the 20th century, women had bigger challenges to overcome like the basic right to vote, a challenge that continues today in some parts of the world.

In my parent's generation, when a woman married in the UK, she was usually expected to give up work because her place was to run the home, bring up a family and attend to the needs of her husband. Generally, this meant that women did not have careers; they had jobs, something that would provide some level of personal income. When married, this also implied that the household could be funded solely based on the income on one earner, the man.

In the latter stages of the 20th century, this all began to change, though primarily in Europe, North America and Australasia, beginning with the international women's liberation movement of the 1960s which campaigned for legal and social equality for women. It continues with both the feminist and post-feminist movements into the 21st century that seek equality in pay, working practices and financial self-reliance. Along the way, social norms changed and even became a requirement that in any partnership, both parties need to work in order to generate income for a desired lifestyle. The price of housing has been a major factor.

DOI: 10.4324/9781003150626-9

Men on the other hand have been accustomed to an almost exclusive male environment for centuries. Where women were present, it was to fulfil a supporting function such as that of secretary or assistant. Men who began their careers in the 1980s are not only still in the workplace, having progressed up the career ladder, they now occupy the top jobs. Their attitudes carry weight and power and inform their inbuilt or unconscious bias. As they retire, attitudes are changing but often at a generational pace.

The business environment is materially changing from the economics of the '80s and '90s. Twentieth-century methods are beginning to struggle in this 21st century world. Reviewing the content of MBAs, leadership development programmes and philosophies right up to the end of the last century show that the fundamentals of accepted business practice were based on competition. This informed vision, strategy, strength, power and decision-making. Companies were built like machines with each part fulfilling its own function, mechanical raw material in, product out; a true reflection of the Industrial Revolution. The business environment in the 21st century requires businesses to be nimble and agile, both responding to rapid change and capable of anticipating what the next shift will be. They need to respond to complexity, wicked problems and apply systemic solutions. Business leaders who will be successful will be those who can ride the wave of this increasingly changing world, harnessing the benefits of globalisation, technology and new societal attitudes to ethics and fairness. They will embrace collaborative relationships and be prepared to be radical in their thinking to build organisations that are fleet of foot and thrive on uncertainty and ambiguity. These leaders will operate beyond their ego, continuing personal development and learning. They will be able to:

- Embed authentic, ethical and emotionally intelligent behaviours into the DNA of the organisation
- Build strong, empathetic, caring and collaborative relationships within the organisation and with all stakeholders
- Develop a performance-enhancing culture that provides sustainability

We call people that can do this Transpersonal Leaders.

What relevance has this to women in leadership? A preliminary review of LeaderShape's research data (Knights, 2013) indicated that women are naturally better leaders for the 21st century. This view is supported by a broad ranging global study by Mercer (2015) entitled 'When Women Thrive, Businesses Thrive'.

More and more companies now recognise that collaborative, rather than competitive behaviour, creates more success and women are well placed to lead in this century. The data show women have all the right attributes, including empathy, change catalyst and inspirational leadership. More than that, there are a number of reports that demonstrate that companies with women on the Board perform better. There are now women on the Board of every UK Financial Times Stock Exchange (FTSE) 100 company. This sounds great, but the 2016 Female FTSE Board Report (Cranfield School of Management, 2016) is typical in showing that out of 279 female held directorships, only 26, that's a mere 9.7%, are executive roles so one could argue the real power is still being controlled by the men. An update of the Hampton Alexander report published in February 2021 shows that women now account for 36.2% of the Board membership of the FTSE 100 companies and 33.2% of FTSE250 companies. However, women still only account for 26.5% of the Executive Committee membership where the true organisational power lies. At the layer below the Executive Committee, women account for a higher 31.2% of the membership, indicating a slow but positive trajectory. Although on the face of it, this looks like good news, alarmingly, the turnover rate of women in those senior roles has risen from 21%/year in 2017 to a staggering 30% in 2020. This indicates that there is something fundamentally at odds with the ability of women to thrive at that level. There is evidence to show that the more women there are on Boards, then the turnover rate decreases, this might be a factor in retaining talented people (Nili, 2019). In the USA, just 26% of S&P500 Board members are women (Spencer Stuart, 2019).

Clearly, men play a big part in women getting the real power in companies. The enlightened ones recognise and embrace the strength and diversity of qualities and opinion women bring. Yet, others steadfastly cling on to the old ways harking back to when they were successful – but in a different context, on another day. Some sectors are worse than others. According to a recent report (Zarya, 2016), most Tech CEOs rate a specific expertise as very or extremely important. While women make up 59% of the total workforce, they account for only 30% in major tech companies. That figure is even worse when you consider it includes both tech and non-tech jobs. At Google, Facebook and Twitter, women hold less than 20% of tech jobs (Garnett, 2016). Technical expertise is return on investment positive, potentially mission critical – necessary but insufficient. What will keep the company ahead is thought diversity. So, having women on your Board and exploiting that thought diversity is what will give you a company that will be around in the longer term. Having women on the Board as tokenism merely adds talking ballast to the payroll.

It's no secret then that there is resistance from some men to welcome women into the powerful positions in senior leadership, but actually that's not all. Women themselves can be their own worst enemy. LeaderShape's data (explained in the next section of this chapter) show that an area where women don't score as well as men is self-confidence. The Leadership and Emotional Intelligence Performance Accelerator (LEIPA) tool, which is based on a 360° format (see Chapter 8) really shows this well. The instrument compares observed behaviour against ideal, so the closer to ideal you are observed, the better you are performing. We find that women consistently mark themselves poorly, so their self-rating shows them to be pretty poor performers across all the EI competencies. But being a 360° format, when they see the scores that colleagues have given them, their hidden strengths (determined by the difference between their own scores and that of their colleagues) shine out and are usually manifold. This in itself can be incredibly reaffirming, but it seems to be a real issue that women will naturally undermine their own achievements, be afraid of being found out and suffer from imposter syndrome.

Writing this in April 2021 during the time of the global COVID-19 pandemic, it is worth noting the impact that the crisis has had on women in leadership positions. Globally, countries with women heads of state such as Germany under Chancellor Angela Merkel and New Zealand under Prime Minister Jacinda Ardern are recognised to have dealt with the crisis better with fewer fatalities per capita. This has sparked recognition of women as great heads of state particularly in a crisis with high levels of empathy and approaches that have been bold in their approach to the safety of human life. See Chapter 16 for more discussion of the role of women leaders in a crisis.

Economies have suffered less as a result. In contrast to the few women leaders, however, the fact is that women have been most affected by the consequences of the pandemic. The burden of home schooling of children has largely fallen to women, and women workers have a higher presence in those sectors that have been more greatly affected by the need for social distancing such as hospitality, retail and the care sector. While it is too early to state the longer-term impact of the pandemic on gender balance in the workplace, the prediction is that it will either slow the process or put it back by a number of years.

Where are the differences in leadership between men and women?

Between the years 2006 and 2020, LeaderShape undertook some original research using its executive development tool LEIPA. Based on a 360° assessment format, LEIPA collects anonymous input from individuals, their managers, peers, reports and others with whom they have a meaningful working relationship. The questionnaire compared observed against desired frequency of exhibited behaviours for all the emotional intelligence (EI) competencies set out in Goleman's model of EI and leadership styles (Goleman, 2000). For more details of this process, see Chapter 8.

Data from 425 individuals were assessed, 37% of which had women as the subjects. Ethnicity was not recorded, but subjects were distributed around the world, including the USA, the UK, India, Switzerland, Italy, Sweden, China, the UAE, Lebanon, Germany, Japan, Côte d'Ivoire, South Africa, Tanzania, Kenya, Kazakhstan and Brazil. The candidates were also spread across the government, public, private and not-for-profit sectors and ranged in age from over 55 to under 24 at the time of the assessment (Baby Boomers to Gen Z). Candidates were mostly C-Suite and Vice President (VP) level followed by Director level.

Although LeaderShape did not set out to focus on gender as a leadership issue, subsequent analysis of the data comparing results from men with those from women indicated some interesting similarities and differences.

The four EI competencies of Self-Awareness, Self-Management, Social Awareness and Relationship Management were broken down into a number of EI capabilities.

Three other capabilities (Trustworthiness, Communication and Conscientiousness) were also assessed which are considered EI capabilities by some authors but not others, yet are considered to be fundamental to good leadership performance.

Data and analysis

The LEIPA survey comprises 92 statements which describe granular behaviours such as "Behaves calmly under stress" or "Identifies opportunities and stimulates individuals to develop to their full potential". They were asked to rate to which level they currently observe the behaviour ("how often does occur now and in the recent past?") and which level they would desire the behaviour (How often would you like this to occur?) to occur. Table 7.1 shows the level descriptors used by candidates and raters.

The difference between observed and desired (The Difference Index) was measured for each individual behaviour which were grouped into 19 EI capabilities. As shown in Table 7.2, a 'Difference Index' score of greater than 0.5

Table 7.1 Absolute levels used by LEIPA raters

Absolute level of 'observed' and 'desired' behaviours	
1	Never or Almost Never
2	Occasionally
3	Quite Often
4	Usually
5	Always

Table 7.2 Difference between observed and desired behaviours and recommendations

Difference between 'observed' and 'desired' behaviours	
Performing beyond expectation	<0
Performing at expectation	0
Performing close to expectation	>0 but <0.5
May need improvement	From 0.5 but <1.0
Indicates need for change	Between 1.0 and 1.5
Significant shortfall	>1.5

Table 7.3 Difference scores of EI competencies for men and women. Results that are statistically significant are shaded

EI competencies	Men	Women	Difference
Emotional self-awareness	0.57	0.44	**0.13**
Accurate self-assesment	0.53	0.45	**0.08**
Self-confidence	0.43	0.48	**−0.05**
Achievement orientation	0.46	0.37	**0.09**
Optimism	0.43	0.36	**0.07**
Emotional self-control	0.48	0.43	**0.05**
Transparency	0.45	0.31	**0.14**
Adaptability	0.48	0.44	**0.04**
Initiative	0.58	0.47	**0.10**
Empathy	0.78	0.58	**0.19**
Organisational awareness	0.41	0.36	**0.05**
Service orientation	0.45	0.32	**0.13**
Developing others	0.68	0.49	**0.19**
Inspirational leadership	0.59	0.49	**0.10**
Influence	0.56	0.47	**0.09**
Change catalyst	0.65	0.51	**0.13**
Conflict management	0.68	0.55	**0.13**
Building bonds	0.45	0.37	**0.08**
Team work and collaboration	0.56	0.44	**0.12**

suggested the individual might need to improve that particular behaviour, and the greater the Difference Index the greater the need for improvement and development.

Comparing the mean Difference Index scores of men against those of women showed that women fared better in 18 of the 19 capabilities as shown in Table 7.3. Of the 18 competencies where women performed closer to desired, 13 produced a significant difference using a confidence interval method. The one competency where men performed closer to desired (Self-confidence) was found not to be statistically significant.

Represented graphically, the chart below shows the difference in performance of men and women. Bars above the 0.00 line indicate women perform closer to desired levels, and that below the line indicates men perform closer to desired levels. The darker shaded bars indicate those results that are statistically significant using a confidence interval method (Figure 7.1).

The capability where men scored better is Self-confidence, although it is not statistically significant. Women scored better in all the remaining capabilities with those of Emotional Self-awareness, Achievement Orientation, Optimism, Initiative, Empathy, Service Orientation, Developing Others, Inspirational Leadership, Influence, Change Catalyst, Conflict Management, Building Bonds and Team work and Collaboration being statistically significant using a confidence interval method.

The final analysis looked at how men and women rated themselves (self-analysis) compared to how their raters evaluated them. On average, both men

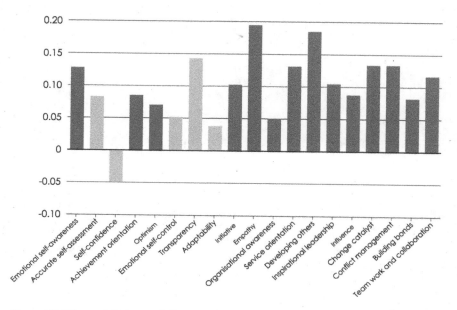

Figure 7.1 EI capabilities – difference by gender (statistically significant findings darker shaded)

Table 7.4 Difference in self rating (numbers rounded)

Self (difference) men vs women

Men	Women	Difference
0.15	0.29	−0.15

and women rated themselves to have a greater difference between "observed" and "desired" than do their raters; however, the gap was larger for men (0.29 against 0.15) than for women (see Table 7.4).

Although this could be attributed to poor self-assessment, it is also associated with low self-confidence. During the feedback process, it is not uncommon for this picture to be a revelation to the candidate in understanding how others see her in contrast to how she sees herself. This mirrors the commonly felt imposter syndrome. In contrast, being presented with anonymous and therefore less biased data on her own performance that is considerably better than her own assessment provides a very positive and reaffirming boost to self-confidence that often equates to a mandate to do more of the same.

Ensuring women reach the top

There are many strong and valid societal and organisational reasons why fewer women reach senior positions and the very top of organisations than would be expected and justified by demographics. What this research study identifies is that women are actually better than men as leaders in many of the EI capabilities that make up the leadership styles that leaders need in the 21st century.

However, the study also shows that there are a few areas, especially around emotional self-control and self-confidence, where women could and should focus to make themselves as good as they can be as leaders in this fast-changing world.

Strategies for building a strong pipeline of women leaders

Despite this study showing that women have natural attributes that when realised make them ideal leaders for organisations in the 21st century, the challenge is to get more women into leadership positions where they can deliver maximum advantage.

These strategies fall into broad categories of:

1 Setting targets based upon sound data
2 Creating the right HR policies that enable the talent to be present in the work environment
3 Developing Organisation Development (OD) policies that recognise the difference in requirements between genders
4 Building a culture that recognises and encourages leverage of the difference that women can make to strategic thinking and performance

Setting targets

While the debate about gender quotas continues, and 15 countries globally have adopted them (Terjesen & Sealy, 2016), others, including the UK have adopted a voluntary business-led approach. Targets provide clarity of goals and a disciplined approach to change. They should be set in the context of a clear action plan, with a specific timeline and a robust measurement process to identify progress. Target setting in this way is a manifestation of vision and a clear communication both internally and externally that the organisation seeks to shift. However, targets should not be set only for the highest level, say at Board level, they should be set to build a strong succession pipeline of talented women. This might include setting proportionality in the promotions process, processes that are designed to minimise unconscious bias. So, say if 40% of the available talent pool comprises women, then it would be expected that roughly 40% of staff promoted to senior positions from that pool would be women, reflecting the available pipeline.

Creating the right HR policies

Mercer's global study 'When Women Thrive' demonstrates that policies such as pay equity and health and benefit programmes impact firms' long-term ability to engage and retain female talent. According to the World Economic Forum (2015), women today earn what men were earning ten years ago, with global average earnings for women being US$11k compared to US$21k for men. This is sometimes a matter of unintended consequences; for example, an organisation whose culture is equally supportive of men having time off options for family and paternity leave are better situated to improve the representation of women. When men take time off for family reasons, this can release the woman to be in work and participate in the talent pool and improve chances of promotion. In Sweden, parents are entitled to 480 days leave of which the father must take at least 90 days. In fact, the fathers take closer to 120 days (Swedish Gov., 2021). Pay equity means that men's roles are less likely to be prioritised over women's for those families required to maximise income to support a burdensome mortgage.

Case Study

In the 1990s, I was on a panel of employees asked to undertake some research by a particularly enlightened General Manager. The context was a Pharmaceutical company, in particular the sales function. It was noted that at the Sales Representative level, the majority of the employees were women, around 75%. At Territory Management level, this proportion went down to 50% women; at Regional Management level, the percentage of women was 25%. The National Sales Manager was, and has always been a man, neither had there ever been a woman on the Executive Team. The task was to find out why this was so and to create an environment where women could be more present at higher levels in the organisation.

We undertook a series of interviews and observed:

- Women made successful sales representative, at least as good as the men
- Where women were in leadership and management roles, their teams performed as well as those reporting to male managers
- Some women eliminated themselves from career progression because they left on maternity leave and elected not to return (within the period of the study)
- Some women had no ambition to seek promotion, this number was similar to that of men
- Some women had a desire for promotion but did not put themselves forward
- Some women sought promotion, but were unsuccessful
- A small number of women sought promotion and were successful.

Digging a little deeper we found that of those in the last three observations:

- Some women did not feel they had the skills to make effective managers from the point of promotion or the self-confidence to put themselves forward.
- There was a bias, conscious or unconscious, for promoting in the image of the promoter. Both men and women who were promoted shared similar preferences in their Myers Briggs profiles with those of their boss. There was also a strong emphasis on social interaction, e.g. sales meetings at golfing venues, a drinking culture.

That led us to take action on two things aimed at a bottom-up and a top-down approach.

- We reviewed OD policy and built in to each appraisal a conversation that asked the appraisee what development the organisation could provide that would make them feel capable of being successfully promoted.
  - The uptake was greater among women than men and included things like Managing a Budget or P&L, Leadership and Management development, Appraisal Skills, Presentation Skills.
  - We also offered a 360° assessment which provided anonymised feedback based on capabilities, and it also recorded verbatim comments. The biggest impact was seen in women who received feedback from raters that was more positive than they had awarded themselves. Being anonymous, there was no agenda and the reaffirmation that the feedback provided was extremely positive in building the self-confidence that someone needed to seek promotion.
- The senior management in the sales function underwent a series of development workshops to develop EI – self-awareness, self-management, social awareness and relationship management. Leadership styles changed, and the emerging culture was less hierarchical. In particular was the realisation that diverse teams were strong teams and that a high degree of homogeneity led to a shared mode of failure.

With a shift in OD policy and development for those in positions of promoting others, we saw rapid change, the number of regional managers reached parity and although the male National Sales Manager remained in post, within a year, we had a woman on the executive.

Reframing OD policy

Most organisations' OD policies are remnants of the 20th century, naturally favouring a male approach to job application and promotion. Women often approach matters in a different way; it is often being said that a man will look at a job application and think "I can do 20% of that, I think I will apply" and a woman will think "I cannot do 20% of that; I don't think I can apply".

Building the right culture

Culture is the factor that determines performance; it is shaped by the leaders in the organisation through the climate they create coupled with the leadership styles they use. Importantly, leaders need to model the behaviours they expect to see in others. Tolstoy's quote: "Everyone thinks of changing the world, but no one thinks of changing himself" is very apt. Data from reports presented earlier in the chapter indicate that women are finding their way onto boards, but the number of those women in executive roles remains stubbornly low and appears in the UK at least to have stalled. This may indicate a sense of tokenism; we have a woman on the board so the pressure to appoint another is off and we will go back to our old ways. The best leaders are recognising that diversity itself is not the point; it is the exploitation of the difference in thinking that the diversity presents that is the key to 21st-century success.

Engaging men

A final word on perhaps the biggest obstacle or enabler depending on which way you look at it. This chapter has been on the benefits women can bring to 21st-century leadership and how the context is right for women leaders to enable their organisations to thrive. At the beginning of this chapter, space was given to statistics and the historical domination of the workplace by men. In order for organisations to benefit from gender balance, something has to change. At the current rate, it will take around 100 years for gender balance to be commonplace. The question is, how can this be accelerated? Most organisations of any size now have development programs designed to develop women leaders. These programs have enjoyed varying degrees of success in achieving their aim. Some have been counterproductive in producing women equipped with the knowledge and knowhow to lead, and then frustrated in being given no-one to lead. In truth, men still dominate the workplace. They are the biggest obstacle and are also perhaps the biggest enabler.

"When accustomed to privilege, equality feels like oppression"

Some time ago, I came across this quote but to my regret I have no idea to whom to attribute it; however, it sums up some attitudes among men well. It is this attitude that provides the block, men feeling that their position and status are being eroded. Thankfully, it is an attitude that is largely generational and so gradually being diluted in the workplace, but it also means that it will take generations to shift.

There is another way to view the phenomenon: that is to engage man in building the gender-balanced movement. No longer a men vs women idea, this is men with women making the difference. In 2018, the UK commemorated 100 years of women's suffrage when some (not all) women for the first time had the right to elect a national government, to vote in a General Election. In the UK, most women and men will know the name Emmeline Pankhurst as the Suffragette most recognisable for being the face of the movement that led to women having the vote. She was an activist. When asked, however, most people do not recognise the name Willoughby Dickinson. He was a Liberal MP credited with steering the legislation for women's suffrage through the then all-male Parliament and onto the statute books. In his own way, he was an activist, a believer in women's rights and made a material contribution to that cause. The equivalent today is to identify those men who would be the activists in each organisation that can themselves collaborate with women to bring about a movement for change. There is a danger that men sign up to support this cause and remain just that, passive supporters. If a step change is to occur, it is the male activists, operating in the transpersonal leadership model, that will actively change policy, listen to the changes needed in workplace practices – including elements like maternity and paternity leave – and create a place where the contribution of women to organisational leadership is not only recognised but nurtured and thriving.

Only when working together will the transformation really reach its goal.

Questions and actions for personal development

1. What cultural issues might contribute to exclusion of women from leadership positions?
2. What might women bring to strengthen a board (see also Chapter 13 for more on this topic)?
3. How might men help to change organisations to encourage new leadership from women?
4. Explore the pay gap and other barriers in your own organisation, and how they are hampering performance as a whole. What are you going to do about it?

References

Cranfield School of Management. 2016. Female FTSE board report. *Cranfield. ac.uk*. https://www.cranfield.ac.uk/som/research-centres/gender-leadership-and-inclusion-centre/female-ftse-board-report, April 6, 2021.

Garnett, L. 2016. The real status on women in the tech industry. *Inc.com*. https://www.inc.com/laura-garnett/women-in-tech-what-s-the-status.html, April 6, 2021.

Goleman, D. (2000). Leadership that gets results. *Harvard Business Review*, 78(2): 4–17.

Knights, J. 2013. *Women: Naturally Better Leaders for the 21st Century*. Oxford: LeaderShape Global.

Nili, Y. G. 2019. Beyond the numbers: Substantive gender diversity in boardrooms. *Indiana Law Journal*, 94(1), Article 4.

Mercer. 2015. When women thrive: A European perspective | Mercer. *Mercer.com*. https://www.mercer.at/our-thinking/when-women-thrive-a-european-perspective.html, April 6, 2021.

Spencer Stuart. 2019. US Spencer Stuart Board Index. *Spencerstuart.com*. https://www.spencerstuart.com/-/media/2019/ssbi-2019/us_board_index_2019.pdf, April 6, 2021.

Swedish Government. 2021. Quick fact: Parental leave | sweden.se. *sweden.se*. https://sweden.se/quickfact/parental-leave/, April 6, 2021.

Terjesen, S., & Sealy, R. 2016. Board gender quotas: Exploring ethical tensions from a multi-theoretical perspective. *Business Ethics Quarterly*, 26(1): 23–65.

US Bureau of Labor Statistics. 2020. Labor force statistics from the current population survey. *www.bls, gov*. https://www.bls.gov/cps/cpsaat03.htm, April 6, 2021.

Wall, T., & Knights, J. 2013. *Leadership Assessment for Talent Development*. London: Kogan Page.

World Economic Forum. 2015. Ten years of the global gender gap. *Global Gender Gap Report 2015*. http://reports.weforum.org/global-gender-gap-report-2015/report-highlights/, April 6, 2021.

Zarya, V. 2016. 1 in 3 Tech CEOs don't think gender diversity is important. *Fortune*. https://fortune.com/2016/02/24/boardlist-women-boards/, April 6, 2021.

8   Learning principles for transpersonal leadership development

Danielle Grant

Tell me and I forget. Teach me and I remember. Involve me and I learn.
Benjamin Franklin

Overview

The key principles enabling embedding and application of leadership learning have been shared before (Knights, Grant & Young, 2018, Chapter 22). The key points that came out of research and trial were that blended learning is essential. Multimodal learning, both synchronous in the form of live workshops with other motivated learners; and asynchronous, in the form of online learning that 'primes' the brain, are key elements of this approach. Reversing the learning experience, so that learners are presented with concepts before they take part in a social learning experience, was found to be key to engagement and real participation. This is known as 'flipping' in educational terms. An opportunity to relate the learning to real work situations and bring the two together is the cornerstone to retention and establishment of new skills and habits. These three principles: blended learning, flipping the learning experience and relating learning to real work situations are the founding principles of the approach used at LeaderShape in the now well tried and tested Transpersonal Leadership programmes. '

In recent years, the development of technology has enabled some practices to be refined and improved. The key area of advance is the greater ability of trainers and trainees to use reliable video conferencing across most of the world, which gives an enhanced opportunity to create stronger learning communities in our cohorts. The global application of these learning principles means that cohorts have strongly benefited from the diverse input and shared experience of people from very different geographies.

This chapter shares our experience of new technology and its use to enrich the experience of learners (and trainers) around the world.

DOI: 10.4324/9781003150626-10

Growth of learning technologies

The growth in the use of remote delivery methodologies resulting from the 2020 COVID-19 pandemic has created greater acceptance of virtual learning; however, many organisations are still learning how to create effective engagement. For some, the move to remote learning has been a new exercise forced upon them by social distancing and has led to first thinking about flexible learning (Zayapragassarazan, 2020). Current research includes new thinking on making remote learning relevant through empathetic design (Xie, 2020). For others, challenges have included new approaches to management of and communication with students (Petillion & McNeil, 2020).

At LeaderShape Global, we have a decade of experience of remote and global learning, so some of these challenges are not new. The fundamental principles outlined previously (Knights, Grant & Young, 2018, Chapter 22) are still valid, namely employing:

- Blended learning – the use of a mix of live sessions, books and other written materials, online interactive learning modules including video and exercises, and group calls – offering learners a mix of ways to engage and maximum flexibility in terms of timing and embedding
- Flipped learning – designing courses to deliver knowledge in advance of live sessions to review, question and embed lessons
- Relevant learning – relating knowledge to real-world situations in work and life, and encouraging application of ideas with reports back on results at subsequent sessions
- Engaging with the learning in short, bite-sized sessions, with space between these, to allow the new neural connections to 'set'.

The increased incidence of remote and online learning has not changed the basic, brain-friendly premise of our work.

The opportunity we see as a result of the increased usage and acceptance of online learning, and in particular ubiquitous video conferencing and calling, is to build communities of learning, or cohorts, spanning the globe and therefore expanding our definition of diversity, bringing added richness to learning.

Online learning cohorts and diversity

Multiple studies demonstrate the best leadership development programmes have cohort learning as it helps to embed this across the organisation (Fifolt & Breaux, 2018). In addition, it offers peer coaching as well as group support and discussion, feedback and emotional engagement. Well-designed cohorts also have the benefit of diversity, and remote technology allows that to be even greater than usual, leading to really rich exchanges.

The benefits of a diverse group in cohorts cannot be overstated. By sharing experiences of others, and their perspectives on the material of the course, our understanding becomes much deeper. The more diverse the group, the larger the number of insights that will be generated and can be shared. It is valuable to unpick personal and cultural assumptions, and hearing from others with very different approaches and backgrounds is the best way to do that. Diversity is experienced in a carefully designed cohort in its broadest sense (not just in terms of the protected characteristics under law, but also style, education, neuro diversity). This drives innovation and encourages new thinking.

Case Study

A recent cohort on the LeaderShape Transpersonal Leadership Coaching course included delegates from the UK, Kazakhstan, Malawi and Tanzania, with contributions from others in larger groups including Japan, the USA and Germany. At certain points, delegates dialled in from Japan, Ireland and America, fitting the training around work commitments and family upheavals. The cohort was a mix of men and women, half each, and at different stages of career from early stages to post-corporate life, combined with a rich set of experiences to share. Comments were very positive and included praise for the richness through diversity, during a shared experience of lockdown as a result of the pandemic. One participant commented:

> The interaction among the participants was the best. I thoroughly enjoyed the diversity of persons and experiences shared. Once we got to 'know' each other, it became easier to anticipate how the dialogue was going to materialize. I genuinely appreciate how our course tutor managed the conversations and provided the necessary prompts to keep us engaged and thoughtful.

The role of advanced learning principles in organisational health and success

In developing transpersonal leaders, we are seeking to impart knowledge, of course – the structured journey and the principles of emotional intelligence (EI), leadership styles and high-performing cultures, for example. However, we work to enable leaders to experience 'aha!' moments of insight. This provides a rush of energy and commitment to apply the insight. This underpins the learner's need to undergo change in themselves, and to do that they benefit from a peer-based cohort approach in a safe facilitated environment. Finally, they need to apply their learning at work, so leaders are given concepts and select actions to implement at work as part of the course. Adult students appreciate the acquisition of practical skills and knowledge that they can use professionally and in their personal lives (Knowles et al, 2005). Having students apply knowledge and skills in a real-life context is known as authentic learning (Davidson et al., 2019).

Crucially, this approach embeds soft capabilities such as awareness of culture, capability, resilience, examining values and recognising and altering behaviours.

- Developing transpersonal leadership is key to the success of organisations. This then reflects positively internally and externally to the organisation. It aligns personal and organisational purpose and values such that greater engagement and discretionary effort are fostered. This, in turn, creates high-performing, sustainable, caring and healthy organisations.
- Traditional hierarchical leadership that features multi-levelled organisations or the more flexible, flatter structures that are becoming more prevalent affects the culture. Flatter, more nimble structures are called for to deliver agile solutions in such a rapidly changing environment. To create these more autonomous, flatter organisations requires us to understand the value of dispersed leadership, so those nearest to the situation are empowered to take decisions. In terms of the practicalities of leaders and pragmatic line management responsibilities, it is crucial that everyone sees themselves as and, indeed, becomes a leader, with explicit understanding of their contribution to the purpose and achievements of the organisation.
- These different organisational structures give rise to either traditional, 20th-century (frequently commanding and pacesetting) leadership. Looking at Figure 8.1, we can see that 21st-century leadership fosters

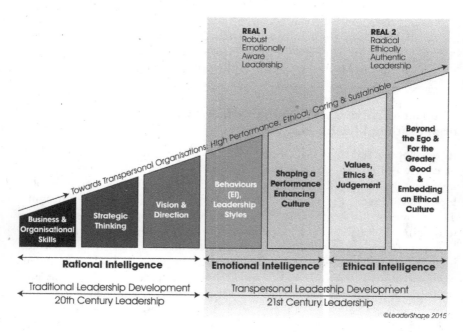

Figure 8.1 Transpersonal leadership journey

the development of EI and builds on that through Personal Conscience and Self-Determination to provide clarity on one's Spiritual Intelligence, a life-long journey. Our programme puts leaders on a holistic journey that deepens their awareness of their default and desirable: behaviours and leadership style. The practical application of this learning provides them with the tools to shape a performance-enhancing culture. Their journey deepens this awareness so their values, ethics and judgement are brought into full consciousness. Challenges and differing perspectives in the group discussions is enlightening as, learners discover, despite deep cultural differences, the fundamentals of human connection on a values basis are pretty consistent.

Blended learning in the new normal

The primary purposes and benefits of blended learning can be understood through several well-established principles. The first principle, known as the trifecta of engagement (Leslie, 2019), represents three types of interaction that must be present for an online course to be considered learner centred (Moore, 1989). These three aspects are:

1 learner–content interaction (online ALIVE prep),
2 learner–learner interaction (cohort plenary and breakout sessions) and
3 learner–instructor interaction, with the Course Tutor.

It follows therefore that the trifecta of student engagement requires that students regularly and meaningfully interact with their course curriculum content, both self-directed, with their peers and with their instructor to be fully engaged in a course.

A further key principle is that of creating a learning community, by facilitating cohort members to establish mutual understanding and real relationships. They are supported by the course leader to introduce themselves as full rounded human beings, with foibles, personal challenges and triumphs, down to favourite foods, pets and other personal life details. This transparency has to be rendered safe by the facilitator. We encourage this by the course tutor also demonstrating their willingness to be vulnerable through example (Iowa State University, n.d.).

Students then have choice and freedom to demonstrate their learning and curiosity through a co-created agenda and process for each cohort session. The Course Tutor starts each cohort meeting after sharing reflection notes for the whole cohort. This allows students to prepare and so enabling the agenda to emerge within the group at the start of the session. Students can request plenary or breakout sessions. This will vary with each group and topic. This results in them experiencing the programme as largely self-directed and increasing their engagement and learning (Merriam & Bierema, 2013).

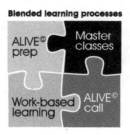

Figure 8.2 Blended learning approach

As has been indicated, the thrust of the work is to provide learners with practical, applicable skills and knowledge that they can apply immediately in their lives and careers. Encouraging them to apply knowledge and skills in a real-life context is known as authentic learning (Davidson et al., 2019). This means the content is relevant. Utilising a constructivist approach, this allows students to make meaning of the course content by connecting it to their own experience (Merriam & Bierema, 2013). During the online course content, learners are asked to reflect and apply the concepts they have seen in the various videos and other materials, to their real-world experience; this is further extended in the group discussions with coaching conversations on their application of those ideas. This builds on the principle of problem-based learning (Barrows, 1996). Figure 8.2 illustrates the blended learning approach adopted at LeaderShape.

The future of learning technology

Building on the use of video and other media available online, what is the future of learning technology and how can it add to our suite of tools? Video conferencing facilities offer opportunities that go beyond just the convenience and effectiveness of functions such as shared whiteboards and breakout rooms (though these alone allow sophisticated analogues for existing forms of work such as workshopping, World Café (Covarrubias Venegas, 2020) and inquiry-based learning. Simulations, using avatars, such as those offered by Mursion (www.mursion.com), can provide new ways to engage and empower learners in a safe space. Our view is that these new technologies are something we very much want to add to the experience we provide our learners. However, we feel they are not yet cost effective enough to be a standard inclusion in our programmes. To make these integral to our approach, the scenarios would have to be able to be set and changed rapidly to match the context of our clients and in multiple languages. The leading players at the present time do not provide these facilities at a price that makes it scalable for us.

Avatar-based learning would supplement and allow for practice and we would see it as being fully on-demand learning. However, since this simply adds another asynchronous element, it does not address the need for social learning and feedback.

The other question we frequently consider is the use of gamification, badges, leader boards and the like. These would fit best in a simulation of the work environment; otherwise, it becomes rather disconnected. Our proven approach is heavily embedded in the human relationships of the cohort group members and their Tutor. It relies on people bringing real work challenges into the group where collaborative working and discussions give rise to insights and commitment to implement these. This totally human process does not really lend itself to a competitive badge-awarding approach. We are aiming to foster collaboration over competition. However, as the technology associated with Avatars and Simulations evolves, so bespoke simulations and a game-based approach can be integrated. The three core principles that would be a prerequisite for this to be successful are (Meister, 2013):

1   **Place business strategy at the heart of the design.** This means identifying and articulating what the business objectives are and how you will measure progress towards a desired business outcome. This is not so easy to do when you are dealing with how individuals manage relationships as the key development need rather than more easily quantifiable hard skills.
2   **Make sure you create the right environment for a game to work well.** This means understanding the demographics and behaviour patterns of the participants as well as identifying and putting into place the right extrinsic and intrinsic rewards. The challenge here is that altering habitual behaviour to develop emotional and spiritual intelligence can only be successful where intrinsic motivation is at play and with intrinsic motivation, the value of gamification and leader boards etc. is far lower.
3   **Use design thinking.** To be successful, a game has to be contextual and relevant for the community. It has to have the right visual and sensory appeal, as well as a relevant storyline. This represents a further challenge in that in a cohort of different individuals with different cultural backgrounds, often from different industries and organisational contexts, it becomes wholly impractical to meet this requirement for everyone. Therefore, this approach is self-evidently most appropriate for a corporate with homogenous scenarios and needs.

Feedback from learners

Here are some examples of feedback, shared in full to give a flavour of the responses of learners to the blended learning experience following our principles outlined above, working with online and remote learning. They provide

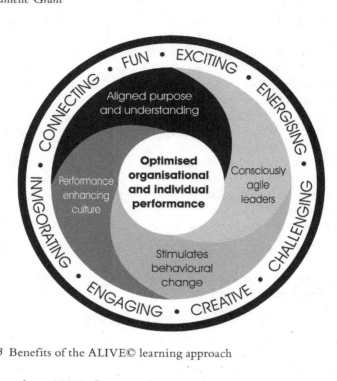

Figure 8.3 Benefits of the ALIVE© learning approach

validation of our ALIVE© approach (Figure 8.3). The average score across six online courses with various cohorts was 4.7 out of 5.

- A very good course to go inside ourselves with courage and honesty.
- I have attended many seminars and read many books on these topics. Again and again, new perspectives on my life and the meaning of life arise. Thank you for this great course.
- This was a thought-provoking and important module – the first on the second part of the journey.
- This has been an amazing experience! I generally hate doing 'homework' but this was a pleasant and engaging experience. One great way of showing what a great leader can do if they make it interesting for the individuals concerned. Well done to all who put this together!
- A good, comprehensive reinforcement of my existing knowledge on leadership excellence, with some useful new ideas.
- What I particularly liked about this course is that it presented different perspectives on things, not a one size fits all approach.
- Excellent experience! Material is fresh and relevant to the practical work environment.
- Informative and thought-provoking with a good mixture of mediums to help consolidate learning.

- The material on Climate and Culture is valuable and instructive. I simply wish that this stuff was mainstream, and that people were required to learn it and demonstrate practical competence in it and commitment to it before being appointed to senior leadership positions. The majority of senior leadership is unaccountable, destructive and incompetent.
- Thank you for this course! Clear, rich and very interesting info and funny :-). But main point is very useful.
- Terrific – an excellent learning experience that reinforces critical issues.
- The course really made me think about EI and leadership and the things I might need to improve if I want to be a leader.
- Excellent course! I have learnt more about EI and leadership styles and about neuro-plasticity in this module, than I have learnt through materials in the past.
- I really enjoyed the course. It was informative, had a good level of detail and had blended and engaging content.
- I really enjoyed the ALIVE prep. The content was highly engaging – various media employed to keep me attentive throughout. Both written and visual media were on-point, insightful and entertaining.
- Very clear and valuable course. As ever, very helpful use of video clips. Structured well to make sure that following the process properly is understood as well as internalising the concept! I am often not good on detailed process following – it was good that this module did not let me off the hook!

Further comments included the following:

- The Transpersonal Leadership Coaching (TLC) programme is not just a way to hone new skills and develop new understanding about coaching. It has changed my view of my own life and given me insights I will continue to develop for the rest of my life.
- I must say it was highly valuable. It got me into thinking of my journey, My Why... awesome. appreciate all your efforts.
- Overall experience – Fantastic! I loved my cohort! It was a well thought out cohort, and I believe we complemented each other well and were very supportive. My course leader was amazing as always and it never ceases to amaze me that I regularly come out having a new insight, idea or thought process from the sessions. I will definitely suggest it to others.
- The cohort was extraordinary and our course leader's facilitation was super.
- The materials are excellent. They provided me with a framework of how to organise and sequence this important developmental work for leaders.
- For me, it was a stimulating, provocative program with so much great, fully researched material. The material is great.

Conclusion

The initial findings of the research used to create the Transpersonal Leadership Development programme are still amongst the most up to date information that exists. The adaptations that have occurred over the past few years are related to the wider availability of better technological solutions that enable greater interaction and personal engagement rather than any fundamental change in the underlying approach. The diversity of cohorts has expanded as a result of the wider adoption of online learning technologies, and the ubiquitous use of video has enabled really rich exchanges and relationship building.

Questions and actions for personal development

1. What are the key principles that need inclusion in a blended learning programme?
2. What are the ingredients that create a learning community in a blended learning programme?
3. Why is it important for learning to be applicable and applied in the real world?
4. What is the trifecta of engagement? How would you enable this in a programme?
5. Which of the principles in this chapter have you experienced and what was the impact?
6. Which is the first concept you can make use of in your learning experiences?
7. What are the benefits and drawbacks of advanced technologies, such as Simulations and Gamification? To what extent might they be of value in your organisation?

References

Barrows, H. 1996. *What Your Tutor May Never Tell You*. Springfield: Southern Illinois University School of Medicine.

Covarrubias Venegas, B. 2020. How to organise and facilitate a virtual World Café?. *barbaracv.com*. https://www.barbaracv.com/blog/how-to-organise-and-facilitate-a-virtual-world-cafe/, March 31, 2021.

Davidson, R., Snelling, C., Karanicolas, S., Crotti, T., & Phillips, B. 2019. Authentic assessment as a tool to bridge the transition between learning and work. In A. Diver (Ed.), *Employability via Higher Education: Sustainability as Scholarship*. New York: Springer, pp. 255–274.

Fifolt, M., & Breaux, A. 2018. Exploring student experiences with the cohort model in an executive EdD Program in the Southeastern United States. *The Journal of Continuing Higher Education*, 66(3): 158–169.

Iowa State University. n.d. Ideas to Create a Welcoming, Engaging and Inclusive Classroom • Center for Excellence in Learning and Teaching • Iowa State

University. Celt.iastate.edu. http://www.celt.iastate.edu/teaching/preparing-to-teach/ideas-to-create-a-welcoming-engaging-and-inclusive-classroom, March 31, 2021.

Knights, J., Grant, D., & Young, G. 2018. *Leading Beyond the Ego*. London: Routledge.

Knowles, M., Holton, E. & Swanson, R., 2005. *The Adult Learner*. 6th ed. Boston: Butterworth-Heinemann.

Leslie, H. 2019. Trifecta of student engagement. *Journal of Research in Innovative Teaching & Learning*, 13(2): 149–173.

Meister, J. 2013. Gamification in leadership development: How companies use gaming to build their leader pipeline. *Forbes*. https://www.forbes.com/sites/jeannemeister/2013/09/30/gamification-in-leadership-development-how-companies-use-gaming-to-build-their-leader-pipeline/?sh=533eb0b65a57, March 31, 2021.

Merriam, S., & Bierema, L. 2013. *Adult Learning: Linking Theory and Practice*. San Francisco: Jossey-Bass.

Michael G. Moore (1989) Editorial: Three types of interaction. *American Journal of Distance Education*, 3(2): 1–7. DOI: 10.1080/08923648909526659.

Petillion, R., & McNeil, W. 2020. Student experiences of emergency remote teaching: Impacts of instructor practice on student learning, engagement, and well-being. *Journal of Chemical Education*, 97(9): 2486–2493.

Xie, K. 2020. Projecting learner engagement in remote contexts using empathic design. *Educational Technology Research and Development*, 69(1): 81–85.

Zayapragassarazan, Z. 2020. Strategies for engaging remote learners in medical education [version 1; not peer reviewed]. *F1000 Research*, 9(273):1–18.

Part 2

Impact of a transpersonal leader

Duncan Enright

> Thou look'st like him that knows a warlike charge.
> To business that we love we rise betimes
> And go to 't with delight.
>
> Antony and Cleopatra, William Shakespeare

(In my words: You look like you have experience of decisive action. For a cause we care about we rise early, and take action with eagerness.)

Overview

By looking at the contribution of transpersonal leaders when faced with a number of challenges, we can observe their value in practice and learn something about their importance and the way they approach situations. Good leaders, no matter what their position in an organisation or team, make a difference. In this section, the role and distinct approach of transpersonal leaders is examined in relation to challenges including digital transformation, managing stakeholders, working across cultures and encouraging diversity, equality and inclusion.

Navigating the chapters in this section

This section explores the benefits of a transpersonal approach to leadership in the face of several common but difficult challenges. First, Jenny Plaister-Ten shares her experience and research to explore how culture influences how we lead (and what we recognise and value in leaders). Jenny introduces the cross-cultural kaleidoscope as a tool to raise awareness and help develop strategies to manage across cultures. Frederick Hölscher and Danielle Grant then prove the value of diversity, equality and inclusion in modern teams and organisations. They then explain how transpersonal leaders are well suited to allowing diversity to blossom; and they share insights to show how leaders can do this most effectively.

As a veteran of multiple digital transformations, it seems to me that in times of change and turbulence, with the huge opportunities but great unbalancing impacts of technology, we need a transpersonal approach to navigate change successfully. By establishing core purpose, and using the technology as a pivot – with board-level support and attention paid to the needs of stakeholders throughout

DOI: 10.4324/9781003150626-11

and outside the organisation – these projects which are often doomed to failure can realise transformative benefits. Finally, in this section, John Knights looks at the relationship with all the different stakeholders in an organisation, and how to work for mutual benefit. Note that a transpersonal leader goes beyond the ego, taking into account all stakeholders, including employees, customers, management teams, shareholders and the wider public (including, crucially in these times of climate crisis, the planet).

During the pandemic, we all became aware of the need for leaders during a time of crisis. This has been a moment in human history that is unprecedented in its worldwide impact, yet crises occur frequently within organisations, sectors, countries and economies – with unexpected impacts. We talk about a world that is vulnerable, unpredictable, complex and ambiguous, a VUCA world. Danielle Grant and I explore lessons learned in many crises but embedded and brought to the fore during our recent shared experience.

Chapters 9, 11 and 12 have appeared in an earlier form as part of the Transpersonal Leadership White Paper Series (LeaderShape Global Ltd., 2019). Here, they are expanded and brought up to date. Together, this collection of work provides a view of leaders facing common challenges and offers insights of value when facing those same or similar situations. It also shines a light on the nature of ethical, effective, transpersonal leadership in action.

How to use this section

If you are reading about transpersonal leadership for the first time, this section answers the question "what would a transpersonal leader do when faced with a particular common problem?" You might find it useful to read the chapter if it correlates with something you are facing, or expect to encounter, in your own working life. All chapters serve to flesh out the role of leadership in our modern world.

If you are a confident leader, the whole section will expand your knowledge and provide ideas to help you be more effective and successful in these situations. The questions in each chapter can help you plan for action and dig out the roots of problems. If you are responsible for the development of others who are struggling with these and other issues, you may wish to share chapters with your own notes about the specific context and find time to discuss this in a coaching conversation. Coaches and trainers can also find useful material here to address client challenges and help them think differently through to solutions.

On a leadership journey, there will be obstacles – difficult terrains to cross, and times when the traditional maps do not offer a safe route. This section of the book offers some notes and advice from experienced travellers who have been this way before.

References

LeaderShape Global Ltd. 2019. LeaderShape–The Transpersonal Leadership White Paper series. *Leadershapeglobal.com.* https://www.leadershapeglobal.com/white-papers, February 9, 2021.

9 Leading across cultures

Developing leaders for global organisations

Jenny Plaister-Ten

We do not see things as they are; we see them as we are.
We do not hear things as they are; we hear them as we are.

The Talmud

Overview

This chapter looks at how our cultural influences impact our values and beliefs and consequently our behaviours and working practices, including leadership styles. It goes on to suggest that different cultures value different leadership approaches and also attach different importance to business goals. This can create confusion, misunderstandings and conflict. Nevertheless, companies with extensive ethnic diversity are more likely to deliver the innovative ideas and the creativity to deliver new products, services and solutions. This chapter explores the limitations and considerations of tapping into that potential and of the importance of doing so for global organisations.

Introduction

This topic holds significant personal meaning for me as I have not only lived and worked in several different countries, but I am married inter-culturally and have raised a son amongst several different cultures. In each instance of being transferred internationally, I was not given any support by any of the companies I worked for at the time. I therefore made my fair share of cultural 'blunders'. My way of 'giving back' is to support others working in complex multi-cultural contexts.

Just as we thought we were making progress as an inclusive society, the UK plunged into a polarised nation that seems to have caused regressive conversations about 'foreigners' and an increase in racially induced hate crimes. Clearly, the British 'bulldog spirit' is alive and well as is a radical form of bias exhibited by the then US President Donald Trump during the 2016 election campaign. (The British Bulldog Spirit is an expression that became synonymous with Prime Minister Churchill during and after the war years

DOI: 10.4324/9781003150626-12

to express solidity and fearlessness. It has since become used as an association with a strongly nationalistic position, viewpoint or person.) Elsewhere in Europe, the rise of 'far right' parties is apparent. Thus, 'in-group' and 'out-group' formation is reinforcing what social scientists have for a long time known – that we typically like and trust 'people like us'. This is explained perfectly in the above quotation from the Talmud. In the workplace, this bias is very often unconscious as most of us think that we believe in an open, transparent, ethical and 'just' world – one that is beyond bias, beyond ego. Transpersonal even.

So, how much are our allegiances hidden to us? In a quotation from Trompenaars and Hampden-Turner (1997), we may begin to understand one of the big paradoxes of cultural bias: "A fish never discovers his need for water until he is no longer in it". Thus, those of us who have not had the opportunity to live and work outside of our home country will not appreciate the magnitude of this quotation. Even those who have had tenures overseas may have simply transferred their way of life into a new country – without really adjusting. Hofstede (2001, p. 18) explains that the difficulty arising from identifying culture-related behaviour is because *"it takes a prolonged stay abroad and mixing with other nationals there for us to recognise the numerous and often subtle differences in the ways they and we behave, because that is how our society has programmed us"*. Hall (1976, p. 58) also states, *"Understanding the reality of covert culture and accepting it on a gut level comes neither quickly nor easily; it must be lived"*. This seemingly implies that to understand other cultures, it is necessary to live outside your own, in multiple, extended and different tenures.

Therein lies a dilemma and perhaps explains why there are so many misunderstandings when operating globally. There are many challenges. How can global leaders, who have not had this depth and breadth of exposure, really understand and appreciate what is going on for someone with an entirely different perspective? How can they make the time to explore the nuances and subtlety of cultural differences? How can leaders operating globally remain authentic whilst exhibiting cultural sensitivity and understanding? How can they be adaptive in the face of so many different cultures and cultural norms?

As this chapter attempts to address these questions, perhaps it would help to first explore the notion of leadership and specifically what is imbued in the concept of 'good leadership' for different people.

The notion of good leadership

At LeaderShape, we define a good leader as operating beyond the ego, working for the greater good (caring) in an emotionally intelligent (EI) manner and within an ethical and purposeful framework. If we explore some of these concepts, we can see how difficulties occur.

1   Beyond the ego. Ego is essentially an individualist construct, borne by individualist cultures. Ego is Latin for "I" and was brought into 'popular'

awareness by Sigmund Freud (1923) – from Germany; an individualist culture. However, there are many cultures who do not perceive the self to be a separate entity. More significantly, concepts of self can vary widely across cultures. A person tending to construe him/herself as an independent individual, or as an interdependent member of a group, is culturally bound. Cousins (1989) devised a 20-statement test to compare self-concepts between students in Japan and the US. Results showed that the Western self-concept is thought of as independent and autonomous, whereas the Eastern is interdependent. This is sometimes reflected in language. For example, the Japanese word for self, *jibun*, means "a share of the shared life space", according to Hamaguchi (1985, cited in Markus and Kitayama, 1999, p. 343). Furthermore, there may be cultures who are more hierarchical in nature who expect a leader to have a strong 'ego' when ego is expressed as strength of direction or force of opinion.

2   If we take 'the greater good' as a concept, then for all parties this can get confusing. Which entity are we referring to when we refer to the greater good? This could be simply the 'other' as in several Asian cultures or it could be the family, the community, the organisation as a whole – or a team or division, it could be a country – or a guiding spiritual force. For those cultures who believe that external forces guide their fate, this is likely to be an allegiance to 'the Gods'. 'Inshallah' translated to mean 'to Gods will' can be very frustrating to those who are internally referenced, from individualistic cultures believing in the ability, acumen or competency of the leader, rather than the fateful 'what will be, will be' approach. It can be equally as frustrating to be pushed towards an outcome or action, when one takes a *'laissez-faire'* approach to life.

3   Lastly, ethics in the concept of culture. If as Bower (1966) suggests, culture means 'how we do things around here', then an EI leader would be attuned into the way in which things work in the local culture and adapt accordingly. But, how far do we take this? Many companies have come unstuck when operating globally when discovering that local cultural norms and expectations run counter to their own moral compass. Bribery in one country can be tantamount to 'connections' in another. Or, in some paternalist cultures, it may be seen as being benevolent towards those who do not have the resources or are not paid 'fairly'; therefore, a 'backhander' may be seen as an obligation or a cultural norm.

The net result of these differences in perspective – on a global scale – is vastly differing views of what good leadership is. In his book, "Leading with Cultural Intelligence", Livermore (2015) explores what the leadership expectations are from different cultural perspectives. Here are just some (Table 9.1).

Thus, we can immediately see potential for clashes when some want empowerment, some want benevolence, some want a highly cultivated style, others want risk-takers, confidence, flair, empathy, aloofness, self-sacrifice,

Table 9.1 Conceptions of leadership by country (Livermore, 2015)

Country	Conception of good leadership
France	Cultivated and highly educated
China	Benevolence. Dignified/aloof but sympathetic
The Netherlands	Sceptical about the value and status of leaders
Brazil	A good relationship builder who demonstrates flair and empathy
Egypt	Treat leaders as heroes. Worship them so long as they remain in power
Japan	Symbolic leadership – *Public responsibility taken for the failures of company (e.g. CEO resigns over a corporate scandal)*
USA	Some like leaders who empower and encourage subordinates; others prefer bold, confident and risk-oriented leaders.

relationship builders and some don't value leaders at all. And those differences are from a list of only seven countries!

Differing values lead to differing emphasis on business goals

Complicating the matter still further, Hofstede et al. (2010), in a study of more than 1,800 MBA students at 21 universities in 17 countries, found marked differences in *perceived* business goals. Perceived business goals mean those that you personally hold to be the most important (as opposed to the ones that your boss or the organisation hold to be the most important). The international top five goals can be seen in this box below:

International top five business goals:

- Growth of the business
- Personal wealth
- This year's profits
- Power
- Continuity of the business

China and Germany were the most dissimilar from the international average. They both placed "Responsibility towards society" and "Respecting ethical norms" in the top five, whereas these were typically found in the bottom five for other countries. China also cited patriotism, national pride, honour, face and reputation as extremely important, and Germany placed responsibility towards employees, creating something new and profits in ten years' time as important.

If on top of all of this complexity we are demanding that leaders are authentic, we need to ask the question, "authentic to what or to whom?"

What is culture?

In a well-known expression, Hofstede (2003) refers to culture as "*the software of the mind*". The question remains, is it the operating system or the application software? If one views culture as 'the way we do things around here', then it may be understood as the operating system. The fundamental roots, or codes, of how things work, understood by members of a group – be that a country, region, organisation, community or social group or family.

These codes are learned from an early age and are therefore largely subconscious to us. A useful analogy is that of the cultural iceberg. Above the waterline lies visible culture. What we can see may include customs, dress, buildings, food, rituals and more, even the way streets are laid out or named. These aspects may be easily changed and may even be temporary or subject to the whims of 'popular culture'. Those aspects of culture below the waterline include our thoughts, attitudes, emotions, expectations, values and beliefs, many of which are enduring yet are difficult to observe and often remain hidden, even from our selves.

The Culture Iceberg diagram below draws on Freud's (1923) work identifying elements of culture that are held at conscious and unconscious levels, known as visible and invisible culture.

Those aspects above the water are more easily visible and understandable, whereas those beneath the water are intangible and therefore less easily understood. On a collective level, the cultural self becomes manifest in cultural norms. Whilst customs, dress, art, dance and music, even the influence of climate, are all expressions of cultural norms, below the waterline is where most clashes occur. Here lie values, assumptions and beliefs. They are less widely known to be the expectations and rules that guide the behaviour of members of a culture and are often held subconsciously. Thus, a leader's beliefs and values will be informing the organisation culture.

If two icebergs were to collide, the impact would be felt below the water line. As with culture, this is where the most damage may be felt and where the potential for clashes lies. It is here that those leaders with an eye on leveraging the potential of diversity of thought need to be most aware (Figure 9.1).

The difficulties of identifying cultural values and beliefs.

Cultural communication patterns, loaded with custom, practice and belief, along with value-laden expectations, are acknowledged to contribute to misinterpretations in a cross-cultural setting. Significantly, however, it is the meaning behind this for the individual that appears to be the area of potential conflict. Triandis (1972) suggests that subjective culture is the cultural groups' typical perception of norms, values and beliefs. But, on the whole,

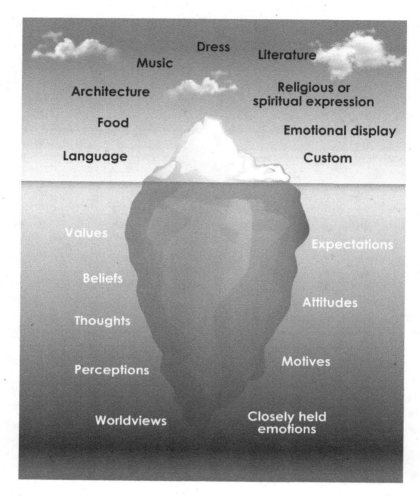

Figure 9.1 The cultural iceberg

we do not know very much about how culture shapes our perceptions and choices; the internal drivers and deeply held emotions of our cultural selves.

If we are not aware of these drivers of differences in perspectives how can we possibly begin to understand the reasons for workplace disagreements or behaviours that can appear subversive, obstructive or intrusive – or just plain rude!

Values-led leadership styles

One key research project that has identified similarities in leadership approaches based on where a person comes from confirms that culture affects

leadership styles. The Globe Study (House et al., 2002, 2004) has identified similarities based on ten regions around the world: Southern Asia,
Latin America, Nordic Europe, Anglo, Germanic Europe, Latin Europe,
Sub-Saharan Africa, Eastern Europe, Middle East and Confucian Asia.
This awareness alone can help leaders orientate themselves towards inherent differences. However, it still categorises people into groups based
on where they come from, increasing the tendency towards 'in-group'
or 'out-group' perspectives and stereotyping. Many emerging leaders and
'millennials' have had exposure to multiple cultural influences before they
enter the workplace, bringing with them a rich tapestry of perspectives.
Therefore, this, along with a growing global middle class, means that a
global mindset is called for when working in multi-cultural teams and
societies.

What remains true however is that attitudes to authority can cause motivated or de-motivated staff, depending on what the expectations of a good
leader are. This can be compounded when we bring organisation culture
into the mix. Organisation cultures are borne out of the home culture of
the original founders, or a merger of cultures in the case of international
mergers and acquisitions. International mergers and acquisitions are no-
torious for their failures, yet are found to be at least 26% more effective if
cultural issues are addressed at the outset (Renaud, 2009). Yet, this is rarely
done.

If cultural misunderstandings are not resolved, this can lead to clashes in
the workplace. In multi-cultural teams, this can mean that productivity suf-
fers; compounded further when working remotely.

Cultural differences may be found in the following approaches to work:

- Attitude to time: with some members showing up at precisely the pre-
  scribed hour and others being late
- Differences in communication styles: with some being very direct and
  others indirect
- A focus on the task or the relationship
- Differing levels of accountability and assertiveness
- Focus on the context or the letter of the law/agreement
- Levels of formality and hierarchy
- Levels of fatalism compared with personal autonomy
- A concern for process or results
- Differing attitudes to risk
- A desire for achievement or balance

These differences mean that in the workplace and in multi-cultural teams
there are differing behaviours around protocols such as how to greet people,
dress and exchange business cards. How to lead a meeting differs in terms
of levels of formality, styles and expectations of how to behave especially

concerning the amount of contribution expected or not expected from team members. Negotiations and the processes/structures involved in decision-making differs widely, with some cultures exhibiting a lot of personal autonomy and others deferring to either the wisdom of the group or the authority of the leader – or both.

Furthermore, preferred organisation structures differ across cultures with gender, rank, boss and subordinate relationships all having a bearing upon the structure. Conflict resolution will also differ as will motivation and reward structures, with some being more concerned with achievement orientation and others with process and consensus.

How can leaders stay authentic across the globe?

With so many different ways of working to navigate, how is it that global leaders manage to stay effective? Little wonder then that the organisation culture becomes touted as the 'tune by which all shall dance'. This too comes at a cost as one party may be seen to impose its way on the other. Think about the impact of a 'Western organisation' imposing its will for engaged, assertive employees in a culture that thinks inactivity is wise lest a mistake might be made. Think about the impact of an 'Eastern organisation' planning for the long term in a context that demands quarterly results.

Certainly, one thing leaders must not do is to stereotype. Cultural norms are simply an expression of the tendencies of the majority and do not constitute observed behaviour in every individual from that culture. An obvious statement, but one that is frequently overlooked. As we enter into a period of protectionist and nationalistic governmental policies, this will become even more important.

EI global leaders seek to understand the perspectives of their global ecosystem by utilising the four pillars of self-awareness, self-management, social-awareness and relationship management (Goleman, 1995). These pillars and their corresponding behavioural competencies are critical in a mono-cultural environment, but even more so when operating inter-culturally. We need to first discern our culturally bound responses (self-awareness), then we need to control the urge to respond according to our own cultural code of conduct (self-management). An awareness of the cultural norms within a multi-cultural environment would support the social awareness pillar and following the protocols and rules of the culture would support the relationship management pillar. However, this should not be at the expense of a leader's own inner purpose or authenticity, factors perhaps more naturally associated with self-awareness and self-management. This approach also needs to take into account the fact that how we hold our culture internally has distinct meanings for each and every one of us (Figure 9.2).

Self-awareness   Social awareness

Self-management   Relationship management

Figure 9.2 The four competencies of emotional intelligence (Goleman, 1995)

It should be noted that EI and the ability to read the 'other' does not automatically translate across borders, factors perhaps more naturally associated with social awareness and relationship management.

Emotional expression differs across cultures

This is because there are strict rules in most cultures for cultural expression with some cultures demanding active emotional expression (as in some Latin countries, for example, whilst others 'hide' it (as in Asian countries such as Japan for example)). As a further consideration, when we see a smiling face, we may assume it is because the person is happy and want to smile back. However, smiling is even frowned upon, literally not trusted in some cultures. That is why you do not see it very often in countries like Russia. Other examples of cultural expression are in the area of self-promotion which is a common expression of confidence in some cultures such as the USA, whereas it is often frowned upon in other cultures such as the UK. Similarly, according to a study comparing the emotional expression of anger in both the USA and Japan (Araki and Wiseman, 1996), found the American levels of expression to be much higher. These studies reinforce the assertion that differences lie more typically in the nuances between cultures. Not so much in the "what" – we all experience the emotion of anger – but in the "how". How it is expressed. Furthermore, according to Tsui (2007) whilst it is universally accepted that most people want to feel good, how they go about that differs widely. Working at the level of these very nuanced differences takes dedication to observe how others behave and respond as well as shining a mirror back on to oneself to understand better our own culturally imbued habitual responses.

So, what can we do to adapt when working globally, whilst remaining authentic to our own sense of self? Here are some ways to help us on the path:

1   In seeking to be authentic, leaders must be prepared to learn and to reflect on the meanings that their own culture has for them and how this affects their attitude to the organisation culture and to their role as a leader. Only with this self-awareness will they be able to recognise a cultural difference. This self-awareness can be helped with a tool such as LeaderShape's Leadership and Emotional Intelligence Performance Accelerator (LEIPA – http://www.leadershapeglobal.com/leipa). LEIPA will help to discern the difference between how a leader sees him or herself and how his or her stakeholders see him or her (Wall & Knights, 2013).

2   Learn to stop imposing our own 'map' onto others. This can be tricky if it is the organisation culture demanding a certain code of conduct that is culturally bound. We can stop compounding this by being very aware of our own cultural norms as stated above. It then becomes even more important to find a way to make it explicitly known that you are doing *xyz* because you are from *xyz* culture. I, for example, am known to say to my more direct Dutch colleagues, "ah, I answered in that way because I was being English and indirect" (in comparison with a typical Dutch person). If you find yourself in disagreement with another, or simply not understanding what happened, try to find at least three reasons for it happening. So, I may have responded in that way because I was being too English, or because I thought that was because my boss expected me to behave in that way, or because I simply was having a bad day. At least three reasons is important, because in that way, our own need to be right becomes loosened – which does not happen if we have only one reason, and if two reasons, the choice becomes binary. Only with three can we start to see other possibilities for the situation.

3   Use a tool to help such as the Cross-Cultural Kaleidoscope® (Plaister-Ten, 2016a, 2016b). The Cross-Cultural Kaleidoscope is a tool that has been developed through research and tested in practice. Its purpose is to raise culturally derived awareness and to facilitate culturally appropriate responsibility (Figure 9.3).

It incorporates the need to take a systems view of the situation in a multi-cultural context. A systems view takes the external factors that a leader has been exposed to over the course of their international career and over their lifespan. It therefore looks at the economic circumstances, the political, as well as historical and legal. It considers the arts and the social context, including national education systems as well as the more

The Cross-Cultural Kaleidoscope™
A Systems Approach

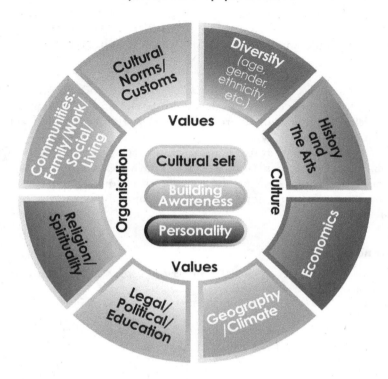

10 Consulting Ltd © 2016

Figure 9.3 Cross–cultural Kaleidoscope® copyright 10 Consulting Ltd

obvious need to identify cultural norms. Diversity and religious and spiritual beliefs are also provided for in the model. It even explores the geographical and environmental factors. These elements are then examined in terms of their effect on the internal world of the leader. A concept known as the 'cultural self'. For example, if a person grew up in a country with a history and family background of slavery, the inquiry delves into how this might have impacted their psyche and affected their leadership approach. Would they be more inclined or less inclined to do as others tell them to do?

4   The last point concerns 'unlearning'. At LeaderShape, we call for Transpersonal Leaders to keep learning. Yet, as global leaders, we need to *unlearn* faster than most. We need to be aware of those patterns that

were formed in a different country or age or context that are no longer appropriate. A contemplation of culture as acquired, or learned and therefore "unlearned", suggests that an awareness of those culturally bound responses no longer serving the situation is mandatory for 21st century leadership. This implies letting go of certain cultural constructs that a leader has grown up with or developed. Yet, a warning from Hofstede "unlearning is more difficult than learning for the first time" (2003, p. 4).

The global stage is a huge playground. Schneider and Barsoux (2003) compare the quest for cultural understanding with an exploration as deep as the ocean. But the rewards are immense. Developing a global mindset and maintaining curiosity about the world and the people in it is surely one of the greatest gifts available to mankind. To work with people from different countries, organisations, sectors and walks of life represents an opportunity to leverage the creativity and innovation inherent within diverse mindsets. We truly hope that you will enjoy the journey as much as we do.

References

Araki, F., & Wiseman, R. (1996–1997). *Emotional Expression in the United States and Japan*, Intercultural Communication Studies, V1(2): 13–32.

Bower, M. (1966). *The Will to Manage: Corporate Success Through Programmed Management*. New York: McGraw-Hill.

Cousins, S. D. (1989). *Culture and Self-perception in Japan and the United States*. Journal of Personality and Social Psychology, 56: 124–131.

Freud, S. (1923). *The Ego and the Id*. Standard Edition, 19: 1–66.

Goleman, D. (1995). *Emotional Intelligence, Why It Can Matter More Than IQ*. London: Bantam.

Hall, T. E. (1976). *Beyond Culture*. New York: Anchor.

Hamaguchi, E. (1985). *A Contextual Model of the Japanese: Toward a Methodological Innovation in Japan Studies*. Journal of Japanese Studies, 11: 289–321.

Hofstede, G. (2001). *Culture's Consequences: Comparing Values, Behaviors, Institutions, and Organizations across Nations*. Thousand Oaks, CA: Sage.

Hofstede, G. (2003). *Cultures and Organizations: Intercultural Cooperation and Its Importance for Survival*. London: Profile.

Hofstede, G., Hofstede, G. J., & Minkov, M. (2010). *Cultures and Organizations: Software of the Mind* (3rd edition). New York: McGraw Hill.

House, R. J., Hanges, P. J., Javidan, M., Dorfman, P. W., & Gupta, V. (2004). *Culture, Leadership and Organisations: The GLOBE Study of 62 Societies*. Thousand Oaks, CA: Sage.

House, R. J., Javidan, M., Hanges, P., & Dorfman, P. (2002). *Understanding Cultures and Implicit Leadership Theories across the Globe: An Introduction to Project GLOBE*. Journal of World Business, 37: 3–10.

Livermore, D. (2015). *Leading with Cultural Intelligence: The Real Secret to Success*. New York: AMACOM.

Markus, H. R., & Kitayama, S. (1999). Culture and the self: Implications for cognition, emotion and motivation. In: R. F. Baumeister (Ed.), *The Self in Social Psychology* (pp. 339–367). Philadelphia, PA: Taylor & Francis.

Plaister-Ten, J. (2016a). *The Cross-Cultural Coaching Kaleidoscope: A Systems Approach to Coaching amongst Different Cultural Influences*. London: Karnac.

Plaister-Ten, J. (2016b). Leading change in mergers and acquisitions in Asia-Pacific. In: C. Barmeyer and P. Franklin (Eds.), *Intercultural Management, A Case-Based Approach to Achieving Complementarity and Synergy* (pp. 95–106). London: Palgrave.

Renaud, M. (2009). *Air France KLM: Lessons from a Successful Merger*. Presentation delivered in York, UK: High-Performing International Teams, 17/9/2009.

Schneider, S. C., & Barsoux, J. L. (2003). *Managing Across Cultures*. Harlow: Pearson Education.

Triandis, H. C. (1972). *The Analysis of Subjective Culture*. New York: John Wiley & Sons.

Trompenaars, F., & Hampden-Turner, C. (1997). *Riding the Waves of Culture: Understanding Cultural Diversity in Business*. London: Nicholas Brealey.

Tsui, J. L. (2007). Ideal Affect, *Cultural Causes and Behavioural Consequences*. Association for Psychological Science, 2(3): 242–259.

Wall, T. & Knights, J. (2013). *Leadership Assessment for Talent Development*. London: Kogan Page.

10 Addressing diversity, equality and inclusion through transpersonal leadership

Danielle Grant and Frederick Hölscher

> Everyone is kneaded out of the same dough but not baked in the same oven.
>
> Proverb

Overview

Dealing with diversity is not a new challenge for leaders. Martin Luther King Jr gave a famous 12-minute speech of 1964 on his American dream for equality and a society that includes everyone on the basis of freedom and justice, which was voted the most influential speech of the 20th century. Nelson Mandela was another 20th century leader to face the challenges of exclusion or 'Apartheid' as it was called. As we write this chapter way into the 21st century, we have been seeing a large number of headlines such as 'Black Lives Matter' and issues around Brexit, even after it has taken place. We see this in terms of the new diversity and inclusion (D&I) framework presented in this chapter. This is essentially about the challenge of recognising diversity and finding different ways of inclusion for self-governing countries. We can consider other challenges in this light, like the controversy around America–China trade relations (among others), sweeping through the world. Above all, we believe ten years from now, leaders will still be measured by how they deal with the challenges of diversity and inclusion, in its wider context. Just as biodiversity is needed for the natural ecosystem to survive, so we believe that diversity in our social ecosystem is needed for our survival as humans. However, humans' inability to deal with diversity, often because of egocentric behaviour, turns diversity into a cause for conflict which threatens our social ecosystem. In this chapter we propose how the art of inclusion turns diversity into a treasure chest of growth instead of a destructive force of conflict.

Introduction

Diversity and Inclusion (D&I) is not only a topic that is continually in the news, but has, over the past ten years, consistently appeared in the top ten human capital trends in the workplace in various global studies.

DOI: 10.4324/9781003150626-13

The D&I debate in the 20th century was fuelled by the humanistic values of freedom, equality, freedom of speech, and fairness. It was mostly an issue for the HR department to fix, and the tools they used were mostly policies, rules and regulations, or awareness campaigns to gain appreciation of cultural diversity. However, the McKinsey report of 2007 on 'Women Matter' (McKinsey, 2007) shows that companies who have a greater level of gender diversity perform financially better than their peers. All of a sudden D&I shifted from the HR desk to that of the CEO. A stream of further research followed to point out that the value of D&I in the workplace is more than just addressing humanistic values; it has the potential to bring financial value to a business, as well as enhances innovation and growth if managed properly.

As Forbes says *"A diverse and inclusive workforce is necessary to drive innovation, foster creativity, and guide business strategies. Multiple voices lead to new ideas, new services, and new products, and encourage out-of-the-box thinking"* (Forbes Insights 2011: Global Diversity and Inclusion: Fostering Innovation through a Diverse Workforce).

Diversity is no longer simply a case of applying humanistic values like fairness, equality and non-discrimination, or something to strive towards to 'score some social points' or to be compliant with some CSR (Corporate Social Responsibility) objectives. Diversity is an imperative, to be embedded in the fibre of every organisation. Human diversity is more than a matter of demo- and sociographics like gender and race; social diversity includes diversity of interest and thinking which brings fresh and different challenges around inclusion. It is necessary to bring it to our awareness and manage it in a way that unlocks the hidden treasures in organisations. This is one of the gifts of transpersonal leadership to an organisation, which is what we want to explore in this chapter. We take a fresh view of D&I in the new world of work, based on the view that organisations not only function as 'ego systems' but also as 'ecosystems', or what has been called complex adaptive systems (CAS) (Knights, Grant & Young, 2018, p. 234).

A new lens on diversity and inclusion

In taking a different perspective on diversity and inclusion, it is important to consider the role of the ego which differentiates humans from plants and animals and, as such, gives a different flavour to the D&I debate.

The human ego is there to give us our identity, to differentiate us from the rest of the world. It feeds our need to be unique and to be free to express our uniqueness in the world. As such it can be seen as the main driver of diversity. Our ego is constantly finding itself in the 'naming' game; it is not only concerned with ourselves, but also others who need to 'have a name'. There is nothing wrong with naming, it helps with differentiation, and factors into our analytical capability, which is essential for our evolutionary journey. However, the risk is that when we create ego-systems and ringfence these identities that we have created using the names as stereotypes, this places people in a sort of social bondage that excludes them from growing together for the common good. This is when the ego loses the plot, becoming self-centred, and uses others to fulfil its own needs. This is when ego slips into its 'shadow side' and becomes a stumbling block instead of a stepping stone for growth.

Transpersonal leadership offers a framework to deal with D&I in a different way, to unleash the full potential of our social diversity as one of the keys for growth. Transpersonal leaders take an ecosystemic view of organisations, communities and nations. It is a well-known fact that bio-diversity is a key for survival of the natural ecosystem, so leaders can do well to learn from 'Mother Nature' in this regard, as Giles Hutchins suggests in his ground-breaking work 'The Nature of Business' (Hutchins, 2012). When we see our societies or our organisations as 'eco-systems' instead of 'ego-systems' a new world of possibilities opens up and this becomes the new lens of the transpersonal leader.

What are the secrets of transpersonal leadership in unlocking the treasures of diversity? This is what we will explore in this chapter.

The chapter in a nutshell

We highlight the benefits of diversity and inclusion and offer a new framework for assessing diversity in an organisation by looking at three dimensions of diversity. We explore four levels of inclusion as the 'other side of the coin' to unlock diversity's full value. In support, we offer some skills and tools the transpersonal leader uses and identify key barriers to inclusion. Through this we show how transpersonal leadership overcomes these barriers in the transpersonal leader's journey of inclusion.

The nature of diversity

Diversity is embedded in the fibre of our society and, indeed, in our very being. We are all different (as our unique fingerprints demonstrate). We live in a world rich in diversity, peopled by a human race, connected as never before but different from one another in every way possible. Consider the picture in Figure 10.1, which illustrates the world as a village of 100 people. The diversity on view, according to these few parameters, is already clear to see. What surprises you about this picture of our Earth and its people?

The fundamental issue we want to demonstrate here are the parameters or criteria used for defining diversity and to what extent they serve the growth (or not) of our ego or eco-systems. Some of these categories may give rise to prejudice or inequality or they may be seen as essential to the survival of our species. Look at Table 10.1, which of these criteria is useful to your society or organisation? (Figure 10.1).

This is one of the first challenges we face when we define diversity in the workplace, because our definition and the criteria will create awareness of these differences; and with it, the challenge to include or exclude people

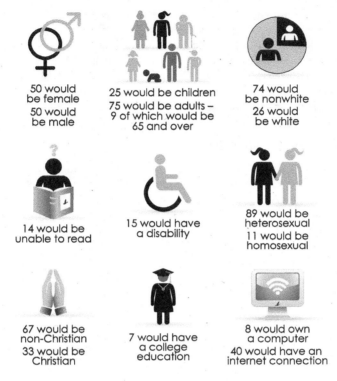

Figure 10.1 The world as a village of 100 people

Table 10.1 Six levels of awareness and full consciousness

1.	Have a logical/analytical understanding of what Awareness is
2.	An understanding of my own self-awareness, especially what triggers things to go wrong
3.	Through being actively empathetic I let people know I understand how they are feeling and the cause of their perspective
4.	I listen to my conscience, values and ethics, and separate it from what I want to do for myself
5.	I listen and take note of my inner self through bringing personal conscience virtues and self-determination values to full consciousness
6.	No longer a struggle between my ego (what I want for myself) and the greater good

who carry a specific 'diversity badge'. In an 'ego system', leaders will, for instance, hire people in their own image, they look for people who have a cultural fit and who the leaders therefore believe will serve the vision of the organisation. Promotion will be the result of how well you comply and fit this organisational blueprint.

As described before (Knights, Grant & Young, 2018), transpersonal leaders operate beyond the narrow confines of the ego, seek continual personal development and learning, and are radical, ethical and authentic while emotionally intelligent and caring. Because transpersonal leaders think differently about the world and organisations, they see organisations as complex adaptive systems that thrive on diversity; they are agile and adaptable. Transpersonal leaders are prepared to stretch themselves, enabling the success of those they lead through creating sustainable, performance-enhancing cultures.

Cultural iceberg: diversity criteria

The following picture of the cultural 'iceberg' provides some clues to the most prominent criteria for social diversity. These are not exclusive but may serve as a framework to sensitise us and create awareness of the richness of diversity. However, the purpose of our argument is not to provide a list of criteria. Each context will determine what is relevant to the situation and how diversity may be leveraged to create value. Some identified criteria may be desirable, but some may not, especially when we have conflicting expectations, attitudes, beliefs and thoughts. This is where the real challenge comes, as we will discuss later (Figure 10.2).

Exploring the iceberg

Robert Dilts (1990) developed a model of what he calls 'logical levels', which explore the cultural criteria of diversity. Each of these levels encompasses a rich variety of diversity.

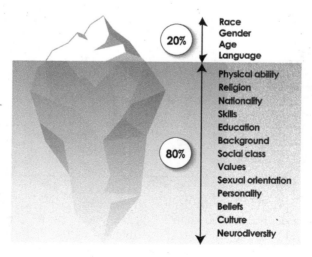

Figure 10.2 Visible and underlying aspects of diversity

In the Iceberg image, it is much more straightforward to deal with the observable elements as we can accommodate, adjust and complement one another, with goodwill.

On the other hand, to understand the 'below the waterline' attributes, we need to be ready to appreciate that they are more likely to be discovered in an exploration of beliefs/values or identity.

When we look at these elements, they are also more deeply rooted in our sense of self, so it is a practice of the aspiring transpersonal leader to develop an understanding of how observable behaviour is anchored in values. And more importantly, how to deal with diverse and even conflicting values, as that is the bigger challenge. Behaviours and practices may be 'managed' through policies and procedures, but that won't necessarily change our values and beliefs about race, gender, sexual orientation, and so on.

The deepest level

This level relates to the question 'who am I?' The observable fact that I am a woman, a man, black, white, LGBTQ+, or differently able because of a physical or neurodiverse condition, is not the final answer to the question 'who am I?' This is where the ego often gets stuck, it stereotypes people and ignores any deeper exploration or understanding of the answer to this question. Transpersonal leaders are able to operate at all levels of diversity. Allowing diversity of 'being' to play out in the workplace is imperative to understanding diversity and inclusion.

We believe that the real benefits of diversity are unlocked the deeper one goes below the waterline, and we explore this further in this chapter.

The benefits of diversity

Since the 2007 McKinsey report (McKinsey, 2007), many more studies have been done on the benefits of diversity in the workplace. McKinsey's 2019 analysis (McKinsey, 2020), for instance, shows that companies in the top quartile for gender diversity on executive teams were 25% more likely to have above-average profitability than companies in the fourth quartile – up from 21% in 2017 and 15% in 2014 (Figure 10.3).

Some of the quantifiable benefits of diversity can be seen in the results of organisations which are effective at creating diverse and inclusive cultures (Figure 10.4).

Why are diverse organisations and teams performing better?

From this it is clear that diversity and inclusion are increasingly important for the profitability and success of a business. In a blog post for Psychology Today (Rock & Grant, 2017) Neuroscientist Dr David Rock has identified

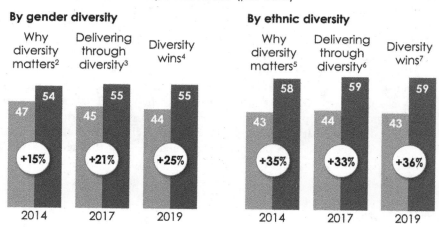

Likelihood of financial outperformance[1] (per cent)

[1]Likelihood of financial outperformance vs the national industry median; p-value <0.05, except 2014 data where p-value <0.1. [2]n = 383; Latin America, UK and US; earnings before interest and taxes (EBIT) margin 2010–13, [3]n = 991; Australia, Brazil, France, Germany, India, Japan, Mexico, Nigeria, Singapore, South Africa, UK and US; EBIT margin 2011–15. [4]n = 1,039; 2017 companies for which gender data available in 2019, plus Denmark, Norway and Sweden; EBIT margin 2014–18. [5]n = 364; Latin America, UK and US; EBIT margin 2010-13. [6]n = 589; Brazil, Mexico, Singapore, South Africa, UK and US; EBIT margin 2011–14. [7]n = 533; Brazil, Mexico, Nigeria, Singapore, South Africa, UK and US. where ethnicity data available in 2019; EBIT margin 2014–18. Source: Diversity Wins data set.

Figure 10.3 Business case for diversity, data according to McKinsey, 2019

that diverse and inclusive organisations are better at focusing and thinking more carefully about facts and are also more innovative, as explained in more detail below:

1   They are better at focusing on facts. Diverse teams are more likely to re-examine facts when there is a disagreement. They're also more likely to remain objective and be willing to scrutinise others' viewpoints. Ensuring people in the workplace work with different groups allows employees to become aware of their own biases, possibly highlighting errors they wouldn't be aware of before.
2   They think about facts more carefully. Not only are the facts more likely to be considered, but greater diversity means those facts are probably thought about more systematically, because having people with different perspectives reduces group think and may make people process information more carefully.
3   They are more innovative. Innovation and adaptability are crucial to business and, the best way to achieve this is by hiring more diverse team members.

Whilst working with similar people is comfortable, this does not actually confer a benefit. In fact, a team of different backgrounds, style, genders,

Organisations with inclusive cultures are:-

2x as likely to meet or exceed financial targets

3x as likely to be high performing

6x as likely to be innovative and agile

8x as likely to achieve better business outcomes

Motivated teams = increased employee engagement.
Hay Group research indicates engaged employees are up to 43 per cent more productive

Figure 10.4 Benefits of inclusive cultures

races, culture, and nationalities contributes to increase the potential and creativity of a business in multiple ways; helping team members in avoiding bias, questioning their own viewpoints and finding new, valuable perspectives.

The final incentive is that Forbes Insights 2017, has found that companies with diverse executive boards have higher earnings and returns on equity. This makes a compelling logical, business case as well as an ethical and emotional one, enabling sustainable success.

Although the demographics of diversity are visible and measurable, it appears that there is more to diversity than meets the eye. Even if we are ticking all the boxes on the demographic compliance chart, we may nevertheless, be selecting men and women, people of different race, ability and sexual orientation, all thinking the same way, how does that lead to harvesting the benefits of diversity?

This is what we want to explore in the rest of this chapter by taking a deep dive into the phenomena of diversity and inclusion.

The multidimensionality of diversity

As we argued above, taking a different perspective on the new world of work and emerging business models reveals other dimensions of diversity. We also mentioned that as biodiversity increases the capacity of the natural ecosystem to adapt, so diversity will increase the capacity of the social ecosystem to adapt to face the disruptions of our day. We have clustered the diversity into three dimensions interacting with each other like three DNA strands. The metaphor of DNA is used to highlight the interdependence of these three dimensions, they feed on each other but also influence each other. The one should not be seen or dealt with in isolation, which unfortunately is the way that many D&I strategies are dealing with diversity.

The following diagram depicts the three dimensions of diversity as interconnected DNA strands, that may be useful in identifying diversity and managing it in the new world of work (Figure 10.5).

Demo- and socio-graphical diversity

As we have seen, this dimension of diversity is currently dominating much thinking and action on this subject. The underlying humanistic values and beliefs built an ethical and moral foundation for diversity and gave rise to anti-discrimination legislation, policies and procedures (Knights, Grant & Young, 2018, p.187). Unfortunately, in many organisations, it became a tickbox exercise, fuelled by the zeal of activists to drive the case for equality and fairness in the workplace for women, race, ethnicity, sexual orientation, disability (or as it has been called, differently-able people, including those who are neurodiverse). This became evident in the classical definitions of diversity which include the following categories:

- The **primary categories** of diversity are the following: age, ethnicity, gender, physical abilities/qualities, race and sexual orientation.

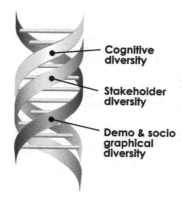

Figure 10.5 The three interconnected strands of diversity

- **Secondary categories** of diversity are those that can be changed, and include, but are not limited to, educational background, geographic location, income, marital status, military experience, parental status, religious beliefs, and work experiences.

The arguments for including these groups in the workplace were initially based on factors like fairness, reflecting the customer/community base of organisations, and to ensure local capacity building for global companies who work all over the world.

Stakeholder diversity

The awareness of stakeholder diversity is the result of a shift in how organisations are viewed. Organisations used to be considered as machines, constructed with organograms of positions and roles, which was a result of the first and second industrial revolutions. Today, we are looking at them as complex adaptive systems that are operating as part of a network of stakeholders.

Each individual is also part of a stakeholder group. Within an organisation one could be an employee or a manager, a contract worker or part of a department. One could be a supplier or a customer, part of a business or government or civil society, and so on. Each stakeholder group has its own interests and is part of creating stakeholder value.

John Knights (Knights, Grant & Young, 2018) refers to this when he introduces the concept of transpersonal practices as complex adaptive systems being a basis for transpersonal leadership. He compares the organisation with nature: 'The whole of nature depends on relationships, patterns, iterations and emergence' (Knights, Grant & Young, 2018, p. 243). Looking at organisations through this lens brings a new awareness of diversity in the workplace. Through this viewpoint, stakeholders include customers, suppliers, government, the community, and (nature) the planet. It acknowledges that all these diverse interests are legitimate concerns for the organisation and that they are all likely to be affected by the business.

Evidence of this shift are the updated ideas around the triple bottom line (Elkington, 2018) and Porter's value chains (Porter, 1985). More recently, Hampden Turner and Fons Trompenaars (Hampden-Turner, Trompenaars & Cummings, 2015, pp. 182–183) make a compelling case for 'conscious capitalism' and show how companies that have learned the secret of creating both internal and external stakeholder value are outperforming their peers by 10.5 times over 15 years, demonstrating the significant value that can be created through leveraging the interdependence of stakeholders.

One of the important points made by Hampden Turner is that profit is a lagging indicator of wealth, and is the result of happy customers, suppliers, and employees. This is why they are producing wealth for the shareholders. If there is no profit, it is almost too late, because it shows that the chain of value creation is somehow broken.

The inclusion of other stakeholders has also been highlighted in the 2019 Deloitte report on Global Human Capital Trends (Deloitte, 2019). It shows a shift from organisations as business enterprises to social enterprises. The key to this shift is viewing the organisation as an 'ecosystem' and learning the art of leveraging stakeholder interdependencies to create value for all.

The 'reset strategy' of the World Economic Forum for 2021 highlights what is called 'stakeholder capitalism' as one of the three focus areas of how they see business and other organisations will survive in the disruptive times we live in.

However, it is not only the external stakeholders, but also the internal stakeholders that hold the key to wealth creation.

Many organisations have long suffered from the handicap of working in silos, especially lower down the organisation, with decisions being escalated to the highest level in the function. This approach is not only time-consuming and inefficient, but prevents the cultivation of systemic thinking.

Transpersonal leaders think of the organisation not as an ego-based system of well-defined positions, roles and responsibilities and structural organograms, but rather, they view organisations as living systems, adapting to challenges and initiating change from the inside out (Knights, Grant & Young, 2018, pp. 234–235).

Cognitive diversity

Cognitive diversity has become a growing 21st century trend in the diversity debate. What is the value of ticking all the demographic boxes but, nevertheless, having people who all think much the same way? It does not automatically follow that a woman versus a man or people of different races always think or approach problems differently from one another.

When it comes to thinking and world views, research shows that there are more differences amongst men and amongst women (especially, for example, if they have similar backgrounds or education) than *between* men and women! Hence the shift towards embracing cognitive diversity in the workplace as a stimulus for innovation and creativity.

Cognitive diversity includes *what* we think, and *how* we think and solve problems.

What we think: different perspectives

The humanistic values of freedom of expression and equality have contributed to individualism and people being proud of their cultural heritage, but also to their personal worldviews. These individualistic values feed the ego in its search to establish and preserve its own identity. The ego also wants to grow its own identity by getting followers. However, the risk is that ego-centric leaders seek others whose views reflect their own perspectives. Transpersonal leaders, on the other hand, will seek to associate with those who have different perspectives because they appreciate that growth comes through embracing differences instead of focusing on similarities.

It is not only the diversity of what we think but also the diversity of how we think that adds to the cognitive variety in the new world of work.

Different ways of thinking: how we think

People who have different styles of problem solving can offer unique perspectives because they think differently. Unlike demographic diversity, which focuses on achieving a mixture of statistical characteristics such as gender or age, cognitive diversity focuses on achieving a mixture of how people carry out intellectual activities, such as making associations or drawing conclusions. This also relates to different personality types (for example, how do you gain the value of both extroverts and introverts, big picture thinkers (right brain) versus analytical thinkers (left brain), and so on). It also embraces the value of neurodiversity, as individuals with conditions such as ADD/ADHD, autism, dyscalculia, dyslexia, dyspraxia or Tourette's offer a variety of thinking strengths. These vary from creativity, ability to think in 3D, observational skills, to holistic (systemic) thinking and more. Which well-informed leader wouldn't want these capabilities brought to bear on their organisational challenges?

Artificial intelligence and human intelligence: a new challenge for cognitive diversity

In the new world of work, a new form of cognitive diversity that needs to be dealt with is the diverse way that human intelligence and artificial intelligence solve problems.

A large banking group told us that they have already created 250 'machine employees' each with their own name and number to work alongside humans to fulfil certain functions in the bank. The team leaders need to monitor and manage these new diverse teams in a different way. The Watson computer from IBM, for instance, outperforms humans by far in some tasks; it can read 200 million pages of information in a few seconds and answer questions. IBM has also employed 'chat bots' as part of their induction process and new employees sometimes find them more helpful than humans. We believe that cognitive diversity takes on new challenges when 'algorithms and humanrithms' as futurist Gert Leonhard (2016) calls it, need to work together.

We believe that these three dimensions of diversity will create a new awareness of the complexities of diversity and open up new opportunities for organisations to excel. However, it is not the diversity in itself that brings the benefits, it is the art of inclusion that brings about the magic.

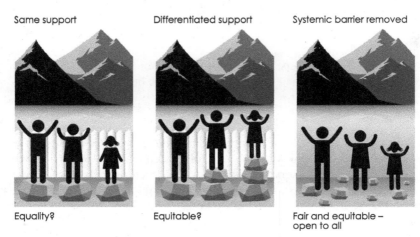

Adapted from Deloitte (The diversity and inclusion revolution, 2018)

Figure 10.6 Equality, Equity and Systemic change

Equality and fairness

Before discussing how to nurture and harness diversity and inclusion, it is useful to consider the nature of equality and fairness. It is not our objective to get into the argument of the relative merits of equality of outcome versus opportunity – but instead to discuss fairness as perceived through the lens of diversity.

Case Study: A true story of three brothers

There were three brothers, one aged 14 and twins aged 13, who were all sent away to a British boarding school. Their mother allocated a fixed budget to their termly 'tuck box' (a box that each child was allowed that contained treats to eat provided by parents each school term). However, one of the twins was diabetic. His diabetic treats cost considerably more than the standard ones. As a result, he had about half as many treats as his brothers did.

    Questions:

- *Was this fair?*
- *Was it equitable?*
- *How else might the mother have allocated her budget to be fair and equitable to all her sons?*
- *What might a systemic solution have been that the school could have implemented to ensure fair and equitable treatment for all pupils?*

Deloitte's report "The Diversity and Inclusion Revolution" (Bourke and Dillon, 2018), presents a metaphor for equality, equity and fairness based on the story of three people looking over a fence. Equally treated, not everyone will have the ability to achieve or experience the same things. Equitable treatment allows equal access through differential action, but a desirable goal for a leader committed to equality is to remove barriers from the start (Figure 10.6).

The magic of inclusion: creating value from diversity

One can say diversity and inclusion are like two sides of a coin; without inclusion, diversity can be counter-productive and could lead to disengagement and even conflict. It's not only about the diversity facts and figures but more about emotions and relationships, inclusion means building the *emotional* and *social capital* of the organisation to make diversity work.

Developing emotional intelligence is a critical part of the journey in becoming a transpersonal leader. The four competencies of emotionally intelligent leaders will enable them to deal with inclusion in a constructive way (Knights et al., 2018, p. 69). However, to become an inclusive leader is about more than developing emotional intelligence; it includes deeper levels of awareness and consciousness (Knights et al., 2018, p. 234).

Knights et al. (2018) introduces an awareness of the world as a Complex Adaptive System (CAS) as the foundation of transpersonal leadership. CAS thinking is an essential paradigm shift for the transpersonal leader, and without this orientation, inclusion will keep struggling in the efforts of the ego to use conformity, compliance and agreement as the basis for inclusion.

In the chart below (Figure 10.7), we introduce the following four levels of inclusion. This corresponds with the journey of the transpersonal Leader in 'taming' or, perhaps more accurately, harnessing the ego to become more useful, instead of trapping the leader in a cage of self-centredness.

The first three levels of inclusion in the bottom section of the chart below, are based on the way the dualistic ego mindset tries to deal with the challenge of inclusion and these three levels include the first part of the transpersonal leadership (TL) journey. Level four includes a fresh rethink of inclusion in the light of the CAS awareness mentioned above. Organisations are seen as eco-systems vs ego-systems.

As we discuss the four levels, we will refer to the appropriate leadership competence and skills required to deal with inclusion as referred to in the journey of the transpersonal leader (Figure 10.7).

Level one (L1): conform

This level is dominated by the human ego's need for identity. It plays the naming game for itself and others, this gives us the perspective that the ego is the author of diversity. The ego sees the world as a well-oiled machine,

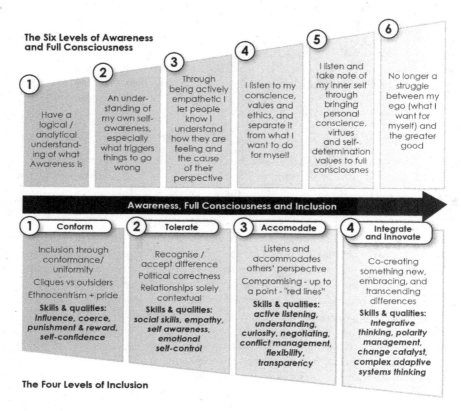

Figure 10.7 Correlating the six levels of awareness & consciousness with the four levels of inclusion

where every part fits in according to the overall design, and this is also the long established view of how organisations work.

Level one operates on an ego–systemic way of inclusion. It creates a sense of pride and self-confidence and a sense of belonging for followers. There are rewards for those who conform and 'fit in' with the culture, however, those who do not conform may be either punished or excluded. This view-point plays on the human needs for safety and security, and a need to belong through conformance. If you do not 'fit the paradigm' you will be excluded; it is a matter of FIFO– Fit In or Fly Off!

This corresponds with the first two levels of awareness in the Table 10.1 above: a logical and analytical (and, we want to add, a dualistic) understanding of the world; an understanding of self and a clear definition of what is right and wrong, what fits and does not fit. Operating at this level, a person believes in a central control system that enforces conformance through influence or even coercion. A good example of this is organisations that work through hierarchical organograms, constraining job descriptions and induction programmes designed to help new employees to find their cultural and structural fit. Organograms are still useful tools to help us to understand lines of command, however transpersonal leaders are aware of the fact that an organogram does not reflect the working of an organisation and see it for what it is. The real organisation is a network of human relationships (and we want to add also non-human or robotic relationships). It has a life of its own despite the efforts of egocentric leaders to control it. As one of the CEOs of a large organisation told us: 'I feel like I am riding an elephant, I try to steer it but it goes where it wants to go'.

Behaviour and skills

In level 1, the behaviours and skills are about analytical thinking, clarity of role definitions and focus, clear boundaries, building self-confidence and pride, influencing and coercion.

The upside of L1 inclusion brings a sense of belonging and pride. Many organisations spend large amounts of money on branding to differentiate themselves in the marketplace. However, the downside of this is that it can lead to an 'in-group-out-group' mindset: ethnocentrism as was seen in the holocaust, to use an extreme example. The typical downside behaviours we see on L1 are bias, stereotyping and making sweeping assumptions. These show up as egocentrism, ethnocentrism where one regards your ethnic groups as superior to others, and racism. It manifests in the workplace as 'silencing' where people in lower positions are not given a chance to speak, and nor are people of different gender, race or other 'out-groups'. Slogans like 'America first' and 'What's in it for us?' are the typical behaviours we see on L1 inclusion.

When organisations are confronted with their self-centeredness and become aware of diversity, they often move to level 2.

Level two (L2): tolerance

The move to L2 comes mostly as the result of the acceptance of humanistic values the development of emotional intelligence. It resonates with level 3 of Knights' et al. (2018) six levels of awareness. People become actively empathetic, recognise differences, and show some understanding. Organisations start to recognise the differences, and stereotypical labels become taboo at L2.

To promote better understanding, activities such as cultural days are often organised. People start to find it interesting to meet others who are very different. They become curious to understand how others eat, drink and dress. We also see programmes, especially in global companies, to encourage people to want to know about the customs of other cultures and to be respectful when doing business across the globe. How do you greet people from other cultures? How do you share business cards? How do you dress for meetings?

But it also goes further in gaining a better understanding other cultures' values and beliefs.

Behaviours and skills

The typical behaviours and skills at this level are related to social skills, respect, empathy, and sensitivity to others. These 'culture' programmes are not without value and enhance mutual understanding and respect. However, understanding other cultures does not necessarily require individuals to accept them as part of their value system.

The next levels of inclusion become more important, and are when we start to become aware of the diversity dimensions of stakeholders and diversity of thought.

Level three (L3): accommodating

Level three becomes more challenging because we need to consider the needs and expectations of others, such as external stakeholders like customers and suppliers, in our plans and strategies. It also requires another look at how we accommodate the views of people in the organisation with different views. It relates to level four of the levels of awareness in the sense that I become aware that there is something more than what *I* want and what *I* think is good. We are now moving beyond our ego-dominated world.

Accommodating refers to a situation where one will expand one's point of view to include that of another person or group. It implies making some compromises to accommodate the views of others. However, there are clear limits as to how far one will go to include another's opinions. One is playing within the boundaries of your own thoughts, beliefs and values which plays an important role in the formation of our paradigms.

To illustrate this, we can use the metaphor of a circle and triangle. When we ask participants in our workshops to bring a circle and triangle together (representing inclusion), without changing its original shape, we get various variations like this (Figure 10.8):

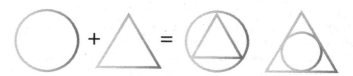

Figure 10.8 Bringing circles and triangles together in two dimensions

Figure 10.9 Another two-dimensional approach to adapting and accommodating

Some will even try this (Figure 10.9):

The fit is not always 100%, we may compromise by enlarging our 'figure' to include others. However, the focus is on the areas of agreement and tolerance for those areas that do not fit. Many conflict resolution programmes are built on this principle of finding common ground and tolerance for the areas of disagreement.

Another example that can serve as a metaphor for L3 inclusion is when salt gets mixed with water to form a saltwater solution. However, each substance retains its own characteristics and can relatively easily be separated again through boiling the water to evaporate and cooling it down again, leaving the salt to dry out and return to its original solid form.

Behaviours and skills

The skills required at L3 are active listening, seeking understanding and having a willingness to adapt in order to accommodate others. It is about negotiation, and 'compromise', 'give and take', but it often implies having 'red lines' which one is not prepared to cross. The main orientation on L3 is looking for common ground and points of agreement or consensus. As the pictures of the circle and triangle suggest, there are some overlaps where we may agree to disagree as long as we have sufficient common ground to work together. Many leaders progress to this level, but get stuck here because the next level requires more than just different skills, it requires a totally different mindset and orientation to life.

This represents a paradigm shift in the journey of the transpersonal Leader which is based on a complex adaptive system (CAS) perspective of the world and organisations.

Level four (L4): integrate and innovate

The fourth level takes diversity and inclusion beyond the previous boundary. This is based on a full awareness of myself as something bigger than my ego identity, as Knights says in describing level 6 of awareness: "It is no longer a struggle between my ego (what I want for myself) and the greater good".

Table 10.2 Eleven transpersonal practices of a CAS

Practice	Description
1. Everyone's a leader	Unlike predictable hierarchical systems, CASs have no central control mechanism. For a transpersonal leader this means delegating and decentralising whenever we can. To achieve this, we need to maximum everyone's potential through development and practice.
2. Value led Sustainability	Providing consistency by acting from principle, based on core values and being transparent in doing so. Actions should be based on what is best for the long term, sacrificing short term gain where appropriate.
3. Emergent thinking	The complex world we live in does not give us the comfort of making detailed plans that he expects to remain the same. We can set direction but need to continually adjust depending on how things develop. We must be much more open minded and intently curious.
4. Holistic approach	We must take the broadest view. Be aware of patterns, relationships and connections. We must be fully conscious so that we can make full use of all our decision-making processes. We must also feel we belong to the system we are involved with.
5. Self-awareness & Self-management	To be aware of our emotions and to be able to manage them effectively for ourselves and the greater good.
6. Balancing Feedback vs Independence	A CAS survives because it responds to the feedback system within. So must transpersonal leaders encourage and value feedback. The balance between accepting and responding to feedback versus standing up for your beliefs and convictions is critical.
7. Adaptive	We must be sensitive to external change by learning, and where necessary recreating ourselves and our organisations to respond. With people we must have empathy and compassion to understand and respond.
8. Managing Chaos and Random Probability	Small changes (random chance or intended) can have huge consequences. Only a CAS can bring order to such a system. For a Transpersonal leader it means the positive use of adversity – learn from mistakes, see problems as opportunities and being resilient.
9. Norming Diversity	In a CAS, each part plays a full role. We must value all other people, cultures and situations in celebration of their difference, not despite them.
10. Vocation	Within nature, humans are probably alone in *wanting* to serve something greater than oneself. It comes from deep within to want to serve others or the Universe. For some, this can happen from early adulthood but for most this comes later in life in wishing to give something back in gratitude for what one has received.
11. Enjoyment	One of the key criteria of a sustainable performance-enhancing culture is enjoyment (see Chapter 8). We can't be happy all the time as we react to everything that happens in our lives but as transpersonal leaders, we should make every effort to bring joy to the lives of others.

This is supported by the 11 transpersonal practices of a Complex Adaptive System (Knights et al., 2018, p. 235) (Table 10.2):

It takes the sting out of conflict and *turns opposition into a space of innovation.* It builds on the previous levels but transcends it.

The whole is greater than the sum of its parts

The challenge for a leader comes when stakeholder diversity or the diversity of thought or becomes paradoxical or polarised, such as when asking "shall we consolidate our business or diversify?", "Shall we globalise or grow our local business?" "Should we focus on our staff or our customers?" "Shall we merge with another business or grow our own?" "Should we centralise or decentralise?"

We call level four Innovate because it refers to bringing different elements or standpoints together to form something new. Here we also need to respect others, but spell it as 're-*spect*' to refer to a situation where one 're-looks' at others, and is curious to find out what others have to say or offer. At this level people search for value in an opposing idea with an open mind, heart and will, and look for alternative solutions which include, and even transcend, both views, to create something new.

To take the metaphor of matching the circle and triangle one step further, we can create a cone from a circle and a triangle if we can enter the third dimension (Figure 10.10).

Another analogy could be when sodium and chlorine (two poisonous substances) come together to form the new chemical compound, salt. Salt contains both sodium and chlorine atoms, but the compound is something different/more than the sum of its parts. Chlorine is a poison, but in the right combination and the following the right process, when combined with sodium (also poisonous), it creates table salt, a precious substance for all humans – it not only brings taste to our food and works in preserving it, but is an essential component for homeostasis in the body.

The really important contribution of D&I in the context of today's complex organisations is to harness that innovation that comes from diverse perspectives. These are integrated into leadership practice in Level 4 so that the whole becomes more than its components.

Figure 10.10 Three-dimensional metaphor for thinking to resolve diversity issues

Roger Martin (Martin, 2009) calls this integrative thinking, which he regards as the quality of 21st century leaders. He gives numerous examples of leaders who had the ability to hold paradoxical thoughts; and instead of deciding what is right or wrong, had the ability to integrate both and come up with a new business model Barry Johnson (2014) calls it 'polarity management' and provides numerous practical tools that leaders can use to facilitate Level 4 inclusion.

Many organisations are trapped in either-or thinking – like shall we centralise or decentralise, shall we diversify of consolidate, shall we go global or stay national? Shall we focus on our employees or the customer? Shall we keep control or empower our people? Shall we focus on the task or the on our people? These are the typical choices that ego-intelligent leaders want to make. Eco-intelligent leaders have developed the ability of thinking 'both-and', holding these paradoxes and creating something that accommodates, but transcends, both.

As mentioned above, Knights et al. (2018), in *Leading Beyond the Ego*, has brought a new direction for the development of transpersonal leaders with the introduction of a new narrative for leadership development in Complex Adaptive Systems (CAS). If we use the CAS narrative to explore diversity and inclusion it brings new exciting perspectives. This new narrative for leadership is also explored by Olivier, Hölscher and Williams (2020) in their work on agile leadership for turbulent times. The authors explore essentially the same space as transpersonal leadership by introducing three leadership intelligences referred to as 'ego, eco and intuitive intelligence'.

Behaviours and skills

We discussed above the 11 transpersonal practices, that lay the foundation for L4 inclusion, and here we show their relevance to diversity and inclusion.

1 **Everyone is a leader:** This refers to the fact that leadership becomes separated from an individual and seen as a process rather than a position. Diversity and inclusion thus become an issue for everyone, not just a specific leader. Those who feel excluded will therefore work as hard as those who exclude to create something new from their engagement. It is almost like giving birth to a new child!

2 **Value-led sustainability:** Every participant, stakeholder or person with diverse ideas should work together to enable sustainable value creation for the organisation.

3 **Emergent thinking:** The 'traditional' linear planning processes, with leaders in charge, often find themselves lacking resourcefulness or the right capabilities in our VUCA world of uncertainty. When the organisation and its leadership are geared to L4 Inclusion it will unleash innovation at a different scale. The ego is well grounded in the use of linear thinking. It requires eco and intuitive intelligence to take the leader

'beyond the confines of the narrow ego thinking' (Olivier, Hölscher & Williams, 2020) to create a space of emergence where diverse ideas can flourish and cross pollinate each other.

4 **Holistic approach**: The inclusion of diverse and even opposing ideas needs a holistic view. A holistic perspective opens up the space for diversity to flourish.

5 **Self-awareness:** To consider opposing views requires an open but not an empty mind. To participate at L4 inclusion one needs an awareness of one's own emotions and thoughts and be able to manage them. Without self-awareness the leader get stuck in their own ego needs and becomes blind to the perspectives of others. One can say that self-awareness is the first step towards liberating the ego to become a servant, rather than the master of destiny.

6 **Balancing feedback versus independence:** One of the key principles of L4 inclusion is the awareness of interdependence versus independence or dependence. Constant feedback between stakeholders and thought leaders is critical to maintain momentum on the journey. Feedback and transparency are the lifeline of ecosystems, because they create the foundation for continuous adaptation.

7 **Adaptive:** When confronted with diverse thoughts and feelings transpersonal leaders will be able to respond appropriately instead being reactive. They will adapt when required. As Darwin said, "it is not the strongest but the most adaptable that will survive on the evolutionary journey". Ego leaders and ego systems find themselves stuck in their definitions of themselves, others, and on a practical side how a business must be run. Transpersonal leadership paves the way out of 'stuckness' to become agile and adaptive.

8 **Managing chaos and random probability:** The transpersonal leader fails fast and learns quickly. When action is required, they take more of an incremental change approach, deliver something tangible and mindful of new disruptive inputs from various stakeholders who are part of the journey. Openness to diversity is a particular strength of transpersonal leaders not only to survive, but to thrive in turbulent times.

9 **Norming diversity:** Transpersonal leaders realise that just as biodiversity is critical to the survival of the ecosystem in nature, social diversity is critical for the survival of business and organisations. They will cultivate it and use it to thrive in the uncertain and volatile world we live in.

10 **Vocation**: In the 20th century it was customary to define vision for the future. The human ego delights in defining the future and creating a set of linear actions to get there; these were called strategies. With the disruptions and complexities of the 21st century, business and work environment visions and linear strategies are often quickly found to be out of date. The new shift in business is to become purpose driven instead of vision led. Purpose is, at its simplest, 'to serve something greater than oneself' (see above). Diversity mostly occurs on the 'what' and the 'how',

but if these are grounded in the 'why' question it gives an opportunity to move beyond the ego.

11 **Enjoyment:** In the research for the 'best company to work for' the answer which correlates the highest enjoyment, scoring 86% (Gostick & Christopher, 2008) was 'This is a fun place to work'. Fun and laughter transcend the uncertainties of diversity. Bringing appropriate humour and exercises that evoke enjoyment, and therefore the bonding hormone oxytocin, promote human connection and a 'towards', creative mindset (Rock & Schwartz, 2008).

Dealing with diversity of values and thought through transpersonal leadership

This case study represents a personal experience of applying the principles spelled out above. It includes thoughts on how diversity manifested on the three dimensions and how we progressed through the four levels of inclusion. We also refer to the 11 practices of a complex adaptive system, where appropriate. It is important to note the shift in this case study from focussing on specific leaders, but rather to the leadership process in the organisation that led to significant business results. We highlight the key concepts as we explain how we applied transpersonal thinking. At the time we did not have the conceptual framework as described by Knights, Grant and Young (2018), however in retrospect it was quite clear how it was applied.

A consulting group applied the principles of transpersonal leadership and Level 4 inclusion during early post-apartheid times in South Africa. The group was asked to address productivity and cost saving in one of the world's biggest goldmines. The gold grades were low, in many cases only about 5 g of gold per ton of rock with the need to go about 3 km underground to find the gold reefs. Working conditions were horrible and often unsafe. Many team discussions were held between 2 km and 3 km underground in unbearable heat. Nelson Mandela had very recently been released from prison, the country was plunged in uncertainty, the black workforce was euphoric, and they had the wind in their sails in the effort to break the back of apartheid. White workers and bosses were plunged into fear and uncertainty. How would they stay competitive in the global marketplace? The deep divides of uncertainty were felt in all three dimensions of diversity. Demographic and sociographic stakeholders, like the communities in which the mines operate, were excluded and, most importantly, the value of diversity of thought was not recognised. The management style was very much ego-centric 'traditional' command and control. Management and unions, in this case the National Union of Mineworkers (NUM), were far apart, and even conflicted in their values, their vision and mission for the mines, and how the workplace should be organised. Leadership was very much in the hands of white Afrikaner males (WAMs) who held the reins very tight. Union leaders were seen as a threat and were not included in the leadership process.

One of the shafts was making a loss of 1.5m Rand (about USD400,000 today) per month, and the shareholders did not like it. The clear instruction from the investors was: "it does not look good on the balance sheet, not good for the cash flow and the share price. Close it down if you cannot turn it around" – a logical shareholder's demand. The stakes were high; closing a mine shaft meant a loss of jobs that would not go down well with the NUM. The Union normally reacts to these business decisions with industrial action or strikes, which could escalate to other mines because they believed 'injury to one is injury to all'. Such a strike could cost the mine up to R40m (around USD10m today) per month in lost production, apart from the reputational damage in labour relations.

Mining engineers developed a 'turn-around plan', but they needed the support of the labour force to implement it. The consulting group were asked to 'sell the ideas', or to get 'buy-in' from the unions. There were a number of unions representing different factions of the workforce. The consulting team also included mining engineers, whilst the consultants were the so-called 'social engineers', working with the hearts and minds of people to improve relationships. This required being seen as 'neutral' in the process. Given how far apart management and unions were in their thinking, there were high levels of distrust and even animosity between the two sides. The conflict resolution 'toolkit' of many consultants in those days consisted of numerous 'agreement tools', like getting everyone to have the same vision, mission, values and strategic objectives - this was called 'stakeholder alignment'.

First the consultancy team used Level 1 consensus tools to create trust, but it did not seem to work. In one of the series of workshops they tried to develop a common mission statement for the mine; and asked, 'what is the core business of the mine?' Management defined it as 'we mine gold to create shareholder value', on the other side, the unions saw the core purpose or mission of the mine as being 'to create jobs'. The concept of 'agreement' was far from their thinking. If management seemed to agree with the unions they were regarded as 'soft', if union leaders agreed with management, they were regarded as 'management stooges' and this could cost them their positions as leaders. The two ego systems were well entrenched in their positions and they needed to look good to their constituencies. All the while, the shaft was losing money.

How to build trust without agreement was one of the big questions to answer. The consultants introduced what was considered an absurd idea at the time. Essentially, they coined a new word in their vocabulary: 'synergy', which was defined as a unity of opposites (this was, after all, the path of the new South Africa). All concerned had to find respect and understanding of each other in order to build the new South Africa under the leadership of the new President Mandela, without losing their own identity. The leadership of the opposing groups had to be convinced that they would not 'lose face' but, instead, work together on a solution that suited everyone – for the common good, taking a holistic approach. The future was not clear, so instead of trying to define it together (common vision), the future was allowed emerge as the various stakeholders became engaged in a generative dialogue. Generative dialogue does not start with consensus as its point of departure; it works towards seeking respect for differences or diversity as the cornerstone of a sustainable social ecosystem or, for that matter, a business. We defined respect as re-spect, meaning to re-look at others and try to understand the world from their point of view. To understand someone, you do need not agree with them.

The first stage was to 're-spect' each other (starting at Level 2 above), to look through the cracks of the stereotypes and search for value in the other. This was followed by efforts to help them 'understand' each other, and the bigger picture. A big revelation for many was that understanding does not imply agreement, but rather stepping into the shoes of the other and looking through their eyes at yourself and the world, without judgement, defence or attack.

A process based on the principles of generative dialogue was established, thereby creating a space of emergence where new ideas could be developed using the diversity of ideas from each stakeholder — 'developing a cone' as it were. It was termed 'dialogical intervention', meaning that the intention of the consultants was not to take sides, but to facilitate a process where all stakeholders collaborate towards finding a solution to the problem of an unprofitable mine shaft.

The steps taken were as follows:

1   Identification of stakeholder and issues.
2   Interviews with key leaders and influencers from both camps: this required individual interviews with them, preparing them for the process of dialogue, searching for those leaders with transpersonal leadership qualities and getting their support for the process.
3   Separate stakeholder workshops: The two mindsets of how to run a profitable business were miles apart and it took some time, especially with the union leaders, to understand sophisticated engineering concepts as well as business principles. To help bridge the gap in understanding, a simple example of a taxi business (which they all knew very well) was used to explain concepts of profit and loss. On the other side, engineers had to be persuaded to use much simpler examples and metaphors in explaining their solutions. It took about two months to create a common vocabulary which is essential for dialogue. The facilitators worked on both sides and set the scene for the dialogue session.
4   All stakeholder workshop — dialogue: when it was felt that the stakeholders were ready, a joint meeting was called for dialogue. Management was prepared to set a week aside where management and unions would design a rescue plan for the mining shaft. Both sides had a proper mandate from their constituencies and had a good idea of the various options. But most

of all they had common vocabulary. An operations room, with posters of various concepts against the walls, was set up, so that all the options were transparent. By the end of the week, a plan was on the table – the 'cone' was built through emergent thinking and taking a holistic approach. It was not a plan that had 'buy-in', but it was a plan that had 'ownership' because it was co-created by both parties – like a child that belongs to both parents.

5   Joint working groups: It was important to have joint working committees to take ownership of certain tasks, and that was a breakthrough for mine mangers who were used to 'calling the shots'. But the process prepared them for that, and the ecosystem started to work. There developed a move to a level of distributed leadership where union leadership was recognised by management as an intrinsic part of decision making, and even execution. Distributed leadership, and seeing leadership as a process rather than a position, is one of the keys to transpersonal leadership in organisations.

6   Monitoring of progress: Feedback is a cornerstone of CAS. Apart from constant feedback from the joint working groups, the bigger forum of all leaders came together every few months to receive feedback and monitor progress. The progress was substantial, the loss of about 1.5m Rand (USD400,000) per month turned into a profit of about 3m Rand (USD800,000) per month. Jobs were not lost, and the shareholders were happy. While supported by humanistic values like equality, freedom of speech and fairness, the focus was on creating *business value for all*. This process also rippled out to joint community projects like job creation and school building, where management and union leaders worked together in the communities for the benefit of all – *stakeholder diversity*. The eleventh CAS practice (see above) is 'enjoyment'. Celebration was very important, and in South Africa at that time white people and black people very seldom mixed socially for eating and drinking together. There were a number of these social events organised and sponsored by the business and these contributed to breaking the pain of social isolation and celebrating diversity.

This process was designed to stimulate diversity and develop the practices of integrative thinking in complex adaptive systems. The political leaders in South Africa at the time were all in dialogue to build a new South Africa, and this approach helped to get the process going.

Summary

Diversity and inclusion are no longer merely key performance areas for HR practitioners. We become more and more aware of the need to recognise diversity and to learn the art of inclusion. The battle for inclusion is part of the international political and global business scene. As we write this chapter, US-China trade, Brexit and Black Lives Matter are dominating the news channels, in between the news on COVID-19.

We hope that this chapter widens the scope of awareness of the various dimensions of diversity. We believe there are more dimensions that will be unveiled as we continue the discussion. We have also offered some thoughts on how we deal with inclusion on four levels which corresponds with the development journey of the transpersonal leader.

Questions for personal reflection and development

1.   Organisational culture

We find this table useful as a framework for discussion. You can do it yourself or invite your team to discuss your experience and perceptions about diversity and inclusion on the various dimensions.

   a.   Look at the D&I strategy in your organisation. To what extent do you address all three dimensions?
   b.   Think about your policies and practices, how do you include the various demographic categories?
   c.   How are you doing with your stakeholders, are they kept at arm's length or are you engaging them in your business?
   d.   Regarding cognitive diversity, how do you deal with differences of thought, personalities, and conflicting ideas?
   e.   Do you have inclusive practices in place to deal with situations where people differ on ideas?

Score yourself out of 5, where 1 is not at all or very little and 5 is completely, on how you are doing on each dimension. Consider the three strands of diversity and the extent to which each is present in your organisation and /or personal thinking (Table 10.3).

Score yourself out of 5 again on the following question, where 1 is never or almost never and 5 is always or almost always.

Table 10.3 Diversity scorecard

	Demographic and sociographic diversity	Stakeholder diversity	Cognitive diversity
L1 – Conformance			
L2 – Tolerance			
L3 – Accommodating			
L4 – Integration and innovation			

2.   Your personal mindset

What is your first reaction when someone disagrees with you?
   •   Do you defend yourself?

- Do you try to explain yourself better to convince the other of your standpoint?
- Do you ask the other inquisitive questions to explore their position? What do you think the transpersonal leader will do?
3. Observe others in your team, what are the most 'used reactions' to differences? Write a brief observation and reflection note on what you notice.
4. Cultural Iceberg — we tend to only see what is above the waterline.
   a. Which of these elements of diversity have you considered when engaging with those who are of different backgrounds?
   b. How have you explored these?
   c. What would you do differently in future?

References

Bourke, J. and Dillon, B. 2018. The diversity and inclusion revolution. *Deloitte Review* (22), pp. 82–95.

Deloitte. 2019. Human Capital Trends Report 2019. *www.deloitte.com*. https://www2.deloitte.com/ro/en/pages/human-capital/articles/2019-deloitte-global-human-capital-trends.html, accessed March 11, 2021.

Dilts, R. 1990. *Changing Belief Systems with NLP*. Cupertino: Meta Publications.

Elkington, J. 2018. 25 Years Ago I Coined the Phrase "Triple Bottom Line." Here's Why It's Time to Rethink It. *Harvard Business Review*. https://hbr.org/2018/06/-25-years-ago-i-coined-the-phrase-triple-bottom-line-heres-why-im-giving-up-on-it, March 11, 2021.

Forbes. 2011. Global Diversity and Inclusion: Fostering Innovation through a Diverse Workforce. *Forbes.com*. https://www.forbes.com/forbesinsights/innovation_diversity/, March 11, 2021.

Gostick, A., & Christopher, S. 2008. *The Levity Effect*. Hoboken: Wiley.

Hampden-Turner, C., Trompenaars, A., & Cummings, T. 2015. *Nine Visions of Capitalism*. Oxford: Infinite Ideas Ltd.

Hutchins, G. 2012. *The Nature of Business*. Totnes: Green Books.

Johnson, B. 2014. *Polarity Management* (2nd ed.). Amherst: HRD Press.

Knights, J., Grant, D., & Young, G. 2018. *Leading Beyond the Ego*. London: Routledge.

Leonhard, G. 2016. *Technology vs Humanity*. Zurich: The Futures Agency.

McKinsey. 2007. Women Matter. *www.mckinsey.com*. https://www.mckinsey.com/-business-functions/organization/our-insights/gender-diversity-a-corporate-performance-driver, accessed March 11, 2021.

McKinsey. 2020. *mckinsey.com*. https://www.mckinsey.com/featured-insights/diversity-and-inclusion/diversity-wins-how-inclusion-matters, accessed March 11, 2021.

Martin, R., 2009. *The Opposable Mind*. Boston: Harvard Business Press.

Olivier, S., Hölscher, F., & Williams, C. 2020. *Agile Leadership for Turbulent Times*. London: Routledge.

Porter, M. 1985. *Competitive Advantage*. New York: Free Press.

Rock, D., & Grant, H. 2017. Why diverse teams are smarter. *Psychology Today*. https://www.psychologytoday.com/us/blog/your-brain-work/201703/why-diverse-teams-are-smarter, accessed March 11, 2021.

Rock, D. & Schwartz, J. 2008. SCARF: A brain-based model for collaborating with and influencing others. *Neuroleadership Journal* Issue 1, pp. 1–9.

11 Digital transformation and change through transpersonal leadership

Duncan Enright

> There is nothing more difficult to take in hand, more perilous to conduct, or more uncertain in its success, than to take the lead in the introduction of a new order of things.
>
> Niccolo Machiavelli

Overview

Examples of successes and failures litter the rocky road to digital transformation, like monuments or gravestones depending on outcomes. Such a fundamental change, in a changing world, poses significant challenges. This chapter offers insights, examples and solutions to leaders. It is instructive to look for reasons for difficulties not in technology or even strategy, but through leadership. The factors of success can be found in understanding and restating the core purpose of an organisation, by looking at the climate and culture of the organisation, which drive behaviours, and by considering the styles of leadership on display.

During digital transformation, high-performing organisations require visionary leadership. In addition, a democratic style within an organisation will liberate talent, and harness diversity in support of transformation, including the perspectives of digital natives. Finally, customer focus (and involvement) is key, and the empathy required to lead beyond as well as within the organisation will play a critical role in helping leaders understand the needs of all stakeholders, including customers and staff.

Too often it is the IT department that is left to carry the project alone and leading the change. To survive digital transformation, leaders need to take responsibility, and that includes transforming themselves.

Introduction

Leaders throughout the public, private and third sectors face the same challenge: to excavate and articulate core purpose, describe how it will be pursued in the new digital world, and plot a course through digital transformation.

DOI: 10.4324/9781003150626-14

Leaders need to become transpersonal – leading beyond the ego. All departments and all staff, as well as partners, clients and customers, contribute to and operate under the climate and culture. In particular, this paper is for the board and the division or team leading digital development, giving insights into the perceived reluctance of other departments and stakeholders to engage.

The culture of our organisations and businesses needs to change, and individual behaviours emerge from the new culture, to reap the benefits of new digital transformation in services and enterprises, and increase confidence in what we do for customers. Digital experts need to engage the whole organisation and be sure to pay attention to the need to change behaviours as well as install technology.

Leaders throughout the organisation need to be confident to explore and back new approaches, experimental services, co-produced services and new relationships with citizens, service providers and partners. This requires a different kind of leadership and working: purposeful, open, constantly challenging without losing focus or friends, and engaged with customers as never before.

The main messages are the following:

- Digital transformation requires us to foster a climate and culture that is confident to face the challenges of change, while safeguarding core purpose and values.
- Behaviours that support innovation and change in every part of an organisation need to be fostered.
- Insightful leaders will recognise the need to change themselves in order to be able to drive change, displaying vision, empathy and using a democratic style to engage everyone in transformation.
- It is crucial to develop a strong senior leadership commitment to developing leaders capable of delivering change and sustaining a climate in which tradition is valued but innovation is nurtured.
- Digital transformation plans must acknowledge and accommodate the latest understanding of the emotional, physiological, psychological and neuroscientific impact of change on people with the behavioural implications of these (e.g. fight or flight).
- Leaders must display empathy and optimism, seeing themselves as champions of customers, active facilitators and supporters of change; having a sense of the 'possible'.
- Practical steps must be identified in each office, department and geography and between them to grasp the opportunities of digital transformation.

Digital transformation

All around us the world is changing faster than ever before. The pace is driven by many factors, and commentators struggle to identify the key elements and divine their implications. For example, Robert Tucker wrote of six "driving forces" in the late part of this decade:

- economic recovery,
- the arrival of Millennials as a dominant demographic,
- brand disruption,
- "real time responsiveness" and convenience as differentiators,
- the adoption of artificial intelligence and
- the decline in deference or "social trust" (Tucker, 2018).

Yet each is just a wave crashing ashore from the huge disturbance of digital transformation.

In developed economies, over 80% of people have mobile phones of which two thirds are smartphones, connecting half the population to advanced digital capabilities. Overall mobile digital technology has reached the point where predictions are being made that poverty, hunger and other Millennium Development Goals may be achieved (GSMA, 2020).

The ruins of former (many long standing) industrial giants lie around us like Ozymandias (Shelley, 1817), conquered and supplanted by agile new competitors or superseded by new activities and enterprises. Table 11.1 lists a number of the fallen, and the victors who have risen in their place, thanks to digital disruption.

Table 11.1 Companies that have experienced disruptive change

Vanquished former Titans	Digital disruption
Blockbuster Video	Offered a chance to acquire Netflix in 2000, this $5 billion behemoth closed its doors because of agile digital competitors like Netflix in 2014 (Downes and Nunes, 2013; Satell, 2014)
Kodak	A Kodak engineer invented the first digital camera in 1975 but was allegedly told by senior leaders to hide it to protect the film business. Incorrectly, the leadership of Kodak believed themselves to be in the (doomed) film chemical processing business (Mui, 2012).
Borders	Despite being well loved and a major and innovative retailer of books, Borders' leadership failed to make their own digital move until too late (Sanburn, 2011)
Encyclopaedia Britannica	The home reference of choice was swiftly replaced by digital references, and was unable to innovate to compete as the Internet emerged as a dominant source of reference (Greenstein, 2016).
Toys 'R' Us	In a final irony for a retailer swamped by online competitors, commentators claim Amazon considered taking over some of its stores (Townsend, Coleman-Lochner and Soper, 2018).
Digital Equipment Corporation	Even the most digital, most innovative companies can founder because of cultural issues (Mangelsdorf, 2011).

Case Study 1: Open Access and Academic Publishing

Academic journal publishing has been a robust and strongly growing sector for the last century, driven by the growth in research activity and the increasing requirement to publish results. In particular, the sciences have driven this imperative through growth, and the number of journal articles published passed 50 million around 2009, and approximately 2.5 million papers are published every year.

The advent of the internet, along with pressures on budgets, persuaded academics and research funders to propose and instigate "Open Access" publishing – articles published free to view online. This posed a significant challenge to traditional subscription journal publishers, of whom the largest is Elsevier (owned by RELX Ltd).

In 2004, at the height of the debate about the best way to publish journal articles, the UK Parliament's Science and Technology Committee called the Chief Executive of Reed Elsevier, Crispin Davis, to give evidence, and gave him a hard time over pricing, quality of research published, and the limits placed by subscription on access.

Reed Elsevier invested in digital technology, changed the structure of the organisation, and introduced shared values across the whole company (customer focus, valuing our people, innovation, boundarylessness, passion for winning), demonstrating a commitment not just to technology but to the culture and behaviours of the organisation. Today Elsevier is one of the fastest growing open access publishers in the World (Elsevier.com, 2020).

Case study 1 describes such a transformative impact on an industry sector, with resulting disruption to organisations, stakeholders and business models, resulting in profound consequences.

Steps to success

Digital transformation projects are fraught with difficulty, and because of their wide reach into the operations of organisations are hard to control. Budgetary and time overruns, unforeseen consequences and catastrophic failure are commonplace. Digital transformation is not completed through just the successful execution of a standalone project. It has become clear that a comprehensive overall business strategy review is an essential precursor of such a transformation. Without an ambitious strategy no transformation project can succeed.

However, the best strategy on its own is still not enough. Too often strategy is decoupled from deeper thinking about development, and in particular culture, values and behaviour. Figure 11.1 illustrates the usual main operational focus (on the left), whereas the developmental focus (on the right) is fundamental but often overlooked.

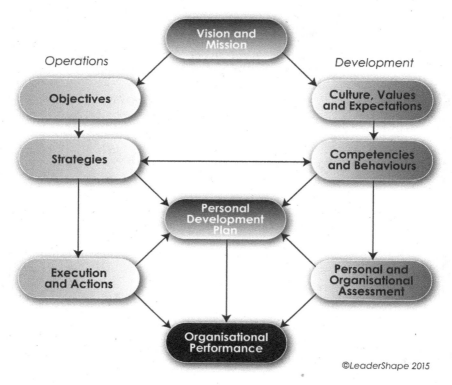

Figure 11.1 Vision to Performance (Knights, Grant and Young, 2018)

Strategic thinking cannot reach far enough to encompass the breadth of its consequences, prepare for unforeseen outcomes, and cope with the inevitable continuing change required in the modern world. Another change must take place; that change is in culture, values and behaviours.

Those organisations undertaking digital transformation projects must excavate a common understanding, throughout their organisation, of shared core purpose. To do this they must engage all stakeholders, address the climate created by leaders, the culture that ensues, and thus shift the very nature of power and control. Radical, ethical, authentic leadership or transpersonal leadership, is required. And that means leaders need to change themselves too.

Leading digital transformation

"The role of a leader is to generate followers, bring them to a place they would not ordinarily go, and to inspire new leaders" (Knights, Grant and Young, 2018, p. 22). Digital transformation means going to new places, but that takes a new sort of leader. It is also critical that the organisational culture is transformed for the journey, and that too takes leadership. A new digital future will not just feel different, it will actually be quite different, and it will demand different things from all stakeholders. Leaders will look to bring customers along on the journey and trust the leaders. Successful leaders will engage staff fully, have a clear understanding of the reasons for change, and be optimistic that the journey is worthwhile during even the most difficult periods of change. The confidence of shareholders or owners will be a priority. Ideally everyone will be inspired, and working towards the common purpose. That takes radical, ethical, authentic leaders – transpersonal leaders.

Transpersonal leadership

By its very nature, leadership is nothing without other people. The concept of and journey to "Transpersonal Leadership" is described inspiringly and at length by John Knights (Knights, Grant and Young, 2018). It is defined as "extending or going beyond the personal or individual, beyond the usual limits of ego and personality". A transpersonal leader uses emotional intelligence, and empathy in particular, to master and deploy six styles of leadership (Goleman, Boyatzis and McKee, 2013). These are shown in Figure 11.2.

In addition, transpersonal leaders exercise ethical judgments, working with and for the interests of all stakeholders. In brief, they make emotionally intelligent choices for the greater good.

The challenges of digital transformation are many, and require radical, ethical, authentic leadership skilled in all styles of leadership, and willing to lead beyond the ego. In particular, a leader will need to display visionary leadership and the ability to create leaders throughout the organisation through the democratic style.

Visionary
Towards a shared vision

Coaching
Develop performance of others

Affiliative
Brings people together

Democratic
Everyone has a voice

Pace-setting
Sets targets and goals

Commanding
Gives instructions and orders

Figure 11.2 Six leadership styles (Knights, Grant and Young, 2018)

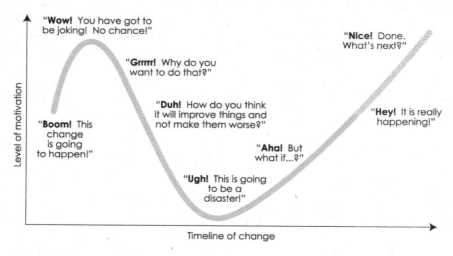

Figure 11.3 Stages of feelings through change

An organisation will need a sustained innovation culture, which will be created and nurtured by the climate – itself set by the leadership. Customer Focus is a core ingredient, with leaders engaging customers and displaying empathy in working with them.

Finally, leaders need high levels of optimism to drive the organisation through the difficult phases of change. A durable model of the psychological process of change was developed by Elizabeth Kübler-Ross in her treatise "On Death and Dying" (Kübler-Ross and Byock, 1969), and this model has been applied in many organisational change settings such as, for example, the introduction of electronic medical records (a difficult element of digital health transformation) (Shoolin, 2010). In the context of change and digital transformation the fluctuations in motivation experienced by a participant are shown in Figure 11.3.

Visionary leadership: defining core purpose, finding the pivot

The six leadership styles are all important in their own right. For example, the Commanding Style, while widely overused (and often seen as a default) is of value in situations when compliance with orders is required, as in emergency situations.

Digital transformation requires intelligent use of the visionary style of leadership. An essential component in any strategy is a vision consistent with the organisation's core purpose (Hanna, 2016) and recognising the long-term nature of the change envisaged. Visionary leaders can create high energy in an organisation based on a motivating shared vision, or story, about the change ahead (Knights, Grant and Young, 2018).

In particular, it is the task of the visionary leader or leaders to engage all stakeholders in the search for 'core purpose', and this is the pivot on which digital transformation can take place. The benefits of building a core purpose and becoming a visionary company are manifold, and cannot all be discussed here, but for more examples of doubling down on customer value and core purpose read *Built to Last* (Collins and Porras, 1998) and Blue Ocean Strategy (Kim and Mauborgne, 2005) as great examples.

Digital transformation is an ongoing endeavour, and like any change programme leaders will seek to protect against fatigue, sabotage or resistance. Visionary leaders carry optimism for the organisation, and maintain a strongly positive influence on colleagues, illuminating the mission and the core purpose.

By tethering core purpose, and describing how it will be enhanced or served by digital transformation, leaders can provide a clear picture for staff,

---

Case Study 2: e-Estonia, leading through vision

In 1991 the Estonian Government faced a huge problem. Its economy had fallen way behind neighbours such as Finland during nearly 50 years as a Soviet state (Marzouk, 2017), and it risked losing ambitious outward-looking highly educated citizens to other richer countries. Without other infrastructure and resources its economy started behind its neighbours but at the birth of the World Wide Web its leaders recognised one domain in which it could compete. "We had to set a goal that resonates, large enough for the society to believe in" said former chief information officer of Estonia, Taavi Kotka (Heller, 2017).

The new government of independent Estonia, a country of only 1.3 million people, had a major asset – trust among its people (Ehasoo, 2017). It chose a deliberate path to create a digital future for the country and now stands at the forefront of digital nations, using technology not just for public services and government but as a strategic national asset. Digital identity is a foundation, but that could only be created and accepted with a shared vision and trust in government (Shen, 2016).

Almost 20 years later, Estonia is a model of the digital nation, with a transparent identity system trusted by its people, services run efficiently, democratic processes offered online, and public services including health, security and taxation now managed digitally through a series of national transformation projects (e-Estonia, 2018).

Thanks to a clear initial vision of a digital society, empowering citizens and involving them in the journey, Estonia has weathered storms and created an efficient, competitive and successful society and economy (Jaffe, 2016).

partners, shareholders and customers alike (Swaminathan and Meffert, 2017). Digital transformation without core purpose is doomed to be a rudderless reaction to technological challenges, and adds little to the overall value of an organisation. What's more, it can be hard to gain understanding and support from across the organisation, which leaves projects prone to failure. Case Study 2 shows the way a clear vision with strong underpinning values and stories can drive even a multi-faceted transformation programme with great success.

Democratic leadership: empowering stakeholders

> Occasionally a leader comes along who has excellent ideas and has the charisma to carry everyone with them without using the Democratic style – but this is a very rare exception to the rule. Not recommended for most of us mere mortals!
>
> (Knights, Grant and Young, 2018)

Leaders can often think they know all the answers. However in the case of digital transformation (as in many highly complex situations) it is unwise to believe so. A Democratic style of leadership builds engagement, commitment and buy-in. This alone is enough to recommend this approach. However, it is also extremely valuable when building a culture of innovation, encouraging employees to exercise specialist skills, or harnessing expertise throughout the company.

One key group to engage, both within the organisation and among customers, is digital natives, those who have grown up, gone through education, and entered the workforce since the ubiquity of the worldwide web. They will be younger – the millennial generation born between 1980 and 1994 along with younger members of the previous Generation Y (unlike the author of this chapter!) constitute a group not usually yet in senior positions, but with a radically different approach to digital technology and a hugely valuable and forward-looking perspective to offer. Only a democratic style of leadership will engage them fully, and only a visionary style will inspire them to contribute (DeVaney, 2015; Frith, 2017).

Note the importance here of using the visionary and democratic styles in tandem. One possible limitation of the democratic style is procrastination, so it is essential to keep things moving by reminding everyone of the goal, and motivating them to reach it. The Affiliative style is often required to get through the tough times during a project with team spirit intact. More detail on the power of the leadership styles is available in John Knights' work, particularly Chapter 8 of *Leading Beyond the Ego* (Knights, Grant and Young, 2018).

Transpersonal leadership approaches, particularly empathy and a democratic style, are key to engaging stakeholders who are considered 'hard to reach'. In the context of digital transformation, in particular, older groups of customers or clients may be excluded if their views are not considered during early stages of the design process.

Sometimes the best source of insight can be suppliers, or partners in enterprise. One company with a great record of innovation is the John Lewis Partnership from the UK. Although the specific word "partner" is used to refer to staff at John Lewis, the company operates in partnership with suppliers (despite the inevitable tensions and demands of the retail environment) as is clear from the supply chain efforts and innovations such as JLab, discussed in Case Study 3.

Coaching: getting the best from your team

One of the least observed and most valuable and positive styles of leadership is the Coaching style. This is never more the case than at a time of great change. Coaching leaders provide support for team members to develop and grow, using their talents to the full. It is a positive style because as well as making space for insights, it has a very positive impact on morale. The Kubler-Ross change curve (Kübler-Ross and Byock, 1969) describes the psychological journey through change. Coaching can help individuals cope with the stages of change they find most difficult.

The successful digital transformation of airline SAS was analysed and is a good example of using a coaching style (Bygstad, Aanby and Iden, 2017). This example, like most other successes, includes a significant level of employee engagement.

Case Study 3: John Lewis: Engaging partners to drive digital innovation

The John Lewis Partnership is an employee-owned company and leading retailer based in the UK. Leaders have developed a Partner Ideas programme (Beswick, Bishop and Geraghty, 2015) to involve the whole organisation in its innovation strategy. John Lewis Partnership has invited start-ups to participate in finding solutions through its JLab programme, accessing the ideas of digitally native innovators. A recent JLab prize winner provides a way for staff to know when a customer enters the store to pick up an order, through their smartphone signal, so the order is ready at the desk by the time they get there (Ghosh, 2015). John Lewis encourages its staff, or "partners" as they are called, to contribute, adding engagement and capturing front-line experience. It introduced "partner devices", tablets to allow staff to check stock levels and product details, through just such an idea. Sienne Velt, director of online product, describes the impact: "This means the partners were really invested in the outcomes" (Brown, 2017).

Customer focus: the power of empathy

Digital transformation means engaging people throughout the business, including customers. Especially customers. A transpersonal leader will always think beyond the organisation and put themselves in the shoes of all their stakeholders but especially their clients wherever possible, involving them in thinking of solutions and contributing to outcomes beneficial to all parties. This is not about using marketing personas to guide product development, nor is it an extension of customer service. Both have an important place, but customer focus goes way beyond this. Diversity at senior levels of an organisation helps avoid groupthink, and allows leaders to reflect the range of customer experiences. Core to the leadership skills is empathy, and it is this which allows an organisation to understand the needs of customers more closely.

Empathy is not the same as sympathy. Empathy is objective, whereas sympathy is sharing the emotions with someone. Empathy involves stepping into the shoes of another person, in this case the customer, and walking with them through their experience.

Leaders can create space for customer focus through coaching, encouraging employees to reflect on their own reactions to what is happening around them, and understand what it is like to be in a customer's shoes. For example, a commonly used proxy for a customer in the marketing strategy meeting is the "persona" which can be built from data. A good leader can coach a marketer to dig deeper into the customer experience and create real empathy through engagement. Ask customers, and you will find out what they really think of you! In fact, marketers who use a coaching style with their customers to find out their issues and their real need will be in an even better position to provide the right solution.

One bank realised something we customers have known for years, which is that the less we see or do with the bank, the better. But at their best they can come to the rescue, stand alongside us, and be on our side through life's adventures (Bloomberg, 2016; The Economist, 2018).

Creating a culture of innovation

Democratic and visionary leadership can lead to a culture of innovation. But it is the climate created by leaders that encourage organisations to perform

---

Case Study 4: DBS follows the customer

DBS is Singapore's largest bank, and on a growth curve thanks to new digital technology (The Economist, 2018). All banks are moving for digital advantage, so what clues can we find behind DBS success? "If you can digitally engage people, they tend to do more. That's the bare bones of our thesis", says CEO Mr Gupta. Focus on and involvement of customers lies at the heart of success (Bloomberg, 2016).

highly. Our behaviour is conditioned by our reactions, many of which are innate – fight or flight reactions to stress, for example. But creativity thrives in a company led by transpersonal leaders who are emotionally intelligent, self-aware, skilled in leadership styles, ethical in purpose and empathetic.

The climate set by the leadership of an organisation is translated, through staff behaviour and values, into a culture that can foster innovation and meet great challenges. The four culture parameters (Knights, Grant and Young, 2018) are based on the work of Charles Handy (Handy, 1993) and are described as Power, Structure, Support and Achievement. It is the last of these, achievement, that is the driver for digital transformation, with a heavy dose of support to prevent burnout or loss of focus. This culture needs to be shared with all stakeholders; the sense of purpose, urgency and consistency with values imbues successful projects, and a fine example of this is in the great survivor of the world of digital transformation, IBM.

Case Study 5: IBM culture of innovation standing the test of time

IBM prides itself, rightly, on its enduring culture built on strong values, as stated up front (https://www.ibm.com/ibm/values/us/):

Dedication to every client's success.

Innovation that matters – for our company and for the world.

Trust and personal responsibility in all relationships.

These values run through the expected behaviour of every so-called IBMer, and contribute to radical thinking and constant innovation (Lombardo, 2017). A company which has lasted over 100 years at the forefront of technology implementation and research, with many tactical switches and strategic moves when required to support their values, IBM remains on a strong and steady course that means managers all over the world still repeat that "nobody ever got fired for buying IBM" (IBMers will remind you that it was customers, not employees, who coined this much repeated phrase!).

Questions and actions for personal development

Digital transformation is a commercial imperative, touching every part of commerce, government, education, services and driven by the convenience, control and efficiency it offers every one of us. New digital entrants find it easier than ever to compete. To avoid becoming a gravestone rather than a monument on the road to the future, it is necessary to take action.

1. Establish the core purpose of the organisation, to act as a pivot during digital transformation
2. Create a vision – and visionary leadership – to inspire and maintain optimism

3. All aboard! Recognise the power of democratic (and affiliative) styles
4. Use empathy, and a deep and detailed customer focus, by letting clients be involved
5. Change the culture, and make digital transformation as a continuous process
6. Pursue transpersonal leadership: leaders must change themselves!

References

Beswick, C., Bishop, D. and Geraghty, J. (2015). *Building a Culture of Innovation.* London: Kogan Page.

Bloomberg, J. (2016). *How DBS Bank Became the Best Digital Bank in the World by Becoming Invisible.* [online] Forbes.com. Available at: https://www.forbes.com/sites/jasonbloomberg/2016/12/23/how-dbs-bank-became-the-best-digital-bank-in-the-world-by-becoming-invisible [Accessed 31 March 2021].

Brown, H. (2017). *What Can We Learn from John Lewis's Take on Innovation?* [online] Drapers. Available at: https://www.drapersonline.com/companies/john-lewis/what-can-we-learn-from-john-lewiss-take-on-innovation/7020695.article [Accessed 31 march 2021].

Bygstad, B., Aanby, H. and Iden, J. (2017). Leading Digital Transformation: The Scandinavian Way. *Lecture Notes in Business Information Processing,* pp. 1–14.

Collins, J. and Porras, J. (1998). *Built to Last.* London: Random House Business Books.

DeVaney, S.A. (2015) Understanding the Millennial Generation. *Journal of Financial Service Professionals,* 69, 11–14.

Downes, L. and Nunes, P. (2013). *Blockbuster Becomes a Casualty of Big Bang Disruption.* [online] Harvard Business Review. Available at: https://hbr.org/2013/11/blockbuster-becomes-a-casualty-of-big-bang-disruption [Accessed 31 March 2021].

e-Estonia. (2018). *e-Estonia — We Have Built a Digital Society and We Can Show You How.* [online] Available at: https://e-estonia.com/ [Accessed 31 March 2021].

The Economist. (2018). *How Digitisation Is Paying for DBS.* [online] Available at: https://www.economist.com/news/finance-and-economics/21738372-singapores-and-south-east-asias-biggest-bank-digital-leader-among [Accessed 31 March 2021].

Ehasoo, E. (2017). *Case Study: How Estonia Became the Global Digital Leader and What Businesses Can Learn from It.* [online] Digital Innovation. Available at: https://blog.rubiksdigital.com/how-estonia-became-the-global-digital-leader-83e1ff576f36 [Accessed 31 March 2021].

Elsevier.com. (2018). *Open Access Information for Journal Authors.* [online] Available at: https://www.elsevier.com/authors/open-access [Accessed 31 March 2021].

Frith, B. (2017). *Millennial Workers Prefer Transformational Leaders.* [online] Hrmagazine.co.uk. Available at: http://www.hrmagazine.co.uk/article-details/millennial-workers-prefer-transformational-leaders [Accessed 31 March 2021].

Ghosh, S. (2015). *Inside John Lewis' Innovation Battleground.* [online] Campaignlive.co.uk. Available at: https://www.campaignlive.co.uk/article/inside-john-lewis-innovation-battleground/1361389 [Accessed 31 March 2021].

Goleman, D., Boyatzis, R. and McKee, A. (2013). *Primal Leadership: Realizing the Power of Emotional Intelligence.* Boston: Harvard Business Review Press.

Greenstein, S. (2016). The Reference Wars: Encyclopaedia Britannica's decline and Encarta's emergence. *Strategic Management Journal*, 38(5), pp. 995–1017.

GSMA (2020). *The Mobile Economy 2020.* [online] Mobile Economy 2020. Available at: https://www.gsma.com/mobileeconomy/ [Accessed 31 March 2021].

Handy, C. (1993). *Understanding Organizations.* 4th ed. London: Penguin Books.

Hanna, N. (2016). *Mastering Digital Transformation.* Bingley: Emerald Group Publication, p. 112.

Heller, N. (2017). *Estonia, the Digital Republic.* [online] The New Yorker. Available at: https://www.newyorker.com/magazine/2017/12/18/estonia-the-digital-republic [Accessed 31 March 2021].

Jaffe, E. (2016). *How Estonia became a Global Model for e-government – Sidewalk Talk – Medium.* [online] Sidewalk Talk. Available at: https://medium.com/sidewalk-talk/how-estonia-became-a-global-model-for-e-government-c12e5002d818 [Accessed 31 March 2021].

Kim, W. and Mauborgne, R. (2005). *Blue Ocean Strategy.* Boston: Harvard Business Review Press.

Knights, J., Grant, D. and Young, G. (2018). *Leading Beyond the Ego: How to Become a Transpersonal Leader.* Oxford: Routledge.

Kübler-Ross, E. and Byock, I. (1969). *On Death and Dying.* New York: Scribner.

Lombardo, J. 2017. *IBM's Organizational Culture & Radical Thinking.* Panmore Institute. http://panmore.com/ibm-organizational-culture-radical-thinking, [Accessed March 31, 2021].

Mangelsdorf, M. (2011). *Lessons from Ken Olsen and Digital Equipment Corp..* [online] MIT Sloan Management Review. Available at: https://sloanreview.mit.edu/article/lessons-from-ken-olsen-and-digital-equipment-corp/ [Accessed 31 March 2021].

Marzouk, Z. (2017). *Estonia's Rise into a Digital Nation.* [online] IT PRO. Available at: http://www.itpro.co.uk/strategy/29868/estonias-rise-into-a-digital-nation [Accessed 31 March 2021].

Mui, C. (2012). *How Kodak Failed.* [online] Forbes.com. Available at: https://www.forbes.com/sites/chunkamui/2012/01/18/how-kodak-failed [Accessed 31 March 2021].

Sanburn, J. (2011). *5 Reasons Borders Went Out of Business (and What Will Take Its Place) | TIME.com.* [online] TIME.com. Available at: http://business.time.com/2011/07/19/5-reasons-borders-went-out-of-business-and-what-will-take-its-place/ [Accessed 31 March 2021].

Satell, G. (2014). *A Look Back At Why Blockbuster Really Failed And Why It Didn't Have To.* [online] Forbes.com. Available at: https://www.forbes.com/sites/gregsatell/2014/09/05/a-look-back-at-why-blockbuster-really-failed-and-why-it-didnt-have-to/ [Accessed 31 March 2021].

Shen, J. (2016). *e-Estonia: The Power and Potential of Digital Identity | Thomson Reuters.* [online] Thomson Reuters Innovation Blog. Available at: https://blogs.thomsonreuters.com/answerson/e-estonia-power-potential-digital-identity/ [Accessed 31 March 2021].

Shelley, P. (1817). *Ozymandias.* [online] Poetry Foundation. Available at: https://www.poetryfoundation.org/poems/46565/ozymandias [Accessed 31 March 2021].

Shoolin, J. (2010). Change Management – Recommendations for Successful Electronic Medical Records Implementation. *Applied Clinical Informatics*, 01(03), pp. 286–292.

Swaminathan, A. and Meffert, J. (2017). *Digital @ Scale*. Hoboken: John Wiley & Sons Ltd, p.37.

Townsend, M., Coleman-Lochner, L. and Soper, S. (2018). *Amazon Has Considered Buying Some Toys 'R' Us Stores*. [online] Bloomberg.com. Available at: https://www.bloomberg.com/news/articles/2018-03-19/amazon-is-said-to-have-mulled-acquiring-some-toys-r-us-stores [Accessed 31 March 2021].

Tucker, R. (2018). *Six Driving Forces Of Change That Will Shape 2018 And Beyond*. [online] Forbes.com. Available at: https://www.forbes.com/sites/robertbtucker/2018/01/10/six-driving-forces-of-change-that-will-shape-2018-and-beyond [Accessed 31 March 2021].

12 Managing stakeholders ethically – and beyond the ego

John Knights

Overview

Managing all stakeholders ethically and fairly requires us as individual leaders to operate beyond our own ego and to enable the organisation, its culture and its people to lead beyond their egos. That is a tall order indeed!

As we described in *Leading Beyond the Ego*, Chapter 15 (Knights, Grant and Young, 2018), part of which is duplicated in this chapter for convenience, managing one's ego and moving beyond it is a critical aspect of Transpersonal Leadership. In addition to each of us dealing with our own self-interest when in conflict with the needs of the organisation we work for, we must likewise ensure our organisation takes into consideration the needs of its stakeholders.

The first step is to determine who the organisation's stakeholders are and then to understand their needs and what we would like from them. In the same way as empathy is so important in building individual relationships, so the organisation needs to have empathy for its stakeholders. That does not mean we should agree with all their needs or always put them first; rather it means understanding their needs and the cause of those needs. Also we need to be clear about the outcomes we expect and consequences that may result. That way it is much more likely we can reach a relationship with our stakeholders that provides a win–win outcome.

This will be easier with some stakeholders than others, as we shall explain in this chapter.

Definitions

Ethical

'Ethical behaviour is acting in a way that is consistent with one's own principles and values which are characterised by honesty, fairness and equity in all interpersonal activities, be they personal or professional; and by respecting the dignity, diversity and rights of individuals and groups of people' (Knights, Grant and Young, 2018, Chapter 5). As discussed in Chapter 5, ethical behaviour is of a higher order than moral behaviour which is merely based on accepted rules of conduct of a group or society.

DOI: 10.4324/9781003150626-15

Ego

Ego is defined as that part of our self that is based on our self-image and only interested in our own personal benefit.

However, although we focused in that book on the negative aspects of the ego because they are the things we need to overcome as transpersonal leaders, there are also positive aspects of the ego which provide drive, intent, commitment and determination to one's purpose, vision and goals. They can be personified through our self-esteem and self-confidence.

Nevertheless, whether negative or positive, the ego is focused on the self. It is only when we go beyond our ego (related to Freud's 'super-ego') that we can focus on the greater good and look to the benefit of others rather than just ourselves.

The same is true for the ego of an organisation. Does the purpose of or vision for the organisation truly go beyond the interest of a few favoured stakeholders and work for the benefit of all?

Stakeholder

We define a stakeholder in this context as anyone (individuals, collectives, organisations or object) interested in, concerned with or affected by the role and/or performance of an organisation.

The list of stakeholders will vary widely for different organisations but usually includes employees, customers, suppliers and, whether acknowledged our not, the planet. Customers might specifically be patients, children, parents, and so on. Depending on the type of organisation it may include shareholders, investors, trustees, the community, freelancers or trade unions. In many organisations "management" would be considered a separate stakeholder because of their different contract with the organisation than other employees.

Is the Universe a stakeholder? A 100 years ago we humans would have been taxed to think of the planet Earth as a stakeholder, let alone the Universe. But how things change. Already the actions of governments has led to dangerous waste materials orbiting in near space. What happens as we inhabit the Moon and colonise Mars? One thing is for sure, we need to start thinking earlier and harder about the consequences of our actions when we take new initiatives or create new realities.

Stakeholder prioritisation?

A really good exercise is to ask individuals in an organisation who they think are their stakeholders based on the definition above. It is not usually too difficult to come up with a consensus, though 'senior management' may not like to be considered a separate group.

Although any organisation may have a unique set of stakeholders, most will be covered in the following list – purposefully here in alphabetical order to eliminate any sense of predetermined priority:

- Customers
- Community
- Employees
- Planet
- Senior Management Team
- Sponsors
- Suppliers
- Shareholders
- Universe

Customers are, in essence, whoever the service or product being produced by the organisation is being provided to. Depending on the type of organisation the word 'customer' may be replaced by patient, pupil, parent, and so on. Employees may include unions, collectives, teams and individuals. Stakeholders may include owners, controllers, investors, trustees, or partners.

Once the list has been agreed, ask each person to list the stakeholders in order of importance. It is likely that different groups, departments, teams and even individuals within groups will have a different order of priority. A conversation to ascertain why there are differences can be very enlightening. These differences might be because of the role of different parts of the organisation but even where this is logical and justifiable, everyone should have an understanding of the relative priorities for the organisation as a whole. Differences may be a result of a lack of understanding of the purpose or vision of the organisation, but can also be connected to unconscious bias.

The resulting insight of most of our clients is that the prioritisation changes according to context and circumstances. Also they find that the relationship with stakeholders is too complex to put in a simple importance or priority list. What is really important is to fully understand the value and importance of the relationship with each stakeholder and to be conscious of how prioritising one stakeholder can be harmful to the relationship with another. It is indeed itself a complex adaptive system.

Then there is the question of dealing with each stakeholder ethically. This requires us to be honest, fair and equitable, respecting their diversity and rights and behaving with dignity. However, being successful in stakeholder relationships also requires working towards win–win solutions that create sustainable relationships. This requires behaviours that demonstrate the ethical and 'beyond the ego' foundation to the relationships. It also requires emotional intelligence. In previous work (Knights, Grant and Young, 2018, Chapter 7), we identified and described 19 emotional intelligence capabilities. Most are important in an organisational relationship context but perhaps

Table 12.1 Behaviours related to emotional intelligence capabilities essential to organisational relationships

---

Transparency
Demonstrating an authentic openness

1. Do what we say we will do
2. Ready to acknowledge own mistakes or error of judgement
3. Our Actions reflect the values of the organisation
4. Honesty is always the best policy whatever the consequences

Empathy
We aim to understand our stakeholders although not necessarily agree with them

1. Listen attentively to what our stakeholders are saying
2. Demonstrates an awareness of how they are feeling
3. Accurately identify the underlying causes of our stakeholders' perspective
4. Express an understanding of their perspective

Conflict Management
Acknowledge feelings and views of all and then redirect the energy towards a shared ideal

1. Handle difficult people and tense situations with diplomacy and tact
2. Spots potential conflict, brings disagreements into the open and helps de-escalate
3. Encourages debate and open discussion
4. Orchestrates win–win solutions

---

the most important are Transparency, Empathy and Conflict Management. The specific behaviours related to these capabilities are shown in Table 12.1.

Following these specific granular behaviours underpinned by the ethical principles described, provides an excellent foundation for sustainable relations with all stakeholders.

The main thing to avoid and overcome is a win-lose mentality which in our experience is still rife within most organisations. This is a natural human default but also very short term as the advantage of one party will often change. Being reasonable and fair when things are in your favour will most often be reciprocated when the balance changes. However, if the other party does not respect this fairness then it is questionable whether they are a beneficial stakeholder for the organisation.

Working with different stakeholders ethically and beyond the ego

In this section of the chapter, we will look at how to handle each major category of stakeholder. This can only be a guide as every organisation will have their own specific context and situation. Every stakeholder relationship has a pendulum of power. As we have demonstrated with our approach to culture (Knights, Grant and Young, 2018, Chapter 10), the lower the power parameter, the greater the engagement of the people, and superior long-term performance will result. We demonstrate that for the organisation to thrive and be sustainable and perform to the highest level, every stakeholder needs to be integral to the purpose and treated in a way that is both ethical and beyond the ego.

Customers

"The customer is always right" may not always be true but it is good default position to hold. When dealing with a customer or client (or in different organisations, the patient, the pupil, the householder, the citizen, and so on) it is important to remember that they are why and how you receive the fuel (e.g. finances) for your organisation to survive and prosper. However, there are many organisations which clearly realise this yet continuously take advantage of their 'customers' – because they can: it may be that their clients have no alternative, it may be because there is a shortage of the services or products on offer, it may be because they have managed to negotiate a contract that is unfair. A typical example is where online organisations are very efficient at taking orders but have a slow purposefully cumbersome process for returns, refunds or handling customer complaints.

In a monopoly situation the real customer may be forgotten about altogether – see Case Study 1. In the short term, this attitude may not have

---

Case Study 1: Stakeholder priority (true and anonymous – under Chatham House Rules)

(Chatham House Rules: When a meeting, or part thereof, is held under the Chatham House Rules, participants are free to use the information received, but neither the identity nor the affiliation of the speaker(s), nor that of any other participant, may be revealed.)

Here is an extract from the interview of the Chairman of a large water utility that has a monopoly in a region of the UK):

INTERVIEWER: *Who is the key stakeholder for your organisation?*
CHAIRMAN: *Our client*
INTERVIEWER: *And who is your client?*
CHAIRMAN: *OFWAT, the regulator!*
INTERVIEWER: *And what about your customers?*
CHAIRMAN: *Who do you mean?*
INTERVIEWER: *The people and companies you sell your water and sewerage services to.*
CHAIRMAN: *Oh, we don't really consider them as customers, except some of the big companies we have to deal with. We don't have any interaction with them. The only organisation we need to satisfy is the regulator.*

consequences but eventually in this example, it could easily turn the voting public against privatised utilities.

To avoid this at all costs and at all levels, it is essential that the customer is considered an integral part of the purpose of the organisation, be it a school, charity, government or private business.

Community

A local community can be a stakeholder of an organisation in many ways. Its citizens become employees so are dependent on the success and sustainability of the organisation. The citizens can also be negatively affected by the operations of the organisation such as transport, effluent, noise and so on. It is important to engage with the community with a mindset of 'what you can do for the community' rather than keeping your distance or, worse, 'what you can get away with'. Apart from minimising the negative impact on the community, reach out to identify how you can help the vulnerable and those in need, including getting involved with local charities. If you inadvertently cause the community to react negatively to some action of your organisation, be humble, be transparent, go that extra step to demonstrate you are a good neighbour – as described in Case Study 2.

A growing number of companies include taking care of the community they operate in as part of their ethos. One of the most famous is the Indian conglomerate, Tata, who state in their Purpose that "at the Tata group we

---

Case Study 2: Working with the Community (true and anonymous)

The manufacture of GRP (Glass Reinforced Plastic) produces styrene as a vapour. There are strict health and safety controls for the levels allowed into the atmosphere in the UK but even below these levels the smell of exhaust fumes is noticeable and for sensitive people this can even affect the eyes.

A leading UK producer of sewage treatment plants started to use a more advanced and efficient process for manufacturing GRP which unfortunately produced more fumes than the old process, even though well within the legal limits. When the wind blew in a certain direction the people in some nearby homes could smell the styrene and a few had eye irritation.

Although the householders had no legal rights, the company immediate adjusted the manufacturing process and increased filtration as well as communicating their actions and intentions in detail to the community. The proactive attitude of the management led to the company being viewed by the community in a positive light.

A year later when the company put in for planning permission to expand its buildings, there were no objections. This was a win-win orchestrated by a transpersonal approach.

are committed to improving the quality of life of the communities we serve" (Tata, 2017). This ethos originated with their founder, Jamsetji Tata, when he established the company in Bombay (now Mumbai) in 1868. However, it is becoming increasingly more complex to maintain such a purpose as the organisation becomes more global. More and more organisations are taking their commitment to their communities and the planet more seriously, but still many others perceive their obligations to community and the planet as being covered by their corporate social responsibility marketing budget.

Employees

In many respects, employees (and their representatives where appropriate) are at the heart of the organisation with their values, behaviour and performance determining the sustainable success of the organisation. We know that productivity is maximised by the discretionary effort of the people in the organisation (Knights, 2019), and to achieve this they must be fully engaged and feel ownership. This requires transpersonal leadership in all its guises.

The one danger is that in some organisations the culture is such that the subconscious purpose is directed inward for the benefit of the employees rather than outward for the benefit of customers and the planet. This can occur where unions or other employee collaboratives are too influential and is seen often in the public sector and professions. Case Study 3 is a good example.

Planet (Earth)

If we go back just 100 years (a very short time in the history of even humans, let alone Earth) virtually no-one paid any attention to the potential impact

---

Case Study 3: Stakeholder priority (true and anonymous)

During an early session of a transpersonal leadership programme for the clinical leadership of a large hospital, we were discussing the importance of their stated vision which puts patients at the centre of everything. However, during the discussion about what this really meant for each individual in the room, it became apparent that really, the loyalty of a number of these leaders was to their colleagues. They felt an obligation to protect each other, as that was the culture they had been brought up with since they were students. While laudable in some ways, we asked how that put patients first. It manifested itself by showing that some operational processes were actually designed for the benefit of the doctors rather than the convenience and welfare of patients.

With this new insight, these very intelligent individuals, with basically noble intentions, realised how their subconscious group ego had undermined their prime role, and set about changing many procedures with the patient in mind.

of human behaviour on the environment, bio-diversity and climate. We only have to go back 50 years to the early 1970s when there was talk of returning to an ice-age rather than climate warming (though this was soon dispelled by increasing scientific evidence (Peterson, Connolley and Fleck, 2008). So, as we humans generally find it hard to change unless there is a crisis, it is not surprising that we have been slow to realise the impact that pollution and our overuse of the resources of land and the sea is having on our sensitive planet. In addition, it is difficult to justify the industrialised world asking the developing economies to make sacrifices when many parts of the former have been exploiting the land for 400 years or more, turning forests into fields or plantations, and mining natural resources.

So far, harming the Earth has only impacted a few of our lives. But that is set to change very rapidly over the next few decades and it requires solutions at a multinational level. However, to be Transpersonal in our leadership we need to be proactive in our approach to save our planet – for the greater good. That means for every action we take as leaders of an organisation, we must consider the impact of and consequences to our planet. Often it simply means bringing what is in our sub-conscious minds into the fully conscious, into the moment, and acting on it. It starts with our personal actions; for example do we maximise recycling, re-use and reduction of packaging in our private lives?

This is truly about caring – for everyone, for nature, for our beautiful planet.

Senior management team

Senior management may not see themselves as a separate stakeholder but in the vast majority of organisations they are. They have special privileges and they have the power to make decisions that impact other employees. In many large listed organisations they have become the most powerful stakeholder, even usurping the traditional primacy of the shareholders. Despite talk of organisations becoming flatter and software allowing distributed decision-making, the reality is that in the last 20 or so years organisation have become more centralised (when was the last time a local bank manager could make a unilateral decision about a mortgage application?). Despite the general un-popularity amongst other stakeholders of the situation in which CEO and Chair position are held by one person, diminishing the scrutiny of the Chief Executive or proper governance, it still remains very common.

A transpersonal leader would demand good governance and expect trans-parency with the board of directors, and distribute leadership and decision-making to those with the direct knowledge and expertise, under a climate of trust and a culture of achievement and support.

Sponsors

This is a stakeholder group that can take on many guises but generally they are providing something to the organisation in return for something else. For the sports team, it will be cash in return for advertising and brand association. For a charity, it will be cash and/or other commodities or assets, in return for being associated with a good cause – branding! Such sponsorship may be purely commercial or heartfelt.

Not so long ago, tobacco companies were major sponsors of sports teams. It only stopped when public opinion made such sponsorships undesirable. Who will be next? Oil companies? Betting companies?

A transpersonal organisation will ensure that sponsorship is consistent with its purpose and values and will study the consequences of the value of the sponsor to society and the planet rather than just its own short-term financial benefit.

Suppliers

Suppliers are an often forgotten stakeholder but amongst the most important. Without a reliable cost effective supply of products and services, an organisation is itself unstable and there are various consequences. At one extreme some companies develop a very close relationship with one supplier and rely on that one company for the delivery of a particular component or service. This can be catastrophic if something goes wrong with the supplier. At the other end of the spectrum, companies have no loyalty to their suppliers and just purchase on price.

The transpersonal leader will work towards a transparent win–win solution and trusting relationship where both the supplier and the organisation have a good level of comfort and work together for mutual success.

One of the least ethical company-supplier relationships which is harmful to society in general, is the insistence of many large companies to pay their small supplier on 90 day terms. In addition their accounts departments build bureaucratic systems that slow down payment even further. Even successful stable small companies then have to go to their bank for loans so they can pay their suppliers, employees and so on. Rather than the large organisation taking a paternal and community oriented philosophy that is fair, they take as much advantage of the little firm as they can. Everyone knows this, and know it is unfair, but in general politicians and senior executives, even the so-called ethical ones, turn a blind eye.

Shareholders (including owners, controllers, investors, trustees, partners)

For as long as I can remember, the shareholder has been at the core of the purpose of business, whether small private or large publicly quoted companies.

A typical purpose has been: 'The purpose of this organisation is to maximise returns for the shareholders'.

Fortunately, this is changing at least in word, if not always in spirit. Of course, shareholders are critical to any organisation. They are often, at least

---

Case Study 4: Supermarkets and dairy suppliers in the UK

This is an example of the common case where the large organisation take advantage of the small supplier, sometime with unexpected consequences. For years the price of milk in supermarkets has been reducing and only very large diaries have the economy of scale to meet the process needs of the major supermarkets. Many of smaller dairies that allow their cows to graze in fields much of the year have been going out of business to be replaced by fewer, larger mechanised diaries where the animals rarely if ever see a blue sky or green grass. Recently, and spurred by COVID, the small dairies that remain are again selling directly to the consumer and able to charge UK 60p a pint more than the retail price in the supermarket, and of course it is fresher. There is no way to know the long-term outcome, but this is case where supermarkets may lose out in the end just because they were able to squeeze and squeeze the little guy (or girl) to offer a lower price to the consumer on what is already a very low cost commodity product.

Next time you negotiate to reduce the price of your supplier, try to think what is reasonable. By all means ask your supplier to be open about their cost/price structure but don't screw them down as far as you can. Our human nature is generally that if we are treated fairly we are more likely to be flexible and strive to do a good job.

---

in the early stages, also the founders and senior executives in the organisation. And of course they are the providers of the capital, without which companies would be dependent on debt.

So my call goes out to shareholders to themselves be more Transpersonal. To measure their returns to some extent in terms of what the companies they are investing in is doing for the benefit of humanity and the planet. I am not against shareholders making profits per se, but I am against shareholders profiteering at the expense of others, often the consumer or employees.

How much pressure are shareholders putting on companies in various sectors to reduce packaging, to reduce the content of harmful foodstuffs, to reduce the likelihood of addiction, be it alcohol, gambling, opioids, or whatever? What pressure are they putting on reducing the use of fossil fuels either directly of indirectly? Yes, it is the role of government to pass appropriate laws but Transpersonal leaders should either avoid investing in companies who are not consistently progressing in a sustainable way for the benefit of humanity and the planet, or at best be proactive in insisting on change. This in turn will attract the appointment of transpersonal leaders to senior positions with all the benefits that brings.

Universe

The universe is an increasingly important stakeholder as we inhabit the Moon and visit Mars and beyond.

It is not long ago that even thinking of our Planet as a stakeholder would not have been considered. Things change quickly. Right now we have tons of debris flying around in the stratosphere and no-one is really taking responsibility to remove it. Over the last 60 years we have succumbed to a typical human default – of not thinking about the consequence of our actions until it is almost too late. Just imagine that the world powers, with the help of the United Nations, had thought about what happens to vehicles and equipment in space when they are needed no longer! Today, we would not have all that dangerous, potentially fatal debris floating around.

Various countries are making moves to take warfare into orbit as reported by the Secure World Foundation (Samson, 2021), an American think-tank. Space is becoming more important to our society. Barriers to access are dropping and many countries and private companies have satellite and space programmes. Already, virtually every person and organisation on the planet is a user of space data services in some form. To avoid future consequences, a global approach is needed now.

Balancing the needs of different stakeholders

An important issue for leaders is balancing the needs or one or more stakeholders against others. It is key to bring to full consciousness the purpose of the organisation together with what is fair. These decisions will often be subjective and based on a decision-making process involving intuition, instinct, insights and ethical philosophy as well as logic (Knights, Grant and Young, 2018, Chapter 16).

Of course, for important decisions where you cannot delegate or distribute the decision-making to the person most competent in your organisation, you will need input from a broad range of both interested and objective parties. In these instances we would recommend using the Visionary and Democratic Styles of leadership (see Chapter 14 for a description of how this works in the context of change; also Knights, Grant and Young, 2018, Chapter 8) and develop a touchstone from which you check that you are making a decision based on the right values and transpersonal qualities (see Knights, Grant and Young, 2018, Chapter 20).

Questions and actions for personal development

1. Who are the stakeholders in your organisation?
2. What is the priority of stakeholders today?
3. Think of examples where your organisation has the right kind of relationship with a stakeholder.

4. Think of examples where your organisation should change its relationship with a stakeholder, and how?
5. How should the order of priority change if you base your decisions on the purpose of the organisation?
6. How should this order of priority change from the perspective of a Transpersonal Leaders?
7. Note the difference between the answers of questions 5 and 6 and explain.
8. What actions will you be taking?

References

Knights, J., Grant, D., and Young, G. 2018. *Leading Beyond the Ego*. Oxford: Routledge.
Knights, J. 2019. The Transpersonal Leadership White Paper Series: The Relationship between Leadership and Productivity. *Routledge.com*. https://www.routledge.com/go/the-relationship-between-leadership-and-productivity, April 2, 2021.
Peterson, T., Connolley, W., and Fleck, J. 2008. The Myth of the 1970s Global Cooling Scientific Consensus. *Bulletin of the American Meteorological Society*, 89(9): 1325–1338.
Samson, V. 2021. Threats to Space Aren't Just Weapons. *Trendsresearch.org*. https://trendsresearch.org/insight/threats-to-space-arent-just-weapons/, April 2, 2021.
Tata Group. 2017. Values and Purpose | Tata group. *Tata.com*. https://www.tata.com/about-us/tata-values-purpose, April 2, 2021.

13 Leading through and beyond crises

Duncan Enright and Danielle Grant

There is no education like adversity.

Benjamin Disraeli

Overview

As we write, the world is still enduring the crisis of the COVID-19 pandemic. However, there are regular times when the world, or our country, or the organisation we work in, or the team we lead, experience difficult periods of turbulence, challenge and change. Our work with leaders has taught us lessons we share with you here about how to lead in a time of crisis, conscious of the impact on others as well as on ourselves.

First, we explore the requirement for leaders with the right temperament and mindset, and in particular the importance of combining rational, emotional and spiritual intelligence. Next, we look at the need for clear communication and purposeful instruction at the start of a crisis in particular, but also throughout a period of turbulence. Everyone needs to be reminded of the core purpose, and to keep their eyes on that throughout. We then review distributed decision making and the democratic style of leadership, as it is only through distributed and supported decision making that we can lead in a time of uncertainty and upheaval, though the leader must remain on top of the situation (and is, ultimately, answerable for decisions). Next, we explore further the need for calm in a crisis, finding leaders throughout an enterprise who are able to remain positive and optimistic. Leaders need to be aware of their decision-making processes and biases, as well as find resilience through relying on their ethical touchstone.

Empathy is required to help others through the situation, which is why transpersonal leaders are valuable and can offer a great deal at such moments. It is also important to look after yourself – leaders need to be resilient and that means also providing for their own needs.

Decision making needs to be crisp but flexible, based on the best evidence at the time but constantly scanning for new information, and admitting when decisions are wrong and need to be changed. Sources of reliable information

DOI: 10.4324/9781003150626-16

are therefore very important, and a dashboard of indicators can help steer a right course.

Finally, we look at an interesting body of evidence from the pandemic which suggests that countries with women as leaders seem to have fared far better — and we suggest why that might be the case.

Using rational, emotional and spiritual intelligence

To become a transpersonal leader, requires the individual to learn to balance their rational, emotional and spiritual intelligence — it is the 'sweet spot' where all three coincide that marks the space a Transpersonal Leader inhabits. As seen in this diagram, the development of Emotional Intelligence combined with pre-existing Rational Intelligence (IQ and personality preferences) enables the leader to initiate and support a performance-enhancing culture. Where Spiritual Intelligence coincides with Emotional Intelligence, a caring and sustainable environment results. Where Rational and Spiritual Intelligence overlap is the arena where ethics are situated (and we have all seen the dire financial consequences for businesses that failed to inhabit this ground) (Figure 13.1).

A crisis calls for clear heads. Those who are aware of the interaction between these three types of intelligence, can recognise them at play in themselves and others, and then put them to work to address situations as they arise, has the mindset and temperament to lead through turbulent times.

Clear communication is crucial

As a McKinsey & Company article stated in late March 2020: "What leaders need during a crisis is not a predefined response plan but behaviours and

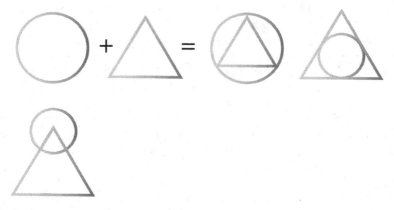

Figure 13.1 Rational, Emotional and Spiritual Intelligence

mindsets that will prevent them from overreacting to yesterday's developments and help them look ahead" (D'Auria & De Smet, 2020).

In other words, it is behaviours developed and the climate created by leaders that provide the solid platform for riding a storm. It is to these that a leader can call when a crisis situation emerges which calls for a commanding style of leadership to be adopted. Because of its overuse, the commanding style has rightly been seen as one to be adopted sparingly. How many of us have worked for bosses who just told us what to do, then were surprised when the results were a demotivated workforce and a one-dimensional strategy? However, when issuing clear communications, it is important that a leader can rely on trust and relationships to issue crisp instructions and a measured assessment of the situation.

If a fire breaks out, someone needs to stand up, don a high-viz jacket, and tell everyone which exits to use. It is the same in any crisis: clear instructions and swift action are required. Not only does this get people moving, but it also provides reassuring clarity in a time of confusion.

Communication does not, however, stop there. Leaders need to provide updates about how the situation is developing. This will inform decisions, provide continuing reassurance, and also remind everyone of the core purpose of the organisation or team. As any navigator will tell you, to steer a course in a gale, one needs to look up at the stars as well as down at the compass (see, for example, Vasshus & Stout Perry, 2017).

Trusting the team

Nobody has all the answers in a crisis. Work from McKinsey includes the astute observation that "during a crisis, leaders must relinquish the belief that a top-down response will engender stability" (D'Auria & De Smet, 2020). The next area to consider is the crucial importance of distributed leadership, which follows naturally from the transpersonal perspective. In a crisis, using diverse perspectives enables the unthinkable to be brought to the table, it avoids the perils of a single perspective (groupthink) and enables more effective solutions (Yim & Park, 2021). Underpinning distributed leadership is a democratic style of leadership. This requires a leader to be self-confident, transparent, a change catalyst and to offer inspirational leadership. It builds engagement, commitment and buy-in by getting ideas and input from team members and beyond. The outcome is not dependent on one person, or voting or consensus, but is clearly built on a wide range of opinions and advice. It is a facilitating underpinning approach to support distributed leadership, where a leader deliberately shares autonomy with a wide range of people throughout the organisation.

One way to devolve leadership in times of crisis is through the organisation of a network of teams that can tackle discrete responsibilities and are empowered to communicate with each other to create a complete picture before coming to decisions. It is essential that they are authorised to take decisions, without a need for approval from the top. You can see why it is important for the top leadership to keep everyone abreast of the latest situation, and remind them of the longer-term objectives which should not be lost along the way.

This same approach can enable a group to be assembled to look at preparedness for the post-crisis recovery. The heightened awareness of the transpersonal leader means they can be freed up from the constraints of dealing with the details of the immediate challenges of the crisis itself. Thus, the transpersonal leader can set the 'future-focused' group up with the autonomy to use their fully conscious decision-making processes to create a myriad of 'what if' options. From this diverse and open thinking comes an agility to take the best actions, as areas of clarity emerge.

To achieve this requires not just humility, leading beyond the ego, but also transparency, trust, and effective communication. A transpersonal leader has travelled a road where these attributes have been developed, alongside a honed appreciation of how to improve judgment and decision making.

A cool head in a crisis – making decisions

The transpersonal leader learns that we have five decision-making processes, of which only one is conscious. Harnessing and bringing into greater awareness the processes that lie below consciousness enables them to detach from their emotional reactions or unconscious biases. This gives them space to take a pause, stand back and allow the distributed responsibilities to be exercised by teams that they have assembled, using all these capacities (Figure 13.2).

Developing the ability to bring these processes into awareness leads to more thoughtful and insightful decisions. Our usual default decision-making process is an emotional one, which we rationalise to make it acceptable to others. The development of the transpersonal approach means working to understand and manage the emotional impulses that are the underlying driver of our decisions, then to mindfully identify what instinctive or other biases we may be subject to and thereby mitigate their effects. In a transpersonal decision, we seek to identify what information our intuition (accumulated past experience) is providing and seek conditions where insights arise (triggered by external stimuli).

In their 2020 McKinsey report the authors make this point:

> leaders with the right temperament and character are necessary during times of uncertainty. They stay curious and flexible but can still make the tough calls, even if that makes them unpopular. They gather differing perspectives and then make the decisions, with the best interests of the organization (not their careers) in mind, without needing a full consensus.
>
> (D'Auria & De Smet, 2020)

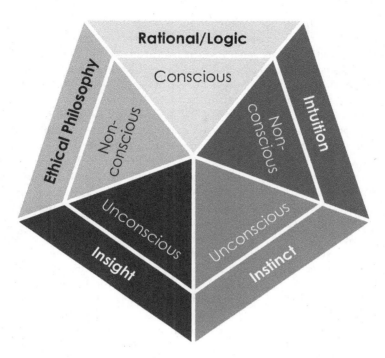

Figure 13.2 The five decision-making processes

Right temperament and character are needed, indeed, but these are not traits from birth or inherited characteristics like hair colour or physical build. While we may have preferences, our behaviour and demeanour are learned and can be developed through self-awareness and emotional intelligence.

For many people insights arise on a calm walk or in the shower or, more reliably in dialogue with an effective coach or mentor. The final area that the transpersonal leader brings into consciousness is their own ethical philosophy. Are they most concerned with the principle, the potential impact on people or the rules that need to be followed? One of these will be the most potent for each individual. In combination they enable a leader to create an ethical 'touchstone' that they can use to guide their decision-making processes despite all the uncertainties that abound (see Chapter 2 on Purpose for more on developing an ethical touchstone).

Checking thinking and decisions against one's own values and the transpersonal qualities is the foundation. This stepping back to gain clarity creates the sound mindset and behaviours that are indispensable in leading through and out the other side of any crisis. It allows boldness to be tempered with just enough prudence to maximise the upsides of the situation.

The transpersonal leader can use their own touchstone of values and self-determination to have the confidence in backing decisions and making any tough calls along the way. Such a leader will appreciate the level of thinking from empowered teams of experts. This shared understanding of how well-considered decisions are made results in both sides trusting the other. The environment of psychological safety and optimism which follows from these principles, becomes an underpinning enabler.

The result of this is that transpersonal leaders are able to make decisions that are grounded in strong self-awareness and emotional intelligence. It means they are able to access their sense of who they are (at their best) and know how they wish to make this manifest in the world. After all, the most revered world figures would be unknown if they had not determined to speak out and show the way forward in the world. This is the area of being transpersonal, where small anxieties and personal concerns or defensiveness are left behind and clarity is acquired.

We realised that leaders could be emotionally intelligent but also manipulative and self-serving. This phenomenon is driven by excessive egos that want power, prestige, recognition, and reward. While there is nothing wrong with these drivers, per se, when they are the dominant force in decisions, rather than the needs of the organisation and its stakeholders (including the community and the planet), then the problems arise. This is when the incidence of corporate scandals increases, as we have all seen in recent years. A transpersonal leader operates beyond their own ego and personal drivers and balances the needs of all the organisation's stakeholders. This means they are making decisions in full consciousness of their sense of purpose, ethics, and values.

This approach self-evidently enables a mindset that offers a long-term perspective. Because, if leaders are balancing the needs of stakeholders in a values-conscious way, they will not cut corners or put short term gains at the forefront of decisions. This meets the need to slow down and not overreact. It naturally gives them the tendency to look ahead at or beyond the immediate horizon. It also means that a leader whose ego is not in the driving seat will have the humility to appreciate that in a crisis (especially), they do not have all the answers and that leadership and decision-making needs to be distributed to those who have the best knowledge and information. Those who are driven by their ego, for example, will take centre stage and proclaim to have the answers, ignoring or side-lining the experts who could give a more realistic assessment of a situation, managing people's expectations. The leader who is transpersonal will value the expertise of those around and enable that to be disseminated to achieve the best outcome.

Empathy, resilience and self-care

Empathy has been shown time and again in our work as the emotional intelligence capability that bears most fruit when developed further. In a crisis it provides a valuable tool in a number of ways.

Empathy is of course not the same as sympathy, nor is it justifying another. Instead, it is the conscious effort to understand another's perspective, yet retain objectivity to reach an understanding together of the cause of that perspective. As the old saying goes, 'don't judge another until you have walked a mile in their shoes'.

A transpersonal leader knows how to read the room – even one on Zoom. They take account of body language, vocabulary, what goes unsaid as what is said. They ask good questions in a coaching style to bring out the best thinking of others. This way they can offer appropriate support to their team, and make plans based on a good understanding of others' emotions as well as good information.

As we have learned during the coronavirus pandemic, not everyone is affected in the same way during a crisis, and not everyone who has the same experience responds in the same way. Leaders need to provide different support to different people. Simply communicating empathy will go a long way to gaining the commitment of others to the work that needs to be done. It will also provide useful insights to help maintain and even strengthen bonds during a period of adversity. Gathering information to guide recovery is a key task, and an empathetic approach is more likely to elicit authentic responses from stakeholders on which to build recovery plans. Stress, anxiety and burnout are all more likely, so a leader will need to be ready to spend time listening skilfully to manage wellbeing and safeguard performance. Some research has found that there are potential pitfalls in a purely empathetic approach, including a tendency to catastrophise or inattention to the need for organisational recovery (König, Graf-Vlachy, Bundy & Little, 2020). Our experience is that, just by knowing this is a potential problem, it will not become one.

Finally, it is the duty of a leader to maintain their own resilience, and practice self-care, to make sure that they see out the crisis. This means pacing yourself, respecting your own needs, taking time away and being aware of your own feelings.

Tools for managing stress

Here we share a range of methods, though everyone will have their own way to manage stress and negative feelings.

Recognise what makes you stressed

Take time when you are calm and away from sources of stress to think about what makes you stressed. Could it be coping with a large workload, a personal issue, a difficult relationship at work or home, or a particular deadline or meeting. Knowing what makes you stressed is a first step to dealing with it. This takes (and the process builds) emotional self-awareness.

Take a break and get some perspective

Stepping away can help you see the issues more clearly, and gain a clear perspective of what is going on. Imagine you are looking on your situation as if you are a kindly but distant friend – what do you see?

Talk to friend (or a coach)

Confiding in someone you can trust is a major step towards acknowledging and dealing with stress. By talking through your situation, you can work through the triggers and discuss ideas for next steps. Even if the advice of the friend is not always relevant or appropriate, it will feel great to share the burden, and know that you are valued. This might be a trusted work colleague who knows the situation, or a friend from outside who can provide distance. Either way, a problem shared is a problem halved.

Manage your time and tasks

Lots of good tools exist to help manage time, and the basics of all of them are

- Defining overall goals – for life as well as work!
- Prioritising tasks to match them to your goals
- Making a list, and enjoying the feeling of ticking items off
- Differentiating between tasks: urgent and important, urgent but not important, important but not urgent, 'elephant' tasks (to be completed in chunks over time)
- Don't be afraid to share, delegate, delete and defer
- Build in breaks to take a breather!

Look for support and advice offered by your organisation

Many employers use Employee Assistance Programmes (EAPs) or have internal policies and systems to help with a wide range of concerns or issues. A business person described how his partner contacted EAP with worries about his state of mind when very stressed. Confidentially, and professionally, they were able to organise help and support, and they returned to work with a spring in their step and a suite of new tools to deal with situations – and hasn't looked back. Frequently such programmes also offer advice on home issues, from relocation to bereavement counselling.

Healthy body, healthy mind

Evidence is plentiful that physical exercise has wonderful effects on our mental state, and provides a great way to expel those negative stress chemicals from the body. A brisk walk, lungfuls of fresh air or a regular class or team session, all help to break down the patterns of thought as well as iron out the physical traces of stress. During a particularly stressful period at work, karate helped one of us throw away the negative feelings, and even imagine some retribution for stress triggers!

Build in wins

Stress reduces in the face of optimism and positivity. Set yourself little wins – a list to tick off is a good start. Having some wins is great for morale. Make one a project you can work on that fits your values, goals and skills – something you can believe in, and keep at it.

Write it down

A senior member of staff was in a stressful exchange with a client. They described how good it felt to write down exactly what was happening. They also kept a constantly updated 'letter' to the person causing the stress! This was NOT to send – never send correspondence when stressed, only do that when logic prevails. This helped collect their feelings, and get on top of their anxiety. It worked – the letter remained secure and private, but contains a clear account which helped them manage their feelings. Of course, if you are in a situation where you are feeling harassed or bullied, a diary provides evidence that may prove useful; more often though, writing things down creates an outlet, a private message to your future self for personal use only. Writing it out helps gain perspective, and reduces negative feelings.

Use awareness exercises and other calming techniques that work for you

This is sometimes called mindfulness. Search for apps that might help (examples include Calm, Headspace and Mequilibrium). Fitbit has a Relax mode with breathing exercises. Be you, experience the moment. Concentrating on breathing, or observing nature, or being aware of everyday events, can help to calm your mood and ready you for the next task. Here are some examples of simple exercises:

- Find a joke online or ask your active speaker for one. Tell Alexa you love her, and see what happens! Laugh out loud, even if the joke is terrible (it will be terrible). Laughing creates and relieves a stress response, leaving a good feeling; it breaks tension; it stimulates your organs; it stimulates blood flow. Even if you are simulating laughter, it does you good (and such ridiculousness can activate a real chuckle!) What's more, it may well cheer up those around you.
- Breathe in through your nose as deeply as you can, hold it for a second, then breathe out through your mouth. Repeat ten times.

Visualise breathing in goodness from the world, and expelling negativity. Doing this once a day has proven benefits for physical and mental wellbeing.

- Pop a picture you like on your desk – either people you care about, something that inspires you, or a place you love. Spend a minute silently appreciating it. Look at every detail, get lost in it. If you need to, replace it regularly.
- Focus on something in nature or the outside world – the view from your window for example. Marvel at the world around you, let all other thoughts disappear as you explore every aspect. Wonder and gratitude have been consistently linked with positive emotions (Brown & Wong, 2021).
- Find a new piece of music, perhaps a random selection on the radio or online. Allow yourself to become lost in its sound, notice how it makes you feel, focus on the ebb and flow of voices and instruments.

Go with the flow

'Flow' is also known as being 'in the zone', becoming lost in a task (often repetitive) – losing a sense of time and of self. Tasks which induce flow are often routine, and can lead to mental wellbeing and satisfaction. You will have experienced this in your life; think of when and capture that memory. Build time into your life to experience flow regularly. For one of us it is doing jigsaws or reading a good book. Others find it in playing music, dancing, playing sport or bird watching – even housework can bring flow. Hobbies and games are a good source of flow (Csikszentmihalyi, 2008).

Visualise then put your worries in perspective

Legendary fictional wizard Harry Potter's classmate Neville deals with his greatest fear, the bullying Professor Snape, by 'casting the Riddikulus spell' – visualising Snape in his grandmother's clothes, then laughing at his nemesis. Recognising what is making you stressed is an important step, but reducing that trigger to its true proportion, using laughter and satire if it helps, can get rid of some of those feelings of stress.

Remember what makes you, you

You are the only person like you out of 7 billion in the world today. Nobody like you has ever existed before; nobody like you will ever exist again. You are valuable, and have a unique set of skills, knowledge and competences. Remember why you do what you do – what you believe in. Build your self-confidence by building your picture of what makes you, YOU. Think of what makes you passionate, and focus on that as a way to stay motivated and remember why you do what you do.

Playfulness

A playful attitude, even at work, has been shown to reduce stress and increase productivity. Research has shown it can provide a positive distraction, assist coping efforts, build social support and foster optimism (Magnuson & Barnett, 2013). If possible, look for 'playful' ways to bond with co-workers (is there time for a game at lunchtime, or to share a joke with colleagues?) Some of the most productive workplaces build play into the day, such as offering regular leisure breaks or even holding creative play sessions when seeking solutions to problems. How about starting a meeting with a round of unusual news of the week? Look online for possible exercises and what others do to free their playful selves.

Serenity aphorisms

Many participants on courses run by LeaderShape (including those of all faiths and none!) find comfort in the prayer, first attributed to American theologian Reinhold Niebuhr: "God grant me the serenity to accept the things I cannot change, courage to change the things I can, and wisdom to know the difference". Others cite sayings that provide comfort or a little light humour, such as "I can't believe they are paying me for this s★★t!" or "The more I do, the more I experience. The more I experience, the more I learn. The more I learn, the better I can manage the daily stresses of life". "Remember, life is a marathon, not a sprint, so pace yourself". Or the old adage: "What doesn't kill you, makes you stronger". Find your own motto that gives you comfort, and stick it on a note on your desk. Better still, get someone you love to write and illustrate it for you.

Seeing stress as helpful

What if we saw stress as our human way of readying ourselves to face challenges? By changing our way of thinking about stress, we can experience positive and not negative results in terms of our health (McGonigal, 2015).

Helping others

Research shows that those who spend time helping family, friends neighbours and others experience none of the negative side effects of stress (McGonigal, 2015). This is borne out by the experience of many volunteers who have helped with the response to the pandemic.

Seeking evidence and solutions collaboratively

Crisis management calls for collaboration with stakeholders, partners, and even competitors. In the confusion and uncertainty following the UK exit from the European Union, many fierce rivals in industry and commerce have worked together directly, and through trade bodies, to influence resulting trading arrangements and to manage new complexities.

A transpersonal leader goes beyond the ego, and is a natural networker. By building relationships beyond the ego, team and organisation, and thinking broadly about shared interests, they can gather the best information in a crisis and act collectively for the common good.

In the search for a COVID-19 vaccine, governments, academic institutions such as the University of Oxford, pharmaceutical companies like Pfizer and AstraZeneca, clinical trial partners in many countries, their supply chain partners like immunotherapy firm BioNTech, manufacturers around the globe, funders from the charitable sector (including singer Dolly Parton) and regulators in every country, collaborated in the development and rollout of a range of highly sophisticated and effective vaccines in record time. In the UK, the National Health Service managed communications (to maximise take-up) and delivery to the adult population in record time. Such collaboration depends on strong relationships developed over years by leaders in the field, united by a common crisis as never before. Perhaps the most positive thing about managing a crisis is the way it brings people together.

Leadership lessons men can learn from women in a crisis

Here are some data and suggested reasons for women leaders to be not only viewed equal to men but, in some cases, be recognised for their superior natural leadership skills. In this way, we can begin to counter the built-in bias which has led to generations of lower representation of female leaders in organisations and governments across the globe. See also Chapter 7 for more on women as more effective leaders for the 21st century).

Since 2008, LeaderShape Global has been collating and analysing results from our Leadership and Emotional Intelligence Performance Accelerator (LEIPA®), 360° feedback tool (see Chapter 6). Over this period, we have identified key emotional intelligence attributes related to excellent leadership, where women score statistically significantly better than men.

Comparing the mean Difference Index scores of men against those of women showed that women fared better in 18 of the 19 Capabilities as shown in Figure 13.3. Bars above the axis show a positive difference of up to 0.2 for women, whereas the bar below the axis shows the one capability where men are stronger. Darker shaded bars are those which are statistically significant. It is striking to see how in this quite large dataset women perform more strongly than men.

The one Emotional Intelligence (EI) Capability where men score better is Self-confidence, though the difference is not statistically significant. The key EI Capabilities where women score significantly better include Empathy, Service Orientation and Developing Others; but also Emotional Self

Awareness, Change Catalyst, Conflict Management, Team work and Collaboration and Inspirational Leadership.

In EI terms, the male strengths cluster in the areas categorised under Self-awareness and Self-management, those of women under Social awareness and Relationship management, demonstrating that on average women tend to be better at dealing with others.

What is it about these capabilities that correlate to women leading more effectively through the crisis? What does this tell us about our need to enable more women leaders to come to the fore?

It is interesting to consider the data around the death rates from COVID-19 in female-led countries during the current coronavirus crisis. In figures from late March 2021, this showed countries led by women had lower numbers of deaths per million of population than those led be men. Table 13.1 shows some interesting comparisons: UK, France and Italy all have roughly double the rate of Germany, the only one of the four largest Western European countries with a female leader. Female-led Serbia has a rate less than a half of its male-led neighbour Croatia. Even in Oceania we see Australia led by a man with rates running much higher than New Zealand led by Jacinda

Table 13.1 Deaths from COVID-19 per 1M population (25/3/21) by country (Worldometers.info)

Country	Leader	Male/female	Deaths from COVID-19 per 1M population (25 March 2021)
Iceland	Katrin Jakobsdottir	Female	85
Norway	Erna Solberg	Female	120
Finland	Sanna Marin	Female	147
Denmark	Mette Frederiksen	Female	414
Germany	Angela Merkel	Female	904
New Zealand	Jacinda Ardern	Female	5
Bangladesh	Sheikh Hasina	Female	53
Barbados	Mia Mottley	Female	139
Serbia	Ana Brnabic	Female	583
Sweden	Stefan Lofven	Male	1318
Netherlands	Mark Rutte	Male	955
France	Emmanuel Macron	Male	1425
Italy	Mario Draghi	Male	1761
UK	Boris Johnson	Male	1855
USA	Donald Trump/Joe Biden	Male	1680
China	Xi Jinping	Male	63
Russia	Vladimir Putin	Male	662
Australia	Scott Morrison	Male	35
India	Narendra Modi	Male	116
Jamaica	Andrew Holness	Male	184
Croatia	Andrej Plenkovic	Male	1429

Ardern. Of the Nordic countries only Sweden has a man as leader, and also has the highest rate by a large margin.

Closer examination shows that there may be many factors at work here. Cultural issues may encourage both progressive social policies and gender-representation policies which coincide in countries, but it could be the former not the latter which leads to better public health management of the pandemic. Geographical issues lead Caribbean countries and New Zealand, for example, to be able to quarantine more effectively. Health data is not collected on exactly the same basis across the world, so this might also provide some problems when interpreting the results (Windsor et al., 2020). However, there is certainly some evidence of a difference, which has led to examination of leadership styles and traits of women. What do the actions of these women leaders tell us about the nature and value of female leadership?

In the response to the pandemic, women leaders have displayed key attributes including the following (Wittenberg-Cox, 2020):

Candour: Angela Merkel was bold with the truth from the start (no denials from her), that this was a very serious outbreak and could develop to have a massive impact on the German population and economy. Testing and tracing were accepted and stages of disbelief and non-compliance were minimised. Candour correlates directly to the emotional intelligence capability of transparency in Figure 13.3.

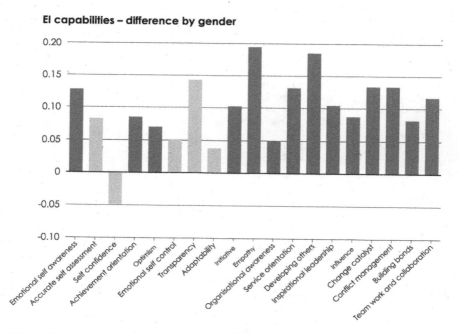

Figure 13.3 EI capabilities – differences between women and men (darker shaded bars show statistically significant differences)

Decisiveness: Tsai Ing-wen, President of Taiwan, acted rapidly and decisively at the first indications of this new illness, implementing 124 measures immediately that avoided a lockdown or explosion of cases. Taiwan is now at the forefront of sending masks to other more adversely affected countries. These actions resonate with the attributes of Change Catalyst and Achievement Orientation. Jacinda Ardern, the New Zealand Prime Minister, also executed a rapid response that was effective in locking down and explaining the reasons for her decision for the immediate and decisive response. Here, her words and example not only resonate with those attributes mentioned above of Tsai Ing-wen, but she also showed Inspirational Leadership and Empathy for her fellow citizens. See Chapter 19 for further reflections on her leadership qualities.

Technology: Sanna Marin (the youngest leader of all) and Katrín Jakobsdóttir, of Finland and Iceland respectively, both embraced new technology. Iceland has driven testing on a scale beyond other countries to create a platform to stop the spread and track the disease to avoid lockdown, shutting schools and other impacts. In Finland, social media influencers have been harnessed to spread fact-based information, recognising not everyone follows traditional news channels. These two leaders demonstrate not only the previously mentioned attributes, but also Service Orientation and Developing Others. In service of their countries, they pushed testing and media boundaries. Thereby they created a drive to develop the skills of those in the community and on social media to address the needs of the country in a new way.

Empathy: Erna Solberg of Norway reached out with empathy and concern to the children of her country, inviting them to ask questions and speak to her directly on television, responding directly to their questions and assuaging their fears.

These real-life examples of empathy, transparency, embracing change, and inspirational leadership throws into stark relief the actions of some of the male leaders of other nations, where arrogance, blaming others, and overweening self-confidence have resulted in a period of denial which, in turn, resulted in less decisive action being taken. Perhaps they thought they would have looked weak or frightened to respond as women leaders did? This is a perennial challenge for leaders, especially those driven by their ego and therefore susceptible to popularity polls and 'optics' (and, as we can see, these are more frequently men).

What are the lessons from women leaders? The following findings reflect recent work (Chamorro-Premuzic & Gallop, 2020) on lessons men can learn from women.

Play to your strengths. Empathy can enable you to take information on board, be transparent and through that bolster achievement, enabling making the right decisive calls.

Know your weaknesses. Knowing when you don't know, rather than feeling you have to have all the answers, is crucial. Then you can take on board advice from a variety of experts and adapt to changing data without any sense of loss of (false) authority.

Motivate and inspire. Women lead best through offering a route to transformation. They align people with purpose and meaning rather than reward and threat. When people feel engaged and that they are contributing, they give more discretionary effort and are more productive (Knights, 2019). Women's territory of hearts and souls, as well as minds, are the key to achievement, as beliefs drive behaviours.

Unlock potential. Women's demonstrable strengths (from Figure 13.3) in developing others and having a service orientation, translates into unlocking the potential of the whole team and workforce, rather than focussing energies on self-aggrandisement.

Empathise. Chamorro-Premuzic and Gallop (2020) say: "twenty-first century leadership demands that leaders establish an emotional connection with their followers". Despite any future changes from automation and AI, so long as humans are involved, they need appreciation, recognition and understanding, especially if they are to embrace rather than resist the introduction of new technology. All of these areas of empathy come more naturally to women than men.

Be a talent agent. Women are more likely to invest in developing, coaching and promoting their employees. They are also more likely to hire more diverse teams and those who may be more skilled than they are themselves. All of these factors create a development and growth environment, leading to more success, and high performing teams.

Be humble. The lower self-confidence levels shown in our surveys show up as greater humility. This attribute, when combined with a growth mindset, allows women to really learn from experience and apply the learning in the future. However, it is important that women develop a greater inner self-assurance, at least partly by acknowledging the contribution they can make as leaders.

And what is the key lesson for men? Value the attributes of women leaders and see them as the strengths they are. Adopt those capabilities where you have further development potential and harness (hire more!) women leaders to bring more of these strengths into being in the workplaces and hallways of power of tomorrow.

Questions and actions for personal development

1. What preparations did your organisation make for a crisis, and how did leaders respond at the start of the pandemic? What does that tell you about the culture?
2. Think of the signs that a crisis might be coming. What information sources can you use?
3. List the advantages of distributed decision making and leadership in a crisis.
4. Why is diversity in a leadership group important in a crisis situation?
5. Which are the key emotional intelligence capabilities that might mean women are better at leading in a crisis? How can men learn to lead in these ways?

References

Brown, J., & Wong, J. 2021. How Gratitude Changes You and Your Brain. *Greater Good Magazine*. https://greatergood.berkeley.edu/article/item/how_gratitude_changes_you_and_your_brain, March 25, 2021.

Chamorro-Premuzic, T., & Gallop, C. 2020. 7 Leadership Lessons Men Can Learn from Women. *Harvard Business Review*. https://hbr.org/2020/04/7-leadership-lessons-men-can-learn-from-women, March 25, 2021.

Csikszentmihalyi, M. 2008. *Flow*. New York: Harper and Row.

D'Auria, G., & De Smet, A. 2020. Leadership in a Crisis: Responding to the Coronavirus Outbreak and Future Challenges. *www.mckinsey.com*. https://www.mckinsey.com/-business-functions/organization/our-insights/leadership-in-a-crisis-responding-to-the-coronavirus-outbreak-and-future-challenges, accessed March 23, 2021.

Knights, J. 2019. How to Achieve Productivity Improvement through Transformational Leadership. *Routledge.com*. https://www.routledge.com/blog/article/-productivity-improvement-through-transformational-leadership, March 25, 2021.

König, A., Graf-Vlachy, L., Bundy, J., & Little, L. 2020. A Blessing and a Curse: How CEOs' Trait Empathy Affects Their Management of Organizational Crises. *Academy of Management Review*, 45(1): 130–153.

Magnuson, C., & Barnett, L. 2013. The Playful Advantage: How Playfulness Enhances Coping with Stress. *Leisure Sciences*, 35(2): 129–144.

McGonigal, K. 2015. *The Upside of Stress*. London: Ebury.

Vasshus, T., & Stout Perry, G. 2017. Navigating the Storm - Lessons from an Old Sea Captain. *Corporater.com*. https://corporater.com/en/navigating-the-storm-lessons-from-an-old-sea-captain/, accessed March 24, 2021.

Windsor, L., Yannitell Reinhardt, G., Windsor, A., Ostergard, R., Allen, S., & Burns, C. et al. 2020. Gender in the Time of COVID-19: Evaluating National Leadership and COVID-19 Fatalities. *PLOS ONE*, 15(12): e0244531.

Wittenberg-Cox, A. 2020. What Do Countries With The Best Coronavirus Responses Have In Common? Women Leaders. *Forbes*. https://www.forbes.com/sites/avivahwittenbergcox/2020/04/13/what-do-countries-with-the-best-coronavirus-reponses-have-in-common-women-leaders/, March 25, 2021.

Yim, M., & Park, H. 2021. The Effects of Corporate Elitism and Groupthink on Organizational Empathy in Crisis Situations. *Public Relations Review*, 47(1): 101985.

Part 3

Transpersonal leadership in action

Duncan Enright

> Remember that it is the actions, and not the commission, that make the officer, and that there is more expected from him, than the title.
> George Washington, Thursday January 8th, 1756

Overview

Leaders operate in every part of the world, at every level in organisations, and in every sector of society, where action is required. Here, we look at transpersonal leadership in action around the world and observe its impact in various spheres of human activity, including politics, remote leadership, human resources (where we provide a manual for the HR professional to apply and promote transpersonal leadership) and in the wider economy. Also included is a perspective on transpersonal leadership comparing it to the ancient ideas that still shape Eastern thought – Confucianism; and a description of implementing transpersonal leadership development in India.

Navigating the chapters in this section

We achieve more together than alone, and we have more in common that unites us than divides us. Wherever action is required, leaders emerge to shape collective effort and find common cause. This section of the book offers a range of perspectives from different viewpoints. The result is an appreciation of transpersonal leadership and its potential to generate energy and activity for good around the world.

Chapters 14–16 build on and take further work which was previously part of the Transpersonal Leadership White Paper Series (LeaderShape Global Ltd., 2019). My work on political leadership starts from the viewpoint that no politician gets everything right, and none are paragons of virtue in every circumstance. Quite apart from the human limits of capability, behaviour and capacity, our political leaders are challenged by events, confronted by competing interests, and often faced with insoluble problems with only partial information. However, by sharing stories of successful and ethical actions, my aim has been to define some traits and behaviours that are desirable in a political leader, and point out some signs that they are on the right path. For example, those that take time and pay attention to developing new leaders to succeed them are worthy of note.

DOI: 10.4324/9781003150626-17

Around the world, as explored in Chapter 9, the ways people describe and approach leadership differ, but the principles don't change. Pavan Bakshi shows in Chapter 15 how transpersonal leadership development can make a significant contribution in India, while Maiqi Ma in Chapter 16 shares learning about East Asian philosophy, and finds remarkable similarities and insights. A growing trend worldwide is towards remote working with teams located outside an office and even around the globe. Greg Young and I apply our thinking to the challenges and opportunities of remote leadership in Chapter 17.

How should a human resources professional develop the ideas of transpersonal leadership in their organisation, and in their own practice? Robert Jarvis in Chapter 18 takes the model developed by the Chartered Institute of Personnel and Development in London and relates it to the concepts of transpersonal leadership, with examples. This is then the basis for a 'manual' or guidebook for those working in HR. Finally, from the perspective of a leader in a large corporation at the heart of the global economy, Otti Vogt challenges us in Chapter 19 to reimagine capitalism to care for the world, to make joy not power our lodestar and to integrate the transpersonal beyond just leadership but into the culture and fabric of our organisations.

How to use this section

If you are reading about transpersonal leadership for the first time, this section answers the question "how do transpersonal leaders act in practice?" Through the stories here, you will begin to spot your own examples – so please share them with the authors. Examples of good practice exist all around us.

If you are a confident and experienced leader, the whole section offers a call to action through looking at the acts of others. You can write your own story about when you acted for positive change or in defence of important values. You can also reflect on ways to improve, where you have struggled to live out your core purpose. International leaders will find the chapters from India and East Asia particularly useful. If you are responsible for the development of others, Chapter 19 gives you a checklist or cookbook of ideas to deploy. Stories of action can give coaches and trainers a way to inspire clients to reflect or act differently. Are any of the examples or ideas here analogies clients would recognise, or can you draw parallels with their situation? We hope so.

This section gives those on the transpersonal leadership journey some stories from others who have passed that way, albeit in different vehicles and perhaps looking at things from different angles. Travel journals are not much use as route maps, but they offer insights a map never can, and flavour to whet our palates for travel and action. And so, to action; rise, and travel hopefully!

Reference

LeaderShape Global Ltd. 2019. LeaderShape – The Transpersonal Leadership White Paper series. *Leadershapeglobal.com*. https://www.leadershapeglobal.com/white-papers, February 9, 2021.

14 Politics beyond the ego

Ethical political leadership for the 21st century

Duncan Enright

"quanto superiores simus, tanto nos geramus summissius" (The higher we are placed, the more humbly we should walk)

Marcus Tullius Cicero

Overview

A Transpersonal Leader operates beyond the ego, generating followers, walking alongside them on a journey they would not otherwise embark upon, and develops the leaders of the future. Leaders need vision of a brighter future. They need to be able to communicate that vision and inspire others to join them in building that future – including, for politicians and leaders of democratic organisations such as co-operatives, winning electoral support. They take account of the many different stakeholders, maintaining a strong ethical framework for decisions and behaviour, creating a climate in which everyone can succeed and grow and promoting a culture of respect, equality and liberating talent, harnessing diversity through inclusion.

Through focussing on the needs of the people they serve, employing and developing empathy in themselves and others, they may not always meet success but they will always offer positive, ethical, effective government. Many inspiring leaders fail to recognise the need to grow new leaders, and their vision is lost. It is essential therefore that they need to inspire and work actively to develop others, to take on the leadership role when they have moved on.

Importantly, political leaders need to adhere to a strong ethical core – to hold values close and remain true to them, make them explicit and invite others to share them and measure decisions against these values. This combination of highly skilled leadership, empathy and emotional intelligence, focus on the needs of others and a firm ethical base is called "Transpersonal Leadership".

Transpersonal leaders are needed more than ever in this time of great change and challenge, not least to the future of our planet. Every political leader can learn to lead beyond the ego, in the best interests of good

DOI: 10.4324/9781003150626-18

government, unlocking the power of democracy, facing the future with confidence and building a world in which everyone can hope to prosper.

Introduction

The great Roman orator, writer, advocate and politician Cicero was one of the first to articulate the principles of politics as we know them today. He described the universality of a law based on nature, including human nature – an inextinguishable and inalienable set of principles that match reason with nature and transcends identity to bind all human beings together. He also described the notion of natural equality, based not on opinion, argument or reason but on the nature of humanity: we are all born for justice, we all possess reason and capacity for experience, we all understand the difference between good and bad. Cicero goes on to describe the State as a natural progression from the human need for social interaction. And of course, such States need conscious "government" – states belong to the people, are created by them to meet their needs, and exist for the common good. The term 'Commonwealth' is coined to encapsulate such a concept (Cicero, 1877). Few governments or politicians would deny these fundamental elements and goals of government.

Our world is governed by institutions, parliaments and senates, all different in the way they work.

The concept of 'liberal democracy' is the system by which most of the Western World has been governed for much of the last century. ('Liberal' is a term which, when applied to politics, is interpreted differently in the USA than Europe, including the UK. Here we are using the European definition of "a form of government in which representative democracy operates under the principles of liberalism, i.e. protecting the rights of the individual, which are generally enshrined in law". Conservatism in the USA commonly refers to a combination of economic 'liberalism' and 'libertarianism', and social conservatism. Its political philosophy advocates only minimal state intervention in the lives of citizens, while promoting more traditional values on social issues.) Liberal democracy is a system under which universal suffrage is used to elect our leaders, who are constrained to respect individual rights and the rights of minorities, and are subject to the rule of law and other democratic checks and balances. This system has various advantages over other forms of government; one is the tendency to encourage the emergence of leaders who have the wider public interest at heart, and who in any case are constrained to exercise power in the public interest. However, this chapter will not differentiate by the nature, form, mode of election or statutory powers of government. Instead it will look at a common feature of them all – they are populated and led by politicians, who are inspired to serve in the work of government, chosen from and by other citizens by means of election or other method of selection, and in whose hands responsibility is placed for the wider good. These politicians are also human, fallible, sometimes inspired, exposed, accountable, and scrutinised.

Politicians are all leaders. They are chosen to be so. The parish councillor in a voluntary and part-time post representing their neighbours, every bit as much as the President of a large country or multinational parliament, has the same responsibility to govern, with consent, on behalf of the people they serve. Alongside their colleagues, they should provide a sense of purpose and destiny for their community. They should play a part in setting the climate and culture of their society. They should work with others, often in a political party, to argue for their values to win through in government. Theirs is not just to keep a steady state, but to pursue a vision of a better world, or at least their bit of it. Politicians should offer vision, inspiration, and take people to a better place they wouldn't otherwise have reached.

It is often said that "all political lives end in failure" (Powell, 1977). It is less noted that by no means all politicians experience success! It is of no value to merely reflect on the career of politicians to seek out more successful ones, and think that success alone is a measure of excellence in political leadership. A lucky politician may never experience the sort of world events and challenges by which less lucky but more talented leaders are defeated. No political leader can claim every action of theirs is virtuous and successful, just as none are entirely without merit. The traits and leadership skills in politics can be derived from the purpose of politics, observed in specific actions and words, and found in the stated preference of the people who put them in a position of power and on whose behalf they serve.

Politics beyond the individual

No successful government can carry on without a sense of direction. The complex machinery of government requires political leaders not only to have a vision, but to be skilled in leading with a visionary style. That means not only having an inspiring vision, but leading people towards a shared vision that everyone (or at least a working majority) has bought into and owns. A visionary style can be highly positive, and can offer clear direction. It requires self-confidence (and self-awareness), transparency and strong relationship management.

In research conducted in 2015, citizens in Canada were asked what they valued in political leaders. The top answers, "Think about what's right for the next generation" and "Understand different parts of the world" indicate a high value placed on visionary leadership. These results are matched by those held by citizens around the world.

The vision of one person, however, is not enough to manage the broad sweep of affairs of state; nor does it match our view of democracy, governing in the interests of all the people. Instead what is required is a democratic style of leadership to support it.

To be clear, when referring to a 'democratic style' of leadership, this does not mean the process of fighting and winning elections through one person, one vote. Nor does it indicate a preference or infer any inherent skills or advantages for parties and groups that describe themselves as 'democratic' (e.g. The Democrats in the USA are no more likely, as a result of their political position, to show this trait than The Republicans!) The democratic style of leadership, in this context, is one that builds engagement and buy-in, through encouraging input and ideas from others. No politician operates in isolation. Political leaders must energise a team of public servants, coordinate a team of ministers within the government, maintain support from a political party, motivate corporate and community organisations, and encourage great thoughts and insights from wider society.

John Knights describes the role leaders play in creating a performance-enhancing culture (Knights, Grant and Young, 2018, Chapter 10). In every situation and organisation we have studied, there has been an appetite to move away from cultures based on power, with its top-down emphasis, and to reduce structures that restrict performance and innovation, and instead promote support-based and achievement-based cultures, getting the best from everyone and enhancing the performance of all. An achievement-based culture is promoted by visionary and democratic styles of leadership.

That combination of visionary and democratic styles of leadership are essential to good government. Signs that this is the case are stable and positive relationships between senior government officials and politicians, attention paid to a wide range of views when formulating policy, clarity of vision and steadfast purpose, and a willingness to engage across political divides and interest groups. Signs that something is wrong include a fast turnover of disgruntled colleagues, summary dismissal of senior leaders, dismissal of contrary views out of hand, muddled messages about direction and purpose, and capture of the agenda by a small number of interest groups. Contrast the turnover of 92% in the Trump White House, compared to Obama, Bush and Clinton administrations with under 75%. Cabinet members fared even less well, with 14 losing their positions in four years compared to three under Obama and only two under George W. Bush.

The democratic style of leadership is potent when working with specialists and high-knowledge colleagues. The commitment generated among such colleagues is essential to good government. If a politician thinks they have all the answers, that is a certain sign that they do not. In a complex world where delivery depends on the expertise of others, a leader using visionary and democratic styles skilfully will maximise the information on which decisions are made, and attract people committed to a successful outcome. It is not about abdicating responsibility, but it involves listening skills and skilful relationship management.

Politics beyond the faction

Ensuring the quality of those we choose to run our government was a prime consideration for the Founding Fathers of the United States. In The Federalist Papers (No. 10) James Madison wrote that government should be delegated to a body of chosen citizens "whose wisdom may best discern the true interest of their country and whose patriotism and love of justice will be least likely to sacrifice it to temporary or partial considerations" (Madison, Hamilton and Jay, 1788).

He also noted "men of factious tempers, of local prejudices, board of sinister designs" might capture the suffrage of the people by "intrigue, corruption, or other means" and then "betray the interests of the people".

In George Washington's Farewell Address of 1796, written with the help of Alexander Hamilton and James Madison, Washington reiterates the concerns about placing faction or party over the government of all people:

> The alternate domination of one faction over another, sharpened by the spirit of revenge, natural to party dissension, which in different ages and countries has perpetrated the most horrid enormities, is itself a frightful despotism. But this leads at length to a more formal and permanent despotism. The disorders and miseries which result gradually incline the minds of men to seek security and repose in the absolute power of an individual; and sooner or later the chief of some prevailing faction, more able or more fortunate than his competitors, turns this disposition to the purposes of his own elevation, on the ruins of public liberty.

The remedy for this situation was envisaged by those founding fathers of the United States to be:

> the employment of careful and deliberative democracy, adherence to the rule of law protecting the rights of the individual (including, perhaps most particularly, those of minorities and in positions of weakness), and constitutional checks and balances to curb absolute power by Federal Government over the States, or the Executive arm over the Legislative or Judicial arms of Government.

These and other matters relating to the principles of democracy are explored in fascinating detail by A C Grayling in his new book The Good State (Grayling, 2020).

John Knights discusses the importance of a change within the leader to match the change they wish to see, transcending personal interests in the pursuit of the best for all stakeholders. Plentiful evidence exists that this form of leadership — ethical, in service to others, mindful of diverse interests and promoting a high-performance culture — is a hallmark of the most successful leaders, organisations and societies. In our world challenged by pandemic, climate and other existential challenges, transpersonal leadership has never been more important.

In elections, therefore, one question voters may ask is which of these candidates is most likely not only to represent me but to represent the whole people? I may be tempted to vote for a person or party who I believe strongly represents my views. However, if they overstep checks and balances, do not have an ethical approach to governing, and don't show intent or willingness to look beyond factional interests, the next such political leader from another faction may use the same approach to act counter to my interests, citing my choice as precedent for their actions.

It is only by choosing to elect those who can best unite the country, or at least attempt to address issues raised by people across the spectrum of opinion, that democracy can be preserved and good government and subsequent success be ensured.

Politics beyond self: for a better society and world

Time after time, studies show that truly effective leaders of high-performing organisations know who they are, and know what they want to achieve, hold ethical values and live them out in their work. This is no mean feat – self-awareness is a foundation stone of emotional intelligence, and provides a basis for personal conscience and self-determination. Without it an individual may lack drive, motivation, empathy and many other essential leadership skills.

But without accessing a higher level of awareness, a leader may make decisions for their own benefit rather than the wider interests of others. For a leader of a country this has profound consequences and can lead to autocratic rule, self-interested denial of freedoms to others, division and mistrust. We face huge challenges – pandemics, climate change, ageing societies, economic disruption, to name a few. We have new forces at play – for example, rogue states intent on chaos in our democracies, partisan media, social media filters driving us apart one demographic from another. I come across people all the time who view events we have both witnessed entirely differently, not only because of our prior perspectives, but because of the media we favour to report the events, and the voices to which we listen. How can leaders bridge these chasms in understanding and belief?

Let's start where we agree. It is not controversial to propose that we all wish to live in a society which offers a fulfilling life free of insecurity, with support for our health and wellbeing, a fertile seedbed for our talents, and opportunities for growth for ourselves and those we care for. At the same time, we hope to enjoy freedom to do as we please so long as it doesn't harm others, cherish our diversity, and be offered tolerance and understanding when we stand out from the crowd. This good society will include the freedom to argue, rant, demonstrate, joke about, and vote against those who preside over the government of our society (or ignore or ridicule them if we so choose!)

Research shows that leadership has a profound impact on the climate of an organisation or society. By distributing power, for example, through consultative and collaborative government, we see diversity of views create stronger policy. It can be seen that countries that have over years been led by democratically elected coalitions such as Germany, New Zealand, Japan or Sweden have a more robust and consistent approach to long-term issues and policies. Those that display partisan and adversarial approaches find such long-term issues incredibly hard to deal with (e.g. the USA, the UK). Those with no formal democratic procedures, and merely rule by decree by a ruling elite, are prone to corruption, riddled by cronyism, and often subject their people to oppressive, intolerant rule, discouraging debate and silencing opposition.

Our government systems can be hijacked by leaders who cannot differentiate between their own ego, and the wider interests of their country. However shining examples, such as the inclusive and forward-looking style adopted by Nelson Mandela in forging a new 'rainbow' nation in South Africa, have resolved generations of conflict and injustice by reconciling interests and laying the foundation of a just and successful society. Jacinda Ardern, the New Zealand Prime Minister, leads a coalition and says of her approach:

> I really rebel against this idea that politics has to be a place full of ego and where you're constantly focused on scoring hits against each one another. Yes, we need a robust democracy, but you can be strong, and you can be kind.

Cindy Wrigglesworth writes in Spiritual Intelligence and Good Leadership (Wrigglesworth, 2014):

> To be a great leader, you must develop a healthy self-orientation – that is, one in which you see the big picture, consider others and also keep in mind your own values and needs. You must access a higher part of your nature – your higher self.

John Knights of LeaderShape Global writes about moving "beyond the ego", enabling personal conscience and self determination to lead and motivate others in the common cause of a better world for us all. In democratic countries we have a choice – to develop and elect leaders, in a system which ensures these values can flourish, in which leaders inspire, develop and share power with others. We need to use that opportunity to choose well, whenever we can.

To find political servants who can lead beyond the ego, we citizens need to encourage active participation and voting, seek those who use the language (and have a record) of empathy and compassion and do not shy away from debate or sharing power, and who develop and inspire others to step up to lead. We need constitutional arrangements that encourage healthy argument, but also value collaboration and consensus. Our leaders must address the issues we face with bravery and openness, negotiate fairly and inclusively, and lead beyond self interest for the good of those they serve and the wider world. We need politics beyond the ego.

What do people want from their political leaders?

The following passage was written with corporate leaders in mind, by Greg Young, CEO of LeaderShape. I have taken the liberty of rewriting it in the context of our world and its political leaders. It expresses really well why we need our politicians to be transpersonal – to lead beyond the ego.

> Imagine you live in a world with a clear sense of purpose that you and your neighbours shared, and that sense of purpose was ethical, authentic and caring whilst also being sustainably successful; taking care not only of a gilded elite, but all citizens. Imagine too, if that sense of purpose and environment allowed world governments to be so nimble and collaborative that they were able to respond to world challenges such as climate change, technological advancement, inequality and natural disaster with successful and radical solutions. An environment where input, initiative and innovation are encouraged; people valued, listened to and cared about with strong relationships between citizens and political colleagues, and civil servants of government highly skilled and trusted to get on with things. Wouldn't that be a place you would want to live?

So often we hear of governments and societies where knowledge is power, where there is a lack of engagement, brought about by politicians relying on carrot and stick methods to force through their agenda, and where politicians often have, for any variety of reasons, their own interests at the forefront of their minds. In addition to re-election and security of tenure, those reasons could include the desire for power, prestige, recognition or reward.

To live in a world that is a great place, like the one described above, it needs to be led by exceptional people. They have become exceptional not only because they are demonstrably great leaders but because they have developed a level of self-awareness of their own strengths and weaknesses. They have also brought into full consciousness who they are in terms of values, ethics and beliefs and they know what they want to do with who they are; their motivation, courage, resilience and aspiration. They know their purpose, and they don't let self-interest get in the way. They are leading beyond the ego (Knights, Grant and Young, 2018).

The news channels and social media are increasingly full of instances where countries are divided, public policy is seen as unethical or uncaring, or they have failed to adapt to a change in context, environmental or societal challenges, or disruptive technology. These might sound quite different things, but at their centre is the political climate set by the top leaders. Their egos are getting in the way, driven either by placing personal reward over ethics, perhaps by the size of their personal fortune or overweening interests, or the fear that being radical will place their own position, power or interests under threat. This is so often echoed throughout a country, mirroring the behaviour of those at the top.

Case Study: What Canadians Look For

The election of Liberal Prime Minister Justin Trudeau in 2015 led to a search for new leaders in the other two main parties. Research and strategy firm Abacus conducted research into what qualities people look for in a political leader. The outcome was surprising: rather than strength or intellect, more of the 'must have' attributes spoke about behaviours and attitudes, including: "think a lot about the future of the world", "ask for help when you need it", and "apologize when you make a mistake" (Anderson and Coletto, 2016).

There's a term for a person who acts beyond their ego, it's called being 'Transpersonal'. Transpersonal leaders have developed the emotional intelligence to lead in ways that mean people follow them, there is empathy, trust and inspiration; all the things that equip someone to be an effective leader. When you have followers, you can afford to be radical in the knowledge that people will stay with you with a shared sense of values and purpose, understanding that you are making decisions in the interests of the greater good. That way countries can thrive in the long term, building a sustainable future, builds trust with its citizens, civil servants, businesses and communities, and other countries and leaders. That's the world I want to live in.

Vision – the essential ingredient

"Politics is the art of the possible, the attainable — the art of the next best", said Otto von Bismarck, the "Iron Chancellor" of Germany. Yet his legacy, a united Germany with a fresh shared identity, speaks of his visionary approach more than his pragmatic words (though it takes both to govern).

Why is vision so important for politicians? There are certainly dangers in judging our leaders based on their vision without scrutiny or expert questioning, as many historic examples of malignant populist visionaries (Hitler, Mussolini) have illustrated, though during election proper process such as public debate, media scrutiny and effective opposition can limit this. Dror (1988) proposes some counter measures to raw populism.

Politicians need to lay out a programme before those they hope to govern. A visionary style of leadership offers optimism, inspiration, and displays the sort of self-confidence necessary in government. As in any enterprise, a distinction is sometimes made between managerial and visionary styles of political leadership (Molchanov, Knight and Masciulli, 2016). A managerial approach to government may be a statement of intent, such as the pledge to pursue 'strong and stable' government (as Theresa May of the Conservatives did rather unsuccessfully in the 2017 UK General Election). It is not sufficient to be a vision, as it has no destination or inspiring direction, and merely describes an inward-looking and process-driven approach – a reductive managerial style of leadership is described. Politicians do not just inspire to get elected or chosen, but rather to provide a clear picture of the future, generate followers, win over citizens and generate momentum towards a common goal.

No successful government can carry on without direction, and that means political leaders should not only have a vision, but be skilled in leading with a visionary style. That means not only having an inspiring vision, but leading people towards a shared vision that everyone has bought into and owns. A visionary style can be highly positive, and offers clear direction. It requires self-confidence (and self-awareness), transparency and strong relationship management (Knights et al., 2018, p. 81).

Case Study: Uniting Europe after War

Extraordinary times encourage imaginative, visionary leaders to promote new ideas that may shape cultural and national identities. Existing identities and histories will necessarily limit the extent to which a new vision can change perceptions – any new vision must resonate with existing opinion. In the same way, a consensus within political groupings based on existing interests around a new vision is a condition of its success. However, at critical junctures visionary political leadership can shift public opinion and sense of identity permanently (Marcussen et al., 1999). Such a moment occurred in Europe at the end of the Second World War and has shaped our world since.

Konrad Adenauer, Chancellor of West Germany from 1949 to 1963, espoused the dream of "the great work of fostering durable international reconciliation and a community of nations for the good of Europe" when Mayor of Cologne in 1919, in the wake of the first terrible war of the 20th century (Buchstab and Schreiner, 2007). Charles De Gaulle, President of France during the formation of a new national identity, allied his vision of a France rebuilt with one of a strong economic and political alliance within Europe, with an outlook tempered by prevailing French notions of nationhood and identity (Moravcsik, 2000). As UK Prime Minister in 1942 Winston Churchill looked forward to "a United States of Europe, in which the barriers between the nations will be greatly minimised and unrestricted travel will be possible" (Ramiro Troitiño, Kerikmäe and Chochia, 2018).

Clearly the coincidence of opportunity, through the need to rebuild and the rejection of open conflict in Europe, coupled with a clear view of national identity and a measure of political consensus, led talented and far-sighted visionary leaders to take a step towards a future that was imagined and then negotiated through decades that followed.

Case Study: Unification of Germany after the Cold War (1990)

Many obstacles stood in the way of the reunification of the Federal and Democratic Republics of Germany (known as West and East Germany respectively) but the collapse of the 'Iron Curtain' dividing Europe from 1945 until the late 1980s created a pivot around which the future of the country, divided at the end of the Second World War, could change. However the political leaders of the time knew they had to act in a concerted manner to resolve the many complexities including unfinished settlement of power in Europe to unite Germany once again. This took extraordinary political and diplomatic skill, and will (Kaiser, 1990). However, it also took visionary political leadership – the ability to articulate a clear picture of the future by Chancellor Kohl of West Germany, UK Prime Minister Margaret Thatcher, American President George Bush Sr, and French President Francois Mitterand, among others, and to pursue that vision by harnessing the enthusiasm and talents of many others worldwide.

In the poll mentioned above of Canadians after an election in 2015, citizens were asked what they valued in political leaders. The top answers, "Think about what's right for the next generation" and "Understand different parts of the world" indicate a high value placed on visionary leadership (Anderson and Coletto, 2016).

Democratic style of leadership

The democratic style, as mentioned above, is one that builds engagement and buy-in, through encouraging input and ideas from others. No politician operates in isolation. Political leaders must energise a team of civil servants, coordinate a team of ministers within the government, maintain support from a political party, and encourage great thoughts and insights from wider society.

The democratic style of leadership is potent when working with specialists and high-knowledge colleagues. The commitment generated among such colleagues is essential to good government. If a politician thinks they have all the answers, that is a certain sign that they do not. In a complex world where delivery depends on the expertise of others, a leader using this style will maximise the information on which decisions are made, and get people committed to a successful outcome. It is not about abdicating responsibility, but it involves listening skills and skilful relationship management.

The democratic style has a particularly positive impact on the culture of government, and in supporting the visionary style. Together evidence shows that these two leadership styles – visionary and democratic – engender an achievement-oriented culture that drives innovation and success (Ogbonna and Harris, 2000).

Many commentators connect the problems of reaching an agreement on Brexit to the lack of cross-party discussions in the UK, at least until the very last moment, whereas the countries of Europe reached a consensus on their approach very early in the negotiations. Longer term issues like providing social care for an ageing population require a broad consensus across the political spectrum and in wider society, and again require a democratic style beyond party and government factions to succeed.

Inspiring leadership through empathy

Empathy is by far the emotional intelligence capability that is most commonly in need of development, with 62% of all leaders requiring work on their skills (Knights et al., 2018). Inspiring through empathy – the ability to

---

Case Study: The UK Labour Party National Policy Forum and democratic inclusion

In 1990, the UK Labour Party established a multi-stakeholder forum to deliberate over policy and take responsibility for the formulation of a manifesto for the forthcoming general election. For the next 25 years, this forum played an important role in allowing elected representatives of the grass roots of the party, along with affiliate organisations such as the Cooperative Party and Trade Unions, to debate key policy issues with MPs, MEPs and Government Ministers including the Prime Ministers or party leaders. The Forum was therefore a group characterised by diversity: including diversity of class, background, gender, geography (delegates were elected by region), political opinion (from all shades of the Labour Party from left to centre) and constituency.

Shortcomings were clear, such as complex relationships with other sources of grass-roots authority such as the annual conference, inability to react quickly enough to debate and influence events as they happened (such as foreign policy issues, notably the Iraq War), limited access to expertise in complex areas, clunky communication mechanisms for much of its existence, and limited coverage of local or multinational policy (Hertner, 2015). However, the National Policy Forum led to a remarkable expansion of policy debate including at regional and local events led by Forum delegates. This improved the sense of party member engagement up to a point, led to coherent programme and policy coverage (rather than atomised 'motions' or 'resolutions', brought forward new ideas from outside Parliament, and influenced leadership positions on issues from healthcare policy to climate change. Most importantly, for much of its time it gave leaders a rich source of (largely positive) insight and opinion.

---

read and react to situations correctly by making the effort to listen to and really understand others – is recognised in many fields as an essential leadership skill (Kail, 2011).

It has been argued (Clohesy, 2013) that

> the relationship between empathy and politics can and should be understood in the context of reciprocity or as elements within a virtuous circle... because empathy provides us with a sense of our duties to others, it allows us to see politics as something that is enabling, necessary, noble and ethical.

In politics, empathy is highly visible and hugely prized in our leaders. On the death of Nelson Mandela, his friend Desmond Tutu wrote of his "incredible empathy" which allowed him to understand the perspectives of former foes as well as difficult allies, and forge the rainbow nation of South Africa out of the post-apartheid confusion (Tutu, 2013).

Developing new leaders

For any leader, the ability to develop new leaders by inspiring, encouraging and providing a role model is an important capability, and one of the core capabilities within relationship management. A true test of a great political leader is the extent to which their work lives on after them through those they have inspired and developed.

Alexis de Tocqueville's examination of democracy in America (de Tocqueville, 2002) shows how an engaged civil society, with many interlocking elements, introduces checks and balances to politics and governance. These do not only restrict demagogues, but also tend to provide a ready supply of

---

Case Study: Lincoln's Empathy Saves The Union

Republican American President Abraham Lincoln was well known as a moral and sometimes stubborn or sorrowful character. However many commentators at the time and since have commented on his empathy (Pruyn, 2005). He brought together a disparate team of talented and ambitious colleagues to operate effectively as a team, through understanding what motivated them. He was able to predict the a ctions of his political opponents, thus planning his own actions to counter them. Thus when called upon to unite a country riven by civil war, his ability to find more in common was a vital tool in binding the United States together again. His famous quote: "Those who look for the bad in people will surely find it" illustrates well his open mind and heart, and another: "I don't like that man. I must get to know him better" shows his belief in the value of empathy to bridge divides.

Case Study: Jacinda Ardern and The Politics of Empathy

In a contribution to a panel at the World Economic Forum in Davos in January 2019, the Prime Minister of New Zealand, Jacinda Ardern talked of a new politics focussed on empathy, kindness and wellbeing (Ardern, 2019). She argued that economic measures alone cannot meet the needs of people, communities and society. Instead government interventions are to look at the gap between economic success measures, and wider measures of what success might include. By looking at the actual lived experience of citizens, rather than traditional economic measures, the hope is that engagement and trust will return to institutions, over the next 20 years or more, and longer term challenges such as climate change and inequality can be addressed.

In response to the tragic mass shooting in Christchurch in 2019, and again during the Coronavirus pandemic, Ardern's empathy was noted as a defining feature of her response.

Ardern is not the only politician to have made wider measures of governmental success important. Indeed UK Deputy Prime Minister John Prescott said in 1998 that "Improving the quality of life for people of this country is perhaps the most important duty of Government". However Ardern is one of the first to couch the goals in terms of empathy.

active politicians ready to challenge and develop – both as opposition and as successors to any leader. To this extent a controversial leader might encourage many others to take up the challenge to lead in their stead. However, politicians who encourage the development of civil society deserve great credit for their role in bolstering talented political leadership in future generations.

Notable contributions come from former political leaders such as US President Clinton, whose Foundation "is committed to cultivating a diverse, new generation of leaders" including a historic partnership between the presidential libraries of President Clinton, President George W. Bush, George H.W. Bush, and Lyndon B. Johnson to cultivate promising leaders from the business, academic, public service, non-profit, and military sectors as they seek to create positive change on the issues confronting their communities.

Promote diversity

Diverse governments are effective governments. A government that shares the diverse background and interests of the people it governs is by its nature better matched to the task.

Case Study: Next Generation Leaders for the Republic of Kazakhstan

The emergence of new countries in the turbulence of the end of the Cold War provide a range of different examples of the development of civil society. One notable such example is the Bolashak Scholarship programme created in the newly formed Republic of Kazakhstan. Bolashak is the Kazakh word for "future". Though some studies have found it hard to pin down the absolute value of the programme (Perna, Orosz and Jumakulov, 2015), it has sponsored almost 12,000 students to study in a range of international universities including in the UK, the USA, China and Russia (JSC Center for International Programs, 2019). Feedback from employers and government, who employ the graduates after their studies for a minimum of five years, is highly positive, with one employer describing the scholars as: "the next generation of leaders of the country" (Perna, Orosz and Jumakulov, 2015). Alongside this development has been the building of a new (and first international) university in the capital Astana, named by the parliament after the first President Nazarbayev, its sponsor and the driving force of the Bolashak program.

The Organisation for Economic Cooperation and Development (OECD, 2019) reports a range of benefits, for example, seen when women play a major part in government:

> An increase of women in public life results in lower levels of inequality and increased confidence in national governments. Figures show that the increased presence of women cabinet ministers is associated with a rise in public health spending across many countries.
>
> Ensuring that governments reflect the diversity of the societies they represent guarantees a balanced perspective which enables an inclusive approach to policy making and service delivery.

Transpersonal leaders reach across the whole population, and make use of the greater insights available through using diversity and inclusion in government, including minority opinions and groups. This does not mean blowing with the wind, but it does lead to a stronger government with greater capacity and clearer insights.

It is very important for political leaders to listen to opposing views, and not surround themselves by those who share their own opinions. Diversity in political leadership groups offers political leaders the opportunity to test ideas, understand objections, and remain flexible in their thinking. The value, for example, of a 'loyal opposition' – an agreed formal role for the principle party not of government enshrined in either rights or constitution (Waldron, 2011) – in democratic countries is to provide an explicit source of challenge and debate.

Diversity exists within political parties, as well as between them. This is noted explicitly in countries that elect their governments by proportional representation, where coalition is the norm, and citizens judge parties by competence (in particular in the economic sphere) (Anderson, 1995) and expect diverse interests to be managed well; citizens find interests represented in more than one party.

Ethical touchstone

For a transpersonal political leader, the choices they make reflect our whole person – choices make us who we are. John Knights gives a fuller discussion of the importance of bringing our whole selves into the choices we make in Chapter 5 on developing ethical leaders: "We can define Ethical Leadership as the process of influencing people to act through principles and values and beliefs that embrace what we have defined as ethical behaviour".

Case Study: British Government, Coalition, Brexit and Diverse Opinions

British Prime Minister Theresa May was unable in January 2019 to avoid a massive parliamentary defeat, the largest by a British Government in modern history, for her plan for the United Kingdom to leave the European Union. Many commentators laid blame at the way she kept the negotiations and planning close to her inner team, lacking the diversity of views and support to be won by involving a wider group, perhaps including opposition MPs, in her discussions (Jenkins, 2019).

In contrast, when faced with minority government in 2010, her predecessor as Prime Minister, David Cameron, reached out to the third party in British politics, the Liberal Democrats, to form a largely stable coalition government that held power for five years. Contrary to expectation, the coalition survived despite following a highly controversial 'austerity' economic policy (Atkins, 2015). The coincidence of interests and diversity of ministers in government delivered solid support, so that despite the collapse in support for the minority partner, the two parties polled 45% of the vote in the 2015 election leading to an unexpected majority for David Cameron's Conservatives.

Example Touchstone

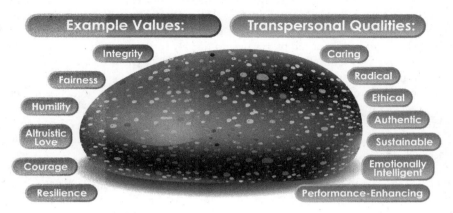

Figure 14.1 Ethical touchstone (Knights, Grant and Young, 2018)

How then do we make choices consistently for the greater good? How do we define what ethical behaviour means for us? Our decisions are the result of the choices we make, and those choices are determined by our perception of the situation, but also by our principles, values and beliefs. In order to make a choice in a way which is free of ego, radical, authentic, ethical, caring, sustainable, emotionally intelligent and performance enhancing, in the interest of those we serve and in full knowledge of those it will impact, we need to bring our full consciousness to bear on decisions. One way to do that is to create a personal touchstone we refer to whenever we make a choice (Knights, Grant and Young, 2018).

A personal ethical touchstone should include core personal values – those virtues we regard as most important to us. See the example shown in Figure 14.1. The values might instead include honesty and trustworthiness, or maybe patience and forgiveness. Alongside these we refer to transpersonal qualities: caring, radical, ethical, authentic, sustainable, emotionally intelligent and performance-enhancing.

On the night before he died, Leader of the UK Labour Party John Smith gave a speech in which he said: "The opportunity to serve our country – that is all we ask". This admirable statement says a lot about the ethical touchstone of John Smith. What is your touchstone?

Resilience

In his work The Presidential Character, James Barber proposes "character, style and world view" as ways to assess the suitability of someone to hold the office of President of the United States (Barber, 2017). He describes four character types: active–positive, active–negative, passive–positive and passive–negative. His view, supported by a rudimentary but effective exploration of those who have held the office of President, indicates that active–positive people do best in the role. The notion of positivity affects very strongly a President's ability, as noted by Barber, to display resilience in the role of leadership, and also lends optimism, along with a focus on the future which is much needed to sustain political leadership.

Resilience relies on strong emotional intelligence, and involves a number of interlocking capabilities and values, such as achievement orientation, self-confidence, adaptability and empathy. It also requires the strong ethical core providing integrity and courage, among other values. It also demands self-knowledge and a measure of introspection (see Figure 14.2).

In his treatise "The Leadership Mystique" Kets de Vries describes two sides of 'narcissism' – which he describes as constructive and reactive. Politicians are usually driven, confident people who might display elements of these traits. Ego is required to be both selfless and safe. The first, constructive narcissism (or a strong sense of self) he illustrates with positive examples of successful leaders and entrepreneurs. Clearly a strong sense of self is highly desirable for leaders – to remain firmly connected to an ethical touchstone and to be resilient in the face of major challenges.

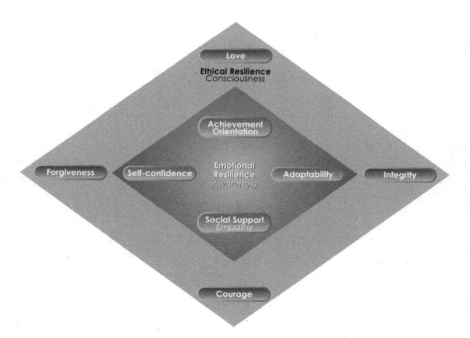

Figure 14.2 Transpersonal resilience (Knights, Grant and Young, 2018)

The latter form, reactive narcissism, is not conducive to good leadership at all; the results of that are described as follows (Kets de Vries, 2006):

> True reactive narcissists tend to have a grandiose sense of self-importance. They habitually take advantage of others in order to achieve their own ends. They also live under the illusion that their problems are unique. Then there is a sense of entitlement, the feeling that they deserve especially favourable treatment and that the rules set for others do not apply to them. Furthermore, they are addicted to compliments – they can never get enough. They lack empathy, being unable to experience how others feel. Last, but certainly not least, their envy of others, and their rage when prevented from getting their own way, can be formidable.
>
> (Kernberg, 1975)

Does that sound like any politicians you know? Does their resilience reflect self-knowledge or something else? Would you describe them as successful political leaders?

Conclusion

In our complex world, we seek political leaders who are prepared to lead in a way that is radical, ethical and authentic – who go beyond their ego to

Figure 14.3 The transpersonal leadership journey

inspire with vision, reach out to others to share power in a democratic style, who show empathy, who develop new leaders to succeed them, who value and encourage diversity, and who have an ethical touchstone visible through the choices they make and the decisions that flow from those choices. They need to be resilient, but not by shutting out all other voices, instead through being highly emotionally intelligent.

In short, we require political leaders who lead beyond the ego: transpersonal leaders. The development journey to transpersonal leadership is not a straight line, nor is it ever completed (see Figure 14.3). However for the sake of each other, and for the planet, this is the journey we need our politicians to follow.

Questions and actions for personal development

1.   What attributes do you look for in a political leader? Do these differ from those you would seek in a business leader?
2.   Think of an example of a time when a political leader displayed empathy. How did you know they were sincere?
3.   Who in the world today shows vision that inspires you?
4.   Develop a personal ethical touchstone. What words describe your core values?
5.   Is ethics essential in a political leader? If so, how can we ensure it? If not, why not?

References

Anderson, B. and Coletto, D. (2016). What do we look for in a political leader? Part 2. [online] *Abacusdata.ca*. Available at: http://abacusdata.ca/what-do-we-look-for-in-a-political-leader-2/ [Accessed 31 March 2021].

Anderson, C. (1995). The dynamics of public support for coalition governments. *Comparative Political Studies*, 28(3), pp. 350–383.

Ardern, J. (2019). New Zealand wants its politics to focus on empathy, kindness and wellbeing (World Economic Forum 2019). [online] *SBS News*. Available at: https://www.facebook.com/sbsnews/videos/381173345998504/ [Accessed 31 March 2021].

Atkins, J. (2015). 'Together in the national interest': The rhetoric of unity and the formation of the Cameron-Clegg government. *The Political Quarterly*, 86(1), pp. 85–92.

Barber, J. (2017). *The Presidential Character*. Milton: Taylor and Francis.

Buchstab, G. and Schreiner, R. (2007). *Konrad Adenauer and the European Integration*. Berlin, Germany: Konrad Adenauer Foundation.

Cicero, M. (1877). Cicero's Tusculan Disputations, On the Nature of the Gods, On the Commonwealth. [online] *Gutenberg.org*. Available at: http://www.gutenberg.org/files/14988/14988-h/14988-h.htm#page-357 [Accessed 31 March 2021].

Clohesy, A. (2013). *Politics of Empathy*. Oxford: Routledge.

de Tocqueville, A. (2002). *Democracy in America*. 2nd ed. Chicago: University of Chicago Press.

Dror, Y. (1988). Visionary Political Leadership: On Improving a Risky Requisite. *International Political Science Review*, 9(1), pp. 7–22.

Grayling, A., 2020. *The Good State: On the Principles of Democracy*. London: Oneworld Publications.

Hertner, I. (2015). Is it always up to the leadership? European policy-making in the Labour Party, Parti Socialiste (PS) and Sozialdemokratische Partei Deutschlands (SPD). *Party Politics*, 21(3), pp. 470–480.

Jenkins, S. (2019). Theresa May must form a one-issue coalition to resolve this Brexit mess. [online] *The Guardian*. Available at: https://www.theguardian.com/commentisfree/2019/jan/18/theresa-may-coalition-brexit-tories-robert-peel [Accessed 31 March 2021].

JSC Center for International Programs (2019). History of the Bolashak Program. [online] *www.gov.kz*. Available at: https://bolashak.gov.kz/en/history-of-the-programme/ [Accessed 31 March 2021].

Kail, E. (2011). Leadership Character. *Washington Post*, [online] 10 June 2011. Available at: http://wapo.st/xD1ExS?tid=ss_tw&utm_term=.7157deeabd49 [Accessed 31 March 2021].

Kaiser, K. (1990). Germany's Unification. *Foreign Affairs*, 70(1), p.179.

Kernberg, O. (1975). *Borderline Conditions and Pathological Narcissism*. Lanham, MD: Rowman & Littlefield.

Kets de Vries, M. (2006). *The Leadership Mystique*. Harlow: Prentice Hall/Financial Times.

Knights, J., Grant, D. and Young, G. (2018). *Leading Beyond the Ego*. Oxford: Routledge.

Madison, J., Hamilton, A. and Jay, J., 1788. *The Federalist Papers*. New York: J & A McLean.

Marcussen, M., Risse, T., Engelmann-Martin, D., Knopf, H. and Roscher, K. (1999). Constructing Europe? The evolution of French, British and German nation state identities. *Journal of European Public Policy*, 6(4), pp. 614–633.

Molchanov, M., Knight, W. and Masciulli, J. (2016). *The Ashgate Research Companion to Political Leadership*. Oxford: Routledge.

Moravcsik, A. (2000). De Gaulle between Grain and Grandeur: The political economy of French EC Policy, 1958–1970 (Part 1). *Journal of Cold War Studies*, 2(2), pp. 3–43.

OECD (2019). Women in Government – OECD. [online] *OECD.org*. Available at: http://www.oecd.org/gov/women-in-government.htm [Accessed 31 March 2021].

Ogbonna, E. and Harris, L. (2000). Leadership style, organizational culture and performance: empirical evidence from UK companies. *The International Journal of Human Resource Management*, 11(4), pp. 766–788.

Perna, L., Orosz, K. and Jumakulov, Z. (2015). Understanding the human capital benefits of a government-funded international scholarship program: An exploration of Kazakhstan's Bolashak program. *International Journal of Educational Development*, 40(January 2015), pp. 85–97.

Powell, E. (1977). *Joseph Chamberlain*. London: Thames and Hudson, p. 151.

Pruyn, P. (2005). Executive Empathy: Lincoln's Antidote to Escalations. [Blog] *The Systems Thinker*. Available at: https://thesystemsthinker.com/executive-empathy-lincolns-antidote-to-escalation/ [Accessed 31 March 2021].

Ramiro Troitiño, D., Kerikmäe, T. and Chochia, A. (2018). *Brexit*. New York: Springer, pp. 33–56.

Tutu, D. (2013). Desmond Tutu on Nelson Mandela: 'Prison became a crucible'. *The Guardian*, [online] 6 Dec 2013. Available at: https://www.theguardian.com/commentisfree/2013/dec/06/desmond-tutu-nelson-mandela [Accessed 31 March 2021].

Waldron, J. (2011). The Principle of Loyal Opposition. *SSRN Electronic Journal*. 10.2139/ssrn.2045647.

Wrigglesworth, C., 2014. Spiritual Intelligence and Good Leadership. [online] *Alchemyassistant.com*. Available at: https://www.alchemyassistant.com/topics/q67bvQKuJCY8nWP6.html [Accessed 31 March 2021].

15 Leadership in India

Keeping pace with India's growth story?

Pavan Bakshi

First they ignore you, then they laugh at you, then they fight you, then you win.

Mahatma Gandhi

Overview

Leadership is a journey and needs to be recognised as one. It also means that, irrespective of the position you hold in your company and how well you have done in the past, the journey never ends. The journey to Transpersonal Leadership is a series of small yet significant steps. It requires humility, perseverance and motivation, not only to reach one's potential (self-actualisation) but to be a traveller in the journey to grow and transcend (self-transcendence) oneself over and over again.

This chapter explains the experiential steps in developing leaders in Indian corporations in the context of India's growth story. Many Indian companies have seen impressive growth over the last few decades with many becoming global organisations.

The International Monetary Fund has projected an 11.5% growth rate for India's economy in 2021. The IMF report suggested that India will be the only major economy to register a double-digit growth this year, followed by China, which is expected to grow by 8.1% in 2021. However, if India is going to achieve its potential, there are many issues that need to be addressed, not least of which is the development of its leaders for the future. In this chapter, we will also identify what we believe are the most urgent leadership developmental needs in India. Given the opportunity, we feel confident that India's next generation of senior leaders will be quick to on board these simple yet profound steps to new transpersonal approaches.

Success will also require strong support and understanding from both the top management and the leadership in human resource departments. Our experience is that participants engage most positively when it includes working in confidence with an external coach or facilitator to discuss their issues and challenges in the context of development. We also need to acknowledge

DOI: 10.4324/9781003150626-19

that people change and develop at different rates and that rewiring of neural circuits takes time, practice, focus and the right environment.

It is also important to mention that many of our findings of the development needs of leaders in India are common across the world – because in the end, we all are human with some degree of variance and differences as per India's unique history, culture and society.

Introduction

Reena walked up to me and told me that the MD and the board of directors were now available to see me regarding the leadership initiative I had proposed for their organisation. As I walked into the meeting room and sat down, Mr Pradhan, the MD, whom I had met earlier, got up to meet me. We shook hands (the Corona virus era was still seven years away and not known to us as of now the normal manners of civility still existed). He introduced me the other five wise men in the room.

Sandeep, one of the directors immediately said: "Emotional intelligent is fine, but we are looking for a real leadership initiative program". I humbly asked him which competencies they were looking to develop in their business heads and their teams. He looked at me and said:

> We want them to be inspirational, show initiative, develop the next level of leaders, understand the needs of clients and their team, be more collaborative and of course then also be more emotionally intelligent- that is that they should be able to manage their emotions in stressful situations.

Most leaders have a misconception that emotional intelligence starts and ends with emotional self-awareness and emotional self-control. Reena had by then uploaded my slides on the meeting room computer and I could see my first slide on the giant screen. I immediately moved to my fifth slide which had the image of the four EI competencies and the 19 EI capabilities. I explained them all, and then placed emphasis on the seven competencies we would be working on. Sandeep was happy to see that the ones he had mentioned were part of the Building Emotional Intelligent Leadership initiative we had proposed. By the end of the hour-long meeting, and after a number of insightful questions asked by the board, we got the go-ahead to commence the engagement. It started with a three-day workshop and then continued for over a year. This resulted in real change, and even to date all the 24 leaders who took part in this leadership journey are always ready to act as referrals to my prospects. The one common theme of the feedback from them was "Pavan this initiative changed me, my life and of all those around me, thank you!"

India's growth story

In its seventh decade of independence, India stands on the pinnacle of major changes: a transformation that could lead to unprecedented economic growth along with radical improvements in the nation's Human Development Index (HDI). (HDI is calculated using the following indicators: Health – life expectancy at birth; Education – expected years schooling for school-age children and average years of schooling in the adult population; Income – measured by Gross National Income (GNI) per capita (purchasing power parity in US dollars).)

The recent electoral mandate for development is a more immediate signal of Indians' desire for growth and for the benefits of growth to be extended to all members of society.

A significant number of Indian companies have experienced impressive growth during the past three decades. Today, many face a daunting side effect: a crisis in leadership. In some ways, Indian companies' fast growth has become a cross to bear. One regional sales head for a mobile telephone handset company pointed out that

> eight to ten years ago, there were only three or four handset brands in the country. Today, there are over 60. Relatively younger managers have had to step up to take on top roles in these companies without having the time to develop themselves for these opportunities.

The case is similar in other sectors where there is a war for the limited experienced talent available in the marketplace.

In support of this, survey data supports this claim, such as the 2018 Manpower Group Talent Shortage Survey (ManpowerGroup, 2018), a global survey of employers, which reported that 56% of respondents based in India had difficulty finding qualified candidates, with senior managerial positions in the top ten shortage areas. A report by Booz & Company (now part of PwC) in 2013 forecasted in an in-depth analysis of India's top 500 companies that by 2017, 15% to 18% of leadership positions in those companies will be unfilled – or will be filled by people underprepared for the jobs (PwC, 2014). This implies that companies will be short of almost one in every five leaders they need, putting both potential growth opportunities and the continuity of existing business operations at risk (Moda et al., 2013). The 20th CEO Survey in India conducted by PWC in 2017 further emphasises the point, with 87% of CEOs citing 'availability of key skills' as a top concern, the number one worry mentioned; with skills identified as important being problem solving, adaptability, leadership, and creativity and innovation (Aashish & Nayantara, 2017).

Current status of leadership in India

Our experience of developing leaders in India together with our research indicates that at least 50% of leaders at senior and mid-level positions have substantial improvements to make to qualify as good leaders. Even the good leaders need to make significant improvement in some areas of their leadership

Table 15.1 Leadership styles

Leadership Style	Impact	Description
VISIONARY	+++	Leads people towards a shared vision
COACHING	++	Enables leaders to build capability in individuals
AFFILIATIVE	+	Provides cohesiveness and harmony to a team, group or organisation
DEMOCRATIC	+	Builds engagement, commitment and buy-in
PACE-SETTING	− −	Sets high standards by expecting followers to "do as I do" and to set meet targets
COMMANDING	− − −	Demands immediate compliance to a leader's agenda and decisions

competence. Indian business leaders have focused on developing technology rather than people. As a senior manager at a large Indian conglomerate put it, "We have quality technical experts, but can't convert them into business leaders". Without a strong leadership pipeline in place, star functional specialists are typically promoted to top roles. These individuals certainly have domain expertise but may not have had the opportunity to develop a broader perspective or set of skills (Moda et al., 2013).

The lack of leadership at various levels of these organisations is leading to a work force that is stressed and demotivated. In India, 46% of the workforce in firms suffer from one or the other form of stress (Bhattacharyya & Vijayaraghavan, 2016). The styles of leadership that continue to be widely used are Commanding and Pacesetting without necessary supporting styles of Coaching, Democratic, and Affiliative (Goleman et al., 2002) as described in the box below (Table 15.1).

This is partly because of the strongly hierarchical nature of Indian society and most businesses. But also, this is due to the natural or default perception of a leader that he needs to know everything and tell people what to do. This largely affects organisational performance and personal lives of employees, thereby reducing sustainable productivity. It leads to a high turnover of staff which results in either the need to rehire new people for the same job or increase salaries to retain key talent. This has two ramifications: first, with India being a cost sensitive market, these companies are finding it difficult to achieve their bottom-line results; and second, India is losing its competitive advantage to other South Asian and African countries.

Our experience in India

Prime Meridian Consulting, as associates of *LeaderShape Global in India*, has conducted numerous leadership development interventions over the last few years, both for multinational corporations (MNCs) and large and medium sized Indian companies. One of the more popular programmes has

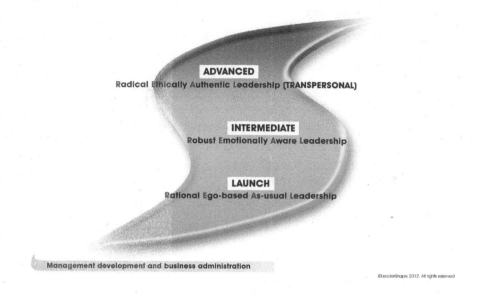

Figure 15.1 The REAL transpersonal leadership journey to excellence

been "Emotionally Intelligent Leadership" to enable leaders to navigate the first leap of transpersonal leadership improvement from the natural default state of "*Rational Ego based As-usual Leadership*" to next level of "*Robust Emotionally Aware Leadership*" (see Figure 15.1).

An individual is promoted to their first position of leadership because of their functional expertise or superior educational qualification (Rational Intelligence). S/he is also result oriented, driven by the need to achieve power, reward, prestige or recognition, or a combination of these. On reaching senior leadership positions, the individual needs to make major shifts in the mind-set from competitiveness (with others in his or her organisation) to collaboration; from self-interest to stakeholders' interest; from goal focus to social focus; and from rigidity of primarily one leadership style to the flexibility of multiple and situationally relevant leadership styles. This entails building a new set of behavioral skills, which move them from transactional to transformational leadership. The journey is shown in Figure 15.1.

The specific seven steps followed in this programme and developed by LeaderShape can be seen in Figure 15.2.

This leadership development intervention takes leaders on a journey of discovery, awareness, and personal development. This leadership development program offering unique journey for each individual, is based on emotional intelligence that focuses on key development areas. It has emerged over the last 20 years, in parallel to greater knowledge about how the brain

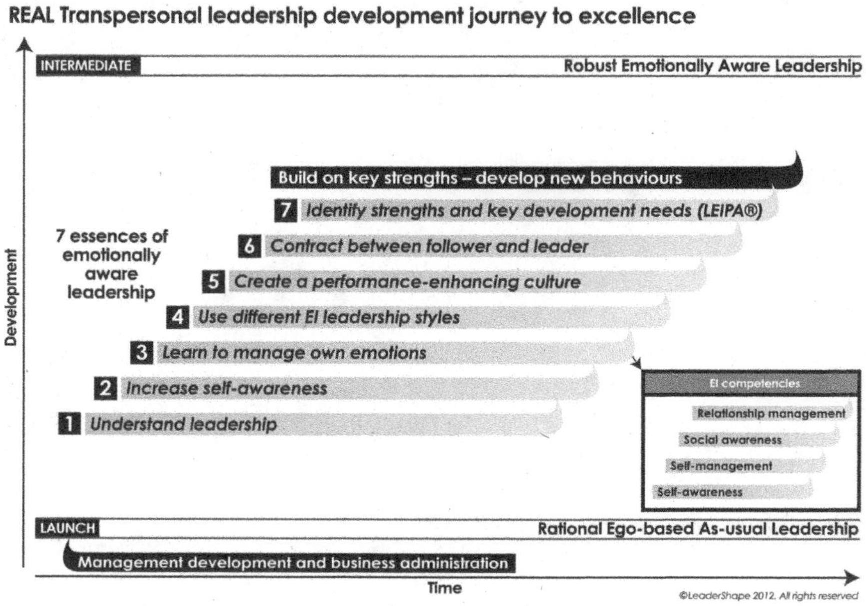

REAL Transpersonal leadership development journey to excellence

Figure 15.2 Steps on the REAL transpersonal leadership journey

works – neuroscience – to become an established form of science now. It enables individuals to better manage their personalities, behaviors, and innate skills towards maximising personal performance and enabling the improved performance of others.

These interventions have been widely acknowledged by participants in India as being extremely relevant and important to their career and personal development.

Endorsements by leadership programme participants

Some the endorsements by the participants are shown below.

- The process of delivery was very good, and I had wonderful insights about my Emotional Intelligence and the need to improve it to become a better leader. This will help me tweak myself in my professional journey helping me to be a better person/leader. **Executive Director, Financial Services MNC**
- The programme really helped me understand the nuances of different styles of leadership and in great depth made me understand the relationship between Emotional Intelligence, Culture, Leadership and Coaching practices. **General Manager, Plant Head MNC**

- Understood the competencies and capabilities of Emotional Intelligence, their connect to Leadership Styles. The big "Aha" moment was the connection I made as to how different leadership styles support the creating of a Performance Enhancing Culture. **President, Large Indian Retail & Restaurant Company**
- Good understanding of EI, its implementation and its importance in organisational growth. **Head SBU, Software Product Company**
- Learned various leadership styles, and how to apply them in various situations. Delivery process was thorough. Case studies involved people. Key learning is various leadership styles and empathy. **VP, Finance, Software Product Company**
- Delivery process was 'inclusive'. We as participants were effectively engaged. Coaching style was my key learning as I am a teacher at heart. **VP, Africa, Software Product Company**
- I learned about leadership styles and their combination to use in day-to-day life. Active Listening and its importance. Lots of things to learn in life and never stop. **Head Design, Indian Retail Company**
- Well-connected and excellent insights. Understood self and how to become a Transformational Leader. **Senior GM, Supply Chain & Material Handling, Large Public Sector Company**
- Very good program. Learned about Coaching/Visionary style of Leadership, Active Listening and Emotional Intelligence. **Senior GM, Finance, Large Public Sector Company**

Self-assessment by Indian leaders

During our leadership programmes, we ask our participants to conduct a self-assessment on seven of the 19 Emotional Intelligence capabilities (see Figure 15.3). This technique is adapted from the model of Daniel Goleman and Richard Boyatzis (Goleman et al., 2002). The capabilities we chose are those most connected to the visionary and coaching style of leadership as shown in Table 15.2, are some of the most impactful styles for performance. At senior levels of leadership, demonstration of these styles supports creating a resonant climate and further enables the development of a performance enhancing culture, which positively impacts organisational performance and its sustainability (Spencer, 2001).

In a recent study we conducted, 457 corporate leaders self-assessed the seven EI capabilities which resulted in identifying the average overall strengths and development areas of these leaders in the visionary and coaching leadership styles.

Analysis of results

This self-assessment suggests that, overall, Indian senior leaders believe they perform well in the areas of emotional self-awareness (being aware of one's

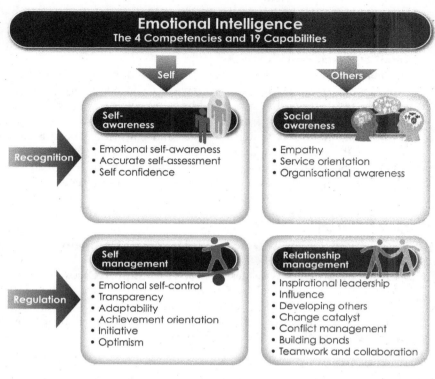

Figure 15.3 Emotional intelligence competencies and capabilities

Table 15.2 Most impactful capabilities for development in India

EI capability	Leadership style	EI competency
Strengths		
Emotional Self-awareness	Coaching	Self-awareness
Self-confidence	Visionary	Self-awareness
Transparency	Visionary	
Development needs		
Empathy	Coaching	Social Awareness
Inspirational Leadership	Visionary	Relationship Management
Change Catalyst	Visionary	Relationship Management
Developing Others	Coaching	Relationship Management

emotions). They also rate themselves high on self-confidence (a good sense of self-worth and capabilities) and transparency (maintaining integrity, being honest and willing to acknowledge mistakes).

While self-confidence is necessary to be a good leader, an excess may make the leader believe they have all the answers and be more directive than necessary rather than open to seeking suggestions from others. In an article in Management Next (Knights, 2013), John Knights (Chairman of LeaderShape Global), makes the observation that

> perhaps the most immediate observation of Indian businesses is that most are still very centralized and hierarchical. This means that most of the people are being told what to do rather than being encouraged to develop their own solutions and take responsibility. Developing others does not seem to be a priority with Indian leadership. The [hierarchical] system can work quite well in a stable world where there is little change. But not in the 21st century that is changing faster by the year and where organisations need to be increasingly nimble. A decision-making process that has to go all the way up the organisation and all the way down again is just not sustainable.

Perhaps the most notable observation of these results is that while these leaders generally believed their Self Awareness and Management was good, they acknowledged that their awareness and management of others was where they needed to focus on development. The capabilities where they acknowledged, they were found wanting were the critical ones of empathy, inspirational leadership, change catalyst and developing others. This is consistent with John Knights' observations.

Reviewing the specific development needs, Change Catalyst may be the most important aspect of leadership in this rapidly changing world. Making change happen in an organisation begins with first, understanding the changes in the external environment and then, responding to them with the appropriate changes within the organisation.

The other specific development needs of Empathy, Inspirational Leadership and Developing others are the three key pillars to enable effective internal changes. The first step for the leaders is to co-create the new vision in collaboration and further enlist the enthusiastic support of employees in achieving it (inspirational leadership). The next step is to become aware of how people are feeling during this change journey, understanding, and acknowledging their perspectives (empathy) and then supporting employees to sustain their involvement in making the necessary changes (developing others), especially the behavioural ones.

Of course, a self-assessment is just that! It is valuable in providing an analysis of how an individual is thinking and feeling but their self-perception is not likely to be totally accurate and will not reveal hidden strengths or blind spots.

I suppose leadership at one time meant muscles; but today it means getting along with people.

Mahatma Gandhi

360-degree assessment of leaders

I was coaching a group of leaders in one of the Big four in India. During our first meeting with the manager and coachee, the manager asked the coachee who I will call Madan to reflect on what areas of improvement he sees in himself. Madan thought long and hard, shook his head and said, "I can't think of any". The manager asked a few more questions to invoke self-reflection but Madan did not seem to be aware of any areas that he needed to work on. After trying everything, the manager looked at me as if to say, "he is all yours now!" I said: "Madan, that is indeed extremely wonderful that you have a high level of self-confidence, which is one capability every leader needs". I then asked: "If you were to think of the next level of leaders in your organisation, what is that one thing you really appreciate in them that you would want to imbibe?" Madan though for a moment and said that there was nothing that he was also not good at. I prodded: "Is their one thing that they have more of that you don't?" He immediately said: "The only thing that they have is that they earn almost twice as much as I do". From the corner of my eye, I could see the exasperated look on his manager's face.

I asked him if he was fine with taking a 360-degree assessment, to which he agreed to immediately. A few weeks later when I debriefed him on his 360-degree report he just broke down, since he realised the gap between what he saw in himself vis-à-vis what others did. This is indeed the first step of awareness followed by acceptance, then commitment and discipline which truly changes people. At the end of over a year, Madan was truly a transformed person and leader.

It has been found that our emotional intelligence and its external demonstration through specific behaviours is best judged by the people around us. To achieve this, we conducted a detailed LEIPA® (Leadership Emotional Intelligence Performance Accelerator) assessment (LeaderShape Global, 2017) – see Chapter 6 – for a number of senior leaders.

In this small study, we assessed 24 senior leaders using 210 raters to assess the 19 EI competencies and 6 leadership styles (see Table 15.1 and Figure 15.3). While this is a small sample, the results are very consistent with other qualitative studies and experience (see Figure 15.4).

As we can see in the graph in Figure 15.4, the largest average difference between observed and desired behaviour (0.49) occurs in the area of Self-Management and Relationship Management, which suggests these are the areas on which many Indian leaders might focus to improve their leadership. The EI competency where Indian leaders are strongest is Self-Awareness.

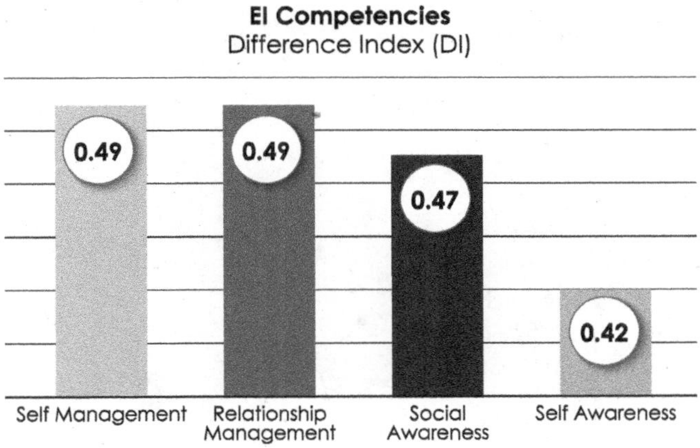

EI Competencies
Difference Index (DI)

Figure 15.4 EI Competencies and difference index for 24 senior leaders in India

Table 15.3 EI capabilities and development needs of Indian leaders

EI capabilities development needs

EI capability	% Above 0.5 DI	Leadership style	EI competency
Initiative	75%	Pace-Setting/ Commanding	Self-Management
Change Catalyst	67%	Visionary	Relationship Management
Empathy	58%	Coaching/ Affiliative	Social Management
Adaptability	50%	Democratic	Self-Management
Achievement Orientation	50%	Pace-Setting/ Commanding	Self-Management
Influence	50%	Commanding	Relationship Management
Conflict Management	50%	Affiliative/ Democratic	Relationship Management
Inspirational Leadership	42%	Visionary	Relationship Management
Developing Others	42%	Coaching	Relationship Management

Digging deeper into the data we can identify those EI Capabilities that are most in need of development. Table 15.3 shows the percentage of leaders assessed who had a Difference Index (DI) of greater than 0.5 in a particular EI capability, which as we know from the box above, signifies a need for development or improvement. The table also shows which leadership style and EI competency each EI capability is connected to.

Analysis of leadership styles

As discussed earlier, the predominant leadership styles in India are Pacesetting and Commanding. LEIPA® raters of Indian leaders listed the six leadership styles defined in Table 15.1 in the following order of importance:

- 1st – Coaching Style
- 2nd – Visionary Style
- 3rd – Affiliative Style
- 4th – Democratic Style
- 5th – Pacesetting Style
- 6th – Commanding Style

What is interesting is that we get the same results around the world for both the most common styles used in organisations and the order of importance of styles according to raters. The only difference is that in more hierarchical cultures the emphasis and levels of difference may be greater.

In a study of the senior leaders in 98 of the largest India-based companies (Cappelli et al., 2010), more than 50% identified the following qualities as the most relevant for their leadership:

61% – envisioning and articulating a path to the future; strategic thinking; guiding change.
57% – being inspirational, accountable, and entrepreneurial.
52% – supporting careful talent selection; grooming; practices that advance business goals.

The first two relate primarily to the Visionary Style. The third infers a coaching style in regard to 'grooming' and possibly any or all of the other styles in reference to 'practices'.

The way forward

> Live as if you were to die tomorrow. Learn as if you were to live forever.
> Mahatma Gandhi

Based on our analysis and experience and supported by the stated needs of CEOs of Indian companies, Indian organisations need to take a fresh and holistic look at their leadership development practices. Their goal should be to develop a sustainable leadership pipeline throughout the organisational pyramid.

This pipeline should also include organisational leadership advancement opportunities for technical specialists. Although it is often assumed that most technical experts will not make good leaders, our experience is that with the right kind of development these intelligent people can learn new behaviours and become more people oriented, often developing into excellent leaders.

The interventions should be based on the needs to develop emotional intelligence competencies and focus on relevant granular behaviours which enhance their adaptability to perform all leadership styles. The leadership change journey is sustainable only when the consequences of the outcome desired are understood clearly by these leaders. Each intervention must enable SMART action plans to be created and followed up.

Far too often, employees are made to go through multiple leadership programs without an overall strategy and without giving them the time to focus on rewiring the learnings into behaviours and then hardwiring them into good habits. In behavioural learning and change it is best to focus on making a few changes at a time but doing them well! It needs focus, attention, and practice – and time! Our experience has shown that sustainable results come from creating small groups to work together after the formal programme is complete. They can then continuously interact, motivate, and learn from each other. The best results come from having a coach to provide direction and challenge the group to keep growing and improving. Because it is not the norm this new approach of very regular and continuous small doses of learning requires the support of the board, the CEO and human resource leaders.

Leaders need to know where they are now in the continuum of leadership development, where they need to get to, and how to impact others. Finally, they need to develop situational awareness and how they can continuously learn and adapt to build sustainable personal and organisational performance.

Arise! Awake! And stop not until the goal is achieved.

Swami Vivekananda

Questions and actions for personal development

1. How do the development needs of senior leaders in India compare to your own experience?
2. How would you advise an executive who could see no areas for development in their leadership practice?
3. If pacesetting and commanding styles of leadership predominate, what will be the results in an organisation?
4. List the top EI capabilities you wish to develop and make a plan to do so.

References

Aashish, M. & Nayantara, S. (2017). 20th CEO Survey: Inside the Minds of CEOs in India. *PWC India*. https://www.pwc.in/publications/ceo-survey/20th-ceo-survey.html, accessed March 22, 2021.

Bhattacharyya, R. & Vijayaraghavan, K. (2016). 46% of Workforce in Firms in India Suffer from Some or the Other Form of Stress: Data. *The Economic Times.*

https://economictimes.indiatimes.com/jobs/46-of-workforce-in-firms-in-india-suffer-from-some-or-the-other-form-of-stress-data/articleshow/52696795.cms, accessed March 22, 2021.

Cappelli, P., Singh, H., Singh, J. & Useem, M. (2010). Leadership Lessons from India. *Harvard Business Review*, March 2010.

Goleman, D., Boyatzis, R. & McKee, A. (2002). *Primal Leadership: Realizing the Power of Emotional Intelligence*. Boston, MA: Harvard Business School Press.

Knights, J. (2013). Indian Leaders Are Short on Emotional intelligence. *Management Next* (vol. 10, Issue 7, pp. 8–9, Jul–Aug 2013).

LeaderShape Global (2017). Leadership & Emotional Intelligence Performance Accelerator. www.leadershapeglobal.com/Leipa

ManpowerGroup. (2018). ManpowerGroup Global. *Go.manpowergroup.com*. https://go.manpowergroup.com/talent-shortage-2018#thereport, accessed March 22, 2021.

Moda, G., Nahar, A. & Sinha, J. (2013). India's Leadership Challenge. *Strategy+Business*. Issue 71 (originally published by Booz & Company). www.strategy-business.com/article/00178

PwC (2014). Future of India–The Winning Leap. 2014 PricewaterhouseCoopers Private Limited. www.pwc.in/assets/pdfs/future-of-india/future-of-india-the-winning-leap.pdf, accessed 22 March 2021.

Spencer, L. (2001). *The Economic Value of Emotional Intelligence Competencies and EIC Based HR Programs*. Chapter 4 in The Emotional Intelligent Workplace. Editors: Cherniss, C. and Goleman, D. (San Francisco: Jossey-Bass).

16 Leadership in East Asia

Confucianism and economics are inseparable

Maiqi Ma

> The supreme leader is one whose existence people are hardly aware of; the next best is one whom people approach and praise; the next is one who is feared, the worst is one who is despised... The supreme leader doesn't talk but act. When his job is done, people say "Amazing, we did it, all by ourselves."
>
> Lao Zi (or Lao Tzu) (c. 571 BC– 471 BC), *Chapter 17,*
> *Daode Jing (or Tao Te Ching)*

Overview

In 2020, our world encountered a major global disaster when the COVID-19 pandemic struck; life, health and safety, social and economic activities were all heavily hit. Whilst governments tried to develop responses to contain and control the pandemic, these measures (perhaps inevitably) resulted in significant economic and societal loss, and the performance of many world leaders has attracted considerable scrutiny and adverse criticism from the media and public. Typically, in the west, initial failures to appreciate the severity of the crisis (at least among the political cadre), and the apparent lack of capacity to develop timely and effective responses to this event, has resulted in significant economic impacts in addition to the tragic human health consequences. One year on, it is gratifying to witness Taiwan's exemplary success in preventing the spread of the virus and that its economic growth reached 2.93%, while many other advanced economies slumped. Japan and South Korea's performance are also relatively better than countries of comparable economic size and range. Each of these eastern Asian countries has a democratic system of government and is heavily influenced by Confucian and Daoist (Taoist) thought. Reflecting on the recent popularity of the study "The Analects (Confucian) and The Abacus (economy) are inseparable" (Tanaka, 2017), (as originally espoused by Viscount Shibusawa Eiichi (1840–1931), a leading figure "who built modern Japan" and has been acclaimed as a paragon of ethical leadership as advocated by Confucius), it's worth taking a little while to discover how ancient Chinese wisdoms were harnessed by China's neighbours,

DOI: 10.4324/9781003150626-20

and how these neighbours embarked on a somewhat different path to both China and the West when developing into advanced countries.

When I started to collaborate with LeaderShape Global in 2015, I found that its Transpersonal Leadership ideas conform to ancient Chinese ethical philosophy. I also endorse its systematic methodologies on how to develop ethical leaders. It convinces me that we can integrate the ancient Eastern wisdom with Western civilisation perfectly. In this chapter, we first explore the similarities and differences between Western and Eastern cultures, and reveal what caused those differences. We also examine the reasons behind China's upswings and descents by revealing deeply rooted cultural merits and failings. Then we will review the Chinese classical teachings on how to develop ethical leadership, and how these teachings may be carried forward in East Asia and possibly in the West. Hopefully, this will provide an alternative thought perspective on transpersonal leadership.

Please note, to avoid confusion, all the spelling of Chinese names and titles are in modern Mandarin Chinese, except some widely recognised names such as Confucius; otherwise, other forms are provided in brackets.

Comparing Western and Eastern Cultures

Simply speaking, the major difference between West and East is "Individualistic" versus "Collective". For example, let us take a quick look at the cultural comparison between the UK, China, and Japan.

From the chart (Figure 16.1) below, we can see that both China and Japan are more collective than the UK. This collectiveness refers to the interests of family or extended family that prevail over the interests of individuals. It does not mean that people from collective societies are better team players. In fact, people from individualistic societies, far less constrained by familial duty and expectation,

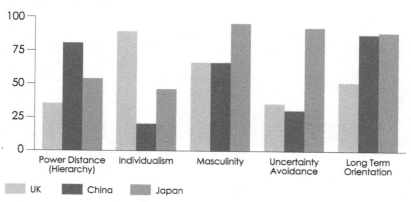

Comparison of Five Cultural Dimensions

Figure 16.1 Five cultural dimensions compared, adapted from Hofstede (2010)

are freer to choose like-minded communities to relate to. This chart also shows that Chinese people have a strong tendency towards clan ties and that China is a relational society. The other more consistent differences between East and West are Power Distance (hierarchy) and Long-Term Orientation. It shows that Chinese people are much more deferential towards perceived superiors. I perceive that this is the consequence of long lasting authoritarian feudal rule. It is interesting to see the big gaps between China and Japan in Uncertainty Avoidance (adventurousness) and Masculinity. These cultural attributes resulted in different leadership styles. For example, incentive schemes: in the west individual incentives are fine but in China collective incentives are common, and in Japan you need to appraise both group and individuals.

Despite the similar "Hierarchy of Needs" of mankind proposed by Maslow (1943), the cultures are so distinctive, why is this? I think that except for influential philosophical thinking, the other reason is the dynamics between those common ethical values and other, differing, schools of teaching. For instance, in China, alongside the Confucian and Daoist, there are other schools of Chinese thought. Specifically, Legalism (Fajia) that synthesised "Fa" – Punishment, "Shu" – Tactics and "Shi" – Power. Fajia played a foundational role in the construction of authoritarian Chinese imperial regimes throughout history and resulted in a greatly centralised government.

Let us first look at the origin of China's ethical philosophy and how it is both similar to and different from the philosophy of the West which is embodied in the economic super-powers of English-speaking countries and those of western and northern Europe. Knights (2016) explained that Western literature on ethical leadership generally refers to the five principles – *Respect, Service, Justice, Honesty* and *Building Community* of Aristotle (384 – 322 BC). On the other side of the world, and a little earlier, Lao Zi originated the concepts of *Dao* 道 (or *Tao*, "The Way"- a kind of eternal existence) and *De* 德 (or *Te*, "virtue").

Lao Zi is the spelling in modern Mandarin Chinese, meaning Old Master: Lao means old or senior and Zi means master. It is an honorific title acclaimed by others. Lao Zi is also known as Lao Tzu or Lao Tsu in the West. Lao Zi's birth name is Li Er, and his courtesy name is Li Dan (when men turn 20 and women turn 16, a capping ceremony will be held to celebrate adulthood, and a courtesy name will be given. This tradition is still kept in today's Japan, it is called Coming of Age Day). Li is the surname. Surnames always come first in Chinese. Many ancient scholars have the title of Zi, e.g. Kong Zi (Confucius), meaning Master Kong; Meng Zi (Mencius), meaning Master Meng.

Following on, Confucius (or Kong Zi, 551BC–479BC) developed the five most important moral ideals – *Ren (Benevolence), Yi (Righteousness), Li (Propriety), Zhi (Wisdom)* and *Xin (Trustworthiness)*.

The name "Confucius" is a transliteration for Kong Fuzi; Fuzi means teacher or scholar in classic Chinese. Kong Zi is the better-known name nowadays among Mandarin speakers. Kong Zi is also an honorific title, meaning Master Kong. Kong Zi's birth name is Kong Qiu, and his courtesy name is Kong Zhongni. Kong Zi is also hailed as Sage Kong, and "Wan shi zhi shi" – Teacher of All Times.

Although the common values in the West and East are similar, its social norms, human and political ecologies appear distinctive. In the west, democracy was born in Ancient Greece and has gradually become a cornerstone of the Trias Politica Model, an approach to state government that aims to separate powers (the typical division is into three branches: a legislature, an executive, and a judiciary). This model has led to a social structure of small government versus big communities, and higher transparency of governance. There are certainly other reasons for the different approaches between West and East such as languages, of which we will see some examples later. Now, let us put the politics aside, and focus on those enlightening classics which have the most enduring impact on Chinese and East Asian life.

Chinese literature of ethics and morality

The Chinese word 道德 (Dao De) is a collective noun for all the good qualities of the inner being, morality and virtue. It is an accomplishment of conscious self-discipline and self-cultivation. It is also a judging standard that is higher than the law. A Chinese person may not know what the law is, but they all know Dao De.

These two archaic characters first appeared on oracle bone scripts around 1271–1213 BCE. (These bone scripts are animal bones or turtle plastrons used in pyromantic divination in the late 2nd millennium BCE and are the earliest known form of written Chinese.) 道 (*Dao*) originally means path or way, but also conveys the idea of 'guiding' and 'trailblazing'. The written form consists of two radicals, one a person's head 首 and the other, the way (or road) 辶. 德 (*De*) originally means acting in accordance with etiquette. It consists of a walking person (denoting going higher), directions (facing a choice of Way), one eye (strong vision), the origin of things (abiding by the rules of Heaven), and a heart (following one's heart, harmony of body and mind).

Lao Zi imbued **Dao** and **De** with philosophical connotations in his masterpiece "Daode Jing" (or "Tao Te Ching", it was originally titled as "Lao Zi". It is Lao Zi's only piece of work). Simply speaking, everything in the universe has its root and rule; this is *Dao*, the Laws of the universe, which is the mother of all beings. It is all-encompassing, invisible, intangible, changeable, speechless, anonymous, and everlasting. To be in harmony with the cosmic world, a social and human need is *De* (morality or ethics). *De* nurtures and nourishes all beings without possessing or dominating.

The book "'Daode Jing' has two parts, the first part is the explanation of *Dao* and the other is about *De*. *Dao* and *De* did not originate at the same time. Later the meanings of *Dao* extended to 'principle, doctrine, method, to speak', and to the name of Daoism, China's original religion. The extended meanings of *De* are "inner strength, integrity, virtue and morality". *Dao* and *De* were first used as a compound word by Xun Zi (or Xun Kuang, 316 BC – c.237–235 BC) and meaning morality and virtues. *Daode Jing* is one of the most translated works in world literature. The most prominent heritor of the Thoughts of Lao Zi is Zhuang Zi (Zhuang Zhou 369 BC–286 BC). His work of the same name together with *Daode Jing* are the two foundational texts of Daoism.

Lao Zi's philosophy strongly influenced the 'Hundred Schools of Thoughts' (zhuzi baijia) including Confucians, Legalists and Mohists. Allegedly, the Emperor Jing of Han (188 BC–141 BC) studied "Lao Zi" and recognised it as a national classic and renamed it '*Daode Jing*'. *Jing* means sacred text. His reign, along with that of his father Emperor Wen, acclaimed as the Rule of Wen and Jing, was regarded as one of the golden ages in Chinese history. Another emperor who highly regarded *Daode Jing* was Emperor Xuanzong of Tang (685–762 AD), who hailed *Daode Jing* as the True Scripture. The Tang Dynasty is considered the most prosperous era in Chinese history.

Along with Daoist works, the Confucians' 'The Four Books' and 'The Five Classics' constructed a systematic doctrine of the importance of ethics and morality and how to cultivate it.

The Four Books refers to Da Xue (The Great Learning, by Zen Zi, 505 BC–435 BC, Confucius' disciple), Zhong Yong (The Doctrine of the Mean, by Zi Si, 483 BC–402 BC, Confucius' grandson), Lun Yu (The Analects of Confucius, 540 BC–400 BC by Confucius' disciples) and Meng Zi (The Works of Mencius, by Mencius, 372 BC–289 BC). And The Five Classics includes Yi Jing (The Book of Changes, 2700

BC–256 BC), Shang Shu (The Book of History, By Fu Sheng, 260 BC–
161 BC), Shi Jing (The Book of Poetry, or The Book of Odes, compiled
by Confucius 551 BC–479 BC), Li Ji (The Book of Propriety, by Dai
Sheng, ca. 202 BC–8 AD), and Zuo Zhuan (The Spring and Autumn
Annals, by Zuo Qiuming, 502 BC–422 BC). The Book of Music has
been lost. These texts are very rich and cover many aspects.

Here, I summarise some points which I think might be relevant to approaches
on Transpersonal Leadership. My comprehension is based on my experience
of learning from "Daode Jing" and "The Analects of Confucius" (Confucius'
disciples, 540 BC–400 BC), which is limited, and I would recommend further
reading by yourselves. Of course, one obvious limitation of all philosophies
(and religions) is that people take from them the ideas and arguments that suit
their own narrative; and ignore or actively reject those that do not. This is true
of both East and West, where societal aspirations and ideals are rarely, if ever,
fully realised.

The power of *Daode*

In Lao Zi's words, the attributes of water are close to that of the *Dao:* it nourishes all creatures without resisting, and dwells in the lowest place which all
men disdain. Thus, although water appears soft and weak, it can overcome
the hard and strong. This is because of the power of *Daode*. With accumula-
tion of *De*, every obstacle may be overcome.

The levels of De (Virtue)

Each individual has different instincts, living environment, desire for learning and action plans, but we can all gain De through self – development.
People will follow those who obtain a higher level of De (Figure 16.2).

The significance of Lao Zi's thoughts is that he perceives humanity as an
integral part of the universe. Every being in the universe is an expression
of the *Dao*. *De* raises them. They exist on a physical entity (*Wu*), and the
circumstances (*Shi*) complete them. The universe is constantly evolving in
response to both inner and outer forces, so too are humans. Therefore, all
things respect the *Dao* and value *De*. Presumably, Chinese relational thinking
is drawn from this Cosmic Centre theory. Lao Zi and later Daoism's influence has been reflected in Chinese tradition, language, and the way of life –
culture. Amusingly, extensive scientific evidence suggests that cultural values
and sustained experiences can affect brain and behaviour: many studies using
functional magnetic resonance imaging (fMRI) show that East Asians, compared with Westerners, respond to visual information in a more holistic way,

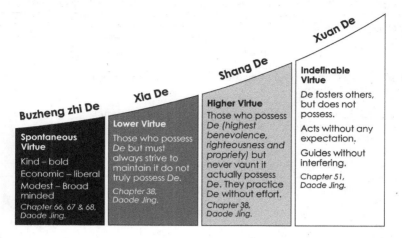

Figure 16.2 The levels of *De* (Virtue), adapted from *Daode Jing*, Lao Zi

considering the relationship between objects and context, whereas Western-ers focus on salient objects independent of the context in an analytical style (Tang, 2018).

It has been suggested that collective responsibility is one of the reasons why the Daoist and Confucian based societies of Japan, South Korea and Taiwan, but including China, have been more successful in the fight against COVID-19 (Van Bavel, 2020). It is estimated that compared with nations with high levels of cultural tightness (such as Taiwan, Singapore, and South Korea), nations with high levels of cultural looseness (Brazil, Argentina, USA) have had nearly five times the number of cases and nine times the number of deaths (Gelfand, 2021).

The portrait and characteristics of a "Sage" by Lao Zi

Lao Zi refers to those who gained "*Daode*" as a sage (Shengren), and although stating that the concepts were difficult to express verbally, the words shown in Table 16.1 were a good approximation.

Did you notice the order of these descriptions? Do you agree, or would you reorder them?

Confucius was about 20 years younger than Lao Zi and he visited Lao Zi three times to learn about *Dao*. To some extent Confucius is a practitioner of Lao Zi's ideology, yet his doctrine has more pragmatic meanings. For instance, he uses the term Gentleman (Junzi) to identify someone with the highest level of *Daode* and specified some codes of conduct and methods to develop those qualities (Table 16.2).

Benevolence (*Ren*) is regarded as Confucius' core thought, and it is the practical development of Lao Zi's *Dao* and *De*. (This might be more usually

Table 16.1 Concepts of sagacity, adapted from *Chapter 15, Daode Jing*, Lao Zi

Sage by Lao Zi (Lao Tzu)	Modern Term
1. Prudent hesitation like wading through an icy river	**Environmental consciousness**
2. Vigilant like being fearful of neighbours	**Social conscience**
3. Respectful like being a guest	
4. Amiable like melting ice	
5. Genuine like uncarved wood	**Self-conscience**
6. Broad minded and modest as a valley	
7. Unprejudiced like muddy water	
8. Calm and mild like the sea	**Behaviour**
9. As elegant as a gentle breeze (and flexible)	

Table 16.2 The portrait and characteristics of "Junzi" by Confucius, adapted from Confucian Analects. The numbers in the brackets shows the chapter and article, respectively

Core values	Closest English Word	Virtuous qualities

仁 *Ren*	**Benevolence**	• Basic
		Filial piety, kind, honest
		• Start to gain benevolence
		learning extensively, have a sincere and determined aspiration, inquiring with earnestness, and reflecting with self-application (*19. 6*).
		• Near to Benevolence
		Indomitable spirit, enduring fortitude, modest and cautious in speech (*13. 27*)
		• Who is Benevolent?
		  • Respectful, tolerant, trustworthy, astute/agile, generous, courageous (*17.6*).
		  • To subdue oneself and return to propriety (*12.1*).
		  • Established in himself and seeks also to establish others; wishing to be enlarged himself, also seeks to enlarge others (*6.28*) …
		• In one word
		Love people
		• A rule of practice
		What you do not want done to yourself, do not do to others. (*15.23*)

义 *Yi*	**Righteousness**	Do the right/appropriate thing (*4.10, 12.10*). Create a justifiable social environment (*6.20*). Treat people justly and with fairness (*5.15, 13.4*); enrich them and teach them (*13.9*).

Table 16.2 Continued

Core values	Closest English Word	Virtuous qualities
礼*Li*	**Propriety**	In practicing the rules of propriety, harmony is to be valued. (*1.12*) In festive ceremonies, it is better to be sparing than extravagant (*3.4*) Propriety is the manifestation of *Dao* and *De*, including moral and ethical norms, ceremonial rites, social and administrative forms, and discipline of behaviours. The texts are collected in *Book of Rites, Rites of Zhou* and *Book of Etiquette and Rites*. Kong Zi praises *Rites of Zhou,* yet he suggests that these rites need to be reviewed.
智*Zhi*	**Wisdom**	Be aware of and admit what you know and do not know, learn what should be learnt and ignore what should not be learnt. (*2.17, 2.16*) Know people by seeing what a person does, noticing their motivation and examining in what things he rests (his soul) (*2.10*). Promote the upright and improve the crooked (*12.22*). Know the force of words. Do not refuse strict admonition; but use it to reform your conduct accordingly. While it is pleasing to hear words of advice gently given, it is unfolding their aim that is valuable (*9.24*). Rhetorical words (to please others) are not benevolent (*1.3*).
信*Xin*	**Trustworthiness**	Be faithful, truthful and keep promises, also trust others.

referred to in current English as 'Caring'.) He tirelessly and repeatedly explained to his disciples what kind of behaviour is *Ren* and how they might gain *Ren*. *Ren* appears over one hundred times in "The Analects of Confucius" which counts as the most frequently used word. 'Filial piety' is a highly important and central Confucian virtue in social ethics and is defined by Encyclopaedia Britannica as "the attitude of obedience, devotion, and care toward one's parents and elder family members that is the basis of individual moral conduct and social harmony".

Confucius acclaims one who possesses all the virtues, and with the highest level of *Ren*, as being *Junzi*. Figure 16.3 shows the relations between these good qualities.

Figure 16.4 shows a sketch of the attributes of *Junzi*.

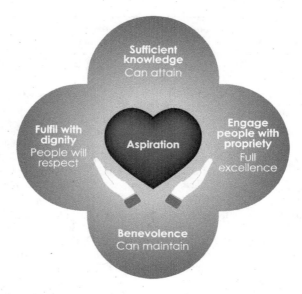

Figure 16.3 The relations between good qualities, adapted from The Analects of Confucius *15.33*

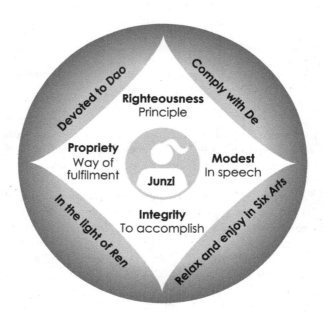

Figure 16.4 Junzi adapted from The Analects of Confucius *7.6, 15.18, 19.7*. The Six Arts taught by Confucius are Propriety, Music, Archery, Driving (horse drawn carriages), Literature/Calligraphy and Mathematics

The characteristics of Junzi by Confucius

Confucius has many words to describe the quality of Junzi, here we just name a few (Table 16.3).

Among these good qualities, courage and boldness were carefully explained by Confucius: "a benevolent man must possess courage, but a bold man is not necessarily benevolent (14.4)". We can gain these virtues from extensive learning (Figure 16.5).

Confucius is hailed as the Teacher of All Times. He advocated that there should be no distinction of social classes in teaching and that people should be developed in accordance with their aptitudes (Figures 16.6 and 16.7).

Confucius praises the effects of poetry, the proprieties and music. He reckons that by learning elegant poetry, one's mind will be aroused; by learning the Rules of Propriety, one's character will be developed; and by learning fine music, one's personality will be established. Lao Zi stated that the ultimate goal of learning and practicing *Dao* is to eliminate extremes, extravagance, and arrogance (Lao Zi, 29). When gaining knowledge, it increases from day to day; while attaining virtues, they diminish from day to day (Lao Zi, *48*); virtue should become part of our nature – in modern words, muscle memory.

Lao Zi considers that our soul is living in our body, and when exercising, our physical body, inner energy and mind should be as one. A strong, soft, and flexible body is regarded as aesthetic. Isn't it interesting to see the contrast with the Ancient Greek teaching of gymnastics to build muscular bodies?

Ren (benevolence), Yi (righteousness), DaoDe (moral, virtue) in China

Ren, *Yi* and *DaoDe* have been regarded as the highest standard of traditional Chinese morality and virtues and the goal of ultimate self-cultivation and the source to influence others. Confucius says, 'he who exercises government by

Table 16.3 Characteristics of Junzi adapted from The Analects of Confucius *20.2, 9.29*

He is/does	But not/free from
Beneficent	but not with great expenditure
Lay tasks on the people	but not outside their capability
Pursue what he desires	but not being covetous
Rest in dignified ease	but not being conceited
Majestic	but not being fierce
Wise	free from perplexities
Benevolent	free from anxiety
Courage	free from fear

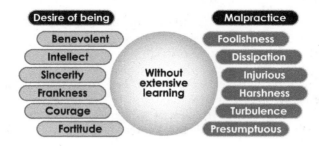

Figure 16.5 The importance of learning, adapted from The Analects of Confucius 17.8

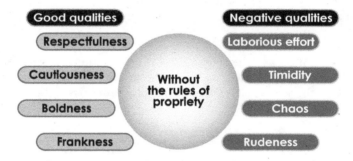

Figure 16.6 The importance of the rules of propriety, adapted from The Analects of Confucius 8.2

Figure 16.7 How to learn and what to learn: aiming to become a Junzi, adapted from The Analects of Confucius 8.8, 2.16, 7.21, 7.25, 16.10, 15.3

means of his virtue may be compared to the north polar star, which keeps its place, and all the stars turn towards it' (2.1).

Ren, **Yi** and **DaoDe** are popular words in the Chinese language, e.g., a statesman who governs with **Ren**, **Yi** and **DaoDe** is called *Ren Jun*. The Confucian doctrine is called *Ru Jiao (Confucianism)*.

The character for *Ru* is儒.

The left part 亻 represents people, and the right part 需 means *needs*. Together the character 儒*Ru* means what human need is gentleness and virtue. 儒*Ru* is also a popular word to address a learned person who possesses **Ren**, **Yi** and **DaoDe**, e.g., a Confucian businessman is acclaimed as *Ru shang*.

Although *Ru Jiao* has been inherited and developed through generations, it has been often ill-fated on the political level. The first catastrophe happened 266 years after Confucius' death. In 213 BC, the first Chinese emperor Qin Shihuang (259 BC–210 BC) carried out "burning the books and executing the *Ru* scholars". Some 460 Confucian scholars were persecuted, most of the classics including philosophic works from Hundred Schools of Thought, poetry and historical records praising the ancient virtuous rulers were destroyed and Confucian institutes were shut (Chan, 1972). Instead, Qin Shihuang implemented the ruling thoughts of Chinese Legalism: weaken people, impoverish people, exhaust/fatigue people, humiliate people and befool/deceive people. The masterpiece of Legalism "the Book of Lord Shang" was only circulated among the princes at the court.

During the New Culture Movement (1915–1923) in China, in light of reflection on the fragmented nation and its partial colonisation by the West, a group of radical Chinese scholars blamed Confucianism for China's backwardness while calling forth Mr. De (democracy) and Mr. Sai (science). These scholars included: Chen Duxiu, one of the founders of the Chinese Communist Party; Cai Yuanpei, the president of Peking (it changed to Beijing after 1949) University at that time; and Hu Shih, a nominee for the 1939 Nobel Prize in literature. This group proposed 'Total Westernisation'. Even though this movement espoused enlightened democratic thought and advocated scientific development, it hit traditional values badly. Half a century later, the Great Proletarian Cultural Revolution (1966–1976) completely smashed ancient Chinese civilisation; Confucianism took the brunt of this attack.

The Confucian businessman **Ru** *shang* was doomed to the same fate. *Shang* means business, commerce, and to extend the economy. In business, profit is the precondition for survival. The relationship between ethics and profit has long been debated, especially when capitalist systems became dominant in the Western world and constantly boosted the economic growth from the mid 17th century until early 20th century (Joff, 2011). It was also at this time that the once economic powerhouse of China started to fall. Max Weber (1864–1920) questioned why capitalism did not develop in China and argued that Confucianism and bureaucratic officialdom had hindered its development in China (Sagers, 2014). His conclusion resulted from his research into religion. He stated that certain types of Protestantism – notably Calvinism – motivated believers to pursue profit with religious ethics, as an indication of their salvation. He reckons that one of the drivers of the capitalist economic system was Protestant religious ideology while a Confucian's goal was "a cultured status position", and actively working for wealth was unbecoming of a proper Confucian (Bendix, 1977).

Once again, I think that our arguments should start from the original words of Confucius. "Wealth and honours are what men desire. If it cannot be obtained in a moral way, they should not be held (*4.5*)". Confucius said,

> who acts with self-interests will be much complained against (*4.12*). When seeing profits, think of righteousness (*14.12*). Being poor without resentment is difficult. Being wealthy yet modest is easy (*14.10*). When a country is well governed, poverty is to be ashamed of. When a country is ill governed, wealth is to be ashamed of (*8.13*).

As mentioned earlier, Confucius stated that one of the qualities to be a righteous leader is to "enrich people". These words show that there is no conflict between Confucian ethics and profit.

Can we accumulate wealth while practicing Confucian values? Zi Gong (520 BC–456 BC) was the wealthiest among Confucius' 3,000 disciples and one of the 72 Good Men. (Zi Gong is also known as Tzǔ kung, his birth name is Duanmu Ci.) He was also one of the most loyal disciples of Confucius. According to the *Records of the Grand Historian* (Sima, 91 BC), Zi Gong came from an unprivileged background and became wealthy through cross-border trading (48.8). Confucius said that Zi Gong's "judgments are often correct (in storage of goods)" (11.19). Zi Gong is the first well acknowledged **Ru** shang. Not only that, but he was also a reputable politician, diplomat, and philosopher. During Confucius' 14 years of life in exile, he was described as a "stray dog", but Zi Gong had always defended his master's dignity, "The Master cannot be defamed. The virtue of other men are mounds which may be stepped over. The Master is the sun or moon, which it is not possible to step over" (19.24). "If one cannot find the door to enter our master's palace (of wisdom), he cannot see its beauty and flourish" (19.23).

Right up to today, many Confucian businessmen regard '诚信Chengxin (Integrity) as their motto. (The dishonest/unmoral trader is called 奸商Jian-shang.) Numerous Confucian business groups contributed to historic Chinese economic prosperity. Notably, Shanxi merchants, one of the largest three, influenced Chinese commerce for more than 500 years. Beside the tea trade with Russia, Mongolia, and Japan, they invented the first bank notes and started the draft bank financial systems during the Ming dynasty (14th to 17th century). The Shanxi banking system was the dominant form of banking in China until the fall of the Qing dynasty in 1911 (Eastman, 1988; Morck and Yang, 2010). In the past century, the Chinese Confucian business-men's destiny got tangled up in political turbulence and left the nation only poignant memories. For example, Zhang Jian (1853–1926), a once forgotten Confucian entrepreneur, politician and educator who founded China's ear-liest textile industry, established more than 20 modern businesses and 370 schools, however he ended up as a "Great failed hero". His early life was con-ventionally successful: studying, attending imperial examinations, gaining the first degree, and being granted a high position at the court. But when he recognised the government's incompetence and corruption, he resigned from office and started his 'industry saves the nation' journey. Starting from textiles, his businesses expanded into salt, flour, oil, soap, shipping, machin-ery, water, electricity, and asset management. Aiming to bring benefits to the people, he built the first common school and museum in China, together with many other public facilities and philanthropic organisations. In 1922, he was elected as 'the most respected person' by the media. But soon after, the soaring price of cotton, an impact from the post-war reconstruction, dragged his most profitable business, textiles into bankruptcy. Without any support and help from the government, his empire collapsed. In 1926 he passed away from fatigue. He also left many works of literature and calligraphy. Zhang Jian is acknowledged as the last preeminent **Ru** Shang in modern Chinese history.

Confucian inspired leadership in East Asia

A contemporary inspirational story happened in Japan. Shibusawa Eiichi, the "father of Japanese capitalism", created "the Analects (Confucian) and the Abacus (economy) are inseparable" theory (Tanaka, 2017), which means an ethical leader should be moral and at the same time, develop economics. As an acknowledgment of his teaching and achievement, his face will be printed on the Japanese ¥10,000 banknotes from 2024.

Born in a village farm, Shibusawa studied the Chinese classics when lit-tle. He first became an activist against the Tokugawa shogun's government (a feudal military government of Japan from 1600 to 1868). Later he served in the new Meiji government's Ministry of Finance. He believed that en-terprises which contributed to the welfare of the nation were compatible with the Confucian values of loyalty and public interest. He left office and started his business career, during which he helped establish some 500 businesses including the Mizuho Financial Group, Imperial Hotel, Tokyo Stock Exchange, Tokyo Gas, Keihan Electric Railway, Oji Paper Company and 600 philanthropic organisations for education, social welfare, and international exchange, including Hitotsubashi University and the Tokyo Chamber of Commerce (Shimada, 2017). In his later life, he retired from all his businesses and gave countless speeches and emphasised that businesses must profit not only shareholders but also the nation as a whole. Morality is an essential part of economic activity. Morality and economy are the two sides of the same coin – Confucian Capitalism. Not only that, Shibusawa also courageously criticised the bureaucracy of government officials, "the characteristic of the current state of Japan that is most deplorable is the poisonous notion of 'revering officials and despising the people' that still must be stopped"; and he noted that "when the people contribute to advancing the nation, their efforts go unrecognised, but praise is lavished on officials for small deeds" (Sagers, 2018). By challenging authority in this way, Shubusawa was following Confucius when he said, "when one gained a higher level of *Ren,* he need not yield even to his teacher (15.36)". Shibusawa has few rivals in Japanese business history (Sagers, 2018). Shibusawa's principles have been attracting renewed attention both in Japan and internationally (Fridenson and Takeo, 2017).

According to Shibusawa's teaching, morality is of two types: passive and active. Passive morality means not acting dishonestly, and not placing one's own interests first. This is different to "it is acceptable that one may pursue one's personal profits as long as one follows the rules" in some teachings. And we have seen that some businesses first accumulated their wealth and only then invested in philanthropy. Active morality refers to doing what one should do; specifically, pursuit of public interests and bringing wealth and happiness to others (Tanaka, 2017). Active morality is the cornerstone for a healthy economy and sustainable society (Figure 16.8).

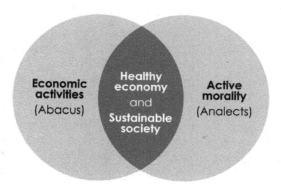

Figure 16.8 Analects and the Abacus are inseparable

What an accomplished new Confucian! Shibusawa cultivated gorgeous flowers on the ancient tree of civilisation. Taking from his legacy, only when leaders from all spectrums – political, institutional, business, and societal – are rooted in morality will ethical businesses be better protected from dishonest rivals; long-term profitable businesses will survive better than those with a 'get rich quick' approach. The whole world will become harmonious and sustainable. To use a current term, it can be said to give "mass immunity" against the vicious circle of competition.

In Taiwan, Japan, and South Korea, "The Analects of Confucius" are taught in schools and universities. For example, a young Japanese business school, SBI Graduate School, "attaches a great deal of importance to moral education". The president of SBI, Mr. Yoshitaka Kitao, CEO of SBI Holdings, is a Confucian follower. Founded in 1398, the South Korean Sungkyunkwan University is perhaps the oldest extant Confucian institute, its motto drew directly from Confucius' doctrine, "*Ren (Benevolence), Yi (*Righteousness*), Li* (Propriety) *and Zhi (Wisdom)*". Mostly sponsored by Samsung and Hyundai, they aim to foster their graduates to achieve these qualities and can demonstrate leadership in the global community.

As a consequence of continuously promoting the principle of "The Analects and Abacus", 75% of major Japanese firms have corporate social responsibility (CSR) committees; 88% of the largest Japanese firms issue reports on their CSR activities; more firms in Japan have been certified as ISO 14000 compliant than in any other country (ISO 14000 is an environmental process standard which is used by many large firms, especially in Western Europe, to select their suppliers); and 132 Japanese firms have subscribed to the United Nations Global Compact (Vogel, 2014). Mr. Mimura (2019), Chairman of the Japan Chamber of Commerce and Industry said, "Shibusawa Eiichi's principle of 'The Analects and the Abacus' will save the Japanese economy".

Conclusion

As science and technology advance, the planet faces even greater threats. Clearly, we remain threatened by chemical, nuclear and biological weapons, but also the greed to attain power, control over others, wealth and self-indulgence is likely to increase. This is fuelled by political hegemony, aided by academic corruption and information monopoly, and exacerbated by environmental damage and disparities in wealth and gender equality. No surprise that Stephen Hawking (2016) warned that "AI (artificial intelligence) will be 'either best or worst thing' for humanity". Moral education and ethical leadership, of which Daoism and Confucianism are without doubt radiant exemplars, provide us a philosophical basis to combat these potential threats. From the examples of Daoist/Confucianist influenced Eastern Asian democracies, we may conclude that a healthy democratic system can help to protect and advance society by instituting ethical governance and the rule of law as a shield to protect ethics. Therefore, learning from each other and equipping ourselves with wisdom from different cultures will help to shape future global transpersonal leadership.

Questions and actions for personal development

1. How would you define ethical leadership?
2. What are the similarities and differences between Confucian teaching and Western culture?
3. Do you agree with the statement that you should "accumulate wealth by all means and then invest in goodwill"?
4. What is your opinion on Shibusawa's idea that "Analects and the Abacus are inseparable"?
5. How would you prioritise or balance private sector profit and public interest?
6. How can you help to shape ethical leadership and create a moral organisational culture?
7. Action plan: How would you adapt the approach given in Figure 16.7 into your practice?

References

Bendix (1977). *Max Weber*. University of California Press.

Chan, Lois Mai (1972). *The Burning of the Books in China, 213 B.C.* The Journal of Library History, 7(2): 101–108, JSTOR 25540352

Confucius disciples (c. 475 BCE). *The Analects of Confucius*. The original traditional Chinese texts refers to He Yan (? -249), *The Interpretation Collection of Analects*; English translations refer to Legge, James. (1861). *Confucian Analects*, Oxford University Press, and the author's own interpretation.

Eastman, L., 1988. *Family, Fields, and Ancestors*. Oxford University Press.

Fridenson, Patrick and Takeo, Kikkawa (2017). *Ethical Capitalism: Shibusawa Eiichi and Business Leadership in Global Perspective*. University of Toronto Press.

Gelfand, M.J. (2021). *The Relationship between Cultural Tightness – Looseness and COVID-19 Cases and Deaths: A Global Analysis* – The Lancet Planetary Health. https://www.thelancet.com/journals/lanplh/article/PIIS2542-5196(20)30301-6/fulltext

Hawking, S., 2016. *Stephen Hawking: AI will be 'either best or worst thing' for humanity*. [online] The Guardian. https://www.theguardian.com/science/2016/oct/19/-stephen-hawking-ai-best-or-worst-thing-for-humanity-cambridge [Accessed 22 October 2021].

Hofstede, G. (2010) *Cultures and Organizations: Software of the Mind*. McGraw-Hill Education.

Joff, Michael (2011). *The Root Cause of Economic Growth under Capitalism*. Cambridge Journal of Economics, 35(5): 873–896. doi:10.1093/cje/beq054.

Knights, John (2016). *Ethical Leadership: Becoming an Ethical Leader*. Routledge.

Lao Zi (c. 571 BC– 471 BC), *Daode Jing* (or *Tao Te Ching*). The original traditional Chinese texts refer to Wang Bi (226–249), *Daode Jing Interpretation*; English translations refer to Legge, James. (1891) *Tao Te Ching*, Oxford University Press,

Mitchell, Stephen (2000) *Tao Te Ching,* Macmillan London, and the author's own interpretation.

Maslow, A. (1943) *A Theory of Human Motivation.* Psychological Review, 50(4): 370–396.

Mimura, Akio (2019). *Shibusawa Eiichi's Principle of "The Analects and the Abacus" Will Save the Japanese Economy — Hopefully, the Will of the "Father of Japanese Capitalism" Will Be Passed on in the New Era.* https://www.japanpolicyforum.jp/economy/pt20190711230502.html

Morck, Randall and Yang, Fan (2010). *The Shanxi Banks.* Academia.edu.

Sagers, John H. (2014) *Shibusawa Eiichi and the Merger of Confucianism and Capitalism in Modern Japan.* Association for Asian Studies.

Sagers, John H. (2018) *Confucian Capitalism: Shibusawa Eiichi, Business Ethics, and Economic Development in Meiji Japan.* Springer.

Shimada, Masakazu (2017) *The Entrepreneur Who Built Modern Japan Shibusawa Eiichi.* Japan Publishing Industry Foundation for Culture (JPIC); 1st Edition.

Tanaka, Kazuhiro (2017) *The "Analects" and the Abacus: The Contemporary Relevance of Shibusawa Eiichi's Business Philosophy.* https://www.nippon.com/en/currents/d00274/

Tang, Yuchun (2018) *Brain Structure Differences between Chinese and Caucasian Cohorts: A Comprehensive Morphometry Study.* Human Brain Mapo 39(5): 2147–2155 https://www.ncbi.nlm.nih.gov/pmc/articles/PMC6625506/

Van Bavel, J.J. (2020) *Using Social and Behavioural Science to Support COVID-19 Pandemic Response | Nature Human Behaviour.* Nature Human Behaviour. https://www.nature.com/articles/s41562-020-0884-z

Vogel, D.J. (2014) *Corporate Social Responsibility: Potential and Challenges.* https://www.tkfd.or.jp/en/research/detail.php?id=353

17 Remote leadership beyond the ego

Duncan Enright and Greg Young

"Far from court, far from care." English proverb, meaning that when one is away from the intrigues and politics of the headquarters, one might be able to relax!

Overview

The COVID pandemic has fuelled an already sharply growing trend towards home working, enabled by technology and seen as desirable by employees tired of commuting and employers looking to expand their talent pool. Before the pandemic in 2020, home working had increased by 140% over 2005; in Spring 2021, over 60% of adults in the UK were working from home. Many benefits in productivity and employee engagement are cited (Bloom et al., 2014; State of Remote Work, 2019), and absenteeism (despite the pandemic) fell dramatically, yet problems persist and the challenges leaders face are many, some new and some enduring, whether sharing a workplace or not.

The world is at a tipping point; it is changing faster and more unpredictably. Society, technology and the climate are changing at unprecedented levels. Successful leaders recognise that leadership has moved on from being authoritative, hierarchical and pace-setting to becoming a distributed leadership underpinned by an ethical, caring, sustainable and performance-enhancing culture. Only Transpersonal Leaders who are both emotionally intelligent and lead beyond their ego can consistently embrace, communicate and enaction these characteristics.

This chapter will examine the challenges faced by leaders in virtual, distributed or remote settings and propose solutions based on leading beyond the ego.

Introduction

In 2019, before the pandemic, LeaderShape created an infographic exploring the growth of virtual organisations. At that time, working from home had increased by 140% over a decade and a half. Reported increases in worker

DOI: 10.4324/9781003150626-21

satisfaction and reductions in attrition rate of up to a half were accompanied by increases in productivity averaging 13% and 91% of remote workers saying they had a better work-life balance thanks to the flexibility it offers. Overall surveys showed full-time remote workers were 22% happier than those who never worked remotely (LeaderShape Global, 2019).

The idea of working remote from a central place of employment is not new. The roots of offices and factories separate from homes are buried in the industrial revolution, and the daily commute to work is a phenomenon familiar to suburban dwellers from the 1850s, but not before. Most of our management practices, including the development of the science of management, date from the 20th century, and our study of leadership has emerged from thinking about this form of central management.

By looking at the growth of centralised practice, we can relearn much of what we know about management, and recognise that leadership skills (in particular transpersonal leadership) are not tied to setting or custom. Instead the seeds of leadership lie within us and can be developed and exercised every bit as much in remote working.

However, the challenges posed by remote working, virtual teams and modern organisations can make certain aspects of leadership more important, and invites us to flex unfamiliar leadership muscles. We know that time and again, all around the world, in all sorts of organisations, when asked, employees at all levels seek cultures shaped by support and achievement rather than power and structure (Figure 17.1). What does this mean for remote organisations? Our conclusion is that the same principles priorities still apply, but perhaps we need to alter our leadership style to meet the needs of remote working.

In this chapter, we use the term 'remote' as it has become widely used to describe a team, group or organisation that is not located in central offices or locations. However this assumes that a central location exists, from which people are 'remote'. Some organisations deliberately choose not to have such a location, and describe themselves as 'distributed', which is quite an attractive and egalitarian notion. Also we use the word 'virtual' from time to time to describe a team or organisation that uses technology to collaborate, communicate, and work despite colleagues being separated – in our view both 'remote' and 'virtual' are largely interchangeable, but the requirement for management and leadership is neither virtual nor remote, but very much real and immediate.

Why do we have workplaces?

One hundred and fifty years ago a home was a workplace. Witney in Oxfordshire, UK, was renowned for three things: bread, beer and blankets. Many of the workers in the neighbourhood of Newland, however, had smallholdings on which they grew vegetables and reared chickens and pigs; alongside

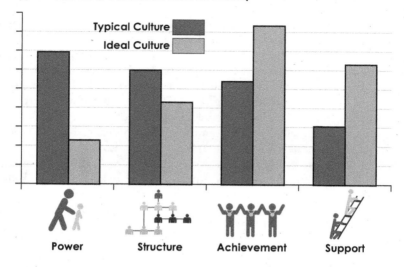

Typical and Ideal Cultures for the 21st Century

LeaderShape Global ©2020

Figure 17.1 Typical and ideal organisational cultures

this many took in 'piecework' for the local glove manufacturers, using locally sourced leather from cattle and, more expensively, deer from nearby Blenheim Estate and Wychwood Forest. Every Monday the work supervisor would bring raw materials, and every Saturday collect finished gloves and dispense wages according to the number made.

The arrival of the industrial revolution led to a move into factories and offices – workplaces where expensive machinery could be used to replicate and outperform the old arrangements. The reasons employers established these costly yet efficient new palaces of industry go beyond the economic:

- New industrial processes required teams of people working together, hence the need to bring them to a single place of employment
- Access to machinery – costly and immobile machines held pride of place in the new factories
- Efficiency and productivity went hand in hand, with the new factories producing far more goods in less time and at lower prices
- Quality control now became easier to manage, with a single point of production and greater opportunities for training and oversight
- Communication of new ideas and methods is simpler in a single workplace, as is the issuing of instructions and confirmation of compliance
- Innovation becomes swifter and easier to encourage through joint endeavour and the ability to share ingenuity and new ideas

In short, the practice of 'Management' was born, both of self, of teams and of wider organisations, with benefits that were only too obvious. Benefits extended to workers too: the establishment of workplaces freed up the home for domestic use (though it took workers out of the home, leading to less time available for chores and a gradual reduction in other activities such as market gardening on the side).

The office in the 20th century

Offices were of course needed to house the ancillary functions of factories: salesmen, overseers, owners and clerks were all accommodated in offices. But it was the 20th century that saw the explosion of office work as a proportion of the workload and the expansion of white collar jobs. The need for warrens of cubicles was driven by the needs of the business but also of machinery. The requirement was for people to cluster around printing facilities, typing pools, filing cabinets, and money management systems such as ledgers and safes. This accelerated latterly (from 1950 onwards) with the increase in demand for computer space. As travel became cheaper and faster, and education improved, the opportunity to travel further and further to work in offices led to a daily commute for many. For me and dozens of others in Witney it meant a journey by car and train; underground or bus, or bike then walk, to central London offices – a daily journey back and forth of over five hours on most days.

It is little wonder that employers and employees saw the advent of mobile computing, and particularly the laptop and the smart phone (and spiralling office costs), as an opportunity for change, and change for the better. Thus, home working became popular, and the need for remote management and leadership emerged.

Remote working: benefits and challenges

As alluded to above, there are many benefits of remote working. These include benefits for the individual, as well as benefits for the team and the organisation. However, these are accompanied by challenges for the individual, the team and the organisation, which also need to be addressed.

Benefits

Working from home or close to it, and organising work to suit their lifestyle, gives employees control in a way not possible in an office. Winning back hours spent on commuting is the most tangible benefit of all for many remote workers. The flexibility allows us to manage home and work responsibilities in ways that suit us, and saving the cost of travel also helps! A home workspace can be tailored to suit the individual and tasks can be organised to match their energy and availability.

When planned and executed carefully, employers can work with their staff to make sure adequate space and appropriate equipment and support are available. For many during the rush to work from home during the pandemic, many physical challenges such as finding space in the modern home have not been addressed adequately.

For employers there are cost savings too. Reduced turnover of staff thanks to greater satisfaction saves time and cost, and the potential to reduce office space and cut rent bills is also not inconsiderable. Employers report a wider pool of qualified and talented applicants becoming available with positions that offer flexibility around location and the ability to manage other priorities such as caring responsibilities. Productivity increases are widely reported, with one study showing that remote workers are an average of 35%–40% more productive than their office counterparts and have measured an output increase of at least 4.4%. In addition greater autonomy leads to employees to produce results with 40% fewer quality defects. Absenteeism falls by 41% as a result of the greater engagement. Turnover falls 12% (and 54% of employees say they would change jobs for greater flexibility where it is not on offer). All of this adds to greater profitability (Farrer, 2020).

Challenges

The most frequently cited challenge for the employee when working at home is losing control of work/life balance. Many report that taking a walk between breakfast and the start of the working day can help, but often we work too hard, don't stop for breaks, and spend too many hours working and not enough time maintaining wellbeing or attending to home responsibilities. Some complain of lack of focus because of distractions at home, and miss the informal interactions and relationships of the workplace. Everyone feels more isolated and for some this can be a significant problem.

For the team, there are issues relating to project coordination and more difficult communication. Many online tools are available, but chat software seems to be the most effective at making sure everyone is working well together (and it can address issues of loneliness).

The organisation as a whole, and leaders in the organisation, have some more fundamental challenges. After all, leadership is exercised through relationships with others, so how can it be maintained in a virtual environment where casual interactions are not happening? How can motivation be maintained and performance be managed? Most importantly, how can a leader make sure the organisation is still following the same core purpose, mission and vision and not becoming fractured?

Managing and leading in a remote environment

Seven principles have been developed to help leaders manage and lead remotely. These are:

1   Remembering to put people at the heart of the organisation;
2   Give first of yourself, sharing vulnerability as well as strength, sharing your stories and letting people know the human you;
3   Model personal discipline particularly on starting and ending the work day;
4   Communicate effectively, frequently and appropriately to maintain relationships and share key messages including reminding people of the organisation's purpose, vision and mission;
5   Care actively and listen attentively, as much as to what isn't being said as to what is;
6   Respect and value difference, as everyone will work differently and the variety lends strength to the common effort; and
7   Keep learning, including from the best at remote working and leadership.

People at the heart

Work should be a supportive and caring environment for everyone. We all do best when everyone is supported to do their best. A transpersonal leader will be aware that a remote workforce may feel 'remote' in more ways than physically. Attention must be paid to making sure that a remotely led enterprise is one which values its people first, and makes sure they know it.

One way to demonstrate this is not to forget to invest in people and their development. Does training in a remote setting hold an important place? Do regular performance management sessions still happen? Can staff members raise issues easily and are they addressed promptly? Do you have a plan to develop careers of everyone who wants to progress in their role (or qualify and move up and onwards)? Every leader you need to show empathy explicitly, and to have regular conversations to make sure you understand how people are doing – and to make sure everyone understands that you are aware of their situation. Empathy is, time and again, the most valuable emotional intelligence capability to develop – and even more so when you don't have the luxury of meeting face to face.

It is tempting to be completely busy with tasks and planning which has nothing to do with your staff. Put time aside to be in touch regularly with everyone who reports to you, and others as well who are important to the team. Make sure everyone is in regular touch with their reports, and establish peer-to-peer support contacts.

Trust people to do the right thing. It has been shown in research that giving people autonomy is a major motivator of better performance, and supporting them to gain skills further enhances their capabilities (Mullenweg, 2020).

The Coaching style of leadership is a particularly valuable way to let people know they are appreciated, as described below. Structured conversations assisted by a coaching style are well suited to remote conversations on the phone (or preferably video).

Give of yourself

Leadership is exercised through trust and strong relationships. It is even more important when leading remotely to be transparent and open about your own feelings and experiences, as they are not visible to the rest of the group. Share your stories, and let everyone see the real human you.

In the pandemic, we all shared sometimes sudden changes of lifestyle and working patterns. By sharing their own story, leaders can be authentic and encourage others to share. It is important to listen to the stories of others too. Stories need to be told with truth; positive stories have particular value in maintaining morale. However being honest is part of building strength, and it can take bravery to share your vulnerabilities. Just remember that people value your leadership more if they know you are authentic and being honest with them about challenges as well as good news.

Be disciplined

As mentioned, work/life balance and overworking is the biggest challenge for many when working from home or remote office. It is your responsibility to model working responsibly. Set a start time that is realistic, finish at an appropriate time, and make sure everyone knows it.

There is an element of self-care in this. Of course, as leaders, we are highly engaged in the business at hand. However if we cannot contain our working hours we will soon be at risk of burnout. Take time to balance work with everything else. Take time to care for yourself. Otherwise you are not doing yourself or the organisation any favours.

Take holiday deliberately and book the time away publicly. Set a good time for a digital dawn and digital dusk – when you can recharge at the same time as the smartphone (my 'on' time is 8 am to 9 pm). If there is too much to do, it is a workload issue which needs addressing, delegation that must happen, or prioritisation not quite right.

Smart communication

Agree appropriate channels for communication, and use them regularly. At LeaderShape we use WhatsApp for team chats and sharing snippets; email for more substantial information sharing and formal notices; FaceTime for watercooler moments and informal chats; and Zoom for business meetings (which we started using in 2016 for the quality of connection and simplicity of use).

A company of 30 people in the UK settled on regular meetings when the pandemic lockdown happened. Each Friday they held all-company informal briefings with contributions from all staff. On Mondays they held formal briefings from the executive team. They established chat forums to replicate discussions held around the lunch table for informal work exchanges about client preferences and project progress; and another for sharing pet and family pictures which became a place to share domestic news including challenges of home schooling and requests for help. Staff reportedly felt well supported, even if on temporary leave.

Good use of communication is the way to maintain the culture of an organisation – sharing 'how we do things round here'. It is also the way to keep everyone focussed on the bigger picture – the core purpose and vision of the organisation.

Active care

Tune in to others and get your radar serviced. In a remote workplace you need to listen very attentively to others and pick up weak signals of conflict or distress. An email can spark disquiet in a way that a remark in a meeting would not, when accompanied by a wink or a smile. Leaders need to warn their colleagues of the danger posed by remote communications. Is everyone copied in to key messages? Sometimes it is noticing what is not said, every bit as much as what is. As with other areas, a coaching conversation can make a big difference.

Respect and value difference

Respect different working patterns. People find different parts of the day more productive. They are also probably juggling other responsibilities which are more pressing when working at home. If work commitments are being met, to the quality and timescale required, you can let people set their own ways of working. You might find the variation is helpful across the team. Also remember the value of difference – see Chapter 13 for more on the value of diversity. If you work across time zones, remember that you don't always need to meet in real time and it is much better to arrange things for mutual convenience.

Keep learning

As in any other field of work or life, keep looking for best practice and advice. Some companies have been working this way for many years. For example, look out for stories by WordPress founder Matt Mullenweg on the value of distributed working (Mullenweg, 2019) based on a global team of self-directed employees.

Coaching style of leadership – remotely

The Coaching Style has a very positive effect on organisational culture, and individual performance, aligning work with overall goals and encouraging insights, ideas, autonomy and innovation. It is a crucial tool for managing and leading remotely, with its positive impact on morale and benefits for the coach and coachee alike, strengthening relationships and building bonds.

Here are some tips for using the coaching style in one-to-one conversations in a remote setting.

1 You can use elements of the coaching style in everyday conversations, but if you want a longer one-to-one give notice so that you can both find time and a place where you won't be interrupted.
2 Use video if at all possible; body language adds hugely to communication.
3 Don't lead: the coach is in charge of the structure of the conversation NOT the subject.
4 Write notes throughout the session under headings Goal, Reality, Options, Will. This ensures each step is covered and gets clarified. (Make sure note taking is brief and does not get in the way of your being 'present' and fully attentive).
5 Stay neutral – it is not up to coaches to come up with answers.
6 Only ask questions – don't give your opinion unless asked for, or unless you really feel the person has a blind spot about the matter; ask permission to offer an alternative perspective).
7 Don't move on to the next step until the one you are on is fully clarified.
8 Stay in control; if the coachee moves off track or jumps to the next stage, pull them back gently.
9 Listen – and show that you are actively listening (nod head, keep eye contact, do not get distracted; if using a phone then indicate understanding with short phrases or verbal indications).
10 Paraphrase to check understanding and meaning – sometimes paraphrasing is more powerful than questioning, so if you are unsure of the 'best' question to ask next, just paraphrase and reflect back.
11 Use silence to encourage more information – if you don't speak they will!
12 Use good questions: The best questions are the simple obvious ones, use open questions – how, what, who, when? (use why? with care, as it can be seen as overly challenging or judgmental).
13 Take time: don't jump in too soon, allow a few seconds after an answer to encourage more thinking.
14 Ask questions with purpose: clarify and flesh out issues, don't be afraid to dig deep, but always ask in the coachee's best interests, never dig deeper just to satisfy your own curiosity.
15 Make space: ask "is there anything else you want to say before we move on?"

To GROW

A useful framework for any coaching conversation is the mnemonic To GROW (see Figure 17.2).

Figure 17.2 To GROW model of coaching

TOPIC: What issues would you like to discuss? Make sure you are very clear about this before you move on. The topic sometimes needs to be 'redefined' later in the session, perhaps after the reality.

GOAL: What do you want to get out of this session? The goal sometimes needs to be 'refined' later in the session, perhaps in the reality.

REALITY: Tell me about the current situation. How do you feel about it? Ask simple, obvious questions to gain detail. Assume nothing. Clarify the topic again before you move on.

OPTIONS: What could you do about it? Options are possible solutions. What alternatives exist? What could be possible outcomes? Rate options in terms of practicality. Assess any possible pitfalls and potential resistance from others, or what support may be needed.

WILL or WHAT NEXT: What are you going to do now? What are the SMART actions and who will do them?

Benefits of remote coaching (ideally video, alternatively audio)

There are some benefits of using technology to enable remote coaching:

- Flexibility: more flexibility on timings, and comfortable and confidential locations.
- Freedom: Both coaches and coachees can be more free to ask, talk, listen, interrupt, rant!
- Notes and resources: easier to take and refer to notes, share documents and resources without breaking the flow.
- Time and time out: flexibility to take a reflective break, easily keep an eye on the clock.

Further research on the comparison between face-to-face and virtual coaching is available in an excellent review (Berry, Ashby, Gnilka and Matheny, 2011) and a pithy article on the comparison has been written by Richard Tarran (2021).

How can remote working replicate office benefits?

What is it that is most important about the workplace which needs to be maintained in a distributed company? One way to think about this is to list the useful physical attributes of an office, and another is to consider the relationships and personal interactions. The following are a list of those physical and social attributes:

- Right tools
- Private places
- Noticeboards
- Informal spaces
- Meeting rooms
- Relationships
- Management
- Training
- Rewards

How will these be provided or managed if people work remotely?

A good manager will make sure that the right tools are in place, which means considering and auditing facilities such as a physical space at home, without constant interruptions, where someone can concentrate. Access to key resources such as relevant information, communication tools and office equipment, and the skills to use them effectively, must be there. A good leader will consider other aspects and key among these are the following.

Reminder of core purpose

Why does the company do what it does? How can everyone stay on the same page? Is the vision still in view, and shared across the whole team? In an office, the walls and noticeboards can be decorated with statements about the purpose and values of the organisation, or more short-term reminders of project deadlines and plans.

How will you ensure the whole team maintains a focus on the bigger picture? Perhaps a slot in each regular team meeting could discuss aspects of the purpose.

Motivation and support

The wellbeing of staff is a prime concern in any setting. However the isolation inherent in home working, or alternatively the pressure of others not engaged in the work (including pets and children!) might also provide a source of stress and discomfort that a leader needs to pay attention to. Many staff are reluctant to use videoconferencing cameras, for a variety of reasons. Some cite their appearance, or that of their surroundings, as a factor in remaining blank on screen meetings. A good leader will determine why this is the case, and work to build confidence. Evidence shows that coaching and support can be very effective in managing wellbeing and reducing stress when delivered remotely (Lungu et al., 2020). However it is my experience that video adds to the attention both parties bring to the exchange. Note however that many people report feeling more tired by phone or video exchanges than would be the case face to face.

Like core purpose, the intangible culture, or 'how we do things round here', can be hard to maintain in remote settings. Often this contributes to security and wellbeing of staff. Perhaps a cross-departmental team could be tasked with coming up with ideas to support a positive culture, flexing where needed to support the needs of the organisation, to introduce new staff members to the culture, and to reassure all staff. A leader will provide their own support for this positive culture by modelling behaviour, and by setting the right tone at the top of the organisation – leaders set the climate, and everyone creates the culture.

Fostering innovation

Those incidental conversations during meetings, or at the coffee machine, fuel a sense of common purpose, transmit a positive (or negative) culture, but also provide a seedbed for new ideas. How can innovation be supported in a virtual environment?

By trusting people to take responsibility for their own work, building autonomy, we can build their creativity and innovation. Some companies even go so far as to schedule days for projects not directly related to day-to-day work, and report excellent and productive results. The combination of autonomy, mastery (becoming really expert at something, emphasising the need for encouragement and continued learning opportunities), and purpose (we see here again the importance of core purpose being communicated effectively in remote working) are the three pillars of motivation (Pink, 2011) (Figure 17.3).

Regular online creativity exchanges can also play a part in trying to mitigate lost creativity of people working in isolation. But there is more to do here to foster creativity and innovation in remote teams, and currently this must be a priority for the agenda of infrequent physical get-togethers. These might operate as innovation conferences in the same way as field sales operative gatherings fulfil a number of corporate requirements for an otherwise dispersed team.

Successful remote meetings

Meetings are not always successful face to face, so don't despair if they seem difficult using technology and at a distance! Here are some ideas for making them work – please add your own.

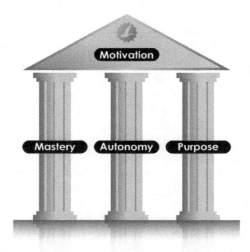

Figure 17.3 Three pillars of motivation (based on work by Pink, 2011)

1 Do you actually need a meeting? Consider whether it is possible to achieve your objective by another means, such as a briefing email, or a series of individual calls.

2 Don't let a meeting drag on. Research suggests at face-to-face meetings attention wanders after an hour. The free 40 minutes on Zoom should suffice for most things. Remember too that online interactions are more tiring than face to face. If needed, cut your meeting into chunks with comfort breaks. A straw poll (my family) indicates it takes on average of 1 hour 20 minutes before you go cross-eyed.

3 Unlike physical meetings, there is no travel time when online to allow participants to refresh their minds and prepare. Build that reflection time into your day, and that of your colleagues, by scheduling meetings to last 25 or 50 minutes rather than a half or full hour, so there is time for participants to rest before the next one starts. This is also a good way of enforcing timing discipline during meetings.

4 Give your meeting a name that describes the objective clearly. Instead of 'weekly team meeting', what about 'The Friday Bonding and Sharing Session'? There is a lot to be said for titling a meeting to match the 'plot' along the lines of Friends episodes: 'The One Where We Decide Whether to Proceed with Plan B' or 'The One With the Board Listening to Customer Feedback'. Or 'The One Where We Check Everyone is OK'.

5 Think hard about your invitation list. Don't invite anyone who isn't able to contribute or who doesn't need to hear. Consider if some people might find it more useful just to see the minutes.

6 Treat the agenda like the listings in the TV guide. Think about where you need to spend most time and give it an appropriate slot in the schedule. Make sure everyone knows by putting times against agenda items. If possible keep the timings visible on screen throughout the meeting.

7 Meeting conduct is even more important online than it is in face-to-face meetings. Establish rules before the meeting as part of the invitation. Rules might include allowing each person to speak once only on every agenda item before asking for repeat performances. It is common practice with large meetings to mute all attendees on entry. This has benefits, but it is fair to let attendees know in advance.

8 Keep to time. Don't allow the meeting to drift. If it seems there are conversations developing, ask participants to have a separate call. If a decision is taking longer than anticipated, consider convening another meeting – clearly it wasn't ready for this one.

9 No distractions. Brief everyone to find a space where they won't be disturbed. If possible ask participants to put a sign on the door of the room where they are working saying "Not Now, Please". Remind them that the meeting needs their full attention, so no checking phones or typing on other screens. If you suspect someone is not engaged, ask them a question and bring them back into the group. BUT...

10 Children and pets allowed! It isn't always possible to stop interruptions. Don't let meetings be knocked off course by the unexpected, just acknowledge it and stay with the agenda.

11 Ask someone to take notes (ideally not you, if you are chairing). Circulate them afterwards. It is rare to find value in recorded videoconferences, so don't do it as a rule. Record decisions, who is doing what by when, in writing.

12 Rotate the chair or facilitator. This is a great development opportunity, and it builds trust and involvement.

Conclusion

The move to remote working is not new, but it is a new challenge for leadership and management. It is likely to become more common in future, and has been accelerated by the COVID pandemic. It has benefits for employees, teams, managers, leaders and organisations, but these are matched by challenges such as retaining a clear vision of the core purpose, maintaining motivation, ensuring wellbeing and fostering a culture that promotes innovation.

A leader needs to develop their emotional intelligence, and particularly hone their empathy, to be able to respond to the needs of a distributed workforce. Leaders need to be encouraged throughout the workforce to assist in the essential work of combatting isolation and stress, and maintaining a positive shared culture. Coaching conversations provide a great opportunity to support staff and build trust.

A few simple rules about how to run meetings, conduct one-to-ones and ensure resilience matter every bit as much as the essential work of auditing home workspaces and applying home working policies. Done well, remote leadership can liberate and motivate employees, empower teams, and lead to innovation and efficiencies not possible in a fixed workplace.

Questions and actions for personal development

1. Which styles of leadership are important when managing a distributed team?
2. What are the main challenges for a leader when not working in the same office as their direct reports?
3. How do the methods a leader employs to motivate a team differ from traditional approaches when not working in the same location?
4. How can leaders ensure wellbeing and high productivity in a distributed organisation?
5. What challenges do hybrid working – colleagues spending some time in the office and some time working remotely – pose for leaders?
6. Think of a way to halve the number of meetings you hold every week, and how you will spend the time productively instead.

References

Berry, R., Ashby, J., Gnilka, P. and Matheny, K., 2011. A comparison of face-to-face and distance coaching practices: Coaches' perceptions of the role of the working alliance in problem resolution. *Consulting Psychology Journal: Practice and Research*, 63(4), pp. 243–253.

Bloom, N., Liang, J., Roberts, J. and Ying, Z., 2014. Does working from home work? Evidence from a Chinese Experiment*. *The Quarterly Journal of Economics*, 130(1), pp. 165–218.

Farrer, L., 2020. 5 Proven benefits of remote work for companies. [online] *Forbes*. Available at: <https://www.forbes.com/sites/laurelfarrer/2020/02/12/top-5-benefits-of-remote-work-for-companies/> [Accessed 29 March 2021].

LeaderShape Global. 2019. Virtual organisation leadership. *Leadershapeglobal.com*. https://www.leadershapeglobal.com/virtual-organisation-leadership, March 29, 2021.

Lungu, A., Boone, M.S., Chen, S.Y., Chen, C.E. and Walser, R.D., 2021. Effectiveness of a cognitive behavioral coaching program delivered via video in real world settings. *Telemedicine Journal and e-Health*. 27(1), pp. 47–54.

Mullenweg, M., 2019. *Distributed.blog*. [online] Distributed.blog. Available at: <https://distributed.blog/> [Accessed 22 October 2021].

Mullenweg, M. 2020. Distributed work's five levels of autonomy. *Matt Mullenweg*. https://ma.tt/2020/04/five-levels-of-autonomy/, March 29, 2021.

Pink, D. 2011. *Drive*. Edinburgh: Canongate.

State of Remote Work Report. 2019. *Owllabs.com*. https://www.owllabs.com/state-of-remote-work/2019, March 29, 2021.

Tarran, R., 2021. Is face to face coaching better than on-line coaching? [online] *Range Advantage*. Available at: <https://www.rangeadvantage.com/News/ArtMID/506/ArticleID/50/IS-FACE-TO-FACE-COACHING-BETTER-THAN-ON-LINE-COACHING> [Accessed 5 January 2021].

18 How to develop transpersonal leadership and transform organisational culture

A guide for HR professionals

Robert Jarvis

> If you make listening and observation your occupation, you will gain much more than you can by talk.
>
> Robert Baden-Powell, The first Chief Scout (1922)

Overview

Fundamentally everything that a human resource (HR) professional does builds, develops and reinforces culture: from building a vision and strategy for diversity and inclusion, drafting a new policy on travel and expenses or even everyday interactions and talent strategy. HR team members are the day-to-day custodians of the culture and a large part of understanding the organisation is in the sphere of transpersonal leadership. HR at all levels from business partners to transactional service providers need to understand and feel how well the organisation is doing and role model the transpersonal behaviours on a day-to-day basis. Often what is not said is just as if not more important than what is said. In this chapter, the concepts of transpersonal leadership are mapped to the HR profession using the professional map developed by the UK Chartered Institute of Personnel Development (CIPD) ("Diversity and inclusion | CIPD Profession Map", 2020).

Listening is the most underrated leadership tool. HR professionals need to role model active listening, as it is the only way you can truly lead beyond the ego. Leadership is not just a hierarchical position in the structure, and management is not always leadership. Leadership can come from any position on an organisation chart and can be contextual to the situation or project being worked on.

Examples: Leaders that can affect culture can be working in any position:

1 In a healthcare (NHS) trust, a CEO spent time with the porters regularly as they touch every department and provide a good sense of how the organisation is doing. They affect and are affected by the rest of the organisation.

DOI: 10.4324/9781003150626-22

2   In another organisation I worked in, the receptionist clearly set the culture for that day, as everyone in the company and external clients walked by their desk and interacted with them every day. Their mood and daily disposition affected the ways others were feeling.

The Global Pandemic 2020 situation has brought to the forefront the need for HR and leaders to step up and use the opportunity to shine. With companies in recovery and having to change the way things are done, to innovate in order to survive and succeed, leaders need to show the way; '*The role of the leader is to generate followers, bring them to a place they would not ordinarily go, and inspire new leaders.*' (Knights, Grant & Young, 2018). It is important for organisations recovery that all individuals act as leaders and become transpersonal leaders, thinking how things are done and what needs to be done. Often in crisis we witness commanding leadership skills taking precedent and they are not necessarily the right ones to display particularly in the medium to long term. Individuals will have all had a unique COVID-19 scenario and the empathetic elements of the coaching style may lead to a better outcome in the longer term.

The pandemic and recovery has also provided HR and leaders the opportunity to show the importance of authenticity: 'act as you truly are'. Showing that the power of human connectivity is so important. It is clear that each individual within a team has different levels of resilience, based on their historical experiences, related to COVID-19. Before the pandemic, the average worker would have a period of time during any day that they were a commuter, a colleague, a friend, a client, a manager, a leader, a partner and perhaps a parent etc. During the pandemic these have all become intertwined. Leadership is about understanding this and using every opportunity to increase the levels of human connectiveness. Connectivity, authenticity and genuine empathy are important transpersonal skills.

Example: The importance of connectivity

3   I previously worked for a boss who remembered the small stuff, kids birthdays, wedding anniversaries, etc. This boosted how connected people felt to him. In contrast working for a boss who didn't remember or care that you had a family had a different impact.

When developing leaders within the organisation, HR need to ensure development is part of a wider succession plan, individuals with potential to be highlighted for their behavioural competencies as well as technical. Often organisations find themselves in a position where hierarchical leaders are in position because of longevity and technical ability.

Example: Leadership versus Management

4   Working in an organisation that had scientists and engineers, actually the chief engineer or scientist may not be the right person to manage

individuals in the sub structure. Leadership in particular the coaching style can be on a professional basis (Knights, Grant & Young, 2018, Chapter 3) There is also a context that HR Professionals must navigate. Sectors have different styles, traditions and ways of working, but particularly in Global Organisations HR must navigate and understand cultural norms and expectations from leadership (see Table 9.1 for more details).

There are times when HR Leaders need to be agile and adaptive to the context in which they find themselves, and over the last number of years each of the six leadership styles outlined by John Knights in Chapter 8 of *Leading Beyond the Ego* (Knights, Grant and Young, 2018) have been utilised, in order to get a positive outcome for the organisation, some more than others:

- Visionary
- Coaching
- Affiliative
- Democratic
- Pace Setting
- Commanding

LeaderShape's LEIPA 360° assessment is unlike most development tools as it combines emotional intelligence with the six styles of leadership. It asks raters to indicate observed and desired behaviours and leadership (Figure 18.1).

In 2018, the CIPD introduced a new profession map after extensive research amongst its members. This identifies core knowledge, core behaviours and specialist knowledge to guide HR professional's in their career. In particular, the nine areas of specialist knowledge for the people function, listed

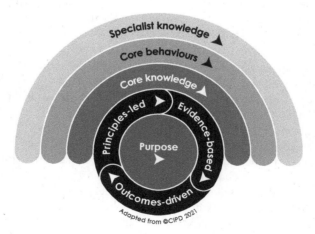

Figure 18.1 Chartered Institute of Personnel and Development Profession Map, with permission of the publisher, Chartered Institute of Personnel and Development in London (www.cipd.co.uk)

below. These could quite comfortably provide the building blocks of an effective HR strategy for an organisation.

> The new Profession Map sets the international benchmark for the people profession. Use it to make better decisions, act with confidence, perform at your peak, drive change in your organisation and progress in your career. No matter who you are in the profession, whether you're a CIPD member or not, the new Profession Map is relevant to you.
> CIPD Website, https://peopleprofession.cipd.org/profession-map

Clearly Transpersonal leadership is integral in this Profession map. In conjunction with the core behaviours, we thought the nine specialist areas could be used to highlight how transpersonal leadership is integral in everything HR does (Table 18.1).

The rest of this chapter will take each of the nine specialist knowledge areas in turn and link them to the CIPD Core Behaviours and Transpersonal Leadership, highlighting areas for consideration for HR professionals.

Organisational development and design

This specialist knowledge area is about systems, processes, structures, and behaviours to drive performance within the organisation. Organisations and businesses have a life cycle from start up to maturity, merger and acquisition and even potential decline. This area considers the development of the organisation and the design implications at each stage. The CIPD describe the expertise in this area as 'hard' and 'soft' which in no way indicates that one is easier than the other:

- Hard: planning, succession, structures and systems.
- Soft: culture, capability, resilience, values and behaviours.

Transpersonal leadership is integral in the success of organisational development and design, and this will reflect positively internally and externally to the organisation. In particular it is essential to make the right design decisions based on ethical and authentic reasons, not driven by egos or historical biases.

Creating multilevelled organisations or flat structures affect the culture. HR professionals need to think of practicalities of leadership and pragmatic line management responsibilities. If the line management responsibilities are not taken care of this affects engagement (simple things like getting holiday requests signed off), but having an accessible leader, role model or coach builds on the foundation for individuals to flourish. This expertise area is about evaluating the current state and creating a future state which reflects Greg Young's quote re leaders taking people to places they would not necessarily have gone, and as stated above this is important in relation to creating robust and resilient organisations in light of the global COVID pandemic (Figure 18.4).

Organisational development and design with transpersonal leadership can take organisations from rational intelligence through to emotional and

Table 18.1 CIPD Profession Map: specialist knowledge and core behaviours, with permission of the publisher, Chartered Institute of Personnel and Development in London (www.cipd.co.uk), including Figure 18.2 specialist knowledge and Figure 18.3 core behaviours

Specialist knowledge	Core behaviours
1. Organisational Development and design.	1. Ethical practice
2. People Analytics	2. Professional courage and influence
3. Resourcing	3. Valuing people
4. Reward	4. Working inclusively
5. Talent Management	5. Commercial drive
6. Employee Experience	6. Passion for learning
7. Employee Relations	7. Insights focussed
8. Diversity and Inclusion (and Belonging)	8. Situational decision-making
9. Learning and Development	

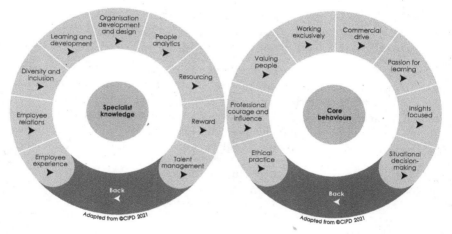

Figure 18.2 Specialist knowledge   *Figure 18.3* Core behaviours

ethical intelligence. The 20th-century leadership has clear understanding of skills, vision, direction and strategy. These are the 'hard skills' outlined by the CIPD. Transpersonal leadership considerations build on 20th-century leaderships and add behaviours, leadership styles, performance culture, values, ethics and in general leading the organisation for the greater good.

Overall, Transpersonal Leadership is inextricably linked to best in class organisational development and design, and HR Professionals leading projects in this area will need to exhibit and coach others to show empathy, authenticity and ethics, to ensure that they are leading beyond the ego. These skills are closely linked to the CIPD core behaviours of commercial drive, ethical practice and valuing people.

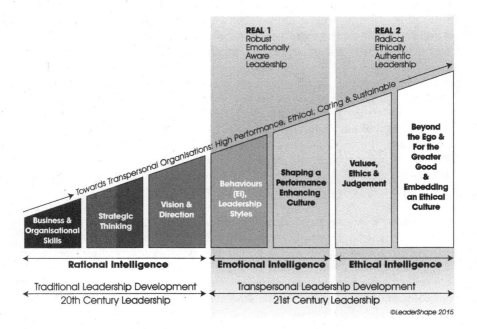

Figure 18.4 Levels of leadership (Knights, Grant & Young, 2018)

People analytics

This specialist knowledge area is about gathering and using quantitative and qualitative data to guide decisions for the organisation. Data literacy is becoming an important part of a HR professionals tool kit, in particular interpreting data in order to make sound business judgement and decisions. There is a thirst for data in all spheres of business and the most important part is knowing what is causing the spike in turnover statistics for example, the data highlights the situation and an inquisitive transpersonal HR professional will be able to ascertain the reason and work on solutions.

The collection and collation of data, often from several sources is a real skill in modern organisations. HR information system providers work hard to ensure their products are as intuitive as possible, but HR professionals have to ensure that they can navigate the system and help develop and build one that is fit for purpose for the organisational context.

Transpersonal Leadership will help in this field in particular with regard to transparency, using data in an ethical way, listening to feedback, not assuming you know why something is happening, and empathetic interpretation. This can be tricky as data often hits the media in the context of increasing regulation from general data protection ("GDPR") and data confidentiality. There have been a number of data breaches reported recently. Data should be treated as one of an organisations valuable assets, and therefore safety and business continuity procedures need to be in place. There is a clear reputational risk involved in mistreating data.

How data is reported, presented and interpreted will impact on your employer brand, and how people view your organisation internally and externally. There is an integral role that data has in building culture within the organisation.

Transpersonal leaders will ensure that statistics are accurate and not creating a scenario to paint the organisation in better light. Data is often a matter of interpretation, and it is important for leaders to get to the bottom of what the data is indicating. This reflects the commonly used phrase "There are three kinds of lies: lies, damned lies, and statistics" (Benjamin Disraeli). Some have even described data science as an art form. Two examples paint this picture clearly:

Examples: People analytics and data interpretation.

- **Gender pay gap reporting UK:** (soon to be ethnicity pay gap reporting also). Many organisations have presented this data with few comments on actions to bring about change. Airlines for example operate in an environment where pilots are predominantly male. This is a statement of fact, but what are the organisations going to do to address this? Perhaps solutions may include creating scholarships or training for female pilots.
- **Salary benchmarking:** For any given data set you can present the mean or median and depending on the different data points, these can be very different, and have a very different narrative attached. Remuneration Committees must work hard to establish an appropriate reference group in order that data presented is meaningful. Transpersonal leaders will bring authenticity and transparency to this.

The CIPD core behaviours of insight focussed, ethical practice and valuing people are connected here to the skills of a transpersonal leader.

Resourcing

This specialist knowledge area is about the attraction and selection of candidates bringing in new talent that drives the business forward. Resourcing ensures that an organisation has the right people in the right place at the right time to meet current and future organisational need. Resourcing and Transpersonal leadership is at the heart of the organisation you are trying to create structurally and culturally.

Resourcing strategies have traditionally looked at technical abilities but it is also important that behavioural abilities are assessed to ensure that the right individuals are being brought in to drive culture and performance. An understanding of emotional intelligence, diversity and inclusion and unconscious bias is important for resourcing specialists. The term 'organisational fit' has been used in the resourcing process for many years, however this can reinforce stereotypes and stifle innovation as fresh ways of thinking are not sought after.

Transpersonal leaders in resourcing will remove barriers, not just from legal standpoint, but from an ethical and cultural perspective too. There is a lot of publicity and debate currently on the barriers certain groups experience in the resourcing process. The empathy displayed by transpersonal leaders is key to breaking barriers and equally important in not creating new ones. Often there are fixed ideas that certain roles are full time and office-based Monday to Friday (9 am to 5 pm). The global pandemic of 2020 has ensured that this is no longer the primary view and virtual working has been successful for large parts of the economy. It is important to note that virtual working does create new considerations for the transpersonal leader, in particular relating to connectivity and performance targets.

Examples related to Resourcing in *Leading Beyond the Ego*

- Unconscious bias: (Knights, Grant & Young, 2018, Chapter 21), Transpersonal leaders will '… increase awareness, changing our unwanted habits, bringing our mind to full consciousness, and making full use of our ethics and values in whatever we do'.

Recently there have been interesting debates on social media regarding unconscious bias and people with tattoos in the corporate workplace. This is in the context that recruitment decisions are still based on first impressions.

The CIPD core behaviours of working inclusively, insight focussed, and ethical practice are involved in resourcing and are also part of the role of a transpersonal leader.

Reward

This specialist knowledge area is about designing and implementing strategies that ensure workers are rewarded in line with the organisational context and culture, relative to the external market environment. It requires specific knowledge in a range of specialist areas to be able to create and shape total reward packages. This may include:

- Executive compensation – which gets a lot of publicity as for listed companies this is published, public information, and often high profile misaligned executive compensation gets a lot of comment.
- Reward – the systems and processes in place for salary and bonus.
- Benefits – the benefits selected to provide employees will reflect the culture of the organisation and the context in which they operate.
- Non-financial reward – the small things that make employees everyday life more enjoyable and rewarding.

Too often the reward policies and systems do not reflect culture that the organisation is trying to achieve, and they reinforce negative behaviours. Transpersonal leaders in this field, truly have to lead beyond the ego and not manage processes based on what they receive. Leading for the greater good is clearly important to the successful application of a reward programme.

The traditional view is that reward drives performance, and to some extent that is the case. If you are being rewarded unfairly and in a non-transparent way, this may lead to negative influences on performance. The reality is that there are other more important factors that drive performance. Feeling valued, appreciated, supported and being aligned with organisational vision and values are perhaps the more important factors in driving performance. Reward can be viewed as a hygiene factor (Herzberg, 2003).

Extrinsic and intrinsic motivation is important in driving organisational and personal performance (Knights, Grant & Young, 2018, p.139). LW Fry describes spiritual leadership for example as 'the values, attitudes and behaviours necessary to intrinsically motivate oneself and others so that they have a sense of calling or membership'. The transpersonal leader will recognise, but not overplay the importance of reward as a cog in the process of motivating a workforce and creating a performance culture.

Example: Reward

* Anecdote: A senior leader, with whom I worked, said that bonus schemes are bad at motivating performance, in fact once paid say in March of any given year, it is forgotten by the end of April. Often you create a culture of expectation, the bonus pays off the credit card purchases that were made in December and January.

A large part of reward is related to managing a finite resource, and it is important for leaders to be clear and transparent on the process. The reality is an organisation is never going to be able to meet every desire and expectation related to reward, but if you are able to explain the process and the rationale, you will reinforce that the process is fair, and that decisions are made on the basis of an ethical and fair approach.

The CIPD core behaviours of ethical practice, professional courage and influence and commercial drive clearly influence this knowledge area and are an integral part of transpersonal leadership.

Talent management

This specialist knowledge area is about using information to ensure that the organisation is fully prepared in terms of succession, contingency, and business continuity planning. It is important that organisations understand what talent populations are needed currently and in the future, and the identification of individuals who are particularly valuable to an organisation.

Scoping out diverse talent pools from within and external to the organisation, takes a great deal of sector knowledge and strong networking skills. Transpersonal leadership is important in this field as it is important that whilst looking for talent, leaders do not compare where individuals are at in their career and where they were at the same age, reflecting negative views of the proceeding generation. It is also important for leaders to not add extra leverage to individuals who attended their university.

The LeaderShape LEIPA® 360° assessment could be a central part of an internal talent management strategy, and developing leaders for the future of the organisation, and ensuring that the leaders for tomorrow take the organisation to the required place with employees fully engaged.

The CIPD core behaviours of valuing people and working inclusively are important here and are linked to transpersonal leadership.

Learning and development

This specialist knowledge area is about creating a culture and environment in which individuals and the organisation can learn and grow. Learning and Development Specialists will work on current and future organisational skills and capabilities and seeking to address any gaps that there might be. A training needs analysis will identify opportunities for learning from within and external to the organisation.

The best in class learning and development programmes can take organisations to another level. Apprenticeships, vocational training, day-release academic qualifications, online and offline learning are all part of a modern learning and development strategy. To ascertain what the organisation and the individual requires, an open people review process should assess career aspirations and any potential gaps in a non-confrontational empathetic way. An approach that looks at the uniqueness of the individual in a collective manner is embedded in a transpersonal leadership style. The CIPD core behaviours of passion for learning and valuing people are clearly apparent.

The LeaderShape LEIPA® 360° assessment could be a central part of an internal Learning and development strategy and developing core behaviours. Being able to accurately describe what skills and behaviours are required is important in order that a Learning and Development strategy is fit for purpose.

The CIPD care behaviours of passion for learning and valuing people are key to the specialist area and are also reflective of a transpersonal leader.

Employee experience

This specialist knowledge area 'is about creating a great work environment for people. It involves understanding the role that trust plays in the employment relationship and making sure people are listened to and have a voice in issues that impact them' (CIPD Website).

This involves ensuring that the psychological contract (Rousseau, 1989) exists in which individuals feel a sense of belonging and are engaged to perform their role to the best of their ability. The role of a transpersonal leader is clear in this specialist knowledge area. Relationships with leaders and managers, and the physical and emotional wellbeing of employees, are important with regard to a sense of belonging. The rhetorical and debatable point often used is that employees join an organisation and leave a manager.

Central in this area is listening, the most underrated and under-used leadership tool. A transpersonal leader will role model active listening and general inquisitiveness on how well their teams are doing. There is a quote that has circulated LinkedIn many times, that has been attributed to Andy Stanley, a pastor, communicator, author, and the founder of North Point Ministries in Alpharetta, Georgia. 'Leaders that don't listen will soon be surrounded by individuals who have nothing to say'.

Wellbeing is becoming an increasingly important watchword for HR professionals – and not just physical, but psychological and emotional wellbeing. Transpersonal leaders will know their team and know when to use one of the six LEIPA leadership styles to ensure that the individual feels a sense of belonging and is striving for their best performance.

Anecdote Wellbeing:

As a HR professional, I walked into a department and saw that a member of the team was not looking as happy as they normally did. I asked the manager privately if anything was going on, and they replied, 'I don't think so, I just think they are having a quiet day'. It is essential for leaders to spot things (even the intangibles) and act. Often tasks take over as the most important element, transpersonal leaders will concentrate on *how* things are done as well as *what* is done.

Anecdote resilience during organisational change:

A huge organisational change, meaning a change of operations, redundancies, and consolidation in locations, involved 'town hall' meetings in which we introduced and revisited the Kübler Ross Resilience Curve (Kübler-Ross & Kessler, 2005) which describes stages of acceptance such as denial, gloom, experimenting, decision and then moving on. This work was originally developed to describe the grieving process, but is now widely applied to describe attitudes and morale during any difficult change. In doing so, leaders were being authentic and empathetic by acknowledging the current experience was not great but trying to make it as good as it could be for each employee, and using leadership styles to adapt.

Example: France Telecom

An example of where employee experiences can go wrong is France Telecom. Accusations of 'moral harassment' ensued when a five-year restructuring reached a nadir, with a spate of employee suicides. Leading executives including the CEO were convicted and received jail sentences.

("France Telecom Suicides: Toxic Management Goes on Trial – Leaders League", 2019)

The CIPD core behaviours of valuing people, commercial drive and is clearly part of employee experience and part of being a transpersonal leader.

Diversity and inclusion (belonging)

This specialist knowledge area is about creating an environment and practices where individuals can be themselves and be supported to work at their best, and is about creating employee experiences for all irrespective of any assumed difference. This involves going beyond the legislation and using ethical, moral, and authentic leadership skills of the transpersonal leader to really make a difference. Diversity, inclusion, and belonging is about genuinely listening in order to break down barriers, and in doing so not creating new ones. The terminology and phraseology used in this subject is very important, and leaders need to be sure not to inadvertently create barriers in the way they discuss this subject.

The CIPD states that diversity and inclusion is about 'understanding and demonstrating the value that diversity and inclusion can bring to all stakeholders across organisations and societies' ("Diversity and inclusion | CIPD Profession Map", 2020). Diversity in its broadest sense (not just in terms of the protected characteristics under law, but also style, education, neurodiversity) drives innovation, otherwise things will be done how they always have been. There is a clear business, ethical and moral imperative for organisations to have an appropriate diversity and inclusion strategy.

Intersectionality or plural identity is a term that describes the overlapping and interdependent aspects of diversity and inclusion. HR need to consider at what point in time (in the employment relationship) is any of an individual's characteristics or differences more important than another. The only way is to be inquisitive and to listen. Don't look, for example, and see a woman of colour and assume that they are the same as others in that category; we are all unique and have unique needs.

In Chapter 12 of this book, Greg Young clearly highlights the important role in what are more generally described as female behaviours, empathy and collaborative working, for example. There is no doubt that the evidence is building that organisations that have female board members tend to make more balanced decisions. A word of caution, there are some males that possess empathy and a collaborative style, and we need all leaders to reflect transpersonal leadership capabilities not just women. Being a man is not an excuse for not embracing the evidence that transpersonal leadership matters and makes a difference.

The terminology and phraseology used in this subject is very important, and leaders need to be sure not to inadvertently create barriers in the way they discuss this subject. An example is using the words 'male, stale and pale' to describe senior leadership within an organisation. In trying to highlight an issue this can create a barrier, change needs to happen across the organisation, and not in certain groups. The last thing organisations need is for individuals who are being described as 'male, stale and pale' thinking that they can ignore the diversity and inclusion agenda as its not relevant to them.

Transpersonal leader will understand the audience and the messages they need to get across.

Transpersonal authentic leaders will always have in mind the unconscious bias that affects the sphere of diversity and inclusion (Knights, Grant & Young, 2018, Chapter 16). Many organisations feel that investing in unconscious bias training is a way to highlight that diversity and inclusion is somewhat under control. However, in isolation this will rarely solve issues, and many organisations are also accompanying unconscious bias with bystander intervention training ensuring that all employees feel able to speak up and call out practices with the company.

Leading beyond the ego and leading ethically with authenticity and empathy is core to diversity and Inclusion. The CIPD core behaviours of valuing people, working inclusively, and ethical practice are all inextricably linked to transpersonal leadership and diversity and inclusion.

Employee relations

This specialist knowledge area is about policies and procedures in place to help create positive working relations. The watch words here are fairness, consistency and transparency which is at the heart of transpersonal leadership.

> People practices will be fairer and more transparent if developed in partnership with unions and employee representative bodies, so the standards encourage knowledge of how to work with employee bodies, and how to ensure that practices represent and are in line with an organisation's brand.
>
> (CIPD website)

The policies and procedures are only a small part of employee relations and authentic leaders will not only rely on policies. It is important to view each situation in the context of what is in front of you and the person that you are dealing with, and therefore empathetic application of policies is a fundamental part of building positive employee relations over a long period.

Anecdote Employee Relations:

As an HR professional I often say to managers that if we find ourselves saying 'the policy states', then we are on the back foot resolving the issue at hand.

Looking at the employee life cycle, exit interviews are an important feedback mechanism for employee relations. The aim is to ensure that mistakes are not repeated and that the positives are re-enforced.

The CIPD behaviours of situational decision-making, valuing people and ethical practice are a strong part of employee relations, and link closely with transpersonal leadership skills.

Conclusion

In this chapter, we have shown the linkages between the CIPD Profession maps specialist knowledge areas and core behaviours and shown that these are inextricably linked to transpersonal leadership. HR professionals and leaders within the organisation need to exhibit embed and coach transpersonal leadership to transform culture and create an organisation that is good for employees, adds value to all stakeholders, drives performance and is resilient to and embraces change.

The core behaviours and therefore transpersonal leadership skills are important to the continual professional development requirements for CIPD members. It could be ascertained that in general HR professionals readily show their authenticity, ethical, spiritual and empathetic qualities, and the focus should be on role modelling and upskilling HR and transpersonal leadership skills across the organisation.

An important role for HR professionals is to roll out effective people management skills in their respective organisations. Anything related to people does not have to be done by HR. The CIPD career map core behaviours and transpersonal leadership are an opportunity to 'champion better work and working lives' (CIPD, 2021) for all.

Questions and actions for personal development

1. Is it possible to deliver an HR Strategy without embracing elements of transpersonal leadership?
2. Think of a HR Leader you work with or have worked with, how do/did they display transpersonal leadership qualities?
3. If you are a business leader or a HR professional think of the CIPD Knowledge areas that you have most interest in, how has transpersonal leadership affected your understanding and interest in this area?
4. What opportunities do you have to introduce and role model transpersonal leadership with regard to how people management is delivered in your organisation?
5. What areas of your current HR strategy would you like to develop in order to introduce more transpersonal leadership?

References

CIPD. 2020. Profession Map. https://peopleprofession.cipd.org/profession-map.

CIPD. 2020. Diversity and Inclusion | CIPD Profession Map. *CIPD People Profession.* https://peopleprofession.cipd.org/profession-map/specialist-knowledge/diversity-inclusion, March 8, 2021.

CIPD. 2021. Our Purpose & Vision | CIPD. *CIPD.* https://www.cipd.co.uk/about/-who-we-are/purpose, March 8, 2021.

France Telecom Suicides: Toxic Management Goes on Trial - Leaders League. 2019. *www.leadersleague.com.* https://www.leadersleague.com/en/news/france-telecom-suicides-toxic-management-goes-on-trial, March 8, 2021.

Herzberg, F. 2003. One More Time: How Do You Motivate Employees?. *Harvard Business Review.* https://hbr.org/2003/01/one-more-time-how-do-you-motivate-employees, March 8, 2021.

Knights, J., Grant, D., & Young, G. 2018. *Leading Beyond the Ego.* London: Routledge.

Kübler-Ross, E., & Kessler, D. 2005. *On Grief and Grieving.* New York: Scribner.

Rousseau, D. 1989. Psychological and implied contracts in organizations. *Employee Responsibilities and Rights Journal,* 2(2): 121–139.

19 Letting go of leadership

A hopeful utopia for corporate realists

Otti Vogt

How Transpersonal Business Leaders enable organisations to become more
ethical, performance-enhancing, caring and sustainable.

A map of the world that does not include Utopia is not worth even glanc-
ing at, for it leaves out the one country at which Humanity is always landing.
Oscar Wilde

Overview

How to put 'transpersonal business leadership into action' and craft ethical,
caring and performing organisations? It might not be an easy conundrum. I
will argue that the concept of leadership itself has become a self-reinforcing
defense mechanism to contain our anxieties about the future and, unconsciously, imprison ourselves in a global status quo.

In order to progress we must embark on a pilgrimage of learning, challenging our societal world views and ethical beliefs, revising our organisational
structures and practices, and examining ourselves. Elaborating on Aristotle's
concept of virtue ethics, I propose a new narrative of a Good Society that
aims at collective aliveness and moral excellence. Combining our know-how
about human-centric and agile learning organisations, I promote a novel Living Organisation metaphor. Building on developmental theory, I suggest that
transpersonal leaders need to embrace a Third Life, letting go of their individual leadership to become part of a unified flow of 'eco-leadership'. Alas,
organisational and societal transformation has never been attainable without
individual transformation.

Indisputably, a transpersonal leader's journey is tough. Infinite pitfalls
of external expectations, complex swamplands of relationships and never-
ending distractions are lurking in the organisational shadows. Torn by inner
demons and propelled by our fearful egos we often unwittingly become stal-
warts of 'managerial arthritis', rather than apostles of organisational redemp-
tion. Yet, there is always light, if only we're brave enough to see it! Indeed,
leadership for me was never just a job. It always was a heartfelt search for that
joyful, sublime energy that arises within and around us when we are in deep

DOI: 10.4324/9781003150626-23

harmony, mutually growing in service of something greater than ourselves; when, all of a sudden, we silently stand in reverence of that profound magic of life. As Ben Zander once said: the only true measure of leadership is "shining eyes" (Zander, 2000). I wish my reflections might serve you well on your own leadership quest: may the spark be with you!

Thanks to Antoinette Weibel, Alicia Hennig, Emanuele Quintarelli, Sergio Caredda, Bryan Ungard, Michele Zanini, John Knights for their contributions. This chapter is dedicated to 'my' #TeamING.

Transpersonal leaders wanted

> Happy slaves are the bitterest enemies of freedom.
> Marie von Ebner-Eschenbach

Are you a good leader? In case you are emphatically nodding, *how* would you know? Regrettably, it has become increasingly difficult to discern what 'good leadership' actually means. Searching Google reveals a mind-boggling 148 million links to the term. Amazon hosts over 100,000 entries. Every day, outfits like Harvard Business Review broadcast ever-varying collections of 'top' leadership traits, behaviours and activities on social media. Such is the nature of the 'leadership industry' – entry barriers are low and armies of self-declared leadership gurus incessantly bombard us with buzzwords galore.

Arguably, taxonomy wouldn't matter much if leadership was actually working. Yet, strikingly, most leadership glitterati do not eagerly reveal which exact problem leadership is solving, how its effectiveness is measured, and how we're currently doing. My friend Sergio Caredda recently compiled over 150 popular leadership models (Caredda, 2020) – most of them inconsistent and seldom backed by research or evidence. Still, if we reasonably assumed that leadership is about mobilising efforts towards a better future, the global leadership profession has – by any standard – largely failed. In spite of humongous investments in leadership development, over 80% of employees feel disengaged (Gallup, 2017); many don't trust their leaders (Pfeffer, 2015); CEO tenure is continuously decreasing; and we reached gloomy records in global inequality and unsustainability. Whilst mankind is facing a historic inflection point, 56% of global citizens believe our (leader-led) "capitalism does more harm than good" (Edelman, 2020).

Alas, leadership, however defined, appears – at least partly – detrimental to our society. A recent paper examining transformational leadership concludes: "Much of the damage done to organisations has resulted from arrogant, unethical behaviour of corporate leaders" (O'Reilly, Chatman, 2020). Nonetheless, most leadership iconophiles seem to suggest that the natural evolution of the profession will gradually resolve our global malaise. Conversely, I will argue that all convenient attempts to smoothen over the shortfalls of corporate leadership – and the anonymous ownership structures behind it – will no longer suffice. The concept of leadership itself has become a perilous problem:

- Leadership cements our current paradigm. Our collective glorification of the role of the leader within an "institutional belief system" (Lee, Edmondson 2017) triggers regression towards existing control structures. "As soon as we call someone a leader", Jeffrey Nielsen argues, "we create a rank-based context that defines power as power-over [...] and hierarchy as the means of transmission of authority from the top down through privileged delegation". As in principle-agent theory, we confer unique privileges to principles whilst assigning duties to inferior 'human resources' — doomed to be sacrificed to "preserve and protect the power and privilege of those designated as leaders" (Nielsen, 2004).
- Leadership nurtures 'learned helplessness' of followers. Simultaneously, "some of the confusion around the concept of leadership", suggest Gemmill and Oakley, "seems to stem from the process of *reification*" (Gemmill, Oakley 1992). A powerful social fiction is turned into an actual observed phenomenon — whenever an organisation is faring particularly well, or badly, we infer it is caused by its leadership. This 'leadership myth' serves as a strong individual and social defence mechanism to repress our own anxieties, helplessness or fear of failure and instead projects these onto prominent leadership figures as 'containers'. Moreover, the leaders' "proposed worldview and self-concept appeal to individuals with high levels of personal uncertainty" and sustain a toxic "*illusio*" (Mergen, Ozbilgin, 2020). As a result, we abdicate our own ownership. If an organisation fails, we conveniently blame its leaders.
- Leadership is stuck. Finally, the narrative of transformational or messianic leadership (Western, 2019) accesses powerful primordial energies of the collective 'Hero' archetype. Whilst successful business leaders are worshipped like modern-day superstars, Jungian psychologist Robert Moore points out that the Hero archetype belongs to an immature 'boy' stage of adult development. Heroes are unaware of their limitations and self-serving in their drive towards success — oblivious that 'conquering the princess will not bring them love'. Moore suggests that modern societies have lost rites of passage towards successful individuation of (male) adults, and immature 'shadow' energies proliferate dominance, violence and weakness (Moore and Gillette, 1990). Sadly, the woman who most needs liberating is 'the woman in every leader'. Adult leaders, as "eternal boys", continue to slumber "in history's unmade bed" (Hollis, 2006), rather than progressing their development towards full, compassionate and regenerative masculinity.

Following this interpretation, the cacophonic chants of a global leadership chorus reflect a deepening collective sense of despair and helplessness, and its seductive gospel reinforces the existing social status quo. Leadership is not the problem: our obsessive clinging to it is. Unbeknownst to ourselves, we are stuck in our own story. In order to reframe leadership as a creative force, we must be willing to 'go on the balcony' and examine the powerful energies that tug us towards the past, and 'presence' the future we desire. As Otto Scharmer suggests, in order to instigate real transformative change, we "have to bend the beam of attention back" from the system onto ourselves (Scharmer, 2016). Only if we are ready to deeply inquire into what the world needs from us and act as responsible stewards on our explorations ahead, will our organisations become true change agents for good. 'We are the system.'

A search for meaning in business

Mostly unacknowledged by their leaders, our enterprises are collectively floating on the forceful currents of dominant 'world views' that skew our conversations and shape our conceptions of how the world works. Unfortunately, if we as leaders fail to examine these systemic narratives, and simply assume 'success' to be 'good', we swiftly find ourselves inadvertently backing a perilous course.

Scrutinising our prevailing socio-political world views (see Table 19.1), we can discern three dominant narratives that are pervasive in society today: we could label these, hyperbolically, as Free-Market, Conservative (Neo-liberal) and Social. Naturally, our political ideologies are profoundly interwoven with our economic world views and large organisations have become prime-time actors on the global stage. Sketching a somewhat extreme version of each paradigm, distinct political, economic and ethical beliefs as well as different "relational models" (Fiske, 1991) become evident:

- The free-market world-view: The libertarian tradition endorses a utilitarian ethics. An action is deemed 'right' if the outcome is beneficial for the majority (so-called consequentialist ethics). However, given the difficulty to accurately assess the 'net' societal impact, an egotistical morality often prevails. The role of the state is minimised and individuals are free to make choices. In a market model based on 'individualist-vertical' relationships, societal relations are oriented by symbols of transactional success such as prices, wages or consumption. Companies are outward-oriented and open to innovation and change, focused on continual self-enhancement. Employees gain access to opportunities based on merit, competence and track record.
- The Conservative (neo-liberal) world-view: In a Conservative or Republican paradigm a legalistic rational logic, based on justice (e.g. Rawls), is emphasised. An action is 'right' if it complies with rules, traditions and duties (so-called deontological ethics), rather than based on its consequences. Public institutions safeguard law and order and citizens have rights and duties whilst pursuing legitimate ends. In a 'collectivist-vertical' model based on formal authority, societal relationships are ranked by the roles people occupy. Companies seek stability and control, leveraging market power, institutional influence and scale. Employees

Table 19.1 Simplified characteristics of alternative worldviews and relational spheres

Societal "world views"	Free-market Democracy (Libertarian Capitalism)	Conservative Democracy ('Neo-liberal' Capitalism)	Social Democracy (Welfare Capitalism)
Concept of society	Market society with minimum state aimed at freedom and efficiency	Civil society aimed at law and order	Pluralistic civil society aimed at social justice and equal opportunity
Most cared about	Merit, Wealth (Outcomes)	Status, Power (Institution)	Harmony, Opportunity (Rights)
Concept of the person	Unencumbered self with "negative" freedoms to pursue private ends	Autonomous self with positive freedoms to attain legitimate ends	Social self with positive rights to attain community ends
Role of state	Individual freedom/ growth	Justice and social order	Social Welfare, full employment
Concept of authority	Market Democracy/ Meritocracy (based on credentials, status, wealth)	(Dominant-party) Democracy (rational-legal based on rules)	Social/Participatory Democracy (based on rights)
Concept of citizen	Property-owning consumer	Political citizen with equal rights/duties	Community citizen with solidarity
Dominant relational model	Market Pricing (Individualist-Vertical)	Authority Ranking (Collectivist-Vertical)	Communal Sharing (Collectivist–Horizontal)
Concept of ethics	Utilitarianism/ Egoism-hedonism, consequentialist ethics	Modernism: Scientific rationality, deontological ethics	Postmodernism: Humanistic, Cultural contextualism (communitarianism)
Concept of life/work	Work is a ticket to personal freedom	Work is a duty – life is work.	Work is opportunity to participate
Concept of economy	Efficient free market competition	Industrial organisation, market power	Regulated market to ensure fair participation/competition
Objective of the firm	Maximisation of shareholder value, competitive advantage	Maximisation of market power, efficiency, scale, barriers to entry	Maximisation of stakeholder value
Success Measures	Market share, profit, share price, cash flow, customer satisfaction	Reputation, Growth, Balance sheet, Soft Power, Efficiency	Stakeholder return, Organisational Health, ESG/SDGs
Ownership	Limited company	Private/Public business	Family business, Coop, B-Corp

Based on Ulrich (2008) and Fiske (1991).

acquire positions in a hierarchy based on political power, loyalty and professional credentials.

- Social world-view: In a Social or welfare society, a humanistic view of dignity and positive human rights (e.g. Kant) is embraced. Actions are 'good' if they respect the rights and sensitivities of all societal groups. The state seeks to attain a 'fair' (re-)distribution of wealth to give all societal groups equal opportunities to participate in society. Relationships in a pluralistic society are based on a 'collectivist-horizontal' model – people treat each other as equal in terms of contribution to the community. Harmony is valued. Companies seek fair and balanced returns for the 'good' of all identified stakeholders. Employees are empowered to participate and influence the organisation collaboratively, and diversity and inclusion are monitored. Ecological topics are often considered, yet balanced with other interests.

Whereas in fact we frequently and unconsciously compromise between these three worldviews, they are, logically and ethically, largely incommensurable (see Knights, Grant, Young, 2018, Chapter 16). Inevitably, we often encounter ideological turf wars, deep awkwardness, or insurmountable disagreements about moral questions. When challenged, intellectual elites are quick to resort to politically correct emotive relativism, suggesting there may not be a 'single truth', or to colourful evolutionary ideologies like spiral dynamics. As a result, schizophrenically, both our anxiety about deeper meaning and the regressive excesses of consumerism have augmented. Whilst "Social Capitalism has widely dominated organisational theory, liberal free-market Capitalism has dominated in practice" (Sison, Beabout, Ferrero, 2017).

Meanwhile, corporate leaders have carefully professed political neutrality and – on the surface – maintained a pragmatic stance. Unsurprisingly, however, the vestiges of our prevalent world views are clearly visible in our organisations. Reflecting these narratives, we can discern three prominent organisational metaphors describing the fundamental principles and characteristics of most contemporary businesses:

- In a Market organisation, all eyes are on clients and competition. The customer is allegedly king (in reality, a profit motive rules). The culture is meritocratic, based on growth and market success, and predominantly individualistic – powered by behaviourist incentives. Organisational focus is on creativity and innovation, stirred by visionary entrepreneurship. Excitement is in the air, the 'game is on', and Sales are in charge.
- In a Machine organisation, order and rules are clear. The CEO is boss and CFOs are second in command. In traditionally bureaucratic organisations, long-term strategic and budgetary planning are highly ritualised. Positional authority is leveraged by leaders who drive for control and pace-setting, continuous process improvement and predictability. Politics abound, conformity is nurtured and the head office sets the tone.

- A Family organisation cares for its constituents and seeks to do both good and well. Employees, customers and other stakeholders are at the top of the (inverted) hierarchy. The organisation values trust and participation, diversity and inclusion, and harmony between different 'types' of employees. Flat structures and empowered teams enable informal collaboration. Leaders act as coaches and therapists. In practice, however, what 'good' looks like is still defined, categorically, by the head office.

These organisational metaphors (see Table 19.2) correlate closely with the organisational cultures described by Knights (Knights, Grant, Young (2018), Chapter 10): Machine organisations emphasise *power* and *structure*, Market organisations embody *achievement* and Family organisations nurture *support*.

Today, traditional Machine bureaucracies are under threat. Businesses are facing ever-faster changes, advances in technology and data, regulation, shortening half-life of knowledge, information abundance and ever greater global interdependencies. In the 'New 20s', companies – begrudgingly – are letting go of the illusion that work can be centrally controlled or predicted in detail, and build organisations that can 'compete on learning'. Ashby's law of requisite variety implies that in order to achieve sustainable performance, businesses must match the increased diversity outside the firm with an increased responsiveness and agility on the inside. Unsurprisingly, the quest for adaptive organisations is intense. Many organisations seek to liberate traditional bureaucracies with agile, empowered or entrepreneurial practices, often combining Family and Market metaphors (and democratic and visionary leadership styles) and extrapolating best practices from allegedly 'enlightened' businesses. Yet, sadly, whilst superficially becoming both more human-centric and flexible, most leaders seem determined to perpetuate our underlying bureaucratic-utilitarian script. Rather than climbing the highest tree to shout out: "wrong jungle!", as Steven Covey once admonished (Covey, 1989), morally mute leaders have often become supporting cast in a global routine that carelessly promises salvation in return for selfish pursuit of profit and fame. In spite of the proliferation of self-managed teams, ambidextrous structures, Kanban boards and post-it notes, a necessary revision of our deeply held world views is dangerously lacking.

Alas, a lot has been written about moral philosophy in the last 2,500 years – of which remarkably little has featured prominently in business education. Post-Enlightenment, a pre-existent belief in normative ethics and spirituality was thoroughly eradicated. Scientific management filled gaps of meanings with a gospel of growth and self-interested profit and stock prices became uncontested ends in themselves. Undoubtedly, postmodern capitalism has unlocked unbelievable growth and innovation, yet at what price? Our organisations have collectively produced numerous outcomes that nobody really wanted: inequality and hunger, burnout and loneliness and ecological collapse. At the same time, embracing global consumerism, we often succumbed to a hedonistic treadmill of money for money's sake. We

Table 19.2 Simplified characteristics of alternative organisational metaphors

Organisational Metaphors	Market	Machine	Family
Strategy	Innovation, Competition, Customer Service, Exploitation of market opportunities	Barriers to entry e.g., scale and standardisation, vertical integration, networks, advertising	Cooperation and co-opetition to 'do good' for all stakeholders, core competencies and culture
Management style	Fail Fast/Rapid iteration, Lean Startup, Agile, Project Management	Business process re-engineering, Continuous improvement, Large-scale restructuring	Management by division, 'Unbossing' and empowerment, purpose and values
Most cared about	Creativity, value-add, bottom line, contribution, extraction	Control and exploitation, predictability, efficiency, compliance	Collaboration, harmony, fairness, trust
Main leadership discourse	Messiah/Visionary Power from (transactional)	Controller/Hero Power over (positional)	Therapist/Coach Power with (participative)
Concept of Employee	Human Capital, Talent	Human Resource, Role	Human Potential, Profile
Culture (Values, beliefs, language)	Founder, entrepreneurial, individualistic, meritocratic, competitive, dynamic, customer-driven, survival of the fittest, ideas, growth, risk-taking, beating the market, adaptive, cutting-edge, 'Speak up for yourself'	Tradition, command and control, efficient, political, loyal, risk-avoidant, standards, turf wars, structure, budget, rational, professional, knowledge is power, problem solving, do no harm, authorisation, delegation, standardisation, 'Please the boss'	Communities of interest/practice, diverse, emotional, dignity, social responsibility, commitment, networks, mentoring, authenticity, shared values, united, one ideal, inclusive, participative, health, wellness, politically correct, personal development, 'Speak up for a group'
Management theory	Standard economics (e.g., Transaction Cost, Principle-Agent-Tournament Theory)	Scientific/Administrative management, Human Relations Theory, Theory X	Humanistic Theory, Theory Y/Z, Workplace Democracy, Stakeholder Theory

Based on various sources including Laloux (2014).

became 'what we have'. In a 'pandemic of busyness' people started to work ever longer hours to attain status, material goods, and wealth, just to find out that it did not really make them happier. Today, the world's few billionaires accumulate more wealth than the 4.6 billion people who make up 60% of the planet's population (Coffey et al, 2020)! Catalysed by a "Fourth Industrial Revolution" (Schwab, 2017) and fuelled by burgeoning financial markets, our work became once again object of global trade – increasingly unbundled, it is sold at the lowest cost or reverse-auctioned on gig-economy platforms. Wretchedly, our postmodern world seems trapped in a treacherous moral 'unenlightenment'. Hence, 50 years after Milton Friedman's famous essay on the responsibility of business, it is time to inquire into the true purpose of work: is society just a 'collection of individuals', and 'social responsibility' really 'undermining the basis of a free society'? Can "collectivist ends [never] be attained without collectivist means"? (Friedman, 1970) *Quo vadis, homo oeconomicus?*

Certainly, suggestions abound. A flurry of well-publicised initiatives is promising to contain the excesses of a gluttonous capitalistic machine: stakeholder or conscious capitalism, business roundtables and Sustainable Development Goals are buzzwords in board rooms and parliaments alike. Sadly, in my opinion all such endeavours are doomed to have limited impact. In our complex globalised world, quotas and taxes seldom stick; negative freedoms will always provoke negative externalities; and extrinsic motivation has limited force. We must have the courage to modify the moral fundaments of today's hegemonic paradigm and rectify its underlying power structures. Simply put, our economy cannot be an end in itself. Money must serve, not rule! Improvements will only emerge if self-determined individuals and organisations voluntarily unite behind a powerful vision for a better society. Sustainable change as Scotty Peck once wrote requires a true and trusting global community: "in and through community lies the salvation of the world" (Peck, 1990). Ultimately, "nothing but the courage and unselfishness of individuals is ever going to make any system work properly... You cannot make man good by law, and without good men you cannot have a good society" (Clive Lewis in: Sandler, 2007).

> The world is a dangerous place. Not because of the people who are evil; but because of the people who don't do anything about it.
>
> Albert Einstein

Remarkably, an alternative ethical theory of pre-modern times could offer us valuable inspiration. In his so-called 'virtue ethics', Aristotle suggested that the ultimate purpose (*telos*) of humans is to attain a 'good life' of well-being and fulfilment (*eudaimonia*). A desire for wealth as an end in itself was deemed unworthy – Aristotle called people who engaged in activities which did not contribute to society parasites (Salomon, 1992). 'Good' people develop 'moral character' by acting habitually in virtuous ways to enable the

Table 19.3 Simplified characteristics of neo-virtuism world view

Neo-virtuism: A Good Society

Concept of society	A Good Society aimed at mutual fulfilment and objective happiness	Concept of ethics	Virtue ethics, Moral Pragmatism
Most cared about	Eudaimonia (good life) and flourishing	Concept of life and work	Work is essential aliveness of unique humans
Concept of the person	Ecological self acting virtuously and with 'moral character' to lead a 'good life'	Concept of economy	Interdependent part of regenerative ecosystems (markets with morals)
Role of state	Enable regenerative flourishing of whole living ecology	Objective of the firm	Flourishing through responsible contribution and co-elevation
Concept of authority	Institutional Democracy (based on distributed power and mutual accountability)	Success Measures	Regenerative value-add, Aliveness, Virtue Ethics Scale (VES), Net Integrity Score
Concept of citizen	Self-determined adult fully engaged across public/private/plural sectors	Ownership	FairShares Commons, Value-to-value alliances/networks

Based on sources including Boyd (2020) and Mintzberg (2015).

reciprocal realisation of our unique human potential. Whilst abused during two millennia of Christian dogma, the notion of a virtuous society that commits to the mutual flourishing of all beings remains captivating.

What if we could recover Aristotle's wisdom to conjure up an alternative vision for a Good Society in the 21st century? What if we would embrace a neo-virtuous worldview (see Table 19.3), founded in a strong belief that all people have dignity and shall be able to collectively express the unique essence of who we truly are. Where mature individuals voluntarily embrace interdependence and co-elevate – in individualist-horizontal relationships – rather than withdraw in fearful isolation. Where work is not just traded for profit, but nurtures a flourishing ecology. Not just bigger, but better. Not just sustainable, but regenerative. Not as a question of marketing or charity, and not even for justice, but to cherish life and our essential freedom to collectively live up to our potential, rather than succumb to a life of quiet desperation. Even in a modern, pluralistic society we must muster the courage to dream anew, if our old models are falling apart. There is always light, if only we are brave enough to be it.

Crafting aliveness at work

> Joy commands the hardy mainspring of the universe eterne. Joy, oh joy the wheel is driving which the worlds' great clock doth turn.
>
> Friedrich Schiller

Accepting the need for both 'de-bureaucratisation' and ethical enlighten-ment, how could responsible leaders craft 'good organisations'? How could we support flourishing at work?

Building on decades of motivational research and neuroscience, "Positive Organisational Scholarship" (e.g. Spreitzer, Lam, Quinn 2012) proposes to define "thriving at work as a desirable and positive psychological state in which employees experience both a sense of vitality and learning." (Kleine, Rudolph, Zacher, 2019) On that basis, we could formalise a novel concept of 'organisational aliveness' (see Figure 19.1) as a composite of:

- Individual vitality: 'Employees who are thriving feel that their current experiences and behaviours at work are intrinsically motivating and sup-portive of self-development and personal growth.' We attain positive en-ergy from our work.
- Organisational learning: The organisational capacity for community and the inherent joy of high-quality relationship 'holds' employees to mutu-ally grow. Learning becomes the central endemic feature and 'glue' of the organisational system, its self-management and its continuous evolu-tion and renewal. Energy is generated in synergic connections between individuals.
- Systemic regeneration: Within the organisation we can spark additional energy by crafting regenerative and life-giving links with the wider ecol-ogy and nature. Surpassing an anthropocentric world view and expand-ing the boundaries of our organisations enables people to attain deeper connection, meaning and transcendence. As Mary Parker Follett once famously noted: "evil is lack of relation" (Heon, Davis, Jones-Patulli, Damart, 2017).

In a neo-virtuous paradigm, the principal objective of the enterprise is to enable the striving for an evolutionary 'good life', across the ecosystem. This does not imply inefficiency, however. It means to act in reciprocate harmony with and across the whole, rather than solely pursuing the business's own survival. Moreover, the proposed conceptualisation of aliveness builds on

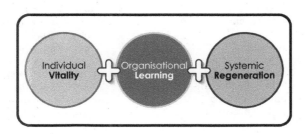

Figure 19.1 Organisational aliveness

an integration of Western and Eastern virtue philosophies – whilst Aristotle focused on individual development, a Confucian virtue approach emphasises social relations and Daoists advocate non-interference and harmony with nature (Hennig, 2016 – also see Chapter 16). We achieve aliveness "in unity, not uniformity": in an organisational system, mature interdependent individuals and teams "co-elevate" (Ferrazzi, 2020) – relationships are as important as individuals, the process of mutual and transformative learning is as relevant as outcomes. Indeed, a neo-virtuous world view seeks to overcome the narrow-sightedness of a materialist narrative, whilst avoiding the limitations of a rules-based collectivist framework: the "subjective and the immaterial are regaining legitimacy and the relation between individual and collective is reorientating itself" (De Vries, 2019).

On this basis, we can sketch an alternative organisational metaphor of a Living Organisation (Table 19.4).

In a Living Organisation structures are heterogeneous, organic, self-managing and networked. The setup is fluid, sensing and adapting continually to enable individual and collective flourishing, in response to requirements, needs and context. The culture is compassionate and curious, based on quality relationships and mutual commitment to enable aliveness at work. Leadership is shared and contextual, and employees act virtuously

Table 19.4 Simplified characteristics of a Living Organisation metaphor

	Living Organisation		
Strategy	Dialogue and reciprocate adaptation to enable positive development across the ecosystem	Concept of Employee	Unique and valuable individual as expression of the living organisational system
Management style	'Holding' for transformation and development, enablement	Culture (Values, beliefs, language)	Virtues, co-elevation, good life, moral character, optimum trust, purposeful emergence, voluntary interdependence, ecology, whole, essence, dialogic, individual self-actualisation and collective meaning-making, reciprocity, regenerative, ecosystem, complexity, networks, organic
Most cared about	Aliveness, transcendence, meaning, quality relationships		
Leadership discourse	Transpersonal/ Eco-Leadership Power through (balanced/ shared)	Management theory	Social constructionism, Complexity theory, trans-disciplinary dialogue

Based on e.g. Wolfe (2011).

with self-determination and relational trust in teams. The organisation embraces deeply regenerative relationships inside and outside the business, to serve a Good Society. 'Appropriate' profit is one signal of efficiency, not an objective.

Sadly, in most traditional organisations employees do not feel alive: "the typical medium- or large-scale organisation infantilises employees, enforces dull conformity, and discourages entrepreneurship" (Hamel, Zanini, 2020). For decades, we have been trained to see humans as strictly rational consumers in economic markets and as self-interested agents with no intrinsic desire for work or growth. In our businesses, we have treated people like easily replaceable human capital or as exchangeable resources to be sourced, allocated and controlled (and 'bribed' with incentives). As a result, not only have the costs of bureaucracy exploded, but, above all, unconceivable amounts of human aliveness have been sacrificed in the mind-numbing rituals of fearful low-energy cultures. In fact, whilst every business has its unique 'energy profile', important 'aliveness gaps' are evident between different organisational types (see Table 19.5).

In Machine' bureaucracies the stated design principle is to 'design and engineer the human out', in order to make work predictable. Consequentially, its aliveness potential is modest. As Bill Gore famously quipped: "authoritarians cannot impose commitments, only commands." Conversely, Family and Market organisations have superior energy profiles: the former endorse community and organisational learning, whilst the latter foster individual creativity and exciting work opportunities. However, only a Living Organisation has the potential to fully unleash individual, social and ecosystemic aliveness. Rather than 'freedom within a frame', it genuinely 'designs the human in', removing barriers to self-actualisation and creating an environment where employees co-elevate and co-create a 'good business' (see also Ingham, 2017).

How can we craft living organisations?

In my experience, in order to enable 'organisational flourishing' and collective leadership, we must have the courage to intentionally re-design work, adapting the context for our teams at multiple levels, and to continuously develop the organisational capacity and motivation for autonomy and dialogue (e.g. Doshi, McGregor 2015). Organisational structures eventually become dynamic 'containers' and 'enabling boundaries' for collective learning and development, continuously both adapting to and promoting the growing agency of the organisation (see Figure 19.2).

Lever 1: from profit to a good life for all

Under a 'virtue ethics' paradigm, organisational purpose reflects a desire for regenerative interdependency across the ecosystem. Rather than drafting yet another prosaic purpose statement we must take a step back and inquire what

Table 19.5 Simplified comparison of 'aliveness potential' by organisational type

Organisational Aliveness: 'Heat map' of different organisational types

Org. Design Principles	Market	Machine	Family	Living Organisation
Structure				
How do we divide responsibilities?	Market-centric hierarchy, shared platforms	Central, functional, matrix bureaucracy	Flat, decentralised hierarchy, incl. self-organising teams	Heterogeneous and fluid network structures, self-managed teams
How is information shared?	Based on market/project	Based on formal role (Need to know)	Based on role and informally	Dialogic and transparent (All there is to know)
Navigation				
How is work identified/planned?	"Beyond budgeting", rolling forecast, opportunity-based	Central budgeting and cascade	Top-down and bottom-up budget interlock	Experimentation and adaptation, developmental, value-based
How is work/resources allocated?	Internal market	Formal processes based on budget or politics	Less formal/more informal processes, consensual	Decentralised matching of potential and development opportunity
How are activities coordinated?	Cross-functional/project teams, Agile, Lean startup	Formal rules, roles, standard procedures	Formal rules and informal team/circle-based activity	Improvisation, continuous exploration and self-alignment

How are decisions made?	Lonely genius, Adhocracy, Meritocracy, experimentation	Autocracy, delegation of authority, "by advice"	Participative/consensus, Tactical decisions decentralised	Dialogic and consent-based, decentralise, common virtues
How does the organisation learn?	Outside-in, innovation pipeline, market research	Continuous process improvement, Lean, Kanban	Professional communities, capability and people-centric	Co-elevation, deutero learning, ecosystemic/networked
Transformation *Personal development*	Creativity and entrepreneurship	Technical skills	Soft skills, personal mastery	Self-determination, transcendence
Culture *What do we care about?*	Extrinsic – profit sharing Intrinsic – interesting work	Extrinsic – compliance, power, performance pay	Intrinsic – community relationships, org purpose	Organic – global caring and transpersonal service to others
How do we collaborate?	Peer-to-peer transactional exchanges	Formal process and structure, based on roles	Formal structures and informal communities	Mutually committed relationship networks, messy coherence

Based on design principles (see, e.g. Thun, 2019).

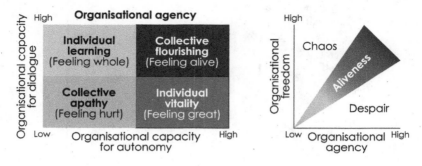

Figure 19.2 Organisational flourishing, based on, e.g., Koning (2019)

life calls us to contribute to the whole ecology, by virtuously leveraging our products and services, resources and capabilities, and relationships. Rather than just measuring net contribution to a 'quadruple bottom line', organisations monitor moral integrity and aliveness and enable continual evolution of all aspects of the organisation to foster collective flourishing. Profit remains one valuable diagnostic to support decisions, but it certainly is not the goal – budget variance is neither measured nor targeted.

Lever 2: from bureaucracy to self-managing teams

Many diverse structures are potentially suitable to implement a Living Organisation. On the one hand, it is critical to enable teams to create value as autonomously as possible, enabling decentralised experimentation, whilst on the other hand, mechanisms are required to manage interdependencies and foster alignment, where beneficial.

Building on agile organisations (e.g. 'tribes and squads'), we are witnessing experiments with adaptive networks of teams like that seen at Buurtzorg (buurtzorg.com), market-oriented ecosystems and micro enterprises like 'RenDanHeYi' at Haier (haier.com), and experiments with interconnected circles based on holacracy and sociocracy (e.g. De Man, Koene, Ars 2019).

Yet, whilst structures remain heterogeneous and dialogic, we must always vigilantly revise the distribution of information and power: in a Living Organisation positional power is (eventually) absent and 'radical transparency' becomes the norm: 'everything is public unless it's harmful', so that strategy becomes a firm-wide conversation.

From domination to dialogue

In a self-managing organisation, teams (or micro-enterprises) autonomously govern priorities, impediments and opportunities and manage the division of work. Sensing and responding to the emerging context, the organisation evolves quickly through experimentation, always in close connection with the communities they serve.

A well-codified governance system, flexible and transparent work designs and resourcing mechanisms, and proactive information sharing are critical to ensure peer-based coordination remains efficient within and across teams (e.g. Lee, Edmondson 2017).

At the same time, in order to support continuous learning and evolution at scale, organisations require both order and freedom – combining 'parental and maternal containing':

- Liberating structures – like common principles, ways of working or rituals – can enable parallel learning and experimentation, play, and generative dialogue, involving as many people as possible.
- Shared standards and agreed interfaces, as well as 'obeya rooms', marketplaces or collective clearing houses can integrate autonomy and demands for quality, efficiency, alignment and compliance.
- Explicit mechanisms are required to manage creative tensions, strategic decisions and conflict. By its very nature, total consensus would overwhelm complex systems. Hence, agreed mechanisms and procedures are needed to foster collaboration across diversity to attain not consensus, but consent (e.g. Rau, 2018).
- In addition, peer-to-peer learning is aided by enterprise-wide knowledge management systems and communities of practice (or 'guilds and chapters').

From egotism to activism

In order to enable personal vitality and thriving in Living Organisations, we must truly put people first. (Yes: clients, second.) We must re-learn to cherish their uniqueness and enable the fulfilment of their basic human needs; that is, their sense of meaning and orientation, autonomy, belonging and self-esteem (see Figure 19.3).

This is not easy. In a world where we are all required to wear many different masks, our public identity has become disengaged from our inner life. It is challenging to relate to ourselves and to each other.

- We must deliberately invest in mechanisms, like coaching, to help people dive below the proverbial iceberg – individually and collectively – and recognise their own biases and anxieties, attachment styles, defense and copying mechanisms.
- Only if people develop personal agency to work with and care for others, can they truly self-actualise and co-generate meaning and value in service of the community (e.g. Sanford, 2019). As Frederique Laloux once said: "We can only go far into the 'we' if we fully inhabit the 'I'" – no one can truly empower others – being empowered is a choice!

Figure 19.3 Five critical human needs in organisations, based on own research and other sources such as Ryan and Deci (2017)

- Moreover, we must nurture our teams' ability to self-manage collectively – combining their capacity for autonomy and dialogue. Teams need to be able to jointly assess options and take decisions; listen deeply, reflect and navigate group dynamics; host discussions and manage conflicts; experiment, learn and evolve; and coordinate implementation.

Eventually, true organisational success is only when every human being at work has the ability to develop, use their creativity and have positive impact: when agency becomes activism. The Transpersonal Development Journey enables this.

From compliance to character

In organisational cultures the souls of our businesses truly show. Rather than being simply 'what happens when the boss is not there', culture is derivative of our worldviews and reflects what we care about and how we treat each other. In order to develop Living Organisations, we must actively nurture an environment that enables collective aliveness and moral character.

- Signature practices can reinforce positive other-regarding emotions like kindness, vulnerability, compassion, caring and awe – and create active connections, communication and community amongst people across the organisation. More than organisational health indices, conversations and stories are the true currency of culture.
- Psychological safety and radical candour facilitate social learning (e.g. Edmondson, 2018): people are not afraid to speak up, commit mistakes or take entrepreneurial risks. Meaningful virtues and shared norms can foster joint accountability and mutual commitment to systemic co-elevation and morality.

- Moreover, we must adapt sometimes anachronistic HR and finance practices. We should always ask ourselves whether our policies, norms and procedures signal that 'we trust each other and value collective learning', or create distance and distrust.
- We need to actively create safe spaces for individual and collective vertical leadership development – such as the Transpersonal Leadership Development Journey – and ensure recruitment and promotion reinforces moral integrity at every single step.
- Ratings and rankings; performance pay and exorbitant levels of executive bonuses; cascaded budgets; traditional job architectures; measures to shame rather than diagnose; delegations of authority – are often examples of the sticky vestiges of managerial arthritis.
- Eventually, we must become intentional about crafting our culture, not only inside the organisation but across our entire ecosystem. As Peter Drucker suggested, "culture eats strategy for breakfast": if we fail to manage our culture, then our culture manages us.

In summary, in order to craft Living Organisations we must enable an environment where people collectively experiment and evolve – not only in terms of how they deliver, but also in regards to how they organise. Rather than a process engineering challenge, we need to start acknowledging organisations also as complex developmental systems, as living organisms, with minds and hearts and souls. Where deep emotional bonds of community and trust matter as much as outcomes and where individuals and teams experience, learn and develop together – in service of a meaningful purpose. Where influence and authority are different from rank and position and where employees have freedom to experiment – where many more people 'become their own CEOs'. So that over time, our organisation become true laboratories of ideas, always sensing and exploring and experimenting whilst we are moving – in teams and in peer communities of learning.

The three lives of a leader

> When you change the way you look at things, the things you look at change.
>
> Max Planck

As a senior executive in global Fortune 500 companies, I've spent most of my career trying to become a 'good' leader. I attended more leadership seminars than I care to remember. I accumulated a library of leadership bestsellers and earned a top-notch MBA. I am proud owner of a vast collection of psychometrics, 360-degree feedbacks, personality analyses, development plans. Yet, I never fathomed that I was largely stuck in a mindset of unexamined ideologies accumulated from the outside, and reactive thought and behavioural patterns developed at the inside – often alienated from a deeper self.

In fact, after joining the ranks of the corporate world, we not only become a productive part of the workforce of our chosen business, but also immerse ourselves into a cultural context of beliefs, conversations and relationships. Swiftly, we find ourselves pulled into a force field between our own personality, the role we have chosen, and the organisational system. During our careers as leaders, we acquire not only practical expertise and the tools of the trade, but also increasing awareness and understanding of our identity and role in a web of relatedness between: (a) organisational culture and relationships; (b) our own personality and authentic self; and (c) the wider context (our world views and moral consciousness) (see Figure 19.4).

During a 'first life of a leader', we progressively understand, master and eventually embody the norms, values and mindsets of the institution. We identify with our role and its visible and invisible associations and affordances. At the same time, we slowly start to examine our own thoughts, emotions and behaviours and hold more and more aspects of our self 'as object' (Kegan, 1983). Growing further, we investigate the deep and often unconscious assumptions, attachments and beliefs we have acquired over time. As a result, we increase our agency and engage with our environment in a more integral manner, reflecting both relational and self-awareness.

Our vertical leadership development typically occurs in several stages – at every subsequent stage, our 'action logic' (Torbert, 1991) and leadership style evolves (see Table 19.6):

- As an Opportunist we enter the organisation and first encounter organisational dynamics.
- As Diplomats we negotiate our way into our role, mainly pursuing individualistic ends as a follower in a team. Our basic leadership style is often commanding and pace-setting.
- Becoming an Expert, often as a junior manager or highly skilled practitioner, we embrace wider relationships within our chosen domain and

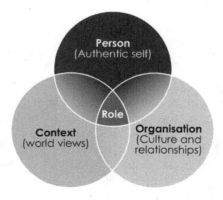

Figure 19.4 Organisational role analysis – 'PROC'

Table 19.6 Leadership developmental stages

A Journey Towards Living Organisations	
Purpose	From Profit to A Good Life
Structure	From Bureaucracy to Self-Managed Teams
Navigation	From Domination to Dialogue
People	From Compliance to Character
Culture	From Fear to Love

Based on Kegan (1983), Torbert (1991), Barrett (2017) and Kohlberg (1981).

make the prevailing norms and beliefs of the profession our own. We develop affiliative and coaching leadership styles.

- Finally, we raise to greater accountabilities and start to identify with our business as whole. As Achievers we take accountability for strategic business objectives and drive ourselves hard to succeed in the eyes of ourselves and others. We combine and balance multiple leadership styles, often becoming more visionary and democratic.

The two most important days in your life are the day you are born and the day you find out why.

Mark Twain

In the passage from our first life as Achievers to a second life as Reformers, the way we perceive our world and what matters to us radically changes (see Table 19.7). Mature leaders, suggests Manfred Kets de Vries, are not only born but "twice born" (Kets de Vries, 2006), through painful 'individuation'. During an often-turbulent and traumatic transformation, increasingly challenged by ambiguity and complexity of our environment, we transcend a mainly institutional frame of mind. We eventually acknowledge that an Achiever mindset does not allow us to authentically express all of who we really are, nor permits us to embrace a greater sense of interdependence and meaning beyond our role, inside the institution. More and more, we develop:

- Self-determination and humility: Transcending the limitations of our role, we overcome outward conditioning and clinging to power, and become inwardly-motivated. Compassionate with our own failures and suffering we grow to know and accept ourselves. From being (re)active perfectionists we gradually become reflective and creative 'imperfectionists'.
- Vulnerability and temperance: Listening deeply, we participate in more intimate and mutually transformative relationships with ourselves and others, and rediscover beauty and wonder in our interactions. We temper our own mastery and start to engage in the moment with authenticity, presence and vulnerability – holding the space for others to attain self-mastery and meaning.

Table 19.7 Leadership developmental stages

The Leader's First Life: 'ME' – I Am My Business (Institutionalised/Reactive)

Opportunist
- Egocentric and driven by self-interest; manipulative and distrustful towards others, rejects feedback
- Agency to regulate simple automatic reflexes; driven by needs, interests, impulses
- Hedonistic/Utilitarian based on personal preferences, obedience to avoid punishment or attain reward; right and wrong based on authority figures

Diplomat
- Individualistic; aware of others but no sense of responsibility for others' needs; relationships are transactional seeking membership and harmony to ensure personal needs are met; observes protocol and avoids conflict
- Agency to regulate competing impulses and appreciate role and perspective of others; develops self-concept and interests; driven by praise/reward for compliance; feels shame if violates norm – face-saving is essential
- Socialised based on duty: conformity with expectations, norms, customs, order (whether right or wrong); loyal to group and willing to follow others who support their viewpoint

Expert, Technician
- Professional community-oriented: (relevant) relationships are intrinsically valuable; cares about others' opinions; wants recognition, but feedback is accepted only from "objective" professionals
- Agency to regulate own emotions, needs, values to balance with needs of others before acting. Identifies with role; no independent, strong sense of self; difficulty to relate to others outside own traditions
- Socialised based on community ethics: self-esteem based on external validation, rationality and intellectual perfectionism. Follows role and derivers morals from professional authorities and relevant groups; not yet developing own value system; critical of self/others based on craft logic; efficiency over effectiveness

Achiever
- Entrepreneurial and business-focused; seeks mutuality not hierarchy; has own vision and work; accepts responsibility, takes stands, set limits, and solves problems within existing strategy; feels like entrepreneur and acts on behalf of whole company; welcomes behavioural feedback and acquires coaching skills
- Agency to reflect on and let go of expert role, relationships and values, but embedded in institution; well-controlled and self-possessed; multiple roles; identify based on success – may seem not to need others; self-initiating, self-correcting, and self-evaluating; feels guilt if not meeting own standards; convinced of "own" theory how to operate – blind to subjectivity behind objectivity; often tries not to display weaknesses
- Self-authoring and social utilitarian/justice oriented but within institutional order; accomplished masters of their careers; values organisational aims above personal power or norms/craft. Morally right and legally right not always the same. Driven by mastery, recognition, status, cause or career in sometimes isolated manner.

Based on Kegan (1983), Torbert (1991), Barrett (2017), Kohlberg (1981).

- Caring and eco-sensitivity: We start to see and sense complex adaptive systems and networks: from being focused on ourselves-in-role, we start to act as ourselves-in-ecosystem. Balancing multiple societal roles and seeking out liminal conversations with others, we extend our awareness and considering to a wider inter-institutional world. We commence a quest to serve a greater purpose, forging connections, community and aliveness (e.g. Logan, King, Fischer-Wright, 2011). From 'being our role', we start to become 'whole'.

For me, personally, everything started to crystallise when at one stage in my career I found myself in unprecedented difficulties to drive change. The situation was hugely pressurised, incentives misaligned, accountabilities unclear, plans complex, personalities plenty. Failure was no option and I pushed hard, yet things only got worse. Frustrated, I started to explore novel approaches and, serendipitously, encountered 'system psychodynamics'. This particular coaching approach combines psychology and complexity theory and puts its focus not on visible behaviours, above the proverbial iceberg, but on the internal system of the organisation – revealing unconscious dynamics within and between individuals and groups, and the organisational context.

I entered an inspiring submerged world. Everything I thought I knew, suddenly took on a different significance. Adopting a 'vicarious listener' stance, I learned to detect and decipher underlying and ever-present anxieties in individuals and teams, and to support others in increasing the quality of their attention, interrogating the systemic relationships within and around them. I discovered, flabbergasted, that 'our inner theatre is our outer theatre' – how early family relationships continue to effect relational patterns in adult life, how societal and organisational expectations shape our 'idealised' egos and how we automatically and destructively protect those 'accidental selves', projecting our shadows onto others. As Jung said "until you make the unconscious conscious, it will direct your life and you will call it fate."

Intrigued by new insights, I immersed myself into practices to attain deeper awareness and self-reflection. Eventually 'hitting my own iceberg' I increasingly realised how profoundly I had construed my own reality. Gradually confronting my own fears and tentatively letting go of my own protective ego and authority, the quality of my relationships rapidly deepened and continuous learning became more important than being 'right' or hitting goals. Promptly, the organisation around me started to flourish. Self-organisation and experimentation thrived. Over time, we launched initiatives to enhance hierarchy with 'sociocratic' circles; deployed signature practices to cultivate kindness, trust and kinship; established reflective peer and team coaching for our executives; experimented with equivalent decision-making by consensus; and started to modify traditional top-down performance management.

Synchronously, my purpose shifted from keenly protecting myself in pursuit of 'success', towards becoming 'systemically responsible', serving others. I began to acknowledge the organisation as 'living being', rather than a deterministic machine, and – integrating head and heart – my role transformed from instructing others (or working overtime myself) into an 'organisational acupuncturist'. Focused on containing, sparking and liberating the invisible energy flows in the organisational body and enabling the system to thrive. Thus, work again acquired profound meaning.

Today, I am thoroughly convinced that sustainable organisational transformation is impossible without concurrent individual transformation, in service of a greater purpose. The maturity of an organisation can never transcend the maturity and consciousness of its leaders. If greater consciousness doesn't operate, a system does not possess the stability to let go of the past and transition to a new model, without losing its sense of identity and cohesion.

Sadly, over 80% of business leaders struggle to progress to their 'second lives' (Torbert, 2020). Only when we eventually acquire the faith to turn inwards, accessing the essence of who we are, with and for others, are we able to let go of fears, authority and the desire to control, so that power becomes mutualistic and shared. Indeed, Reformer leadership is not about individual traits or behaviours, but about entering a self-transforming stage of adult development, where deep clarity of self-awareness and self-regulation springs from a spiritual motive to serve others. We start to build sustainable organisational systems that ultimately and naturally succeed ourselves.

> We hold these truths to be self-evident, that all people are created dependent—on each other, our earth, and its climate—endowed with the inalienable responsibility to maintain justice, liberty, and affiliation for all.
>
> Declaration of Interdependence, Henry Mintzberg

Yet, evolution towards transpersonal leadership requires a further passage to a Third Life (see Table 19.8). Most adult development frameworks seem to suggest that we will continue to develop towards ever higher stages of spiritual consciousness, one-ness and wholeness (e.g. Wilber, 2000). Expanding our identity and awareness further and further, we care for an increasingly more extensive ecosystem within which we operate, across time horizons and ideologies – eventually embracing unconditional 'salvific' love. Deep relatedness informs our actions.

However, whilst expanding our perspectives ever further is necessary, I contend that synchronicity alone will suffice to create good organisations and a Good Society. In order to enable collective flourishing, we also need to courageously embody a moral stance. Our third life as leaders invites us to deeply investigate our interrelated societal world views, organisational and personal values, and to accept personal responsibility to 'become the change in our world'. Ultimately, Leadership is ethics – where ethics is a fundamental choice between alternative futures – not just about right and wrong, but about vision and purpose. Embracing a neo-virtuous paradigm, excellence in leadership is to enable the interdependent flourishing of the whole. We are not

Table 19.8 Leadership developmental stages

The Leader's Second Life: 'WE' – I Am Because You Are (Inter-Institutional/Conscious)

Reformer	• Inter-institutional and systemic: responsible for systems rather than to systems; management challenges are complex/strategic; leader leads to learn; embraces ambiguity, opportunities to grow, intimacy and emotional expression; open for negative feedback to uncover authentic self and mutual transformation; engages in liminal dialogue with others holding different worldviews; actualises sense of purpose by guiding and cooperating with others for reciprocate learning and fulfilment
	• Self-determined and self-transforming. Agency to let go of own ego identity, attachments, authority and institutions; during transition often deep interrogation of meaning and identity triggered by previous overidentification with institution and success; recognition of lack of true intimacy; seeks internal cohesion and meaning; develops deep self-knowledge and "individuation"; understanding of organisational psychodynamics and relational patterns; displays vulnerability and establishes trust; rarely before age 40
	• Development as freedom; realises that success/current life system does not reflect all of who they are; during transition often sceptic, critical and in contrast with institution; ethical relativism; values paradox and tension between thought systems; holds multiple perspectives; seeks to construct synthesis and 'higher' universal moral rules, holds questions, rather than fixing problems; deep examination of alternative worldviews and development of strong moral compass; risk to rely on powerful new theory

Based on Kegan (1983), Torbert (1991), Barrett (2017) and Kohlberg (1981).

separate from but part of our corporate communities within an interconnected ecosystem – our ability to craft 'good' companies depends on our capacity to transcend our individuality to nurture regenerative union. Ultimately, leadership is not a tribe of special individuals with special traits, and not even a role, but about letting go of restraining paradigms to unleash the unique potential in everyone. About developing eco-leadership – where people are no longer passive victims of circumstances, but jointly thriving in the creation of new possibilities. About learning together how to lead a good life (Western, 2007).

What does this mean? Aristotle suggested that in order to attain *eudaimonia*, we must acquire practical wisdom (*phronesis*) to act virtuously. Similarly, Bill Torbert describes transpersonal leaders as 'alchemists' who master the delicate art of 'action inquiry' (see Figure 19.5): attuning themselves moment-to-moment with their own self, their relationships around them, and their moral intentionality, they "cultivate the development of the systems in which they participate" (Torbert, 2004). Being fully aware and present in the moment allows us to interact with moral character – practicing appropriate virtues, we can develop vitality, friendship and mutual learning, and embrace deeper meaning as part of something bigger – in ourselves and others. "The mastery of the moment is mastery of life."

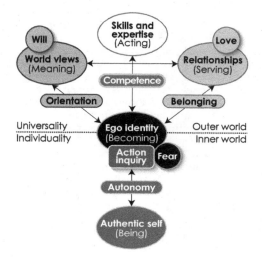

Figure 19.5 Action inquiry

Rather than values or policies, virtues are habits which we consciously and repeatedly enact in our daily relation with others. Virtues, also referred to as 'personal conscience values' in *Leading Beyond the Ego* (Knights, Grant, Young, 2018), seek to enable the best in ourselves and others – in profound acknowledgement of our mutual interdependence. In fact, contrary to what free-market ideologists would like us to believe, maximising self-interested 'surplus profit' or amassing social goods is a myopic moral strategy. Humans have never primarily been individual players, but always thrived in social relations. Our "self-interest is…tied to that system of virtues that makes us good citizens and contributes to the well-being and happiness of others as well as our own." (Salomon, 1992). We are fulfilled by loving relationships, more than goals and outcomes, and friendship, trust, fairness and solidarity are present in every successful organisation in the world. Hence, any rational morality that mismatches trust and interdependence must eventually fail.

From a single-minded focus on maximising profits, the emphasis of our actions shifts towards enabling a living ecosystem. Crafting synergetic 'give-give' relationships, whilst 'satisficing' outcomes, rather than maximising transactional 'win-wins'. Doing good, rather than just doing no harm. On that basis, we can envisage a preliminary set of universal corporate virtues that support organisational aliveness (see Table 19.9). In practice, more work will be required by organisations to craft an effective list.

Hopefully, virtues could eventually provide those simple behavioural principles that enable interdependent actors in a complex global system to act with integrity in service of 'purposeful collective emergence'. In fact, virtues are both *normative and contextual* as they offer general rather than specific

Table 19.9 Illustrative Virtues

The Leader's Third Life: 'US' – I Am The System (Transpersonal and virtuous)

Transpersonal Leader	• Ecosystem-wide awareness: Continuous expansion of awareness to sense the interdependent ecology; embraces mutual dependency as life-giving and self-evident; deep and embodied caring for mutually transformative relationships; systemic awareness of emotions, thoughts, actions in the present • Self- transcending: Understands identity as being part of the wider system; embraces integration of independent beings and nature, without losing own sense of essence; actively seeking patterns and dialogic development; holds space for continual emergence and mutual transformation as expression of being alive; ambiguity, suffering or lack of resolution is accepted and valued as part of relationships; ability to proactively combine inquiry and responsible action in the moment • Meaning-making: spiritual reframing and willingness to serve life's calling for the greater good; deliberate embodiment of moral character and commitment to enable and embody system-wide thriving. Able to navigate complexity seeking universal coherence through pragmatic contextual actions

Inspired by Aguirre-Y-Luker, Hyman, Shanahan (2017).

rules and enable 'abductive' local decisions. We could imagine a voluntary 'declaration of interdependence' – within and across businesses – that settles the virtues we owe to each other, from adult to adult, as individuals and organisations. This serves not only to mitigate questionable business practices and transcend self-serving competitive rhetoric, but to overcome the sickness of purpose and dehumanisation of our organisations.

Ultimately, a Good Society will only emerge if businesses and business leaders actively care and commit themselves to serve the living potential of their communities and consumers, nations and ecosystems. Contrary to prominent management literature, excellence in business has never been just about *what* we achieve – it always was also about *why* and *how* we act.

Letting go of leadership

A new world is trying to emerge. We can feel it deeply in our bones. Underneath the visible symptoms of crisis in society and environment, tectonic shifts of a collective unconsciousness are producing powerful primordial tremors. The wounded soul of a maternal ecosphere is knocking at the doors of our postmodern egos. Voicelessly, it is beseeching us to hold back and reflect. We have ruthlessly remodelled the globe into a mining ground for resources to feed an ever-expanding population. We are crafting technologies that could blight mankind on its ever-faster pursuit of profits and growth. We are funding mind-boggling progress with ever-greater entrenchment of our own lives. Two centuries ago, our enlightened great-great-grandfathers liberated the world from the shackles of religious dogma. Today, we find ourselves enchained once again: our individualistic and materialistic narrative has repressed the indispensable energy of loving interconnectedness and is threatening to quench the essential spirit of our humanity.

Yet, whilst our planet is burning, most of us remain stuck in the phantasy that the world is a lonely, dangerous place and change is impossible. We are plagued by guilt of feeling unworthy and absorbed by fear of attempting anything truly great. We are caught up in the hubristic illusion that one day we will possess more than all the others, and feel great about ourselves.

Together, we must eventually face our collective leadership mid-life crisis and let go of leading to start serving! In order to heal our world, we must stop polishing leadership icons on the altars of modernity and accept personal accountability to create a better future for all, as trustees of an endangered eco-civilisation. We must roll up our sleeves and jointly craft the organisations, processes, and cultures needed to attain both individual flourishing and the emergence of a Good Society. Yet, above all, we must 'lead beyond the ego' and, selflessly and virtuously, let go of our own leadership to spark the unique potential in everyone. From doing to being. From great to good. From fear to love.

Transpersonal Leaders of the world, unite! We are not leaders, because we rule. We are leaders, because we truly care.

Questions and actions for personal development

> Act as if what you do makes a difference. It does.
>
> William James

1. Revising your purpose: what does life 'call for'? How can you virtuously serve the system you are in? How can you measure aliveness? Who do you need in your (extended) 'team' to progress? Where can you further connect the ecosystem to spark mutual growth?
2. Nurturing organisational agency: How could you create '*solidarity groups*' and safe spaces for vertical leadership and community development, using for example 'system psychodynamic' coaching for individuals, peers and teams?
3. Co-creating a virtuous culture: How could you develop a 'pledge of interdependence' to promote virtuous acting, across the business and for each department? Where could you use signature practices and rituals to promote trust, kindness and co-elevation?
4. Adapting organisational design: Where can you enable bold team experimentation with self-managing structures and processes? How can you support teams with knowledge and good practices (e.g. sociocracy)?
5. Removing blockers to aliveness: Which organisational 'patterns', stories, structures, procedures and systems constrain aliveness and trust? How can you address them?

6. Nurturing the rebels: Who are the innovators who bring new and dissenting opinions? How can you nurture a group of 'musketeers' to foster bottom-up dialogue and engagement?
7. Standing up: How can you enable moral integrity in your organisation? What are the 'red lines' of your own integrity? What is your 'plan B' if they get challenged?

References and further reading

Aguirre-Y-Luker G., Hyman M., Shanahan K. 2017, Measuring Systems of Virtue Development, in *Handbook of Virtue Ethics in Business and Management* (Sison, ed.), Springer, pp. 723–747.

Barrett R. 2017, *The Values-Driven Organization: Cultural Health and Employee Well-Being as a Pathway to Sustainable Performance*, Routledge.

Boyd G. 2020, *Rebuild: The Economy, Leadership, and You*, Evolutesix Books.

Caredda 2020, https://sergiocaredda.eu/organisation/leadership-models-the-theory-and-the-practice/.

Coffey C., Revollo P. and Harvey R. 2020, *Time to Care*. Oxford: Oxfam international.

Covey S. 1989, *The 7 Habits of Highly Effective People*, Free Press.

De Man A., Koene P., Ars M. 2019, *How to Survive the Organizational Revolution*, BIS Publishers.

De Vries, B. 2019, *Engaging with the Sustainable Development Goals by Going beyond Modernity: An Ethical Evaluation within a Worldview Framework*, Cambridge University Press.

Doshi N., McGregor L. 2015, *Primed to Perform: How to Build the Highest Performing Cultures through the Science of Total Motivation*, HarperCollins Publishers Inc.

Edelman. 2020, Edelman Trust Barometer. [online] Available at: <https://www.edelman.com/trust/2020-trust-barometer> [Accessed 22 October 2021].

Edmondson A. 2018, *The Fearless Organization: Creating Psychological Safety in the Workplace for Learning, Innovation, and Growth*, Wiley.

Fiske A. 1991, *Structures of Social Life: The Four Elementary Forms of Human Relations: Communal Sharing, Authority Ranking, Equality Matching, Market Pricing*, Free Press.

Ferrazzi K. 2020, *Leading without Authority: Why You Don't Need To Be In Charge to Inspire Others and Make Change Happen*, Penguin Business.

Friedman 1970, The Social Responsibility Of Business Is to Increase Its Profits, *The New York Times*, September 13 1970.

Gallup 2017, *State of the Global Workplace*. New York: Gallup Press.

Gemmill G., Oakley J. 1992. Leadership: An Alienating Social Myth?, *Human Relations* 45, 113–129.

Hamel G., Zanini M. 2020, *Humanocracy: Creating Organizations as Amazing as the People Inside Them*, Harvard Business Review Press.

Hennig, A. 2016, Three Different Approaches to Virtue in Business—Aristotle, Confucius, and Lao Zi, *Frontiers of Philosophy in China* 11(4): 556–586.

Heon, F., Davis A., Jones-Patulli J., Damart S., 2017, *The Essential Mary Parker Follett Ideas We Need Today*, 2017, Published by Heon, Davis, Jones-Patulli, Damart.

Hollis J. 2006, *Finding Meaning in the Second Half of Life*. New York: Gotham Books.

Ingham J. 2017, *The Social Organization: Developing Employee Connections and Relationships for Improved Business Performance*, Kogan Page.

Kegan R. 1983, *The Evolving Self: Problem and Process in Human Development*, Harvard University Press.

Kets de Vries M. 2006, *The Leader on the Couch: A Clinical Approach to Changing People and Organizations*, John Wiley & Sons.

Kleine A., Rudolph C., Zacher H. 2019, Thriving at Work: A Meta-Analysis, *Journal of Organizational Behavior* 40: 973–999.

Knights J., Grant D., Young G. 2018, *Leading Beyond the Ego*. Oxford: Routledge.

Kohlberg L. 1981, *The Philosophy of Moral Development: Moral Stages and the Idea of Justice*, Harpercollins.

Koning P. 2019, *Agile Leadership Toolkit: Learning to Thrive with Self-Managing Teams*, Addison-Wesley.

Laloux F. 2014, *Reinventing Organizations: A Guide to Creating Organizations Inspired by the Next Stage in Human Consciousness*, Nelson Parker.

Lee M., Edmondson A. 2017, Self-Managing Organizations: Exploring the Limits of Less-Hierarchical Organizing, *Research in Organizational Behaviour*, 37: 35–58.

Logan D., King J., Fischer-Wright H. 2011, *Tribal Leadership: Leveraging Natural Groups to Build a Thriving Organization*, HarperBus.

Mergen A., Ozbilgin M. 2020, Understanding the Followers of Toxic Leaders: Toxic Illusio and Personal Uncertainty, *International Journal of Management Reviews*, 00: 1–19.

Mintzberg, H. 2015, *Rebalancing Society*. Oakland, CA: Berrett-Koehler Publishers.

Moore, R. and Gillette, D. 1990, *King, Warrior, Magician, Lover*. San Francisco: HarperSanFrancisco.

Nielsen J. 2004, *The Myth of Leadership*. London: Davies–Black.

O'Reilly C. 2020, Transformational Leader or Narcissist? How Grandiose Narcissists Can Create and Destroy Organizations and Institutions, *California Management Review*, 62(3), 5–27.

Peck S. 1990, *The Different Drum*, Arrow Books.

Pfeffer J. 2015, *Leadership BS: Fixing Workplaces and Careers One Truth at a Time*, HarperBusiness.

Rau T. 2018, Many Voices One Song: Shared Power with Sociocracy, Institute for Peaceable Communities, Inc. and https://sociocracy30.org/.

Ryan R., Deci E. 2017, *Self-Determination Theory: Basic Psychological Needs in Motivation, Development, and Wellness*, Guilford Press.

Salomon R. 1992, *Ethics and Excellence Cooperation and Integrity in Business*, Oxford University Press.

Sandler R. 2007, *Character and Environment: A Virtue-Oriented Approach to Environmental Ethics*, Columbia University Press.

Sanford C. 2019, *No More Feedback: Cultivate Consciousness at Work*, InterOctave.

Scharmer O. 2016, *Theory U: Leading from the Future as It Emerges*, Berrett-Koehler.

Schwab K. 2017, *The Fourth Industrial Revolution*, Portfolio Penguin.

Sison A., Beabout G., Ferrero I. 2017, *Handbook of Virtue Ethics in Business and Management*, Springer.

Spreitzer G., Lam C., Quinn R. 2012, *Human Energy in Organizations: Implications for POS from Six Interdisciplinary Streams*, Article https://www.researchgate.net/publication/267411272.

Thun F. 2019, *Liberated Companies How to Create Vibrant Organizations In The Digital Age*, BoD – Books on Demand.

Torbert W. 1991, *The Power of Balance: Transforming Self, Society, and Scientific Inquiry*, SAGE Publications, Inc.

Torbert W. 2004, *Action Inquiry: The Secret of Timely and Transforming Leadership*, Berrett-Koehler Publisher.

Torbert W. 2020, *Warren Buffet's and Your Own Seven Levels of Transformation*, Global Leadership Associates Press.

Ulrich P. 2008, *Integrative Economic Ethics*, Cambridge University Press.

Western S. 2019, *Leadership*. 3rd ed. London: Sage Publications.

Wilber K. 2000, *Integral Psychology: Consciousness, Spirit, Psychology, Therapy*, Shambhala Publications Inc.

Wolfe N. 2011, *The Living Organization: Transforming Business to Create Extraordinary Results*, Quantum Leaders Publishing.

Zander B. 2000, *The Art of Possibility: Transforming Professional and Personal Life*, Harvard Business Review Press.

Index